Barbara Eaton

Mrs Sherwood
'So Rich in Children'

Mrs M. M. Sherwood (1775–1851),
Kelly, 1854

Barbara Eaton

Mrs Sherwood
'So Rich in Children'

A biography of the 19th Century children's writer
Mrs M. M. Sherwood (1775–1851)
with excerpts from Captain Sherwood's diaries

Francis
Boutle
Publishers

First published by
Francis Boutle Publishers
272 Alexandra Park Road
London N22 7BG
Tel/Fax: (020) 8889 7744
Email: info@francisboutle.co.uk
www.francisboutle.co.uk

ISBN 978 0 9935344 7 8

Acknowledgements

I am most grateful for the generous help which I have received from the following organisations and people: Shropshire Archives, Shrewsbury; Shropshire Regimental Museum, Shrewsbury; Worcestershire Archive and Archaeology Service; Berkshire Record Office; Dorset History Centre; Department of Early Printed Books and SpecialCollections, Trinity College Library, Dublin; Dr. Leonard Smith, University of Birmingham; Penelope Rundle of The College of Matrons, Salisbury; Steven Barlow for transcribing selections from material at Berkshire Record Office; Jane Grierson and Tess Barlow for so generously reading and commenting on my drafts. Special thanks to my publisher, Clive Boutle, for his enthusiastic support, and his designer, Kate Tattersall.

Above all, my husband, Tim, who painstakingly transcribed Henry Sherwood's diaries: a Herculean task. Without his enthusiastic input and research this book would not have been the same.

Thank you all.

For Samuel, Sophie, Daniel, Beatrice, Louise and Alice

Contents

List of maps and illustrations

Maps

Permissions

Illustrations from books out of copyright are shown by reference to the book author, see Bibliography. Credits as web image are open source or of unidentified provenance. Other sources below are reproduced by kind permission.

Darton: p20, 282, 336

Master and Fellows of St. John's College, Cambridge: p204

National Maritime Museum, Greenwich: p113, 169, 182

Shropshire Regimental Museum: p108

Trustees of the British Library: p174, 222

Web image: p36, 177, 235, 315

Who's Who

ENGLAND
Mary – Mary Martha (Butt) Sherwood (1755–1851)
Married her cousin Henry Sherwood and travelled out to India with
him. Stationed in Bengal 1805–16. Wrote stories from an early age and
became a best selling writer, over 300 tracts and books.

Henry – Henry Sherwood (1777–1849)
Imprisoned in France in his early teens during the French Revolution.
Fell in love with his cousin Mary and married her. Captain and
Paymaster, 53rd Regiment of Foot. Served in the West Indies and India.

Mary and Henry's children
  Mary Henrietta (1804–?)
  Born in Morpeth, England (left in care of Mary's mother and sister,
  Lucy, when her parents set sail for India in 1805. She did not see them
  again until 1816).
  Henry (1805–7)
  Born in Dinapore, died in Berhampore, India.
  Annie (adopted 1807)
  Left with Daniel Corrie and his sister Mary in India, 1809.
  Lucy Martha (1807–8)
  Born in Berhampore and died in Cawnpore, India.
  Sally Pownall (adopted 1808)
  Came to England with the Sherwoods.
  Lucy Elizabeth (1809–35)
  Born in Cawnpore, India.

Emily (1811–33)
Born in Cawnpore, India.
Mary Parson (adopted 1812/13)
Henry Martyn (1813–1912)
Born in Meerut, India.
Sophia (1815–99)
Born in Meerut, India. Later her mother's biographer as Mrs Kelly.
George (1819–20)
Born at Wick, Worcester, England.

Rev. Dr. George Butt (1741–1795) and **Mrs Butt (née Martha Sherwood) (1753–1817)**
Mary's parents. Martha Butt was Henry Sherwood's aunt. The Butts had three children:
Rev. John Marten Butt (1774–1846)
Known as Marten. First married Mary Anne Congreve – 8 children, and later Jemima Hubbal – 4 children. Mentally ill in 1829, committed to Spring Vale Asylum 1833.
Mary Martha Butt (Mrs M. M. Sherwood)
See Mary, above.
Lucy Lyttelton Butt (1781–1858)
Married Rev. Charles Cameron, 12 children. Wrote children's books and tracts as Mrs Cameron.

Henry Marten Sherwood (1754–1803)
Henry's father. Children: Henry and Margaret, with Margaret (Maskall) who died in childbirth. Later married cousin Mercy Taylor, 6 children. Henry and Margaret were severely neglected.
George Annesley 1769–1844)
Lord Valentia's son, later Lord Valentia and Earl of Mountnorris. A pupil of Rev. George Butt and close friend of Marten and Mary. Married Anne Courtenay. Owned Arley Hall. Highly publicised scandal and divorce proceedings.
Henry Salt (1780–1827)
Mary's cousin. Artist, traveller and diplomat.

Sir Edward Winnington (1728?–1791)
M.P. Close neighbour of the Butts, lived at Stanford Court. Rev. George
Butt's financial problems stemmed from an agreement with Sir Edward
to rebuild Stanford Rectory.

Isaac Hawkins Browne (1745–1818)
M.P. At Westminster School with Mary's father. Lived at Badger.
Henrietta, his wife, was close friend of Mrs Butt.

Dr. Richard Valpy (1754–1836)
Headmaster of Reading School and friend of Rev. George Butt.

Monsieur St. Quintin
Ex-diplomat and heavy gambler; became a French teacher at The Abbey
Gateway School in Reading. Married Miss Pitts who was joint partner
with Madame Latournelle (aka Sarah Hackett) at the school.

Mrs Slaney
Mary's somewhat irresponsible godmother.

INDIA

Rev. Henry Martyn (1781–1812)
Evangelical chaplain with East India company in Bengal. Close friend
and religious mentor to Mary.

Rev. Daniel Corrie (1777–1837) and **Miss Mary Corrie, later
Mrs Sherer**
Close friends in India of the Sherwoods. Annie was left in their care
when the Sherwoods left for Calcutta in 1809. She remained with the
Corries after the Sherwoods returned in 1810.

Colonel and **Mrs Mawby**
Mawby was Henry's commanding officer in Bengal, later a General.

Genealogical tree of the Butt, Marten, Sherwood and Ashcroft families

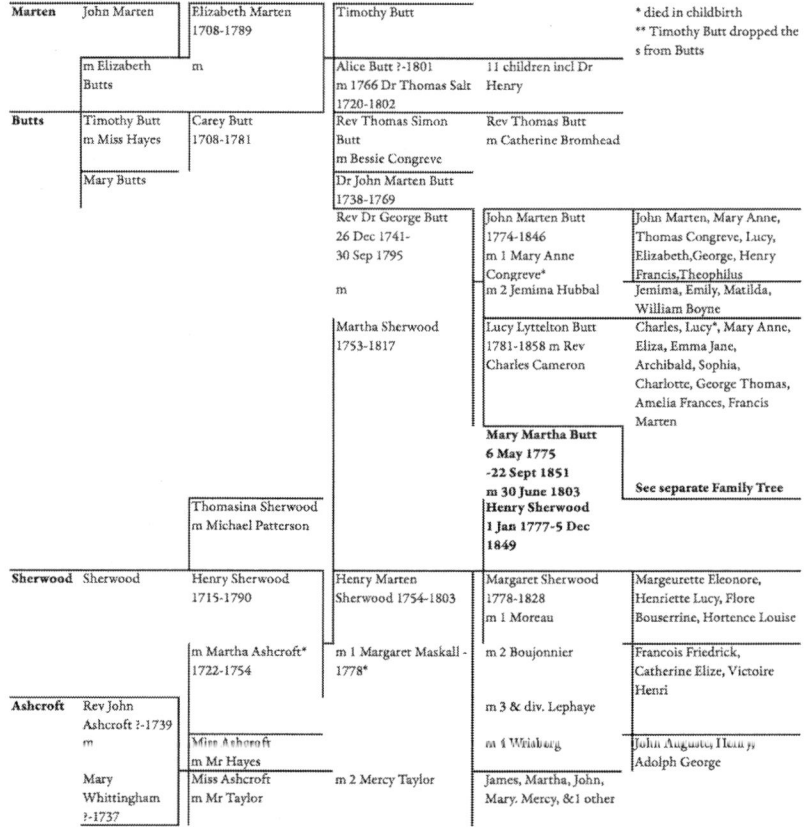

Marten	John Marten	Elizabeth Marten 1708-1789	Timothy Butt			* died in childbirth ** Timothy Butt dropped the s from Butts
	m Elizabeth Butts	m	Alice Butt ?-1801 m 1766 Dr Thomas Salt 1720-1802	11 children incl Dr Henry		
Butts	Timothy Butt m Miss Hayes	Carey Butt 1708-1781	Rev Thomas Simon Butt m Bessie Congreve	Rev Thomas Butt m Catherine Bromhead		
	Mary Butts		Dr John Marten Butt 1738-1769			
			Rev Dr George Butt 26 Dec 1741- 30 Sep 1795	John Marten Butt 1774-1846 m 1 Mary Anne Congreve* m 2 Jemima Hubbal	John Marten, Mary Anne, Thomas Congreve, Lucy, Elizabeth, George, Henry Francis, Theophilus / Jemima, Emily, Matilda, William Boyne	
			m	Lucy Lyttelton Butt 1781-1858 m Rev Charles Cameron	Charles, Lucy*, Mary Anne, Eliza, Emma Jane, Archibald, Sophia, Charlotte, George Thomas, Amelia Frances, Francis Marten	
			Martha Sherwood 1753-1817	**Mary Martha Butt 6 May 1775 -22 Sept 1851 m 30 June 1803 Henry Sherwood 1 Jan 1777-5 Dec 1849**	**See separate Family Tree**	
		Thomasina Sherwood m Michael Patterson				
Sherwood	Sherwood	Henry Sherwood 1715-1790	Henry Marten Sherwood 1754-1803	Margaret Sherwood 1778-1828 m 1 Moreau	Margeurette Eleonore, Henriette Lucy, Flore Bouserrine, Hortence Louise	
		m Martha Ashcroft* 1722-1754	m 1 Margaret Maskall - 1778*	m 2 Boujonnier	Francois Friedrick, Catherine Elize, Victoire Henri	
Ashcroft	Rev John Ashcroft ?-1739 m	Miss Ashcroft m Mr Hayes		m 3 & div. Lephaye		
				m 4 Wriaberg	John Auguste, Henry Adolph George	
	Mary Whittingham ?-1737	Miss Ashcroft m Mr Taylor	m 2 Mercy Taylor	James, Martha, John, Mary. Mercy, & 1 other		

Mary and Henry Sherwood's Family

John Marten Butt 1774-1846 m 1 Mary Anne Congreve* m 2 Jemima Hubbal Lucy Lyttelton Butt 1781-1858 m Rev Charles Cameron	Mary Henrietta Sherwood 20 Apr 1804 Morpeth m 1826 Rev Thomas Dawes	9 children incl. Lucy Elizabeth Dawes
	Henry Sherwood 25 Dec 1805 Dinapore - July 1807 Berhampore	Sir Edwin Sandys Dawes KCMG
Mary Martha Butt **6 May 1775-22 Sept 1851**	Lucy Martha Sherwood 25 Mar 1807 Berhampore - 2 Sep 1808 Cawnpore	m cousin
	Lucy Elizabeth Sherwood 10 Aug 1809 Cawnpore -May 1835* m 1834 William Bagnall	Lucy Emily Bagnall May 1835-?
married cousin **30 June 1803**	Annie Childe adopted 1807 left in India	
Henry Sherwood **1 Jan 1777-5 Dec 1849**	Sally Pownal adopted 1808 India m 1828 Thomas Bird	
Margaret Sherwood 1778-1828	Mary Parsons adopted by 1813 India	
& step-siblings	Emily Sherwood 20 Jul 1811 Cawnpore -8 Oct 1833 m 18 Nov 1829 Dr Robert Streeten	Henry Sherwood 1867-1923 m 1895 Annie Gerty
	Rev Henry Martyn Sherwood 1 Jul 1813 Meerut -21 Jan 1912 m 1 1834 Sarah Sleigh Barber m 2 1866 Mary Emma Taylor	Mary Martha Sherwood 1869-? m Rev Peopleton
	Sophia Sherwood 20 Feb 1815 Meerut m 1 Dr Robert Streeten -1849 m 2 Sep 1851 Dr Hubert Kelly	Annie Emily Sherwood 1870-?
	Catherine Elize Boujonnier 1810 Brussels, Henry's niece fostered 1817	Mabel Sophia Sherwood 1873-?
	George Sherwood 31 Jan 1819- spring 1820	

Preface

Comments and criticism of Mary Martha Sherwood's canon have centred on her life and the different influences on her writing: Evangelism, Millennialism, Calvinism and finally her own religious precepts. But one of the most important influences has been given little space in biographies: that is of course Henry Sherwood, her husband for forty-six years. Mary's marriage to this young man changed her life. He had been abandoned in his youth by his father in revolutionary France, survived imprisonment and desperate poverty there during the French Revolution, and had then saved his father and family for which he was given no thanks. After her marriage Mary exchanged a close-knit loving family in the known and privileged world in which she had been brought up in Worcestershire for the itinerant life of a soldier's wife first in England and then in far-off Bengal.

Mary followed Sarah Trimmer[1] and Hannah More[2] in spreading the message of moral improvement for the disadvantaged by promoting religion and literacy through Sunday School attendance. She became not only a prolific writer of religious tracts, but also of didactic moral stories, text books and novels in the first half of the nineteenth century. Her books remained popular into the twentieth century. Her narrative and descriptive power as a writer still captivate the reader; her didactic religious message to her readers is overt. Although she wrote tracts, as did her younger sister Lucy, for the moral edification of her Sunday School pupils, it was in India that she found her métier and, with the help of Lucy, her first book *Little Henry and his Little Bearer*, was published. It combined a strong narrative, descriptions of the India she knew at first hand and a strong Evangelical message. The central child character, as in so many of her books, has to make a moral decision in the face of opposition from well-meaning adults. The book became a bestseller when it was published in 1814 by Houlston of Wellington, Shropshire. Many of her books create a minatory atmosphere – often far greater than in the fairy tale which had by then fallen out of favour: Mary and the Evangelicals strongly disapproved of them.

Mary continued to write until her death in 1851: latterly with the help of her youngest daughter, Sophia Kelly. In this biography of Mrs Sherwood I have included unpublished material from Henry Sherwood's diaries which contain delightful line drawings, detailed accounts of his financial struggles, observations of flora and fauna, the weather and wind speed, tides and river conditions and the dramatic events which coloured his life. Excerpts from his diaries appear very briefly in Mary's autobiography which Sophia edited for publication in 1854 as *The Life of Mrs Sherwood*. I have included in greater detail: his time in France when a boy; his time as a young officer in the West Indies before his marriage and his time in India after his marriage. Henry readily admitted that his syntax and spelling were weak but, like his wife, he writes with a freshness of observation which is cinematic in its evocation of the local scene.

Mary also kept copious diaries in which she recorded her thoughts and observations which reveal much about her character and the times she lived in. I have taken the anglicised spelling of place names from the Sherwoods' diaries.

Where original handwritten letters and diaries have been transcribed they have been indented and ranged left. The original spelling, syntax and punctuation have been largely kept.

I have used extensively: Darton, (1910) *The Life and Times of Mrs Sherwood*; Kelly, *The Life of Mrs Sherwood*, (1854 and 1857 editions) and Cameron, (1873) *The Life of Mrs Cameron*. There is a large collection of Sherwood papers at the UCLA Library, USA which I have not been able to access because of the prohibitive cost of copying them for study.

Prologue

A Different World

B ells rang out in celebration. The girls, dressed in muslin dresses, Indian shawls and caps trimmed with lace, could not understand why they were the centre of such interest as they stood shivering on the bustling noisy quayside where large crowds had gathered to greet the arrival of the first passengers permitted to land at Liverpool from an East Indiaman.

When Mary Martha Sherwood, with her husband, Captain Henry Sherwood, late paymaster of the 53rd Foot, their four surviving children, and three adopted European girls from Captain Sherwood's regiment, landed in Liverpool on Saturday June 1, 1816 they had left behind their familiar life in India. Their voyage from Calcutta on board the *Robarts*, an East Indiaman, had lasted four and a half months and had involved hardship and dangers. Eager to escape from the chaotic scenes of drunken lascars and contraband goods being smuggled overboard by the officers, the family disembarked in the early morning from the *Robarts* and travelled in a fishing boat across the Mersey estuary from Hoyle Lake moorings. For the bewildered children the sights and sounds were far different from the ones they had been accustomed to at the various Bengal cantonments where they had been born and lived. But for their father, now on half-pay and facing financial uncertainty, and his wife Mary, it was a bitter-sweet return. Two of their children had died in early infancy in India. The high mortality rate among European children – especially newly weaned babies – led the Sherwoods, on medical advice, to make the decision to return to England to safeguard their remaining children's lives. Now they were looking forward to being reunited with their first-born child, Mary Henrietta, whom they had not seen since they left London for Portsmouth to set sail for Calcutta on April 9, 1805. Born in 1804 she had been left in the joint care of Mary Sherwood's widowed mother, Martha Butt, and Mary's sister Lucy, who was now married with four children of her own.

Part One

Worcestershire

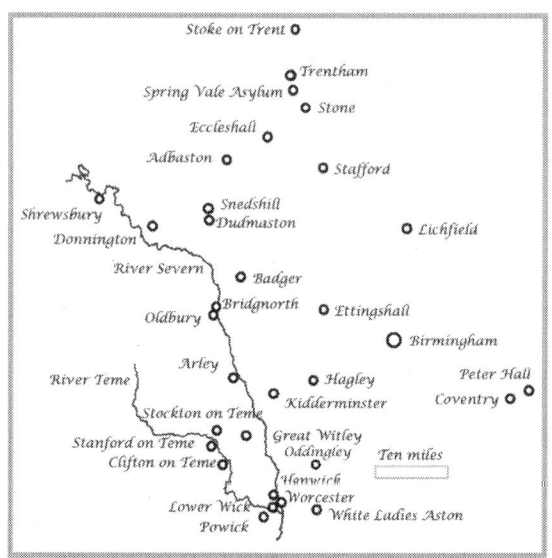

The Sherwoods' West Midlands

A Happy Childhood

In 1773 the Reverend Dr. George Butt married Martha Sherwood, the daughter of a wealthy Coventry silk merchant. George was born in 1741 in Lichfield, Staffordshire, where his father, Carey Butt, was a surgeon. George was highly educated having been sent to Westminster School in 1756 where he became school captain in which capacity he walked in the procession at George II's funeral and George III's coronation. He went up to Christ Church, Oxford and in 1765 he was ordained Deacon. Sir Walter Bagot[3] gifted him the living at Leigh in Staffordshire. George was a scholarly, amiable, handsome young man and a great wit. He had a lively imagination, was extremely open – sometimes too much so – and excelled in the art of conversation which made him a popular guest at the dinner tables of the local nobility. Because of these qualities and his education he became a private tutor in 1766 to Edward, the only son of Sir Edward Winnington.[4] He became Edward's public tutor at Christ Church, Oxford in 1767. Other fathers also sought him out as tutor to their sons, partly to safeguard them against the pitfalls of the non-academic attractions on offer at Oxford.

Martha Sherwood's mother, also called Martha, had died in childbirth in 1754 leaving two children: a daughter, Martha, and the baby, Henry Marten who '...suffered from this early bereavement all through life; neither did he suffer alone, for his conduct caused all those to whom he was near and dear much trouble and anxiety.'[5] The baby son remained at home but Martha was despatched at a tender age; first to school in Nottingham, paying visits during the holidays to her father, Henry Sherwood, at his houses in London or in Coventry. At fourteen she was removed from her school in Guildford and placed with Mrs Woodhouse, a widow living in Lichfield with three beautiful daughters.

George Butt still had close ties to Lichfield and its society. At Lichfield there was an intellectual circle with Anna Seward,[6] the poet, at its centre. Erasmus Darwin, the grandfather of Charles and the author of *The Botanic Garden*; Richard Lovell Edgeworth,[7] the writer on education; Thomas Day, another educationist; Major Sneyd; Dr. Johnson and David Garrick, were all members. George was drawn into this circle and it was on one of his visits to Lichfield that he fell deeply in love with the second Woodhouse sister, Mary. Tragically Mary died. George had met Martha Sherwood as a member of the Woodhouse household and at just twenty, she was drafted in to replace Mary Woodhouse in George's affections. How she felt about this arrangement so soon after Mary's death can only be surmised. Whereas Mary Woodhouse had been beautiful Martha was not blessed with beauty. She was small and bore the scars of smallpox and, perhaps because of this, lacked social confidence preferring to keep in the background. Her appearance must have been in cruel contrast to the three beautiful daughters of the household, close to Martha's age. Her daughter describes her as a 'meek and gentle spirit'. Her beautiful hands were her one redeeming feature. What she did bring to the marriage was a fortune of ten thousand pounds (on her death in 1817 her estate, by then worth fifteen thousand pounds, was divided among her three children). The marriage, so advantageous for George in purely financial terms, was arranged by her father and George's father, Carey Butt. When his daughter, Alice, married a local surgeon, Dr. Salt, Carey Butt settled at Pipe Grange, an estate in Longdon just one mile from Lichfield, where he farmed without much success.

In 1773, the year of George's marriage, Sir Edward Winnington presented him to the rectory of Stanford on Teme, sixteen miles west of Worcester, and the vicarage of Clifton on Teme, an adjoining parish. Winnington was Lord of the Manor at both Stanford and Clifton. At his home, Stanford Court, Winnington had major landscaping plans in mind. In 1768 he had decided to create a large lake of 25 acres in the 75 acre park. This submerged the church which was rebuilt to the east of the original site. The new church, St. Mary's, stood high on a bluff in order to provide a point of interest in the view from Stanford Court. However, because Sir Edward had further landscaping plans at Stanford Court, he wanted to demolish the old rectory so it did not obstruct the view. George Butt was persuaded to enter into an agreement by which Sir Edward would help by underwriting some of the costs of building a new rectory to the west of the church. This would later land George with a large debt 'of many thousands, which was never entirely liquidated till within a year of his death.'

It was at Stanford on Teme that the young couple began married life. Martha:

> ... was not much more than of age when she was married and came to Stanford, where the young people began life in considerable style, a style which they retained till I was five years old, or somewhat more, at which period they began to retrench and lived with greater economy till I was twelve years old, where a change took place in their affairs and arrangements.[8]

Martha's fortune and the two livings at Stanford and Clifton on Teme ensured that the couple were enjoying an enviable life style when their three children were born: John Marten Butt, born on March 10, 1774, known as Marten by the family; followed by a daughter, born on May 6, 1775, named Mary Martha – Mary, after her mother's great friend and her father's first love, Mary Whitehouse, and Martha after her mother. Their youngest child, named Lucy Lyttelton, was born on April 29, 1781. Her two Christian names were chosen because of her father's friendship with Arthur Annesley, later Lord Valentia.[9] Valentia, an extremely handsome man, had married the young and beautiful Lucy Lyttelton, the daughter of Lord Lyttelton.

~

The Butt children grew up in a close-knit and loving family and during their early childhood enjoyed an idyllic life in the small rural village of Stanford.

Here in the peaceful and beautiful setting of rolling hills, woods and deep valleys the family flourished. From the house views to the south stretched across parkland and towards the Malvern Hills. Gracing the front of the house was a large lawn with orchards beyond, and, half a mile away, the banks of the River Teme. But for the two siblings it was the north side of the house which held most delight. Mary recalls many years later:

> ... it commanded a deep dingle, or valley, rich with orchards and cultivated fields, from the bottom of which arose a lofty ridge of land which presented its

Stanford Church and Rectory

> side to the eye, and which in its character, as far as it went, had all the
> appearance of some vast mountain, being partly covered with thick coppices
> being almost precipitous in the manner in which they were disposed... those
> haunts of childhood, those haunts which were never fully explored even by me,
> because there were certain bounds over which I was not permitted to pass
> alone, or with my brother.[10]

George's former pupil, Edward Winnington,[11] with his wife Anne, was
living at Stanford Court where the children of the two families played
together forming close bonds.

One family which Mary's mother often visited was the Stokes in
Lichfield. Mrs Stokes was a close friend of Anna Seward, 'the Swan of
Lichfield.' Mary, who was an attractive and engaging child, had been
taken to Lichfield on several occasions. When she was four and on a visit,
with her parents and brother, to Anna Seward at the Bishop's Palace,
Richard Edgeworth and Dr. Erasmus Darwin were also guests. Her
brother was picked up by Darwin who examined him like a specimen.
Mary comments:

> as I have seen a Frenchman take a frog by one leg, exclaiming at the same time,
> "What a noble animal!" Mr Edgeworth's eye then fell on me, and, having looked
> at me for some time, he paid some compliments to my parents on my well-
> nurtured animal nature; he then patted his own forehead, and added, with no

great tenderness to their feelings, "But you may depend upon it, Mrs Butt, she
wants it here," and the little taps on his own brow were repeated.[12]

Not an opinion shared by her father who referred to her as a genius from
an early age and who had high expectations of her as a writer.

When Mary was four her uncle Henry Marten Sherwood's children
came to stay at Stanford over Christmas. Her cousin Henry, was born on
January 1, 1777 so was now aged almost three, there was just sixteen
months age difference between him and Mary, and his sister, Margaret,
was one. On this first visit Henry and Mary played happily in the nursery
where Henry, blonde and blue-eyed, drew in his favourite red pencil on
the chimney frame. The scribbles remained for many years, a memento
of his visit. But Henry and his sister's childhood was not happy. Their
father, Henry Marten, had married his cousin, Mercy Taylor, after the
death of his first wife in childbirth bearing Margaret. Their stepmother
resented the two children of the first marriage and proved later to be an
extremely uncaring and cruel stepmother. Her husband was a head-
strong man who was extravagant by nature causing his father, Henry
Sherwood the elder, much heartache and anxiety. When Henry Marten
became involved in a variety of financially ruinous schemes Mercy
encouraged him and quarrelled with her father-in-law.

Mary and her brother adored each other although some of her
brother's exploits sound highly dangerous. She recounts how her brother,
when she was five, would put her in a drawer and kick it down the
nursery stairs; how he would pile up chairs and tables (presumably
nursery-sized) and seat her on the top before knocking them down, and
her with them. He would put a horse bridle on her and, holding a whip,
drive her round the nursery. In spite of these games, in which she was the
willing victim, she survived relatively unscathed. One of the gentler
pursuits was Marten's reading *Robinson Crusoe* to her. He would put her
at the bottom of the stairs and with each new page they would move up a
stair. They also had a ritual at the beginning of each month when they cut
notches into two sticks and then hid them in a hollow tree in the woods
next to their house.

When Mary was almost six two events changed the dynamics of the
household: her younger sister, Lucy, was born and their father took a
pupil in order to supplement their income. The latter was necessitated

by the great cost incurred by relocating the rectory. Mrs Butt had taken over the management of their everyday expenses and any money her husband earned he gave to her. Dr. Butt set up a classroom in a nearby mill cottage that was vacant. His pupil was George Annesley, the son of Lord Valentia (later Lord Mountnorris).[13] George was almost five years older than Marten and became part of the family: 'a tall elegant boy, one of the most warm-hearted and affectionate human beings I ever met with. He soon became another brother to me, and no elder brother could ever have conducted himself more kindly or more affectionately through life.'[14]

The two boys included Mary in their imaginative games: building dens in the woods; making wooden boats; collecting and classifying snail shells by colour and garlanding her with wild flowers. She was also co-opted into acting fairy tales involving dragons, which the boys could slay in a heroic manner, no doubt saving her, as a princess or queen, from certain and horrible death. In 1784, while they were at Stanford Mary's father was made a Chaplain in Ordinary to King George III. Each November he was required to be in attendance at St. James's Palace where he would preach. His sermons were eloquent and well-received: on one occasion in 1788, when the King's life was in danger, moving the congregation to tears. So great was its impact that Dr. Butt was encouraged to publish his Court Sermons by subscription. They appeared in two octavo volumes in 1791. He would return to his family with tales of life at court, the manners and etiquette of the royal family and the gossip of the nobles. He insisted on good manners from his children: courteous behaviour and respect, irrespective of age or social standing.

Initially both children were educated at home by their parents. Mary describes them: 'my humble-minded, sensitive mother, a lady of literary and accomplished mind, whose rare integrity and excellent principles were congenial with my father's sense of virtue.'[15] Their mother had taught them both to read from an early age. It was a pastime they enjoyed together, re-reading the same books in the nursery before moving on to their father's considerable library. Mary was a highly imaginative child who loved making up stories. Her creative imagination, which would serve her so richly in later life, began to reveal itself early in the stories she wove as a child; first to her mother, who would write them down on a piece of slate, and then to her younger sister, Lucy. Her father, convinced that both children were geniuses, encouraged both Mary and her brother to write. Mary records his shutting them in his study for several mornings with instructions to write a story each. Until she was six she was given the freedom to develop this gift with the encouragement of both her parents. When Mary turned six her mother took on the daily role of tutor. She taught her daughter in her beautiful dressing room where she kept a dead pet canary in a little carved Indian box, which intrigued her young daughter. Discipline was strict. Here for the next seven years Mary would stand in stocks with an iron collar round her neck and a backboard strapped over her shoulders while her mother taught her. Dry bread and milk formed her diet, yet she was a happy child. Her Aunt Alice wrote to her in 1782:

> Dear Mary,– I am glad to hear you are so good a girl and so much improved, and I have sent you some little playthings for you and Lucy to play with. Give my love to Martin [sic] and Lucy. I hope we shall see you next summer.
>   I am yr. affect. Aunt. Alice Salt.'[16]

Her brother, Marten, was a lazy pupil. His father exercised little discipline over his learning which took place in his study, whereas under her mother's strict guidance Mary was keen to learn and soon made such progress in Latin that she overtook Marten and helped him as he struggled with Virgil. Marten's education as a boy was carefully mapped out. In 1784, when he was ten, he left the confines of his father's study for the wider world. He was sent first to Reading School where the headmaster, Dr. Valpy, was a friend of Dr. Butt, before going to Westminster School in preparation for Christ Church College, Oxford. Marten departed very unwillingly leaving Mary without any close playmate near her age. George Annesley had left the same year and Lucy, who was only three and a delicate child, was too young to join in Mary's make-believe games outdoors or run around in the woods as Mary did with her favourite companion, a doll tied to her pinafore.

When Mary was eight, Charlotte, Madame de Pelévé, who was separated from her French husband and had fled revolutionary France, came to stay. Charlotte was the daughter of Robert Butts, the Bishop of Ely, a distant relative of Dr. Butt. She was a vain woman in her forties. Mary watched in amazement as this exotic creature descended from the carriage dressed in the manner of Marie Antoinette. Her hair was built up, curled and powdered with feathers or flowers on top of a cap. Her opulent clothes with trains of silk, her wardrobe of hats, and the ribbons tying her shoes were a source of fascination to the little girl. Heavily rouged, Charlotte never appeared till two in the afternoon when she would entertain company with amusing stories of life at the French Court of Versailles. The following year, much to Mary's delight, Margaret, her cousin, who was two years younger than her, came to stay at Stanford. Here was a companion she could play in the woods with, and tell long stories to, some of which continued for months. Margaret was a beautiful and very affectionate little girl who had been neglected by her stepmother and father. After a happy eighteen months together the two girls were parted when her father and stepmother collected Margaret and 'carried her off to misery and ruin.'[17] Poor Mary felt the loss of someone close to her age in the household and mourned her departure.

Madame de Pelévé appeared on the scene once more when Mary was twelve and stayed for several months. She discomfited Mary who was tall for her age and had very long curly auburn hair and red cheeks. Although Mary had attended the annual balls at Stanford Court she had never danced at one. The private ball was an event keenly anticipated by the local gentry where the social accomplishment of dancing was viewed as essential. Here a young woman could display herself to advantage to a not uncritical audience and have contact with young men. Mary had no intention of dancing at the Christmas ball at twelve but a young man by the name of Wylde invited her onto the floor. Too shy and embarrassed to refuse she accepted but when they stood ready to dance he was distracted by something and Mary, seizing this opportunity, slipped away into a hiding place she knew. She watched as the perplexed young man searched for her before finally giving up. To her horror the next day Wylde's tutor, Mr Severne, appeared at the vicarage and disappeared into her father's study. Mary was called in to explain her conduct. She confessed that she had hidden herself between two doors in order to escape from dancing. The tutor insisted that she send an apology to the disconcerted and embarrassed young man which she did. Such were the perils for an attractive twelve-year old girl who looked older than her years but had no wish to dance, only to observe.

When Mary was entering her teens she was often taken to be much older, a mistake Wylde had made, causing her much embarrassment on social occasions as she was naturally a shy young girl in company. Her interests remained those of a child:

> The girl grew so quickly that at thirteen she had attained her full height, which was considered above the usual standard for women; and as she was still always dressed in a long pinafore like a child she was much annoyed by the family acquaintances crying out that she promised to be a giantess. As her only companion of her own age was small and delicate she was thoroughly abashed at her own appearance, and was therefore never so happy as when she was out of sight of visitors in her own beloved woods of Stanford.[18]

Here she would delight in her freedom and let her imagination dance with characters and stories which she would tell to a large doll that she continued to love in spite of being told she was too old for such a companion. Later in life she would use many of these happy memories, incidents and settings from her childhood in her fiction for children.

Kidderminster

arly in 1788 Mary was excited when her parents told her of their
plans to move to Kidderminster sixteen miles north of Worcester.
Her father had been given the living there by Lord Foley, Anne
Winnington's father. It was decided that a curate could replace Dr. Butt at
Stanford. His wife, however, was not so happy about moving to a town:
she enjoyed the solitude of the beautiful countryside; taking her children
for long country walks and calling on her neighbours. Lucy remembered
her mother crying 'when the poor cracked bells of Stanford were ringing
for my father's appointment to the living.'[19] The family were exchanging
a peaceful rural life for a town where there was abject poverty. In
Kidderminster the dyed worsted trade predominated and the smell
permeated the town. But for the ever-generous Dr. Butt, the opportunity
to show true Christian benevolence by dispensing money to the poor
and needy within a larger parish in Kidderminster, was irresistible. His
financial generosity was something the Butts could ill afford at the time
and his wife tried to keep it within check. There were also many dissenters with whom he was resolved to be friendly and always treated with
respect, kindness and charity.

The move proved to be detrimental to Martha Butt's happiness and
health. After the initial paying and receiving of visits in the neighbourhood she ventured out little. Gone were the happy days at Stanford which
Mary would look back on with such pleasure in later life. Gone too were
the days when the children would listen to their mother singing and
playing her guitar. Their mother retreated into herself; very probably
suffering from depression. Mary's lessons were neglected; the confines of
stock and collar were forgotten and it was largely left to Mary to take
responsibility for Lucy who had escaped wearing stock and collar
because of her delicate health. The girls were up by six in the mornings,

like their mother, and played outside until breakfast. Then lessons, which included learning passages from the Bible, Latin and French translation, geography and history and reading aloud, began. However, Lucy was much less studious than her sister. Mary would continue studying when their mother left the room whereas Lucy would take the opportunity to leave her place, wander round and generally distract; she was after all only seven years old and could be naughty and obstinate: character traits which Mary did not share. Lucy later regretted her lack of learning.

~

At the Kidderminster vicarage Mary and Lucy shared a bedroom which looked out on a street. From their window they would watch people going about their everyday business. This was a source of interest and entertainment for the two sisters. In spite of Mary's now being thirteen she still loved to play with dolls, for which she carefully fashioned clothes, much to Lucy's admiration. There was also a much-loved dolls' house in a closet in their room. Books were hoarded and read and reread. The family had brought their two white cats from Stanford and their father had bought a gig which, harnessed to his quiet horse, Mary would drive somewhat haphazardly around the neighbourhood with her mother and sister. Mary's talent for creating absorbing narrative and lively characters continued and now Lucy was old enough to participate. On walks together the two sisters spent hours talking to each other inhabiting the characters of two queens who both had large families. Into these roles Mary incorporated adventures and fairy tales whenever they left the house.

Mary was taken by her father to visit a newly married friend at Badger, seven miles north-east of Bridgnorth in Shropshire, whose wife, Henrietta, was the granddaughter of Thomas Hay, 7th Earl of Kinnoul. The friend, Isaac Hawkins Browne, Lord of the Manor of Badger, was MP for Bridgnorth and lived in some style with a coach and four. Mary's father had become friends with him while both were pupils at Westminster. Father and daughter travelled by gig with a man-servant riding alongside. When they arrived Mary was instructed to change into her 'very best dress' for dinner as a large number of important guests were coming. Still unhappy with her gawky appearance matters were made even worse by her being made to wear a shepherdess hat made of pale blue and silver tiffany. This had been made for her by Madame de Pelévé who was living in lodgings at Kidderminster close to the Butts. A maid servant was sent to help Mary dress. The hat was placed on one side of her head with long pins to keep it in place. Her beautiful long, rich auburn hair was arranged in curls to hang down the other side of her head. When she appeared to the guests assembled in the drawing room she saw that she was the only child present. To her embarrassment one of the male guests paid her particular attention, taking her in to dinner and then giving her his arm when the guests strolled in the garden after dinner. Mary bolted into the shrubbery!

It was on their return to Kidderminster that Mary met her cousin, Henry Sherwood, again. Mary's uncle, Henry Marten Sherwood, and his second wife, Mercy, had taken their children to France in 1787 fleeing financial ruin and in the hope of living more cheaply there. The family settled in Boulogne in lodgings opposite the market. Mary's uncle held republican sentiments espousing freedom and liberty. His naivety over the political situation in France would cost the family dear. Grandfather Sherwood had grown increasingly concerned over the political situation in France, the extravagance of his son and the welfare of Henry and Margaret. He decided he must rescue them from their neglectful father and spiteful step-mother. In January 1788 Henry and Margaret were brought back, first to London, then to their grandfather's in Coventry. He placed Margaret in a school in Coventry and brought Henry to Kidderminster to live with the Butts where he continued his chequered education at a Free School in the churchyard. Mary had last seen Henry when she was four. He was now ten but very small for his age whereas his cousin Mary was very tall. The cousins were delighted to be reunited. Henry was a quiet boy and very much in awe of his aunt. He may have wondered how his aunt would treat him when his stepmother was so uncaring towards him and his younger sister. His loving aunt was only too relieved to offer him a home away from his wayward father and his neglectful stepmother, Mercy. Mary regarded him with some admiration and wonder for he had travelled to Calais when his father had taken the family to France; far further than she or any member of her immediate family had been. Henry stayed with the Butts until he was sent to school for a short time in Warwick before being enrolled at Merchant Taylors' school. He remained there until April 1790, on the death of his grandfather, when he returned to France to join his family at Calais; his father assuming that he would inherit and be financially secure. Henry resumed his education: 'My parents sent me to school to a monastery, where the monks could not understand a word I said, nor I what they said. A Virgil was put into my hand, but any one may conceive what little use it was. Thus my education was finished, I being then thirteen.'[20] The family soon moved on to St. Valéry-sur- Somme, a port between Calais and Dieppe.

> During the winter I was often employed in sawing wood for the fires, and sifting flour. One day, when I was thus employed, an English gentleman arrived. He, it appears, had been sent over by my grandfather's executors, and came to remonstrate against the neglect of my education, and, if possible, to take me back with him to England. We than learnt that my grandfather had left me and my sister a property which ought to have amounted to between three or four thousand pounds each. My father, so far from permitting me to return, set off himself to England, and brought my sister to France, and to a house not fit for her reception, which was worse. Our step-mother, having become jealous ever since she knew the extent of my grandfather's bequest, rarely admitted either my sister or myself into her presence.[21]

Conditions for Henry and his sister were extremely harsh. They often went hungry and their father rarely spoke to them. He was extremely unkind to Margaret 'for there was a deadly feud between her and her step-mother and sisters.'[22]

Meanwhile Mary had discovered two new passions. In 1789 she started dancing lessons and was introduced by another pupil to the delights of the novel in the form of *Cecilia* (1782) by the young writer Fanny Burney[23] who had taken the growing reading public by storm with her novel *Evelina* in 1778. Inspired by the the talent of Burney, Mary began to write a novel but never got beyond the title page of *Lady Harebell*. Undaunted, her next literary foray was a play which her father pronounced good although its readership was limited to her family. Lucy adored her sister for Mary was extremely patient and sweet tempered with her. Inspired by Mary's writing Lucy also began to write and the two sisters each continued to write plays for the next few years.

Dr. Butt continued to enjoy the society of the nobility. One day he was invited to dine at Lord Stamford's seat, Enville, near Kidderminster. His servant, John, had laid out Dr. Butt's best suit in the study for him to put on later. His other clothes were in a wardrobe. Busily engaged in writing that day he decided to change early into his best trousers and placed his old coat and waistcoat where the best ones had been. Then he went back to writing. When told that the horses were ready to set off he hurriedly put on his waistcoat and jacket. Then with his greatcoat on he set out for Enville. On arrival, when the butler was helping Dr. Butt out of his coat, he exclaimed that there was a hole in the jacket at the elbow through which the white lining was visible. Dr. Butt, realising that he had picked up his old coat by mistake, turned to the butler for help to avert the impending embarrassment. The butler took him into his room and inked over the white elbow, much to Dr. Butt's amusement. At the end of the dinner he could not contain himself any longer. He turned to the butler and asked for his permission to tell the company. The butler shook his head but he ignored him and related the story to the dinner guests causing much hilarity. The butler was not so amused!

At fifteen Mary was still a child in her interests: she was writing her plays and fairy tales, a genre she would later decry, and still playing with, and making clothes for, her beloved dolls. Her social life among her parents' friends continued to flourish. She was now taking dancing lessons once a fortnight at the assembly room in Kidderminster and enjoyed herself. Dancing was an important accomplishment for a young girl to acquire and Mary excelled at it. She continued to visit Badger, which she loved, and in 1789 recounts meeting there two officers from the 53rd Regiment, stationed at Bridgnorth. All the officers of the regiment were invited to a ball at Badger but were prevented from going by a flood. Little did Mary know how important this regiment would be in her later life.

That year Anna Seward paid a visit to Mary's mother and invited her and Mary to visit her at the Bishop's Palace at Lichfield where she lived. After a long family discussion about the quality of Seward's literary output it was decided to accept. Mary was immediately taken by two portraits of Anna at the Palace: one showing her with black hair as a younger woman while the other one depicted her with golden auburn hair when she was older. Mary examined Anna's hair and decided as its colour was not natural she was wearing a wig. Anna was entranced by the colour of Mary's hair, taking it into her hands to display to the company. She complimented the young Mary saying she had heard 'that there was the promise of genius in me, and she addressed me as an elderly phoenix might be supposed to address a young one.'[24] Mary was shocked by the older woman's vanity and her need to be the centre of attention. The visit impressed upon Mary's mind that if indeed she did become a writer as her father so often predicted she would not encourage a sycophantic coterie around herself. She was also highly disapproving of the relationship between Anna and a Mr Saville who had been present at her visit. Although a married man he spent most evenings having dinner at the Bishop's Palace. He and his wife lived in adjoining houses in the cathedral close but never spoke.

~

In 1789 Mary's paternal grandmother died aged almost ninety. On her death the estate 'for which my mother's fortune had been paid, came to us, but as some little remains of the old debt were still standing, not a penny of it was used.' The debt Mary refers to is the cost incurred in the rebuilding of the rectory at Stanford which still weighed heavily on her parents.

Then in June 1790 Mary lost her maternal grandfather, aged seventy-five. By his will, proved on July 13 that year: 'Henry Sherwood the elder of the City of Coventry Silkman,' left £10 each to his son, Henry Marten Sherwood, and daughter, Mrs Martha Butt; £5.[25] to his manservant; £15 for the servants for mourning clothes; £270 to his sister; and £20 each to his executors. His granddaughter Margaret was to receive his six Oxford Canal shares and she and her brother Henry were to each receive half of a £500 loan given to their grandfather's brother-in-law and partner Michael Patterson who dealt in ribbons from a Coventry warehouse. The remainder of the estate was to be shared equally between all his grandchildren: Henry and Margaret Sherwood, John, Mary and Lucy Butt and all other grandchildren alive at the time of his death. Until the grandchildren were twenty-one years of age they would have the income from their shares applied to their education and maintenance.

Grandfather Sherwood's widow was left the rents from the several estates devised to her by the will of her late first husband, a Mr Garrett. By common law in England, since the Normans, wives were *fem couvert*. Married women's earnings and property were owned by their husband until the Married Women's Property Act of 1870. At the time of her marriage any woman of property lost title and needed a deed of marriage settlement to show her interest so that she might reclaim it on her husband's death.

Mary's grandfather was prescient in safeguarding Henry Marten Sherwood's children's inheritance for later their father would be in dire need of money. By leaving his son, Henry Marten, and his daughter, Martha, only £10 each, her grandfather effectively skipped a generation which would become a cause of much family discord.

Added to these two bereavements the reckless behaviour of Henry Marten, further upset Mary's mother who was concerned about the welfare and education of Henry and Margaret in France. Before Mary met her cousin, Henry, again he would experience great deprivation and hardship because of his father's irresponsibility towards the two children from his first marriage. In later life Henry regretted the paucity of his often-interrupted education. Compared with his cousin, Mary's brother Marten, who was now at Westminster and would continue his education at Oxford, Henry was largely uneducated.

In 1790 George Annesley, the former pupil of Dr. Butt, came with his young bride, Lady Anne Courtenay[26] to live close by at Arley Hall, seven miles north-west of Kidderminster. George was almost twenty and Anne almost seventeen. Neither George nor his wife was wealthy yet they set about completely renovating and refurbishing their new home on a luxurious scale. Servants were taken on to maintain this lifestyle. Mary's mother regarded George as a second son who could do no wrong and when George took her by chariot and four to meet his wife the two women got on well. However, Mrs Butt was alarmed by some of the couple's practical jokes which they loved to play on their guests. Mary recounts how, when her mother was invited to dinner one day, George and Anne took their places at either end of the table. When the meal was placed on the table the pair took hold of each end of the table and pulled it apart. Down crashed glass, china, candles, silver and food into the gap. Mrs Butt fainted! The young couple roared with laughter. Mary resumed her friendship with George but did not take to the very beautiful but spoilt wife. On one occasion Mary, Lucy and their father were invited to Arley to celebrate Anne's birthday. However, their hostess did not appear to greet them. Instead George entertained them to breakfast and then lunch. Finally, after bonfires had been lit in celebration, Anne appeared, beautifully dressed. The party moved in to dinner. When in the middle of the meal George turned to Mary and paid her a compliment about her teeth his wife dropped her knife and fork and appeared to faint. Clearly she was jealous of the attention paid to Mary by her husband. After that Mary kept her distance although Anne always made a great show of loving Lucy.

Boarding School in Reading

W hen Mary was fifteen in 1790 her parents decided that she should be sent away to school that September. She was beginning to find the restrictions placed on her by her parents tiresome. She longed to enjoy parties and dancing and, when thwarted by her parents, took refuge in tears.

En route back to Kidderminster from London, where he had been in attendance at St. James's Palace, Dr. Butt visited Dr. Valpy (rumoured to be 'one of the hardest floggers of his day').[26] He took Mary's father to visit the Abbey Gateway School for girls which was housed in the old Abbey at Reading. Both Cassandra and Jane Austen had been pupils from 1785–86 when it went by the name of The Reading Ladies Boarding School and had an excellent reputation. Dr. Butt approved of the boarding school for girls and it was decided to send Mary there for a year. Lucy, who was now nine, was given Flora, a small dog with a silver bell round its neck to keep her company when Mary left home. Now instead of Mary for a companion on morning walks she had Flora but she no doubt missed the conversations with her sister as the two busy queens.

The headmaster of the Abbey Gateway School was Monsieur St. Quintin. Born into the nobility in Alsace, he had been a diplomat to the Court of St. James. With the advent of the French Revolution he became a French teacher at Reading School before moving to the Abbey Gateway School, close by. Soon he had married Miss Pitts, who was then running the school with Sarah Hackitt, aka Madame Latournelle, who claimed to be the widow, or fiancée, of a Frenchman. Mary describes Madame St. Quintin:

> Madame was in person tall, and largely and majestically formed. She carried her head royally and fearlessly, and if she did not use art, her complexion was bright brown and red carmine, her eyes bright, her nose not too bad, and her

teeth white. She had fine dark hair, and a beautiful hand and arm. She danced remarkably well, but with too much of the Scotch style, which was then in fashion. She played and sang, and did fine needle-work, and she spoke well and agreeably in English and French without fear. In short, she was known to be a fine woman, and believed to be a very clever woman, and she was really the most hospitable, generous, and affectionate of human beings. This warmth and generosity had captivated my father, although it did not render her the exact kind of person to whom to entrust the education of a young girl.[27]

As the atrocities of the French Revolution gathered pace fleeing émigrés began to take up residence in and around the school. Here they found sanctuary at 'a little French court.' It was into this environment of impoverished French exiles that the naïve Mary found herself landed. The school, which was separated from Reading School by a green, was flourishing at this time and had more than sixty pupils. She recalls:

> The Abbey House had been a school longer by far than any person now living. ... The house itself was exceedingly interesting. It consisted of a gateway with rooms above and on each side of it a vast staircase of which the balustrade had been gilt. The gateway itself stood without the garden walls, upon the Forbury, or open green, which belonged to the town, and where Dr. Valpy's boys played, but the rest of the house was encompassed by a beautiful old-fashioned garden, where the children played under tall trees in hot summer evenings.[28]

The very nervous Mary was the first to arrive. The St. Quintins were not yet back from London so she was welcomed by Madame Latournelle who:

> ... was a woman of the old school, a stout woman, hardly under seventy, but very active, although she had a cork leg. She was only fit for giving out clothes for the wash and mending them, making tea, ordering dinner, and in fact doing the work of a housekeeper. She had never been known to have changed the fashion of her dress; her white muslin handkerchief was always pinned with the same number of pins, her muslin apron always hung in the same form; she always wore the same short sleeves, cuffs and ruffles, with a breast bow to answer the bow on her cap, both being flat with notched ends.[29]

Mary was taken into a wainscoted parlour with chenille hangings depicting tombs and weeping willows. Here she warmed herself before a fire. She was joined by another pupil wearing 'a blue satin cloak trimmed with fur' which impressed Mary. The two girls went upstairs to their room in which there were six beds. Their other room-mates would arrive

The Abbey Gateway School, Reading

later in the week. Mary was a parlour boarder, a pupil who had special privileges: she ate with the family, and as such was treated with great respect by the other pupils. Supper was a lively meeting where French was spoken, politics discussed and gossip exchanged with the frequent guests. Madame Latournelle loved the theatre and would hold forth in English – she refused to speak French – about the latest productions and theatre gossip. The shy Mary, away from home alone for the first time, found this difficult and would much have preferred to eat with the other pupils.

During the following week, as the other pupils began arriving, Mary had every opportunity to observe both them and some of the teachers, one of whom, a Miss Bournany, was a 'dashing, slovenly, rather handsome French girl, and ran away with some low man a few months afterwards.' When the embarrassed and nervous Mary was interviewed by St. Quintin in front of his class to decide in which class to place her she realised how little she knew and was covered in embarrassment. Having admitted that her knowledge of French, and all the other subjects he asked about, was scant he finally asked her: 'Tell me, Mademoiselle, what do you know?' To which the highly discomfited Mary responded: 'Latin-Virgil' before bursting into tears. St. Quintin put her in his class. Time out of class, of which there was plenty, apart from the mandatory two hours with St. Quintin in his study, was spent in the garden and in gossiping. When the summer holidays arrived Mary stayed at first with Mrs Valpy, as a companion, Dr. Valpy being away in Jersey. Mrs Valpy was extremely deaf and nervous about sleeping alone so Mary was drafted in as her bedfellow. All went well until one night there was a fire close by. Mary slept soundly throughout the ensuing drama. The next day her night-time duties were taken over by a servant.

Mary's mother and Lucy were visiting friends in Lichfield so, much to Mary's delight, her father joined her in Reading. She was taken on visits to the races at Ascot, Henley and to various friends who had made fortunes in India and were referred to as 'Nabobs'. Her father decked her out in: 'a blond cap with pink ribbons, and a white ostrich feather, which, with a white frock and pink sash, I thought very superior'.[30]

When Mary returned to school after the holidays she discovered that she was to share a room with two other girls, one of them a newcomer. Mary was not enamoured of her, observing her to be common with few manners. She and another girl started bullying the unfortunate girl until Madame St. Quintin took them aside to reprove them about their behaviour. A new teacher, Monsieur Pictet, had joined the staff: an elderly, wrinkled, tall, white-haired man who wore a silk wrap and slippers when teaching. He had been a secretary to Catherine the Great, spoke many European languages but his spoken English was poor. He took Mary under his wing and worked with her privately in his study – where he smoked – on improving her French as well as teaching her some philosophy. He had the habit of putting his feet up on the fireplace when teaching the girls, a habit for which St. Quintin admonished him as being improper. Pictet rejoined that it was perfectly acceptable for Catherine's Prime Minister to sit with his feet high up on the stove in St. Petersburg in the great woman's presence. Later that term Mary suffered illness and lost all her beautiful auburn hair, an upsetting thing to happen to a teenage girl now very much aware of her looks.

Her time at the school was drawing to a close with Christmas fast approaching. When her father and brother, down from Oxford for the vacation, arrived to take her back to Kidderminster, Mary said her tearful farewells to her school friends and deaf Mrs Valpy of whom she had grown fond. Lucy was delighted to have her sister home again and observed: 'She brought with her many new acquirements, was much improved in outward appearance, and had lost none of her sobriety and purity of mind and thought...'[31] Lucy persuaded Mary to pick up their long conversations in the roles of two queens again which Mary was still not too old to enjoy once more.

Realising that her elder daughter might feel bored with the limited social activities available in Kidderminster, Mrs Butt had contacted some local families and set up dances and supper in their homes. Mary appreciated this extension to her social life.

In September 1792 Mary's parents decided not only to send her back to school in Reading but also to send Lucy who was then eleven. This time there were other parlour boarders though Mary was friendly with only one of them. However, Lucy was deemed too young at eleven to be a parlour boarder. Lucy recalls her initial unhappiness at the school and being mocked for her unfashionable dress. She did, however, have Mary to intercede on her behalf when spiteful girls attacked her with their cruel tongues. The situation in France was worsening and St. Quintin became subsumed under anxiety both for his king and country, and his mounting debts. Unfortunately St. Quintin was addicted to gambling which began to affect his ability to run the school. This led him to neglect his duties over academic standards as headmaster. His wife was 'almost always in tears.' The atrocities in France had driven more exiles to Reading, some of whom took up residence in the school. However, the autumn term promised to bring entertainment for the girls: there was to be a grand ball at Reading town hall organised by the dancing master, Monsieur Bigot. At this event a quadrille was to be danced by forty pupils. The two tallest pupils, Mary and another girl, were to lead the dance. Precious hours were spent perfecting the forty dancers' performance. Added to this the girls were then to perform a play, La Bonne Mère, by the popular children's playwright, the Comtesse de Genlis. The play was to be acted in French. The shy Mary was cast in the role of Cèlie, the elderly kind aunt. She pleaded not to act but her protestations were overruled. Hours of rehearsals followed. When the time for the two performances arrived at the end of term Dr. Valpy brought his pupils across from his school. Numbers were further swelled by brothers and proud parents. Princess Amelia's governess accepted her invitation and graced the audience one evening. Princess Amelia was the youngest daughter of

George III. After the performances everyone enjoyed supper. On the last night of term the grand ball took place. Mary danced and enjoyed herself. She was flattered when a young man asked her to dance after the quadrille and remained her partner for the rest of the evening. However, on getting back to school she began to feel unwell.

The next day she felt much worse. Measles was diagnosed. Soon there were six other cases including Lucy. The girls were quarantined in one room: some became very ill and one younger girl died. Mary was extremely ill and remained at school until she was stronger. In order to cheer her up when she was fully recovered Madame St. Quintin took her to London where they stayed at the home of a former pupil in Charing Cross. Lucy remained in Reading under the care of Madame Latournelle.

Once in London Mary enjoyed a hectic social round. She went to Drury Lane to see the celebrated actors, Sarah Siddons and Charles Kemble, in *Macbeth*. Lady Macbeth was Sarah Siddons's most famous role. Also in the audience that evening were the King and Queen accompanied by their three elder daughters. Mary seems to have been more impressed by the members of the royal family than two famous actors! She also met up with friends from school who lived in London and, chaperoned by Madame St. Quintin, visited the British Museum and other London landmarks. Less educational but certainly very enjoyable for the seventeen year old were the dances at various friends' homes. Dancing was top of Mary's favourite activities and she never seemed to lack partners.

The gaiety of London was in sharp contrast to the news that Louis XVI had been guillotined on January 21, 1793. The atmosphere at the school on Mary's return was sober. The number of French noble émigrés grew rapidly in Reading with the Abbey Gateway School becoming the focal point for many previous members of the court at Versailles who were understandably deeply depressed and hugely discomfited by their present predicament. But for Mary they were a source of interest and entertainment although she had difficulty in understanding them as they poured forth their feelings in French with such force, anger and incredulity over their straitened circumstances. The on-going political situation in France was of course their major preoccupation. Mary was highly amused by one Chevalier in his attempts to learn English which foundered in spite of her best efforts. Even less teaching took place during the summer term. Instead, time was occupied by dancing in the garden to the accompaniment of a harp, walking with the French ladies and listening to their conversations as well as taking note of their fashions. They were, as one teacher put it, enjoying *la vie de château*. At the end of the summer term there was again a thespian production: this time two French plays. There was a repeat of *La Bonne Mère*, which was followed by *La Rose de Salencie*. Mary was to give the prologue which had been specially written by her father. Poor Mary dreaded having to be the centre of attention in front of an invited audience and begged to be excused but without success. She duly learnt it off by heart but when Dr. Valpy attended a rehearsal she froze on the stage. Furious at her inability to speak, and forgetting that she was not his pupil, he sprang onto the stage and hit her with his cane! The prologue was given to another pupil who did not suffer from stage fright.

When Mary and Lucy left the school that summer Mary had left behind the shy and gawky girl she had once been. At just eighteen she was an attractive, self-confident young woman, who loved going into society. This did not go unremarked on her return to Kidderminster. George Annesley of Arley Hall had been elevated to Lord Viscount Valentia on his father's being created Earl of Mountnorris. George's wife, Anne, was nearing her confinement with their first child. George was determined to go to a ball at the new assembly room in Bewdley, a few miles from Kidderminster, and invited Marten and Mary to accompany him. After dining at the vicarage George took it upon himself to put flowers in Mary's hair. The three departed in the chariot drawn at high speed by four horses. George enquired whether anyone would know Mary at the ball. When she replied in the negative George announced that she was to be called by a fictitious name with the title of 'Lady'. On arrival at the assembly room on George's arm she was introduced as such. The couple then progressed through the guests and opened the ball with no one any the wiser as to the subterfuge. What George's jealous wife made of it, if she ever knew, Mary does not reveal.

Mary was of highly marriageable age now. Attractive, reasonably educated and articulate and from a good family she could make a catch. Shortly after the adventure with George, Mrs Butt and her two daughters were invited to Lichfield to stay with an old friend, Mrs Sneyd, whose daughters were much admired for their beauty and elegance. There Mary was advised on her dress and taken into company and attended balls where she was often partnered by a baronet, a rich and fun-loving widower of over six foot. He decided to hold a masked ball in Derbyshire to which Mary was invited. It was decided by Mrs Sneyd that Mary should go as a shepherdess, a role she had so unhappily inhabited many years earlier. To her amazement she was partnered at the huge ball in sumptuous surroundings by her handsome host which did much to boost her sense of self-worth in society.

Lord Valentia's marriage was turning out to be very far from a happy one, much to Mrs Butt's dismay. She regarded George as another son and took any unhappiness of his to heart. Lady Valentia and George were by 1793 leading very separate lives and kept separate meal times. She did not rise early and had breakfast at two in the afternoon whereas her husband ate his at nine in the morning. He retired to bed soon after ten at night while she had supper at midnight and went to bed at three or four the next day. To add to the marital problems debts were mounting up as a result of the young couple's profligate spending on improvements to the house. Matters came to a head when the entire Butt family were staying at Arley Hall. A vicious argument broke out between the young couple in the drawing room after dinner one night much to the discomfort of the Butts. Their language was so intemperate that the Butts retired to their rooms and left the following morning. That was the last time they saw Lady Valentia at Arley.

~

In the summer of 1794 Mary's parents decided to leave Kidderminster and return to their beloved Stanford. When they arrived at the rectory Mary found a beautiful Italian greyhound and a selection of rare plants on the front lawn. These were gifts from Lord Valentia. He had also left a substantial number of books, including very valuable ones, in the care of his former tutor, Dr. Butt, who had a large library housed in his study among the chaos of sermons, manuscripts, poems and letters, overseen by a favourite cat occupying the only vacant chair. The Butts also had access to Sir Edward Winnington's library at Stanford Court which boasted one of the largest collections in England. Mary had begun writing *The Traditions*, a Gothic novel, in her spare time at school and while staying with Lord and Lady Valentia at Arley Hall with her father. Here she could shut herself in her own room away from the domestic discord which raged around the house. Very probably Mary would have read Horace Walpole's Gothic novel *The Castle of Otranto* (1764). Dr. Butt was even more convinced that Mary would become a writer: 'my father encouraging me, and everybody about me leading me to believe myself most highly gifted by Nature.'

> … my father had impressed upon my mind from a mere baby that I was to turn out what he called a genius, and therefore the idea was so familiar to me, and the conviction that it was a fact so strong upon my mind, that it never came upon me by surprise. It was a matter of course that I was to write. It was also a matter of instinct … But I had, from seeing Miss Seward and reading the papers in the Tatler respecting Miss Jenny Bickerstaff[32] got a horror of being thought a literary lady; it was, I fancied, ungraceful, unlike a heroine, and, in short, I did not desire at all to be known as an authoress. I was far less established in the idea of my own good looks than of my talents, and one word in favour of them was more precious than thousands in praise of any supposed genius.[33]

When the not entirely unexpected news of St. Quintin's catastrophic financial ruin reached Dr. Butt he proposed that *The Traditions*[34] should be published by subscription for the benefit of St. Quintin. Mary was alarmed at being thrust into the public eye so soon:

> I was very unhappy; but then again, to disappoint my father in his benevolent scheme, and to withhold a helping hand from the friend I so dearly loved, was impossible. I could not, and I did not utter a denial; but really and truly I was thoroughly vexed. Many, many tears I shed in private.[35]

Her uncle, Dr. Salt, a surgeon in Lichfield but about to move to Birmingham, undertook to prepare the manuscript for publication in two volumes. Its success enabled St. Quintin to start a small school in Hans Place, Chelsea. He and his wife were naturally full of gratitude to Mary. Mary herself deeply regretted the publication of *The Traditions* for, although published anonymously, it was widely known to be from her pen. She felt that her private love of writing and her immaturity had been exposed to the public eye when she was not yet nineteen – although she longed to begin writing again.

There were now two servants in the household at Stanford and the atmosphere was a happy one. Mrs Butt was once more among friends and in the countryside. The house was quiet after the bustle at school so the girls welcomed visits from family, friends and the local gentry – especially their friends the Winningtons at Stanford Court. Marten was at home for the vacation from Oxford; their uncle, Dr. Salt stayed with them and other friends visited. It was Lady Winnington who cheered up their social life by arranging dances at which Mary was invariably partnered by the son and heir while Marten danced with the Winnington's eldest daughter. Lucy was less lucky: 'Tommy Berry, often my sister's partner, rather appeared to wheel along than to dance, throwing himself back, and looking, in his white waistcoat, worn for these grand occasions, not unlike a sack of meal set upright on a truck and pushed about the room.'[36] An apt description as Tommy Berry was the miller's brother. Looking back on these carefree days, Mary observed: 'I am ready to laugh to this hour when I think of these balls. I obtained high celebrity then and there for being something very superior in the dancing line.'[37]

The summer had been a happy one with a whirl of social events for Mary and Lucy. With autumn came heavy frosts and the rhythm of their lives became less hectic. The sisters took Bonne, the Italian greyhound, on walks which, because it felt the cold badly, would climb into Mary's long muff with its head peeping out. The family dog, Lion, a Newfoundland, let it sit on his back in the warm kitchen. Friends and relatives departed, leaving the family of four to enjoy their own company. Gothic novels were much in fashion and Mary and Lucy read Mrs Radcliffe's *Mysteries of Udolpho* aloud with their mother in her dressing room. After the publication of *The Traditions*, which one friend of Dr. Butt criticised for being the work of a young and inexperienced author, Mary wrote: 'I wished that I had never known the use of a pen, and tried to resist the longing desire which I had to write again.'[38] The desire to write was too strong: 'I had secretly resolved never to print another book, though I had already planned another, which I began the ensuing autumn...'[39] It was now that Mary began her second Gothic novel, *Margarita*. Several of the characters were based on family and friends some of whom recognised themselves. She also incorporated scenes at Stanford and the countryside. Her father took great interest in the book, partly because of a character named Canon Bernards who closely resembled him. Mary sold the novel for £40 in 1799[40] and 'if I gained nothing else by the exercise, I certainly acquired much command of language. I shall ever love that book, because its earliest sheets were written in my father's study, and because he smiled on the undertaking.'[41]

The autumn brought the tragic death in childbirth at thirty-four of Lady Anne Winnington. She had married at fifteen. The baby, a son and her twelfth child, survived. Her death cast a sombre shadow over the Winnington family and the Butts. Mary's mother had been a close friend so missed her dearly. The gaiety of the balls and dancing, which Mary had enjoyed so much, ceased at Stanford Court.

When the warmer weather came in the early spring of 1795, Mary's godmother, Mrs Slaney, invited her to Bath: 'My godmother never lived a year together in one place; she had a constant succession of intimate friends, who were all that is charming – for a few months, more or less.'[42] There was much to amuse Mary in Bath. She was taken to the assembly rooms where she danced 'in plain muslin dresses, and danced for the pleasure of dancing.' Taking the waters, bathing in the Cross Bath, attending concerts and card parties, offered amusement at which the young and beautiful had ample opportunity to display themselves in a potential marriage market. Bath was a place to see and be seen. Gossip and friendships were made and broken in the structured setting of the season at Bath. For someone of Mary's age, attractive, intelligent and extremely fond of dancing, a close and vigilant chaperone was essential to safeguard against any unwise alliance or scandal which could damage a young woman's reputation. Mrs Slaney did not fit the role: 'there could scarcely have been on many accounts, a more unfit woman with whom to entrust a girl, among persons accounted decent, than my poor godmother'[43] was the opinion of Mrs Sherwood much later in life when she was herself a mother of daughters.

Mary had a keen eye, a writer's eye, for critical detail. At Bath she describes how two beautiful sisters:

> … used to sing at public concerts, and go through all the manoeuvres to attract notice so frequently described in novels; but being quite at the head of their line, they utterly despised common attentions which, in some way or another, did not answer either of their purposes, one of which was to obtain for themselves splendid establishments and the other to attract men to their mother's card parties.[44]

She also observed how beauty fades and, even with the help of rouge and white paint, a Miss Broughton, who had been a renowned beauty when Mary was four, now only 'looked very well by candle-light.' Mrs Slaney soon tired of Bath. The next stop was the Hot Wells at Clifton where they stayed in a boarding-house which was full of French émigrés. Mary was less impressed with them than was her godmother who thrived on making new acquaintances.

On her return to Stanford Mary learnt that Lord Valentia had been to Stanford and 'kidnapped' her beloved greyhound, Bonne, by buttoning her up into his waistcoat. She was heartbroken. However, there was also good news in that at last the debt that had hung so heavily over her parents had finally been paid off. There was also further good financial news. St. Quintin's school in Hans Place was flourishing and, although much smaller than the Abbey Gateway School, it now had a good number of pupils. St. Quintin came to stay with the Butts and expressed his gratitude to them and to Mary. Both Mrs Butt and Sir Edward Winnington found him to be a charming guest.

That autumn an old friend of Dr. Butt, Dr. Holmes, came to stay. They had known each other when they were both boys but they had lost touch. When the time came for Dr. Holmes to leave, Dr. Butt accompanied him as far as Kidderminster. That day Mary's father had a paralytic stroke which left the once highly articulate man of fifty-four with severely affected speech. Dr. Salt, his brother-in-law, came from Birmingham to care for him before he was moved home to Stanford. He suffered two further strokes and died on September 29, 1795. Mary's beloved father was dead and the effect on Mary's mother was life-changing for all the family. Mary was then twenty and Lucy just fourteen.

'Far greater danger in Bath'

The grieving family moved to stay at the parsonage at Arley which had been promised to Mary's father who, with George Annesley's permission, had passed it to his brother, Mary's Uncle Thomas. Here Mary's mother contemplated their future. She ignored the advice of Sir Edward Winnington who strongly recommended a move to Worcester where she had friends. Instead she made the decision to move to Bridgnorth, between Arley and Badger where her close friend, Mrs Hawkins Browne, lived. Her brother-in-law found a house in Bridgnorth: 'an old, miserable, cold wretched place in the High Church Yard.' He also found another house, which was much preferable, but Mrs Butt decided to take the first one. Her decision was based on financial anxieties – the first house was cheaper. Yet she had no need to be anxious on that account for she had a good income. However, she was persuaded to remain at Arley until the following spring. In the middle of January 1796 Mary was invited to Bath again by her godmother. Mary was eager to escape from the unhappy associations with Stanford and her mother's depressive withdrawal from life and financial anxiety.

> I was certainly placed in a very unfavourable position at Bath; but had I had a proper feeling I ought not to have been there at all. I ought to have remained at Stanford to support and console my mother; but I did as most girls would do under the circumstances! I fled from the present and most dreaded evil, the bitter associations and remembrances always arising before me at Stanford, to a state of more cheerfulness indeed, but one of far greater danger in Bath.[45]

This time, however, it was not a happy visit. Her godmother became jealous of any attention paid to her god-daughter and quarrelled with the other people in the house where they were staying. Mary was by now a very striking young woman, tall and with beautiful auburn hair but had grown vain about her looks and appearance. Bath was a heady place for a

young, ill-chaperoned young woman to be. Mary was still wearing
mourning and not participating fully in the attractions on offer. It was
here that Mary became unwisely involved: 'I had for many weeks been
associated with a young gentleman who was an avowed infidel, and he
had so far prevailed, mixing up his poisonous principles with much
flattery, that I had almost begun to hear him, at least without indigna-
tion'.[46] Fortunately for Mary her godmother became bored and it was
decided by the ever-restless old lady that they should move on, first to
Oxford and then to London. The two set off in a post chaise spending a
night en-route at an inn. The old lady talked non-stop regaling Mary
with stories which helped pass the time. Marten was still at Christ
Church:

> He came, all joy, to meet his sister, and before he had been in the room many
> minutes, he presented me with an elegant Testament… I can never forget the
> feelings with which I received that present… If that sweet brother could have
> the slightest suspicion of the conversations to which his sister had lately
> harkened, of the books she had lately read, of the utter carelessness of religion
> in which she had lately lived, what would he think? how would he be pained?
> and my beloved father could he but know how his daughter had fallen, what
> would he feel? With these divinely gifted thoughts I retired to my room, and
> wept most bitterly.'[47]

Mary's remorse was extreme.

Not only was Mary in the company of Marten but she also met several
other undergraduates. Her godmother bloomed in this youthful
company and lapped up the attention paid to her. On Mary's first visit to
Bath a young man who was a Fellow of Merton had shown an interest in
her but her godmother had refused to allow a third meeting between
them. Fearing that they might meet up again in Oxford she forbade Mary
to visit Merton. Mary felt uneasy in Oxford: 'It is not a place for young
women…' As there were no women undergraduates she would have felt
outnumbered by the young men's admiring attention. She was also
feeling chastened about abandoning her mother when her grief was so
raw. She was anxious to leave and go to London but her godmother
announced they had nowhere to stay there. She preferred to remain in
Oxford where she was enjoying the attention of the young male
company. Mary was desperate to leave so contacted St. Quintin. The
ever-grateful St. Quintins found them lodgings in Hans Place close to his

home and his small boarding school. Much to Mary's relief her godmother liked St. Quintin and he very quickly became a great favourite. Unbeknown to Mary and her godmother the St. Quintins were in debt again. When Mary's godmother paid fifty pounds to them for their board and lodging Mme. St. Quintin dropped in a faint to the floor. She later confided that had they not had that fifty pounds their financial crisis would have overwhelmed them once more. On hearing this Mary's godmother immediately gave their hosts another one hundred and fifty pounds thus forestalling any further imminent financial problems.

By 1793 the Valentia's marriage had been all but over. The Butts had observed the stresses between the couple who by then had been married for just over three years. In February 1794 Lord Valentia went abroad to escape his creditors. His wife was to follow but in March she refused to leave England. The reason for her refusal was that she had started an affair with John Bellenden Gawler,[48] a close friend of Valentia. She maintained that her husband knew about the affair and had turned a blind eye. The lovers went to his father's house at Ramridge in Hampshire where they continued their affair and she became pregnant by Gawler. When her husband returned in April 1795 she refused at first to sleep with him knowing that she was pregnant but then admitted she had been unfaithful. However, there was a limit as to what a cuckolded husband would tolerate: she had become pregnant while he was out of the country. There was a strong suspicion that her first child, a daughter, was also Gawler's. Valentia left her and sued Gawler. His marriage to his capricious wife was over. She took their daughter to her sister in Shropshire.[49]

It was while Mary was in London in 1796 that she saw both Lord and Lady Valentia. They were now separated. Lady Valentia was living in Sloane Square close to Hans Place. With her she had her illegitimate son of whom Lord Valentia was trying to get custody. He was desperate for a male heir – legitimate or not. Hearing that Mary was in London he visited her often in Hans Place, partly in the hope of snatching the baby from the nurse on their daily walks. Once he almost succeeded but the nurse managed to escape with the baby and Lord Valentia arrived in a distressed state at Mary's lodgings where she calmed him.

In the House of Lords, in 1796, Lord Valentia sued John B. Gawler, his wife's lover for 'criminal conversation' with his wife. In order to dissolve a marriage an Act of Parliament was necessary at this time. On the first reading of the Bill, under cross examination, a servant who had been employed by Gawler and then by Lord Valentia, described how he heard someone step across to Lady Valentia's bedroom and in the morning he found her bedroom door unlocked and could hear John Gawler's voice. She was in her dressing gown which aroused his suspicions. The servant reported both incidents and his suspicions to Lord Valentia.

> Once there they aroused the suspicion of a servant after she saw Lady Valentia leap from Gawler's lap when she entered one of the rooms in the house. The lovers' conversations in Lady Valentia's room were also overheard. She took a house near Ramridge, and Gawler visited her. Lady Valentia was soon confessing to her friends that she was pregnant by Gawler. Valentia returned to England in April 1795, but did not visit his wife until July 21 after he had settled his affairs with his creditors. Lady Valentia at first refused to sleep with him (he was twenty-five, she twenty-two) and told him it was because she was afraid to have more children. But when he complained the next day, she confessed she had been unfaithful and was pregnant. They separated. That was Valentia's story. Lady Valentia had a different tale. She insisted that Valentia had known of her affair long before July 22. It had started in 1793 before Valentia went abroad. Nonetheless, Valentia had invited Gawler to visit and had left him alone with his wife. Valentia had frequently said he wanted a child to prevent any branch of the family of Sir Henry Cavendish from inheriting his property, and that provided that his wife bore him children, he "did not care who the devil got them." Valentia had seen Gawler's attentions to his wife, and in November 1793 had asked Gawler if he or his brother had been intimate with her. Valentia had also declared that he knew that the child Lady Valentia had borne was Gawler's. He had even told Gawler not to become venereally infected so that the disease would not be passed along to Lady Valentia. Gawler, Valentia said, did all his business for him with Lady Valentia. Lady Valentia's story has a plausible ring about it. If it was true that her first child was Gawler's, Valentia must have decided that he could nonetheless plausibly claim paternity and make the child his heir. But then she became pregnant when her husband was out of the country. The legitimacy of any child that she now bore would be in doubt. and it may be that Valentia was not really prepared to have another man father his children, no matter what he may have said. In any case he left her immediately after he knew she was pregnant. He successfully sued Gawler and received £2,000 in damages and £366 in costs. He began his divorce in the consistory in November 1796, but it was not concluded until April 1799.[50]

However, when it came to the second reading of the Bill:

> Upon reading the Petition of the Right Honourable *George Annesley*,
> commonly called Lord Viscount *Valentia*, in the Kingdom of *Ireland*; setting
> forth, "That a Bill has been presented to this House to dissolve the Marriage of
> the Petitioner with the Honourable *Anne Courtenay* his now Wife, and for
> other Purposes therein mentioned, which has not been read a Second Time:
> That some of the Witnesses, which the Petitioner is advised it is material
> should be examined on the Second Reading of the said Bill, are now out of the
> Kingdom, and cannot be produced until after the End of, or at a very late
> Period in, the present Session of Parliament;" and therefore praying their
> Lordships, "That his said Bill, now depending in this House, may be
> withdrawn:"
>
> It is ORDERED, that the Petitioner be at Liberty to withdraw his said Bill, as
> desired.[51]

The trial was a source of salacious gossip and conjecture in London. The divorce trial collapsed and the couple had to settle for a legal separation which blighted both their chances of remarrying. Mary blamed the advice that Lady Valentia was given by her lover which prevented the divorce. Mary suspected that Gawler did not wish to marry Lady Valentia and become her legal protector. Or did Valentia suspect that her version of events would carry the day? Anne was cast out of London society, still beautiful but with her reputation ruined. Mary never saw her again. Anne died in 1835.

Part Two

Henry Sherwood

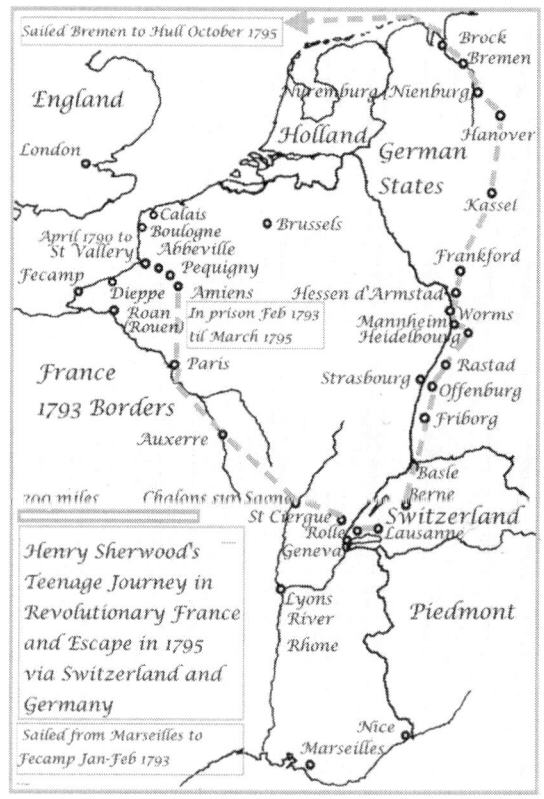

Henry Sherwood in Revolutionary France and
Escape Route 1790–95

Catching up with Cousin Henry

Mary remained in London for six weeks and while there she received a letter from her mother asking her to make contact with Henry Sherwood, her cousin, who was in London too. Henry was now nineteen; Mary was twenty-one. Henry had lived in France during the First Coalition of the French Revolution when Britain was at war with France. He and his sister, Margaret, had been deserted by his father and stepmother; imprisoned as enemy aliens and been reduced to penury. Then, through his own resourcefulness and courage, Henry had saved the family. In contrast Mary had led a sheltered and privileged life. Her social life revolved round visiting friends of her parents, visits to Arley and Stanford Court where she enjoyed dancing at the parties and private balls. Reading and above all writing were important to her enjoyment – she was now a published author. She had visited London, Bath, Oxford and many parts of Worcestershire for short holidays. Unlike Henry she had received an uninterrupted education; first under her mother's guidance and then been sent away to school in Reading where she had mixed with French nobility. When the two cousins met again after so many years Mary was eager to catch up with what had happened to Henry since she last saw him when he was eleven.

Henry had returned to England from France in October 1795, aged eighteen, and made his way to Coventry where his great-aunt Mrs Patterson lived. Thomasina Sherwood had married Michael Patterson, his grandfather's former partner and friend who gave Henry employment in his silk company in London: Henry was unable to benefit from his grandfather Sherwood's will until 1798 when he would be twenty-one. He attempted to make contact with his father and second family who were now living in a very poor neighbourhood, near the brick kilns in Bethnal Green, London. Henry was not welcome: 'he generally drove him away with the most violent abuse.' In spite of this he did take Mary to visit his father, which was the last time she saw her uncle. While they were both in London the cousins saw each other regularly. Mary reassured Henry that her mother would welcome him to her new home in Bridgnorth. She also introduced him to the St. Quintins, who issued an open invitation. He was also a welcome guest of the Reverend Gerrard Andrewes, who was rector of St. James's, Piccadilly, for dinner every Sunday. Andrewes had married a cousin of Henry's father and would in 1809 become Dean of Canterbury. At Mary's request, Henry wrote her a letter and an account of his eventful life since they had last met. Punctuation, syntax and spelling reflect Henry's limited education yet his account of his life in France during the French Revolution is vivid and moving: his resourcefulness in the face of extreme hardship and starvation mark him out as a remarkable young man. There is some debate about the date of the letter (annotated, after both he and Mary were dead, by Sophia, their daughter) as being 1796: the account covers his life from 1790 until 1796 and was published as an edited version of Sophia's edition in 1981 as *The Value of Bread*.[52]

~

Copy of a letter, without date, but written probably in 1796.

[This note was added by a different hand presumably Sophia's.]

To Miss Butt,
Bridgenorth.

Dear Cousin,
    You have forced me to send you this Account but I am afraid you will be punishing yourself more than me, but that is none of my business, I have obeyed you & that is enough. I have omitted many circumstances, which I might have told you but they cannot be written. I have, as you desired, avoided mentioning family concerns more than necessary for carrying on the tale. I can assure you that, had it not been yourself that commanded it, I would not have undertaken it, for I know very well that I am incapable of doing it properly, neither have I the time. You must consider that I am employed from half after six in the morning till eight at night, after which I am tired & not fit to write good sense or Grammar. In my situation I never shall have occasion either to write Histories or Voyages, or even letters except those in set forms in

which the same words are always used, you must therefore content yourself with this poor performance which I only wish better because you are to read it.

I have not kept a copy myself, fearful that some time or other I might be tempted to shew it & be laughed at. I therefore beg that you will not let anyone see it, & I should wish that you would burn it when read. I must also beg that you will not laugh at me yourself for I am conscious that I deserve it.

You know that, when I left you at Kidderminster, my Father placed me at Merchant Taylor's School where I remained only going twice to France till April 1790, the Year of the French Revolution. At that time I went to France as it appears to remain there altho I did not expect it at the time. My Father remained at Calais till June & then he proceeded with his Family to Bolougn, which place we left in August for St. Vallery intending, as I have heard him say, to proceed to the South of France. At St. Vallery my sister, Mercy, was taken ill & we could not go no further. She at length died here in 1791. &c &c &c

I am with love to Lucy,
Your affectionate Cousin
Henry Sherwood Junr[53]

In September 1790 My Father went to reside at Saint Vallery sur Somme, a Sea Port on the Coast of Picardy, on the River Somme about 10 miles from Abbeville. The French Revolution then wore a promising appearance, particularly to those who had been accustomed to look on the American Revolution as the cause of Liberty. I was too young to judge but I observed that my Father was led, in some degree to adopt the new doctrine from a difference in opinion from his Father who was a supporter of the British Government during the American War.

My Father had other reasons for leaving his own Country. He had been extravagant &, altho still possessing a good Income, he thought he would be able to live in greater style in France than he could in a country overburthened with debts & sunk in slavery, as he represented England to be. In June 1790 My Grandfather died & being displeased with some part of the Conduct of his family, he left his Property in very unequal divisions, a much greater part coming to me than was thought just by my Father. I was not (then) 14 years old & consequently under my Fathers control. My StepMother also shewed a degree of unkindness to me which made home unpleasant. Soon after our arrival in Saint Vallery my Father purchased an Eighth part of a Brig. He wished, as he said to form Connections & to identify himself with the <u>Nation</u>. He also bought Houses & LANDs.

One House in the town of St. Vallery & a Benedictine Abbey at a little
distance. The latter was a most Charming Spot, more like a Palace
than a House. There were thirty comfortable rooms in it, & the
Gardens & Grounds were laid out luxuriantly in Groves & Walled
Gardens like a Noblemans domain, here I might have been happy had
it not been for the constant jealousy of My Mother which increased so
much that I could not appear in her Presence or even dine at the table
with the family. Under these circumstances I was glad of the
opportunity offered of being constantly on board the Brig, while
fitting for Sea & the Kindness of the Captain who treated me as a Son
of an Owner won upon me so much that I expressed a wish to go the
voyage with him, which my Father agreed to without the least
hesitation, indeed seemed very happy that it should be so. The Brig
was indeed very small not more than 120 Tons & so old that she was
sold to be broken up. The eight Share did not cost more than forty
pounds. On examination however it appeared that the Vessel was not
fit for sea which caused much delay & hesitation on the part of the
Owners for I believe the Captain had used influence amongst friends
to procure a proper number of subscribers & probably
misrepresented the state of the Ship. So much was this the case that
they refused to pay their quota to the Repairs. These difficulties kept
the Ship a Year in the Harbour sometimes fitting & sometimes
dismantling, which gave me great Interest in her & the difficulties
which the poor Captain met with made him more Civil to me. The
poor fellow's perseverance, at length, overcame all Difficulties & we
sailed for Marseilles on the 22nd July 1792.

Henry's voyage to Marseilles on L'Etoile Mignion. [sic]
The Bay or estuary of the Somme at St. Vallery is about six miles from
the Sea & being 3 miles across & sometimes rough in high winds, I
had fancied that by sleeping on board I had become a Sailor, but I
soon found the difference between a Ship at anchor & one moving. I
crept under the Boat & was most miserably sick & like Robinson
Crusoe, wished myself at home again. The Captain had often joked
with me while in harbour by saying if you go with me you must be
made a Sailor & work hard & I thought it would be a fine thing, but
being sick & placed on a Watch four Hours on deck & four below

alternately I found the difference between work & play. I could not reconcile myself to getting up as I fancied as soon as I got into a pleasant sleep.

The first night indeed, altho posted to a Watch, I was allowed to go below but my sickness was worse there than on deck. In the morning I left my Hammock & went on deck we were close to the Isle of Wight. It looked like a three cornered Hatt & when the sun rose it had a beautiful appearance. As the Sun rose higher we lost sight of the land, not because we were farther off but by reason of the Vapour rising from the Sea.

The day was very fine but warm & the Sea was covered with English Pleasure boats, several with bands of music on board. I lost my sickness & began to think that the sea was more comfortable, but a Storm succeeded this Calm & we were tossed about for several days & my sickness returned. I longed for Shore. We approached, in one of our tacks the Lands End & saw the windmills very plain. The next day we were near to Ushant & saw the light House there. The storm carried us thro the Bay of Biscay rolling us about & when off Cape Finisterre it fell calm. The weather was now extremely Hot, we smelt the Land & the Birds came on board the Ship. I could almost fancy myself on Shore. Off the Rock of Lisbon it was again calm & we harpooned several Porpusses & caught thirteen young sharks with a line.

The Captain employed all hands in cutting up the Porpusses & Sharks, cutting the flesh into long thongs & hanging these thongs to dry & in pressing out the oil from the fatt. The Frenchmen had no other food while this lasted but I could not touch it & therefore I fared Badly. One of the young Sharks seized the dog by the foot & bit it so nearly off so that the poor fellow was thrown overboard. The water was so transparent that we saw the fish as in a Glass biting the bait & drew them in more by observation than feeling, indeed had time been given for their feeling the hook, I have no doubt they could have snapped off the line.

We lay becalmed off Cape Saint Vincent close in with the Shore. On the edge of the percipice is a large Monastery possessing a Battery, as I was told, to protect Vessels running under the guns from Sallie Rovers,[54] formerly very common about here but now seldom seen. I believe the harbour of Salee is, they say, nearly choked up. A Rock is situated in the Sea at a very little distance, yet we passed between it & the shore, so near that we could easily have thrown a stone So as to touch it.

We had a most pleasant sail from St. Vincent to Cape St. Lucia, where we left the land to stretch across the Bay to make the Streights of Gibraltar. We saw Cape Spartel on the 7th Aug. & entered the Streights in company with a Spanish Man of War. The African shore, to which we had approached nearer than to Spain, had a pleasant appearance much more inviting than the Rugged Coast of Spain.

On passing along we saw a Fort which I suppose to have been Tetuan but, owing to the winding of the Streights, I did not see Gibraltar till we had nearly reached it. We still kept on the African side, Mount Atlas appearing close to us, although I am told it is sixty miles off. The Captain quizzed me about it calling it the Mount of Monkeys & giving me a telescope bade me observe the animals. At first I looked out with all my Eyes, but I soon found out that he was laughing at me.

The French Sailors have a custom of (as they call it) christening a Freshman when he passes the Streights or he may purchase his toleration to heathenism. I had no money & was forced to become a Christian. I was placed in a Tub &, with a Common Funnel water was poured down each sleeve & then down my back & afterwards a bucket-full thrown on my head; Gibraltar & Mount Atlas being Sponsors but which was my Godfather I do not know. It was pleasant enough in August; I should have objected much more in January. I now promised Six Livres, which the Captain became responsible for at Marseilles or I might have suffered more. They dipped the Cabin boy in the Sea. The current now sent us over to the European side close under the Rock of Gibraltar & we could see the Sentry on Europa Point. Clearing the Rock, we saw the back of the Peninsula like a Spadeful of Earth towards the Mediterranean. We saw Ceuta, an Island on the opposite shore but in possession of Spain. We kept near the Spanish coast, the Mountains of Grenada being seen in the background. I felt some difficulty in believing the Captain when he told me that they were always covered with snow. We passed Malaga, which we saw & from thence to Cape de Gate where the French say that the wind always changes blowing from different quarters on each side. I believe that the same wind will not carry you round which brought you there, but the sailors are ignorant of the play upon words, if it is so intended. It was with us a dead calm & the current drove us out to sea.

The calm lasted a week, after which a breeze arose which carried us to Ivica, an island off the coast of Valencia, where we saw the remarkable Cleft in a promontory of the mainland which is called The Coup de Sabre de Roland. Reported to have been cut in two by the famous Paladin of that name with his sword Durandal. We were on the lookout for Turtles. I sat all day in the Fore Top looking for them but without success, for this place is famous for them, there being a River called The River of Tortoises here it being a bad time of year. The next day we saw Mountserrat, a mountain in Catalonia. We drifted out to sea again & towards evening saw Cabretta. one of the Balearian it is the most western. Next morning we passed between Majorca & Menorca which had a low shore, many land birds coming on board. We were nearer Majorca which had a low shore with beautiful groves of oranges.

The eastern end of these Islands was rugged rocks which having cleared we stretched over to the North & made Cape Rosas which is a Promontary formed by the Pyrrenees & which separates France from Spain in the whole breadth viz from the Gulf of Bayonne on the Atlantic to Cape Rosas in the Mediterranean.

We had rough weather crossing the Gulf of Lyons & two days afterwards were off Toulon where we were becalmed two days in what is called a dead calm & as there are no tides in the Mediterranean we did not move. The wind arose at the end of two days but boisterous & unfavourable which drove us to Corsica where it changed & we reached Marseilles on the 22nd August. A Fisherman came on board as Pilot. He related to us the dreadful Massacre at Paris on the 10th & he said the Aristocrats were hunted & seized every day. We entered a Large Rocky Bay, with several Islands in its mouth. Here we observed Ships laying which we were told were performing Quarantine. These Islands appeared altogether barren, not a blade of green to be seen. A Fort appeared in one which the Pilot called St. John. He said that the Duchess of Orleans with two of her sons were there confined. We passed close to the Rocks in very deep water. The Rugged appearance of these rocks, as we passed close under them, was tremendous. Our Yard Arms almost touched them as we sailed along.

The City is not seen until you enter the Harbour the entrance to which is narrow & winding. When we were fairly in the number of shipping appeared really astonishing & from their being no tide or current the water was thick & dirty & we could not tell how we had got there from being busy at the time I had not observed our course & I could not perceive any inlet.

The fish called Pilot-fish, which had followed our ship ever since we had been in the Mediterranean died in this dirty water & floated on the surface.

The Port has a fine Effect as you have a view of its whole length terminated by a Broad fine Street, perfectly strait & the Houses, 6 Stories high, are built uniformly. This street is crossed by another called The Course, planted on each side with Plane trees & Fountains in the Center. This Latter is the fashionable walk on Sunday's.

The city with its harbour is surrounded by hills. On the South is the Fort & Chapel of Notre Dame de Bonne Garde with the Signal Post. To this Chapel all our Crew went to return thanks for safe arrival on the first Sunday. I forgot to say that whenever we had bad weather at Sea our Captain kept a candle burning to our Lady of Bonne Garde which was always to be supernumery & not used for profane purposes. Indeed great care was taken that its light might not be serviceable for any thing. The chapel is full of images in wax & paintings of Ships in Storms. The offerings for dangers escaped or Limbs saved by the manifest assistance of the Dame de Bonne Garde. Her image generally appears in the Clouds in each of the pictures offered.

From the terrace of this chapel, you have an extensive view of Sea & Land but the latter apparently burnt up only bare rocks, probably the season is unfavorable for verdure. Here & there in the Vallys a few stunted Firs. The appearance of the City & Harbour is very fine.

On returning to the city & while walking about at a Corner of the Street, I fell in with a mob having Prisoners whom they were going to hang a la Lanterne. One of them was so tall that his head appeared clearly above the heads of the populace. He had no hat on & was dressed like a sportsman in a Short Shooting Jacket & splatterdashes. He was pale but looked with contempt on the Rabble. I followed the mob without knowing what they were about until a Man let down a Lamp which hung across the street & having taken it off, hung the poor Man with the Rope. The mob were singing & dancing & I found myself surrounded & held by the arm & I was afraid to attempt getting away.

They hung one of the Prisoners whose name I heard was Vasque by his feet & opened his body & afterwards cut him down & dragged him round the City by his feet singing all the way. As soon as I could get away I ran off to the Ship & on my way saw several People hanging on different Lamp Cords. When I got on board I intended to keep there & go no more on shore if I could help it.

The Captain, soon after this, struck a Sailor & as the doctrine of Equality was now the order of the day the Powers in Authority decided against the Captain, & as Sailors are generally discontented all our crew left the ship except a Boy & the Mate & myself.

We three took the rigging down, tarred it & put it up again. This was very hard work & my hands became ingrained with Tar & dreadfully swelled. When this was finished I was sent on Shore to look for the Captain. Here I also slept & had an opportunity to be at the play every evening. The Acting was very good & the Entrance Money very small indeed. You might almost go in for nothing. One day, whilst I was employed in my office of Cook, I heard a noise in the street & English Oaths used. On which, I went out & found an English Sailor drunk & quarrelling in the street. He either could not, or would not, understand the People who were trying to pacify him. Upon which, I addressed him in English. He suddenly turned round upon me & said Who are you? I answered An English boy. What & serving with the French, you little Renegade. You leave these French rascalls immediately & go to England. He then went away.

Two or three days afterwards, I met the same man again. He recollected me & addressing me said You are the little English Boy who spoke to me the other day. I warn you to leave this city immediately. If you remain a fortnight longer you will see the blood running up to your knees in the streets. He told me that he belonged

to an English Brig in the Harbour bound for Smyrna & that the ship
was employed to carry valuable goods away belonging to people of
consequence & that they had chests of dollars sunk in the mud in the
harbour at the ship's head.

I did not believe the Man for I thought such a Man could not have
been trusted with such a secret but I have reason to think he spoke
truth. The Captain of *L'Etoile Mignion*, [sic] our Ship, not being able
to obtain a freight at Marseilles sailed for Cette at the bottom of the
Gulf of Lyons, 30 leagues from Marseilles, & as we sailed out of the
Harbour the Citizens were attacking Fort St. Nicholas which was the
beginning of an act of Rebellion for which that part of France suffered
severely.

All the time I was at Marseilles the town was in a dreadful state
scarcely a day passed but that some one was not put to death by the
mob. The Sufferers were generally tried & acquited after Execution. I
saw the Guillotine here first. It was carried about in procession. The
Marseillois hymn was quite new at this time & I have seen the People
fall on their knees in the streets with clasped hands & with all the
appearance of the greatest devotion crying Liberte Liberte cherrie.[55]
At the theatres, the actors invariably knelt & affected to pray to
Liberty.

The Return Voyage.
On sailing out of the Port, we were becalmed all night. Towards
morning a Gulf breeze sprang up, ie a sea breeze. We sailed 10 knots
& reached Cette in 9 hours. We had scarcely got into the Port before
the wind increased to a Hurricane &, the Harbour being much
exposed to the Sea, we were in alarm all night, there is a strong
current running thro the harbour which made it the more dangerous.
The waves from the sea actually came over the Pier into the harbour.
Had we been a few hours later we must have inevitably perished for
we could not have brought up anywhere in this Cul-de-Sac of a Bay,
or found our way into the Harbour, the Pier being hidden.

At 8 in the morning I was coming out of the Cabin & saw a small
ship outside called a Tartan in these seas. She came safe in, as by a
Miracle, & when safe within the harbour, a shout was set up by her
Crew & the People on Shore which made one thrill. A little more than

an hour afterwards a Ship appeared with English Colours hoisted for Quarantine.

The Captain of our ship scarcely had time to say She is lost before she struck so close to us, that a stone might have been thrown on board of her but she was without & we within. The wave cast the ship so high on the Rock & she fell on her side, but seemed fixed, beaten & covered almost by each Wave. But it so happened that she struck on the very point & it was possible almost to reach her bowsprit under the lea of a Rock. An English boat attempted & succeeded in getting very near & receiving the crew but was taken by a heavy sea & swamped. The Sailors saved themselves on a part of a rock which stands in the middle of the harbour, & there remained for neither French nor Dane would venture to help them. Probably the Quarantine was one great reason. The Wind & Sea calmed towards evening & so quickly did they both fall that before night the sea was as smooth as a pond.

The weather was very rough all the while I remained at Cette & I understood that the Gulf of Lyons was very subject to storms. The Country round Cette seemed to be very rocky but covered with vines, figs, olives & all kinds of Fruit Trees. We took an English Sailor on board to replace one of our men who left us at Marseilles. On the 4th of January 1793 it snowed very hard which was reckoned uncommon. On the 9th, having completed our cargo of brandy & wine we sailed in company with a Brig bound to Dieppe determining to keep Company. It blew very hard when we sailed & the next morning our companion made a signal of distress. On our going down we found that she had sprung a Leak & was making Water fast. All hands were at the pump. The Captain begged that we would not leave her. She detained us very much as the Brig could carry but little sail & otherwise sailed badly. We had but little wind & we crept along the Catalonian Shore within view of objects on shore from Cape Rosas to Barcelona, where we left our companion; she going into Barcelona to repair. We almost entered the harbour with her for she made water very fast.

The City of Barcelona appeared fine from the Sea, with a Hill to the West called Mount John much like the entrance of Plymouth. The weather was very warm, altho January. The day after we had looked at

Barcellona as a fair wind sprang up & we were in hopes of being in St. Vallery at St. Blaise[56] the wind however increased to a violent storm & we had scarcely any sail set with a high Sea crossing the Gulf of Valentia.

The wind being fair we were running at 10 knots. The night was dark when about 12 oclock the Savoyard boy at the head cried out "a sail" & we had scarcely time to be alarmed when a Bowsprit appeared over our deck & flying rapidly by caught our main shrouds but as it did not come directly across us the Bow struck our Quarter Gallery & carried it away leaving the Gib boom on board. This was a most narrow escape. A shout was uttered by the men of both Ships & we parted in a moment. Every Sailor on board put up a bit of the boom as a memorial of our escape. We knew nothing of the other vessel or of what Country it was. Our damages in the morning were found to be great. We got round Cape de Gatte in the morning, & soon afterwards neared Gibraltar we saw the surf again against the Rock & the Sentry on Europa Point. We passed a Portugese Fleet cruizing against the Algerenes. We were carried through the Streights with a Levant Wind which carried with it a thick Fog, & as it blew strong, so we were soon clear of the land. Our vessel was very deep in the water & we felt the waves in the Atlantic being unable to carry sail, we were drifted to the Westward. The Vessel's planks were so open that the Water ran through the deck & sides; my berth was quite wet at all times but I was wet for 21 days without having a dry rag on.

The storm increased so much that we lay to under our Mainsail with the Tiller lashed up & the hatchway fastened down. We were obliged to watch an opportunity to run below & pull the door after us. At the end of our 21 days the wind abated & we got our foresail up & entered the Channel. The Feast of St. Blaise arrived & we danced indeed but against our Will. We heaved the lead but I much expect the Captain was ignorant of the soundings. We saw an English ship & made signals to her & hoisted our colours but she bore away. The Captain was very angry & said he had never found the English uncivil before. We had no observation & were afraid to advance so we laid to at night having all hands on Deck. This was Shrove Tuesday.

At daylight we saw a fishing Boat which informed us that France was at war & on being asked "with whom", the answer was with all the

World. A high cliff was ahead of us which turned out to be Fecamp. The Fisherman said, Point D'Enfer (Hell Point). The Captain, thinking it wrong to advance as war was declared, entered Fecamp & he had good reason, for the Ship would have run a great risk of being taken.

On entering the Harbour I went on Shore & took a look at the Ship & she did indeed appear a wretched object. The Captain gave me leave to proceed immediately to St. Vallery & I therefore set off in diligence to Rouen, but before I quitted the Ship, the Mate was put in prison for striking a Sailor & was in danger of being beaten by the mob, who thought it but just & right for a Sailor to beat the Mate or Captain but the Sovreign People must not be touched by their former superiors. From Rouen I passed through Dieppe & Ville D'Eu to St. Vallery. 22nd February 1793.

Arrest and Imprisonment.

In the month of February 1793 I returned from a voyage of the Streights from Marseills to St. Vallery Sur Somme. I was then Sixteen Years of Age, on my arrival I found that War had been declared between England & France during my absence & that all communication was closed between the two Countries; in consequence of which our remittances from England were stopped and we felt very great inconvenience from want of Money to which was added the jealousy among our neighbours from our being English & possessing the largest house in the town. It is well known how high the Spirit of Party at that time ran in France & what absurd tales of England & of Mr. Pitt's Emissaries were current & generally believed. We, however, contrived to get credit & avoid any very disagreeable dispute until April when the tradesmen of Town became urgent for a settlement of their Accounts & not receiving what they required, they said we were spies of the English & living in a Sea Port the better to betray the country. My father became alarmed & returned Inland & went (I believe) to Paris. I do not know what his plan was but he soon returned & settled in Pequiny, a Village between Abbeville & Amiens, twelve miles from the latter town. Owing to some misunderstanding with my Father & the offer made me by an old Servant of supporting me for a short time in hopes of a Peace I remained at St. Vallery. I had indeed another reason which was that at that time the French Nation was Arming in mass & marching toward the frontiers.

Now St. Vallery, being a Sea Port was considered an advanced Post & its population retained for its defence, I was consequently enrolled & stationed at a gun-boat but as the gun-boat was not built I received no pay (!). There being a Free Navigation School in the Town I attended it regularly every morning until the 22nd September when a Decree was passed by the National Convention for confining all foreigners, particularly English. At this period of the French Revolution every Act of the Government was made to appear as arising from some great discovery of a Plot or Conspiracy & when put into execution by the Municipalities was always accompanied with as much Stage Effect as possible. In the town of St. Vallery, besides myself & my only maternal sister, who had also remained with an old servant of the Family, were two young English girls whose Aunt had married a Frenchman.

When the Decree arrived the Gens D'armes were called out & a solemn procession set out to arrest us all. I was the only male, age 16, & my sister Margaret was scarcely 14. They seized me first. Now St. Vallery being out of the way of Grand Sights & Revolutionary Exhibitions, such an opportunity was not to be missed. I was pinioned with straw bands rather I believe out of a joke than anything else & marched between two soldiers, a mob accompanying us to the house where my sister lived. She they only arrested but did not insist on leading her about. They only gave her notice that she must prepare to go to prison. They left her to pack up what things she had & then the Gens D'armes proceeded to the Uncle of the other Ladies living about a mile from the town. The old gentleman remonstrated & said that having adopted them they ought to be considered French. The Municipal Officers seemed so little "acquainted with what they were about that I have no doubt they would have released us all had it not been for their losing their holiday & revolutionary Shew. They therefore did not insist on taking the young Ladies but returned with me singing Ca Ira[57] to the town hall where my Sister soon joined me. It was now twelve o clock & according to the French custom, dinner hour, but we had nothing to eat, indeed the Municipality had so far obeyed the Decree of the Convention in arresting us, but they did not seem to know what further to do, they therefore held a consultation what further was to be done & (as there was no Prison at St. Vallery) they determined to send us to the Chief town of the district, Abbeville. A Gens d'Arme being ordered to conduct us was preparing so to do when my Sister complained of Hunger. She was only attended to by the Guard who gave us some bread. The Secretary, with a deputation from the Municipality went to my Lodgings & placed a Seal on all my Papers these were only a few books on navigation.

About five o'clock the Guard came to conduct us to Abbeville. He persuaded me not to take my clothes with me, giving me a dreadful account of the Prison discipline saying I should be robbed of all I took with me & offering to take care of any thing which I might entrust to him & that I should have them safely returned to me when I regained my liberty, for he seemed to think that I could not remain in Prison long.

We were ordered to walk, but the distance being 12 miles my sister complained that she was unable to perform the journey on foot. She was, however, answered that she must try. She begged to have a Horse by paying for it.

The Soldier went out to endeavour to hire a Horse but returned unsuccessful & we were obliged to proceed on foot at about half after five oclock. Before we reached the half-way House, from want of food we were both much exhausted for I had eaten nothing & my sister but little. She indeed was so much fatigued that I know not how she could have proceeded, when fortunately the Gentleman before mentioned, Uncle to the two English Ladies, had considered our situation & sent a Servant with a Horse, who overtook us here. It was now dark & the latter part of the way I felt much fatigued. On reaching Abbeville, we went to the District House & to the Office of the Procureur Syndick to whom I was known. He gave an order for my being delivered over to the Concierge of the Hotel St. Blimond.

I told him I had no food nor money to procure any. He said he would speak to Monsieur Picot who, from a Taylor remarkable for a due attendance on Religious duties, had now become an Infidel Jacobin,[58] & for his Violent professions of love to his country & hatred of tyrants & the Bloody Pitt & Cobourg, was appointed Ruler of the Prisons.

At the Hotel St. Blimond the Gens D'arme delivered us over to the Concierge, who just introduced us into a courtyard, shut the door upon us & left us. We walked about for some time in the dark, tired & hungry, but could find no way out of the Yard. At length a door opened & a light appeared. We went towards it, entered a Room in which we found a Guard of old men sitting round a peat fire. Some Englishmen were playing at Cards on an old Butcher's block which served for a Table & two or three bricks piled together to serve for seats. A few spears served for Arms & to poke the fire with these were all the furniture of the place.

An Englishman (whom I afterwards found to be a Sailor that is a smuggler) from Bolougne came up to me & asked whether I was a Countryman & on my saying that I was, he entered into conversation & told me that he had been confined already a fortnight, that he slept on the floor without so much as a little straw or any covering, that he had but little money, yet he was not allowed any food. On hearing this I became uneasy as not knowing what would become of us, the whole amount of my property being three livres & the Clothes I had on. I had however put two clean shirts on.

My first thought was how I should keep my Clothes clean & in the morning I commenced operations with an attempt to wash a neckcloth, for which purpose I borrowed a bowl & began washing, but the more I washed the dirtier it seemed to become & at length, I rubbed holes in it. My sister had been placed with the Women in another part of the house. While I was at work some young English girls, who had been in Convents for their Education, passed by & laughed at me but kindly undertook to wash for me which they did as long as we were together.

My friend the Procureur Syndick had given an order to the Concierge to give me food – at his expense – until something could be settled by the District. I had hopes that this might have been continued by the Government but many other English who were in distress seeing that I was provided with food & wanted to procure the same, mentioned my Name as being furnished with provision whilst they were starving. This brought out an order for one Pound of bread being issued to the prisoners per day. In the same Prison, besides Fifty English, there were about a hundred nuns. The house in which we were confined was the Town Residence of the Marquis St. Blimond, a Nobleman who had Emigrated. The House was old & large, but much out of Repair. On Entering by large folded doors we came into a yard around which the House was built. We had a guard of superanuated veterans who were paid 1/5 a day each, by the more wealthy prisoners. A sentry was placed at the Gate & a space chalked out as bounds which we were not to pass to hold conversations with strangers at the Gate but this was only a form for the Windows of the first floor opened onto the Place D'Arme & we could have jumped out without much difficulty.

The clothes of which I had only those on my back began to fail & I procured a small quantity of Canvas from the Concierge, & sitting up in my room, I pulled my old Trowsers to Pieces & by them cut the Canvas into some kind of Shape I made another pair.

One day soon after my arrival a Person called to one of the English Sailors, when we were all in the Garden & asked him to shew him how to kill a goose in the English fashion. He was desired to throw it over the wall. When it was received the Sailor chopped its head off & turning round said there it is Gillotined & now you may see how we shall all look by & bye. As there were quite as Many Women as men present, one of them fainted & another had fits, the garden was soon in a state of the utmost confusion.

As the winter approached, I felt the cold very severely for I had nothing but the floor of a Garret to sleep on. The House was old & the Rafters were double, one under the other, & coming down to the floor. We contrived to get a board, & putting it to stand against the lower rafter, formed a Kind of Weather board at about Two feet from the Wall. This, in some measure, kept the wind from me & before the cold set in very strong a Government Depot was formed in the Stables belonging to our place of confinement & I got some straw.

There was a stove in the Room & by some accident we found a Trapdoor above our Room which led to the top of the House, in which was some old wood. One day they made me, as being the smallest, get thro' the door & I was Jumping on some old wood to break it when the wife of the Concierge came in & caught me. She put herself in a passion & enquired what we were doing. At first we were all silent but when she addressed herself to me, as the only one who could speak French, I answered that when we had destroyed the wood, we intended setting fire to the house. The Woman went immediately & brought in our little Taylor, as he was commonly called, & I was ordered with three others into a dungeon in the common gaol, where we remained one day, after which we were brought back again.

We were now worse off than ever for fuel & felt the cold very severely. Yet we afterwards hit on a plan which was either ring the bell violently or otherwise by some means, alarmed the Guard, for it must be remembered that our Guard was of the oldest & poorest of the People & they were no wonder much alarmed at the times. On hearing the bell, they would all rush out together & we took advantage of the bustle to take their turf which was carried out of the Kitchen by a back door into the Garden & hid until an opportunity occurred of carrying it into our Room. My shoes & stockings were now worn out which saved me some trouble in washing. I went barefoot. We were however very happy which I have observed is often the case under circumstances of trouble, for the mind some how or other habituates itself to its condition & I do not know whether it does not particularly in youth enjoy difficulties. We found that one of our Guards understood a little bit of music & could play on the Violin. He brought his Instrument & we gave him bread, a very small piece from each was enough to satisfy him, for the history of that time informs us that famine was known in France in all its horrors & therefore in some respects the Prisoner was better off than his Gaoler. As there were many young Ladies we used to dance in the Guardroom all Night. I believe I mentioned before that the young Ladies had been boarders in French convents, how they came there I know not. We were induced to dance in this Way partly to keep ourselves warm & I must say that I felt so little my situation that I almost liked it. The truth is, I fancied myself in love with one of the young Women. We were, however, often brought to a sense of our situation by the little Taylor who amused himself by alarming us. Sometimes he would come & say that we must prepare for Paris & at other times, which touched me more, he said that the Men were to be sent to one Prison & the Women to another. At first these reports frightened us but after awhile we found him out & laughed at him.

Our Guards would sometimes insult us. One of them, at one time, made some rude remarks on the English, on which I pushed him backwards into the fire. He, of course, was indignant & threatened all the vengeance of the great Nation. He however never took any farther Notice of it, probably fearing that he might be removed from his station of guard.

Another time we were all dancing & in high good humour when, several of our Guards were asleep, we blacked their faces with oil from the lamp. By this means a coolness arose between the Guard & us & we were obliged to keep more to ourselves.

It became necessary to think of fuel for an hour or two each day. One of our plans was to exercise with a Pike or Halbert. At the word Charge we would come down to the charge with the Pike, advance against a Turf in the Corner & then Shoulder it off to another behind us. This was always performed in the dusk, before the lamp was lighted. We could of course not get much fuel in this way & it may appear extraordinary that I use the word we as if all the English were concerned, but I must observe that I only allude to my own immediate Companions in the same Room, who were like myself utterly without money. Most of the other prisoners had Private Friends. Two in the room with myself were I believe Smugglers. That is, one a Sailor Smuggler & one a Landsman receiver of the goods, One a Journeyman Stationer from Leeds. If I am not much mistaken the Smuggler was Johnson afterwards so well known by his Escape from the King's Bench.

Our room was a Garret but of only one Story high, with Garret Windows looking towards one of the Great Squares of the City, the Place D'Arme. In this Square whatever Troops were in Abbeville was their place of Exercise & all Rejoicings & National Fetes were celebrated under our Eye, for at that time the French were fond of Spectacles such as a renewal of the oath etc etc, which was continually happening, of all of which we had a commanding View. On the 22nd of December the Fete de la Raison was celebrated in this Square. The Intent was to Shew the Superiority of Reason to Religion. A horrid Monster called Superstition was Painted on Canvas & a funeral Pile prepared, on which little Images of the Virgin, Crucifixes & all Manner of Popish trifles were hung. Then a Woman of noted bad Character, an Actress & Mistress of Andre Dumont, personating the Goddess of Reason set fire to the pile & in a Moment the Monster was consumed. The Stage Effect was to shew how quickly Superstition that is religion vanishes before Reason. Yet at this very Fete & in presence of the Representative, numberless relicts were snatched from the flames by the lower ranks & preserved, in spite of the guards who perhaps felt a secret horror at the act they were employed in. Several of these very Images were shewn in our Prison in the course of the evening & our Guards joined in Cursing the Nation. Meaning the Government, & wishing for the old order of things.

While this Mockery of Reason was carrying on, my Name was called & on descending I found my little Taylor who said, Reason required that at my Age I should not be answerable for the sins of your country. I was therefore to be released. I answered that release could be of no service to me as I could not return to England & I had no means of supporting myself. The man appeared kind & said "take your Liberty at any Rate & then come back again to the prison. You can then do what you like". Seeing that my Sister, to whom the same offer was made was very anxious to accept it I went with him to receive my Liberty in form.

He conducted me, with my Sister & many other Prisoners both French & English to the largest Church in the Town where 1 found a platform Erected in the great aisle on which stood Andre Dumont Representative of the People. On his right hand stood the Woman above mentioned acting Goddess of Reason. Behind her was an Actress, whom 1 had seen on the stage, prompting her how to act. Dumont was making a speech as I entered. He was talking of the Harlequins among the Priests while he at the same time with three large Ostrich feathers in his hat, was out Harlequinning them. He said that there was neither Hell nor Heaven, neither Resurrection, Angel or Spirit. He said in particular that a fate attended us but he knew not from whence or how it happened that if God ruled the Earth with justice, why did Louis 14th die in his bed & Louis 16th on the scaffold. 1 thought & why do you stand here & why does Robespiere live & Barrère Hollot D'Herbois.

When Dumont had finished his address, the Prisoners who were to be released were brought up to the Platform on which stood Dumont, the Goddess of Reason & the Actress prompter. We were to go up on one side, pass over the Stage & descend on the other. To each one, some speech was addressed & the Goddess of Reason dressed like Minerva with a spear in her hand touched us as in a Pantomime & our fetters fell.

The only difference, that I remarked, between Reason & Wisdom was that the former had on her Crest a Cock (Gallus) instead of the owl & on the Point of her Spear was the Cap of Liberty. When she moved her Train was held by four of the Municipality (Corporation) As she passed there was an affectation of falling on the knee in imitation of the passing of the Host" in former times to the Sacrament. I have since observed that the affectation of devotion as in kneeling while a stanza of a song is sung is not peculiar to France. I have observed in England an appearance of the same devotion whilst invoking Apollo in the hymn to that false Deity. The Woman personating the deity was an abandoned Woman, wife to an old man, General Tachfire. I had the Honor of the accolade Fraternel & was declared free but at that Moment the stage shewed symptoms of giving way & I was hurried off. The Goddess however followed & I had more Notice that the rest. I was embraced & Symptoms of Pity appeared in her Goddessship for such a youth. She condescended to ask whether I would serve the Nation on board a French Ship. I said I would never fight against my Country. Dumont spoke in favour of my Country but said that it was governed by a Tyrant. I answered that there were more Tyrants than one and that Tyrant as our Ruler was, he had not shut up the French Residents in England in Prison. Dumont replied that He ought to have done so. I passed on & returned to my Prison, not knowing what else to do. Having related to the English Prisoners what had passed, I asked advice & acknowledged that I must go on board a French ship or starve. No advice which I could follow being offered, I joined myself to the other English released, who were all of the lowest rank viz my Companions, the Smugglers, Pocket Book Maker & Gentlemans Servant.

With some others we left our Prison, the Smuggler, Pocket Book Maker Servant & myself thinking that we ought to get to England in

some way or other but we were not one in heart. The Servant had
formed Connection with a French Woman, the daughter of a Farmer
who could not speak a word of English or he of French, and when we
came to Fermontier in the Forest of Cressy, he would go no further
but at the same time he spaliated [announced?] his defection by
saying that he could escape much easyer by seizing a Boat on the
coast near. This broke up our Party. Some engaged with Farmers in
the Neighbourhood & I returned to Abbeville again, to my Prison.

On my arrival I was allowed my bread ration as usual & after a time
a Captain Forster or I believe Lieut Forthley, offered me his assistance
that is offered me food for my services. With this Captain F I lived
until February. I must have been of use to him as I was not considered
a Prisoner but could go in & out whenever I pleased & this, others
could not do.

The confinement of the English was now much relaxed & many
got their liberty, some by bribing the Taylor, other by sick Certificate
which was readily given by the Medical Men. One Lady, wishing to
gain her Liberty had written a letter to Mr Picot the Taylor to which
she had attached a silver snuff box but before she found an
opportunity of presenting it, she lost it in the Garden, where it was
found by some one who to make mischief, posted the letter against
the door of the Yard during the night. This caused suspicions
amongst the English which broke out into a degree of violence &
Enmity never got over while I remained with them.

This disputatious spirit led several families to wish French
company sooner than English & probably in consequence of
representations made to the Municipality, our Taylor began to lose
his Credit. Forster was removed at this time to the old College of the
City, now abandoned by its Scholars & Professors the Nation wanting
the services of the first in the field & pensions of the first to pay their
troops.

A Charge was now made on the English for a considerable Sum by
way of further remuneration for the Guards who had been employed
& the plea was the great lenity shewn us, whereas they, the French,
had been led to believe that the English had put the French
Representatives to death at Toulon, yet they had not put us to death. It
had no effect to say well then according to your own Account, we

were unjustly confined. Their answer was, the thing is done & the men must be paid. The English had a meeting in consequence & Sir Digby Dent, an English Admiral, being the one looked up to, decided that it ought not to be submitted to & so it was determined, but the Municipality frightened the old Man & he paid his Quota. The rest soon submitted on the promise that we should all be immediately released, as I really had no money, so had nothing to pay.

The Release did not however happen as it had been promised. In this College there were still some day students with whom I formed an acquaintance & by their means was enabled to read in their Library in which were a great Number of books, all those originally belonging to the College & those of different Monasterys & of the Emigres. One of the Professors gave me permission to sleep in a Chamber of the Establishment & sent me a Pailass & Blankets so that had I had food enough I should have been happy. but I had only half a Pound pd[59] bread.

Captain Forster assisted me a little & some of the scholars also. I did not enjoy these comforts long, for the College was cleared of Prisoners & I, among others sent to a New House, the very next door to our Former abode, the Hotel St. Blimond. Here I got a room to myself in which was an old Bedstead & I got still what books I wanted from the College. But now we began now to be terrified by Robespier's actions, for at that time, France was in a dreadful state & this wretch was at the height of his Power. There had been a general massacre in the Prisons of Nante's where two English families had lost their lives even Infants had been murdered when under two Months old but the History of these times will no doubt record these Cruelties. We were of course much alarmed. I had opportunities of seeing the newspapers every Night, where in I read the decrees & I found that we were not in much danger of being put to death by any other process & the Prisoners had made up their minds to resist to the last any sudden attack & we had also hopes of being able to escape to the Forest of Crecy. At this time a Prisoner was brought in, who had been confined in Amiens, & he gave a circumstantial account of the death of my Father. He described his Person, his Family & related some part of his History, where he had lived etc. I could not doubt the truth of his assertion for what interest could he have in deceiving me.

My Father had never written or sent me a Message since we had
parted altho I had several times written to him & I began to fear that
the Report was true. I wrote now to my Mother but received no
answer from her. The Man who had related the account of my Father's
death now mentioned the Name of an Englishman in the same Prison
whom he recollected as an acquaintance of my Father's. Upon which I
wrote this Man whose name was Dawson & was answered by my
Father himself, who said that he had never received any letter from
me.

A Report being raised in our Prison of the death of Robespiere[60]
we were dreadfully alarmed for we had heard such reports having
been raised before, as traps to observe how the Prisoners would
behave. When we first heard the report, it was whispered among the
Prisoners with some kind of pleasure, but we very soon began to
doubt the truth & then our anxiety was to escape the imputation of
having raised the report for it having been whispered in confidence
was difficult to trace it. But when the Post arrived it was confirmed
with a great outcry against him & his accomplices & particularly
charging him with cowardice but we shall hear more truly what led to
his death at some future time. After the death of this Tyrant our
Prisons were no longer Watched and altho we had no formal release,
we walked in & out as we pleased.

This winter was very severe & many poor died from Cold. I lived
with Captain Forster who contrived, by means of Jews to get some
money from England but I believe at a very great loss. The cold was
exceedingly severe. I remember a Hamper of Wine being frozen altho
packed in straw & placed under the Sideboard in the dining room.
We had a Regiment of Hessian Prisoners in the town with whom I
made acquaintance. The old Soldiers had served in America.

The famine was also very severe. I have stood for hours at a Baker's
door in a Mob like the crowd endeavouring to enter the London
Playhouse on an extraordinary Evening & no one could get a single
pound of Bread without an order from the Municipality for to enable
the Magistrates to give the Proper orders every family was registered
& the Number & Names affixed to the doors of their houses in some
conspicuous place, together with their ages. We were only allowed a
quarter of a Pound of Black bread for each Individual. A Member of

the Convention being in the Town told the poor People that they ate too much & a Poor Woman called out that she was starving. He said I myself can live on an ounce a day. They shouted out We shall starve. "Well", he said, If you die of Hunger, you will not die of the Plague. What would an English mob have said to this? The French Mob was silent.

Escape across Europe, 1795.

My situation now was very unpleasant & I began to meditate on an escape. Many thoughts came into my head but I should perhaps have feared taking such a step had not my Father passed through Abbeville on his way to St. Vallery. He told me that he was determined to try to leave France & asked me to join him, to which I readily agreed to as I could not run the greater risk through remaining at Abbeville. My Father's plan was to go to St. Vallery & endeavour to raise Money on his Property there & he succeeded but in what way I know not for I was not in his confidence.

At St. Vallery, my Father sent for my Sister but received her in such an extraordinary manner that I was not in the least surprised at her declining to accompany him.[61] I asked to have had some private conversation with her, but he would not allow it, calling on me to follow him or he would disown me as his son. I followed him as he bade me, not being aware of the Short Stay that he intended making & hoping that I might find another opportunity of speaking to my sister but on leaving her it seems that he had finished his business at St. Vallery for he departed for Abbeville & without delaying there passed on to Pequiny where his family had resided since the English had regained their liberty.

We reached Pequinay on Sunday at 11 oclock in the Morning & so anxious were we to commence our retreat that every article in the House was either packed up or sold before night & a covered cart hired on which to proceed to Paris at daylight in the morning. Having still my passport I will copy its translation here only marking that I have kept to the original spelling of my name.

District of Amiens
Department of the Somme
Canton & Municipality of Pequinay.

Allow freely to pass Henry Sherwood fils resident in the
Commune of Pequinay district & department, as aforesaid,
aged 17 years, stature 4 feet 10 inches, hair & eyebrows
chestnut, forehead medium, eyes grey, nose short, mouth
medium, chin ordinary, countenance pale—He has declared
himself a traveller in the department of the Somme & other
departments of the French Republic & asks our help &
assistance in the Canton of Friburg.
Delivered in the Maison Commune of the said Pequinay,
This day the 28th March 3rd year of the Republic.
The said Henry Sherwood signed in our presence
Sanguir Agent Beguin off. M.
Sherwood fils Montigny off. M
Have seen the citizen Enri Churrood
A Roussa 30th March Jean off M of the Guard

I was despatched before at four in the morning to Amiens & the
remainder of the Family came up in the Afternoon. We were badly off
for food there being no bread publickly sold. Amiens was full of
Prisoners of War, mostly English & Hessians. The 87th Regiment
which was taken at Bergen-op-zoon was there besides many
detachments & a considerable number of Officers of other Corps.

The Republic de la Mort

On the 1st April we left Amiens by the Paris road. I was not told where
we were going & my heart misgave, I remember on reaching a hill near
Amiens, & looking back on the Town, I thought of the day & wished it
might not prove to be a fool's day to us. We travelled about 30 miles this
day in the same Pequiny Cart & endeavoured to stop at a farm house,
but they would not receive us except we had our own bread with us.
After some time we succeeded in getting admittance into another
Farmer's house whose Inhabitants appeared to be friends to the Exiled
King, & I believe, were inclined to receive us on that account.

The 2nd April. We moved and reached Clermont at night & there we saw a fine old castle on a hill & the Duke de FitzJames' house. The fine Park & beautiful Woods which once surrounded it, were greatly damaged by the wanton mischief of the Republicans. 3 of April to Chantilly. Here in the Palace of the Prince of Condé was established a Pottery by an Englishman of the name of Potter. We did not see the Palace, it being full of English Prisoners.

Paris

4th April we entered Paris by the Port St. Denis. No question was asked us at the Barrier, nor indeed were our Passports once enquired for on the road. We were, however, informed that we should not be allowed to quit Paris without them. Paris did not appear to advantage for the famine raged. We could get no lodgings & the Bakers' doors were surrounded by Mobs waiting their turns to receive the small allowance of bread granted to each cityzen by paying for it. At length we were admitted into an Inn in the Rue St. Denis but we had not a bit of bread the whole time we were in Paris which was three days. The City of Paris did not appear to me to be any thing equal to London. The streets are narrow & no flagged Foot Paths. The houses, in the Part where I was had no stairs case within but you went up by Stairs on the outside of the House uncovered & very slippery in rainy Weather. But the time in which I saw Paris was very unfavourable. We were all in agitation, for the horrors of the Revolution were by no means over. The very day we arrived Twelve Deputies of the Convention had been arrested. I saw the gardens of the Thuileries but now all was litter, the trees cut down & the basins of Water empty, the Statues defaced & under a kind of canopy lay a death like ghastly image of Voltaire crowned with flowers. The windows of the Louvre were all broken & Moss growing round them.

Our principal business in Paris was to obtain Passports for England, for which purpose we attended the Comittée de Salut Publick, but there were so many persons on the same Errand, there appeared but little chance of our getting an Audience of any of the Members. By the Advice of a Friend of my Fathers, an Italian whom we had formerly [known] in London, we were determined to slip out of Paris if possible & make our way to Switzerland for as we had reached Paris without trouble we might in like manner reach Geneva. His advice was to take our Passage in the boat which went regularly between Paris & Auxere in Burgundy every day. My brother James & myself accordingly took our Passage in the boat. My Father & the rest of the family having got out of the city by means of the Boat, soon after went on shore & took a carriage, leaving my young brother & myself to continue our way. It rained very hard at the time of the vessel's getting under wey and, there being nearly 200 people on board, Market People & others, our Passports were never inquired for. Had they been asked for, I fear they would not have been deemed sufficient as they were from Pequiny & simply allowed us to Travel without any determinate Point. Indeed I now wonder how we could have ventured with such deficient documents.

I have often said that we could get no bread but I had with me a large Cheese, on which my Brother & Myself subsisted never tasting bread for two days or indeed any kind of Vegetable, but simply cheese & I now know the value of Bread. At the end of two days I got on Shore & procured some bread at a farm house but only four Pounds weight.

We were four days in reaching Auxerre, 90 miles from Paris, we travelled night & day. This 4 lb of bread was all that my brother & myself had. We left Auxerre the same day on which we arrived & I firmly believe that the want of bread was now the impulse for my mother in law [stepmother] seemed so much overpowered, that she would readily have remained wherever the sole of her foot could have found rest.

We passed on to Chalons sur Saone, a most delightful Country where wine was in Abundance but no bread. My remark, written about a year afterwards, was "If there had been bread we should not now have been in England. From Auxerre to Chalons we travelled in a Tilted Cart & on our arrival at the later place, the same man undertook to carry us to Geneva not much more than 40 miles & he asked 1000 livres. The sum appeared enormous but the Livres in Paper had now sunk to so little that I have bought 100 livres for a small crown or 2/6. When we had agreed for this sum & provided our food for the road, we should reach Geneva without a farthing in our possession.

In our Journey to Geneva a most providential circumstance happened. We had not advanced far from the town towards evening when we came to a fork in the road. Our Auxerre Carter had trusted to meeting People on the Road but, no one appearing, he at length determined on taking the left hand & what was more curious, we met no one on the road for several miles. The first house that we came to confirmed us in the Idea which we had held for some time from the appearance of the road, that we had taken the wrong one but it was too late to turn that night & we took up our rest at this house, it being a small Publick house.

Our Coachman & the People in the Common Room having well considered the advantages & disadvantages of a Return & in the morning we found it settled that we should continue our rout & pass over Mount Jura by a more direct pass altho a more difficult one & I have reason to think that by this Providential mistake we were able to get out of France. We approached the foot of the mountains before evening & I was astonished at their height. I really thought it impossible to pass over them. I now speak from Memory, having no written remark. They seemed like a Wall, to touch the Clouds. We began to ascend by a very circuitous road cut out of the Solid Rock. We were obliged to walk & carry stones in our hands to prop up the wheels at every short distance. The Precipice on one side was so perpendicular that I dared not approach that side. We had far rather our driver had taken two additional Horses. I think that if it had not ventured too far to return we should have gone back but we got over much better than we expected, for the road was in very good repair & the foundations good. At night we were on the top of our range & we found that maize was the only corn grown there.

Our next day's journey was short but very fatiguing for my Stepmother's timidity was such as not to allow her to ride, yet she had never been accustomed to walk, & her appearance was truly distressing. In this manner, we were three days before we descended into Switzerland. I can only remember that in one place we were placed in a long room with beds running along like pigeon holes at the two sides or more properly like the cabins on board a Dover Packet boat.

The women wore caps edged with fur; something like a Knitting

Needle running on one side of them with little Balls at each end fitted
with something like a Child's rattle & from some conversation that I
held with them they appeared to be much alarmed at the idea of
Spirits. These Mountains are still covered with Snow altho the valleys
in France which we had just left were in full Spring & the heat rather
excessive. The sudden change from one Valley in particular was very
striking. We had approached so near to the Mountains that the lower
ones hid the higher & the appearance seemed as if we were only
under ordinary Hills. In the Valley the Cows were uneasy from the
number of flies & the reflection of the Sun against the bare rock was
excessive, but on proceeding on the road we found Snow & before
long the Snow began to fall with a Cold East Wind, biting in the
extreme. The Inhabitants appeared very very poor & were draped in
fur. On the top of one of the Hills I remarked a small round Tower of a
Castle. It was remarkable as we scarcely ever lost sight of it for three
days. It is said to have been built by Charles the Bold Duke of
Burgundy in his Wars with the Swizers. When we reached the most
advanced post of the French there was a custom house but the officers
duty seems to have been restricted to the examination of Boxes &
they did not stop us but sent us to the Mayor to revise our Passports.
The Mayor was out at Supper & we passed on. It was an accident more
than any thing else, our road which we had taken really by mistake
thro a Country not only in itself unfavourable for Military
movements but it lead to a petty State entirely under the Control of
France.

Our first thought in ordering the Cart on was really without
consideration, but merely that the Cart might have some head way
before we followed but waiting a long time for the Mayor we strolled
on scarcely knowing whether we were right or wrong until we had
cleared the Frontier. The road to the highest elevation from the
Village was scarcely three miles yet it took us four hours to ascend.

I had never at that time seen such Mountains & was naturally
much alarmed at the frightful precipices. My Brother so much so as
actually to be incapable of walking & we were obliged to put him into
the Cart where he soon fell asleep. The Road was narrow & in general
round the Mountain the perpendicular side was of immense height &
very few steps receding would have precipitated the Cart from top to

bottom. We carried stones in our hands to prop the Cart whenever the Horse appeared to give way. On the top of the Mountain we saw numbers of goats. The vegetable production in very small quantity of Grass peeping from under the snow & forests of Fir Trees. On the Summit of the Mountain we met a number of French men driving Horses. They addressed us civilly with the usual salutations of Citoyen. My Father could not bear this but said Monsieur if you please & fancying himself clearly out of France he pulled his Cockade from his staff & jumped upon it, a very inconsiderate act for we were in the power of these men in this place which altho not French was certainly no other Country & we ought to have known that France controlled Geneva & indeed all Switzerland and a band of men in a Border district are always to be feared. They however only laughed which shewed that the Days of Terror if indeed if Terror was ever the order of the day among soldiers was at an end.

Switzerland.

The snow became now very deep, but even in this elevated Region we found a Swiss Village of St. Cierge. It was Sunday & here the change was so sudden it could scarcely be believed. We were stopped by a kind of Militia with Yellow & Red Cockades who would not permit us to move thro the Village until the Protestant service was over. I, poor foolish fellow, thought this nonsense & was for abusing the arbitrary Government.

Paper money now was of no use & we were obliged to sell some of our Clothes for food but here as elsewhere the Sunday was only kept by the laws & not by the People. They would buy & sell on that day. After Church we proceeded & on leaving the Village, which I found was on the descent of the Hill, we found the same kind of road as we had come up from, I believe Morges & we rapidly descended from Snow & Ice & fir trees to warmth, Cherries in blossom into a very Garden, delightful in itself but more so from Contrast. Here we found fine Roads with Gentlemens carriages on them. So complete a contrast could scarcely be conceived even had we dropped from the Clouds, no Paper Money nor dirty citoyens but something like regularity. But even here, everyone wore a Cockade & too many had the appearance of Soldiers.

We were now in the district of Lausanne and from what we heard we wished not to leave it, except to go on the direct road to Germany, but unfortunately Geneva had been pointed out as the place most easily attained & we had formed such arrangements that it became necessary to go there to find friends to enable us to reach home. I believe we had not the value of half a Crown at this time. The reports spread about here were not very consolatory. Geneva was represented as in a State as bad as France itself, which proved too true but we had no alternative & we proceeded.

Towards evening, at the turning of a Road we were saluted with the French Challenge of Qui vive & saw the Tricoloured Flag. The surprize was great, for with oceans of advice & caution, nobody had ever hinted that we must pass through France on our way to Geneva, but we might have known by the map that the French Republic reached to the Borders of the Lake of Geneva. The French Officers were very civil & did not give us much trouble, though they frightened me a little by pretending to suppose I was a French Recruit endeavouring to escape. But on my speaking English with all my might we were allowed to pass. The ferocity of the French soldiers was always much less than that of the Jacobins & even of the Town's People.

Geneva

The gates were shut before we could reach Geneva & we halted at the English Hotel without a demi Ecu in our pockets; more than this we owed 1200 Livres to the Carter. To travellers at home this might have caused some uneasiness, & if I said it did not trouble us I should say what was not true but we met with so many difficulties that we were not overpowered. At the same time, I have remarked, that I have often met with difficulties & also diseases & have found that towards the end of the troubles you seem acutely to feel either disappointment or pain, probably because of having made up my mind to have no more of either.

In the morning, my Father proceeded into the City & introduced himself to a Mr Mar, a Banker. This gentleman, on hearing names of Genevese mentioned by my Father as being in some degree of intimacy particularly the name of Lucadiri, who was in partnership with Mr Troughton my Grandfather's most intimate Friend, advanced us sufficient money to pay our Charioteer. He further lent us a little House in the East of the Town about half a mile from the City, overlooking the Aar. The Bank on which this House was situated over hang the River almost perpendicularly & on the other side, in the Territory of Savoy, was a French Camp. The Government of Geneva is always so very jealous that there is no stranger admitted to remain in the Territory above a certain time & now that time is restricted to a Week, but by the exertions of Mr Mar, we were permitted to remain a Month. The City is very much confined many of the passages vaulted or at least narrow passages under houses. The Rhone running thro it is very delightful, a beautiful transparent green looking Stream.

We could not judge much of the Manners of the People for the State was in disorder & the influence of the French Revolution had rendered it a very unpleasant spot to dwell in but indeed I may accuse the French Revolution unjustly, for I am afraid that the horrors of Democracy had their chief defenders & promoters in Geneva before they reached France. They have lost their Religion once so strict, they have destroyed their Churches & also their public Monuments. One representing a Duc de Rohan merely because the French required it & they now acknowledge that they will soon be obliged to submit to France which indeed they now do & be incorporated into the Great Nation.

They are indeed treated very ill by the French, who allow no Provisions to be brought into the Territory, which, as they command the whole surrounding country, they can prevent. The Lake is a most beautiful piece of Water nearly sixty miles long by about twelve miles in breadth at Lausanne. Geneva itself is situated at the extreme point where the Lake issues into the Rhone. In old books, which I have read it is asserted that the Rhone runs through the Lake without mingling its waters, which seems ridiculous as the Water of the Rhone is very shallow & seems nothing more than the overflowing of the Lake. It is true that rivers run into it, one even called the Rhone, but there are many others as well. It is also said, in these Books, that a commerce is carried on between Geneva & Lyons by the Rhone. Now the Rhone is not navigable within 12 miles of Geneva & you may walk over it up to your knees. We were alarmed one night by the Ringing of Bells, the

Beating of Drums etc. but as the Drawbridges were drawn up we could not ascertain the Reason & we were not allowed to enter the city until noon the next day when we found that two of the Republican or Jacobin party had been killed during a Riot but the Rioters had escaped before the Gates were shut. No Persons were allowed to enter the Gates without Cockades in their Hatts & I was obliged to Mount a French one. Twelve Young Men of the first families were banished for wearing, we were told, Green Handkerchiefs. 6th of June [1795]. Our first remittance from England arrived, affairs were in so unsettled a state that we were ordered to leave the City. Our friend, the Merchant, Monsieur Desaellar being unwilling to interest himself in our favor to procure a longer pass, we were therefore obliged to leave. The first day's journey was most delightful, the Season of the year fine, the fruit ripe & the Lake of Geneva unruffled on our right most delightful & the Alps appearing on the other side of the Lake covered with snow & the Jura mountains on the left & the intermediate space most beautiful. The lower acclivities of the Hills were covered with vines & mulberries & not a wave on the Lake. I do not know whether the resemblance was just but I thought of Catalonia, as I had seen it from a very imperfect view, as we sailed along its Shores. We had, according to my calculation, fifteen Hundred miles to travel before we could reach England & I believe all the money we possessed for 9 of us was less than £20. Soon after leaving Geneva we came to the French Guard Room where we had been stopped on our way to Geneva but it was now abandoned, the troops having advanced into Savoy.

This night we halted at a most delightful place called Rolle, on the banks of the Lake. The weather was fine which, of course, will help to make every place delightful. I do not know whether I have a perfect recollection of places, but it struck me as being like Sittingbourne in Kent yet Rolle was a compleat level & I think Sittingbourne is on rising ground. Here, for the first time, we observed the white Cockade of Royalist Frenchmen worn in publick. We also saw the Green emblems of aristocratic Geneva, for to this place the Banished Genevese had resorted in numbers & the Towns people spoke with great detestation of the French & Genevan Jacobins.

Lausanne.

Dined at Lausanne, a fine old town in the Commencement of the Hilly Country. The streets very steep & narrow with fountains of water, & a running stream in the centre; a most delightful old town. We left the Lake about a mile before we reached the town. The rise of the Hill presented most beautiful views. We slept at Meudon in the Pays de Vaux, a very old town taken from Duke of Savoy by the Swiss about a 100 years since, with the fountain in the Streets & a Stream of Water running down the Middle. The fountains having a Statue of some eminent Patriot standing in the Centre. We slept in the Ancient Town Hall in a fine old Room, where was an old Picture & many old French inscriptions relating to the capture of the City.

The next morning passed the Lake of Morat & saw the monument enclosing the bones of Charles the Bold of Burgundy & his Army or said to be so by the natives which I doubt.

The dress of the Peasants here is quite different from that of the Genevese. The Women wearing their Hair drawn tight from their foreheads & plaited backwards into two tails hanging down, with the addition of ribbon, to their heels. We passed a curious hanging Bridge, over a most rapid river, built of wood & covered over. The Cart going over caused a tremendous motion which, added to the noise of the Torrent below, was rather terrific. It was late in the evening & we saw but little of the bridge, indeed I should scarcely have remarked any thing extraordinary in the Bridge, only that we were told the next day that it was so. I think, however, that the Bridge must have been very long. The German language began to be spoken to the north of the Bridge.

Berne.

A great many English names were written on the Windows & Walls of the little Inn & we were told that many English came to see the Bridge. This morning to Berne, where we only staid to procure a Passport from the English Chargé D'affair & proceeded after Dinner. I was much pleased with Berne, the Situation delightful & the cleaness of the streets surprising. The Prisoners were working in irons to keep the streets clean. A broad stream of water ran rapidly thro of each with the customary Fountains at short distances.

On leaving the City & ascending a Hill we had a fine View of it (the town) with the River almost surrounding it like a Horse shoe. From Hence to Basle, we passed thro a rugged mountainous road, but money running short & not knowing where to procure more, I confess the views were only a very secondary consideration.

Basle.

The Rhine at Basle is a Noble River but I know not its breadth, having other things to think of for here we had intended stopping until our Banker at Geneva should have sent after us the next remittance from England, but, what we had expected for some time now became certain, that there was no resting place for an Englishman in Basle.

The Influence of the French was so great that no exertion on our part could obtain permission for our remaining more than two days. Our money was now gone & we went to every Banker in the Town to endeavour to get cash for a Bill but they had been so accustomed to the distress of the French Emigrés that we could not succeed in procuring money for Bills. At last one Banker advanced six Guineas but he would not take the Bill saying that if it was paid in London it was well, if not he would lose without regret. The Austrian Ambassador advanced 10 Guineas on a Bill. At Mid day we passed the Prince of Condé's army. Our Resident Colonel Crawford was absent but it was pleasing to see the politeness of the French Royalists. We reached Friburg in the Boisgaw [Breisgau] in the evening.

Germany.

In Friburg German is spoken and as we were unacquainted with the Language we had great difficulty in making ourselves understood. Here my Father proposed remaining until we heard from Geneva & he also drew Bills on England & gave them to a Banker who expected to have answers in the course of a Month. We took lodging for that time but were obliged to pay in advance & having little money we felt the extremes of hunger before the remittance from England came, for we never received any letter from Geneva.

I often walked into Cornfields & Vineyards & ate the ears of corn & green grapes. We sold all our Clothes & were literally starving. From some hopes of getting relief from Colonel Crawford who was with the

Prince of Condé's army, I walked over there twelve miles, but Colonel Crawford was at Frankfort. I slept in the Guard tent and returned.

On my arrival I found that an order had been received from the Governor for us to leave the Town in 24 Hours. Our distress was now at its height, without Money, with 5 small children & not understanding the language, I wished myself back in France again, for there we had bread. I wandered into the Fields not knowing what to do. At length I returned home & found that my Father had determined on going with his family to the Governor's & we set off in procession, having Mr. Wickham's passport with us. On being admitted we were shewn into a small room. The Governor came to us with a most savage frown. He asked what we did in Fribourg. He had our passport in his hand and, of course, he knew what we did there. My Father was obliged to go thro his history, which having finished the Governor began in French, By order of His Imperial Majesty, whose Person I represent, no stranger is to remain in a fortified Town without the Governor's permission. We explained that on our arrival we had produced our passports at the Gate and from our ignorance of the language we were not aware of any further necessity of applying to him. My Mother began to cry, upon which he slapped her on the shoulder & in good English desired her to fear nothing & Graciously gave us permission to remain. He even lent us ten shillings until our remittance might arrive.

We were again taken before the Governor a few days later on suspicion of taking plans of the Fortifications, but the plan, appearing to be a very rude sketch of the Church, we were again released. We now felt extreme famine & had no bread in the House when the Governor's wife called & seeing our distress, sent us a Louis d'or & a Crown. When this was gone (there was still) no letter from England, we were one whole day without food. On application to the Banker, he, for the first time, advanced a Louis & seeing that my mother had no shoes on, he sent her a Pair. The next Post day I waited for the Post's arrival but no letter came & I gave up all with a heavy heart. I called on the Banker, not expecting any thing, but I found £22–10 sent to me, but nothing to my father his Bill having been refused by my Grandfather's Executor.

No time was to be lost for if we remained the money we had would

scarcely last until we could write again to England & receive an
answer & we had given up all thought of hearing from Geneva. My
Father determined on advancing to Frankford immediately for we
should at any Rate get more money among the English & nearer
home. He bought an old Landau for £6 & hiring two Post Horses we
started immediately, having 15 Louis D'or in cash. I, however,
prevailed on the banker to risk £5 on a bill of mine and, with Twenty
Pounds, nine of us proceeded on a journey of 1000 miles. A delightful
country to Offenburg where my Mother wished to pass the night but
the Innkeeper said that he had no room. Probably glad to get rid of so
large and, apparently, so poor a family. It was fortunate on the whole
for it forced us forwards & altho we suffered for the Moment, when
we awoke from our Nod in the Carriage, tho tired we were between
20 & 30 miles nearer home with the money which our night's
Lodgings would have cost us, in our pockets. The Young Children did
not feel it.

We saw Strasburg Steeple & more all by the light of the Moon. This
is said to be the highest Steeple in the world. In the morning we
entered Rastad the Capital of the Prince of Baden apparently a fine
City. In the Market a large statue of the Prince of Baden, a General at
the time of our Marlborough. Here they refused to carry us on with
two Horses but a French Emigré wanting two the same way with
some difficulty we got on.

From Rasted to Baden the Road quite strait with Rows of Fruit
trees on each side to Baden. The French Gentleman kept close to us &
assisted us in procuring horses at the next stage. From this to
Dourlach the road being shaded all the way by Apple trees. The
country most level as far as the eye can reach & there being no hedges
the wheat like a calm sea seemed to overspread the whole Country for
there was not a hill to be seen between Fribourg & Heidelbourg. We
met on our road many French deserters going to join the head
quarters of the Prince of Condé. They said that the distress of the
Republican Army most severe & that they had eaten Horses at the
Siege of Mayence.

Very heavy rain came on at Bruscal, the residence of the Bishop of
Worms & we could not proceed in our open carriage. The splendour
of the Roman Priests & their servants was here to be seen in all its

glory. The dress of the Bishops Servants was all covered with Lace. The Protestant States & the Roman States join in all directions & the only mark of division between Worms & Baden is a Land Mark of wood. The Protestants on one side & the Romans on the other side are as distinct as if they lived 1000 miles asunder. The change of Religion in Germany if not everywhere else was brought about by the Princes & not by the people. I am afraid generally interested motives either accelerated or retarded the profession of Faith. France alone kept her religion in opposition to her King but Henry the 4th was not the immediate descendant of the former Kings & had been in disgrace & his Friends destroyed in the former reign.

We passed very near Manheim now in the possession of the French.

Heidelberg.

At Heidelberg we waited some time for Horses, crossed a beautiful bridge at Heidelberg with three turnpikes on it. On the bridge was a statue of Charles Theodore, Elector Palatine, with Minerva at the other end. One of our Horse a wild Hungarian, nearly threw us all into the River. The city of Heidelberg is a fine old place with three religions amicably settled therein viz—Calvinist, Lutheran & Roman.

The Roads now became bad, sadly cut up by the March of the Armys & we were obliged to take an additional Horse. At a Post House I heard a Man singing an English Song. He had been at St. Omer at the College & from thence had made his way to England & was now on his way home. We had left almost the same point & were now crossing. He said that all our English fellow Prisoners English in France were released & head home, so it would have been better had we staid in Prison. We passed Hesse D'armstad but the Post House was outside of the gate. I just looked in & saw the Parade with numerous bands of music & drilling Recruits; more than I should conceive the State would require. Reached Frankford to dinner without any money in our Pocketts.

Frankfurt.

Our difficulties now if I may so say commenced afresh. We were not admitted within the Gates without great difficulty. It is true we had advanced 200 miles but we were still very far from home. At the Inn, the Servants would not let us enter until the Master came home, he fearing that he should not be paid & told us that we might have a Room paying a florin 20 a day for it. There were no Letters at the Post Office for us although we had written both to Geneva & England, requesting to hear from both places. We could not find any Banker who had heard from our Friends at either place.

We lived on Bread for a week going every day to the Post Office but no Letters. The innkeeper became tired of us, & as the fair was approaching in which all his rooms would be wanted, he warned us to leave his house & in this distress we knew not what to do. At the end of a week, we received a letter written by the Attorney, Mr Farr by of my Grandfathers Executor, informing my Father that his bills drawn in Geneva were all paid but desiring him that he would draw no more as Mr Smith would not pay another farthing until our arrival in England.

We now lost hope as our bills from Geneva were of no avail, for altho paid, the Banker retained the Money & we had no hope of hearing from him after so long a silence. The Banker thro whom this Letter had come, delivered it open & it appeared that he had read it. He I suppose from the tenor of the Letter, naturally thought we were extravagant people. He said that, seeing we were English & hearing our story, he might have been induced to advance us six or eight guineas on a Bill but that now he could not do it, as he had warning that any Bill of ours would not be paid. After leaving him, he, of his own accord, sent a Clerk with a present of two Louis D'or & advised us to try other Bankers in the City.

My Father took his advice but no one would take our Bills altho they all gave us something so that after paying our Bills we had 6 Louis in hand. As we could not expect any more in Frankford, we again proceeded with that small sum. Our first stage cost one louis. Of course, we could not get far with six.

It was the commencement of the Great Frankford Fair & the Road was full of Pedlars & Jews. We pushed on thro bad roads, with bad horses & without eating until the last livre was spent, which happened at a small village at 12 oclock at night. The Post Houses are not of necessity Inns & the one we were set down at was a private

House. Fortunately the Post Master could speak French, which is no common thing in this part of Germany. We slept on the floor of the room destined for travellers to sit in while the Horses were changing, under the pretence of being over fatigued but at five they called us to say that the Horses were ready.

As the post houses are paid in advance, we knew not what to do. It was full thirty miles to Hessen Casel & there was no person who had any means of assisting us, as we understood, between this & that City. On the attendant wanting to be paid, we asked to see the Postmaster but were told that he had sat up late & must not be disturbed. As we sat still in the room, every now & then, a Servant came in to say the Horses are ready. At last, I believe they thought we did not understand them & they put the horses to & pointed to them shewed us that we had nothing to do but pay & be off. Some fresh travellers arrived. My Mother said she was ill, on which our Horses were removed & put to the other Carriage. The Wife of the Post-master soon saw our state & called her Husband. To him we told our difficulties & offered him cloths or all that we could give him to help us on. The carriage was our own & that we offered. He not only refused, but told us his room was not an Inn & we must immediately leave it.

Destitute on the Road from Frankfurt to Kassel.

My father, with his family, left the house & proceeded on foot & I stood by the carriage leaning against it I believe, crying. I stood thus for a very long time. I do not know how long. I knew not where the rest of the family had gone but I was convinced that they could not walk far & my feelings were of course much hurt. The villagers, who had heard our story, stood round the carriage. At length the innkeeper wished us away & sent to a Carrier who had spare Horses & made a bargain with him to take us to Casel for the Carriage provided that we could not otherwise pay him. The man, having examined the Vehicle, seemed inclined to break off his bargain, while we were in the heat of Argument, two Officers passed us, a Prussian & an Hessian. The Hessian addressed me in French & asked the meaning of what he saw.

I related to him our present difficulties & to prove to him that what

I said was true, I gave him an account of Colonel Bezenrod's
Regiment, the officers of which Regiment had been in prison with me
& with whom I had been on terms of Intimacy. This Gentleman
immediately interested himself for us & soon found a man who
undertook to conduct the carriage with the family, if they could be
found, to Casel. The two Officers gave us two French crowns 10/-.
The man brought his horses & I proceeded, expecting to overtake the
rest of the family without going far. We soon set off & very shortly
overtook the family who were not a little pleased at seeing me
perched in the front of the carriage. We were soon caught by a violent
storm & wet through & were glad to get into a Jew's House to dry
ourselves & pass the night for it was late in the evening before we had
procured the horses.

The Jew gave us some good Ham for supper & we lay on the floor
in our cloths, still wet, yet caught no Cold. The Jew was the cheapest
Landlord we had ever fallen in with during our travels. On reaching
Cassel, the Carrier offered to leave our carriage if we would pay any
reasonable sum for his trouble. Not being able to do so, he left us in a
decent inn sans sous.

Kassel.
On enquiring what English were in Cassel, we heard of only one, a
Major Le Grand. Who or what he was I do not know. He either did
not believe what we told him, or affected not to do so, because from
the State of France there were many distressed persons all over the
Continent. He however said that if we could prove what we had told
him, he would do what he could.

Now it happened that the only letter we had to shew was Mr. Farr's
letter refusing to pay any Bill and, of course, that would not do. Going
down stairs I met a Soldier, who I recognised as a fellow Prisoner, & I
returned with him but the word of a Private instead of doing service
rather made things worse.

Looking out of the window I saw a General Officer, Colonel now
General Bezenrode. I ran to him but he was the Commanding Officer
on the parade.

He only told me to come to his House, but his manner was such
that, on my return to Major Le Grande, he was completely convinced.

Something however, struck him with respect to my Father. I do not know what, but he did not say anything to him. There is little doubt to me now that all the cares & anxieties he had experienced had affected my Father. Perhaps remorse at having brought his family, by his strong Republican notions, into such great Troubles.

Whatever it was, Major Le Grande lent me 5 guineas saying it was as much as he could spare. On my return to the Inn, I met the Surgeon of the Regiment whom I had known intimately at Abbeville. He was very anxious to hear how we had escaped & promised to call at the Inn in the evening & hear our adventures. He came & brought with him a Captain. They remained with us to supper, & having paid our expenses, gave me as much as they could well afford namely one guinea. They begged that we would not leave Cassel the next day for they thought we might procure an order from the Elector for a free conveyance in the mail cart & that, by mentioning our circumstances on parade, many of the Officers who had known me in France might be inclined to assist us.

Hanover.

I do not know how it was but my Father would insist on going away in the morning, which we did and, though we arrived in Hanover the same day, all our money was expended. My Father was always sanguine & he thought Hanover was England. We found that the Hanovarians had distress enough among themselves & were as badly off, if not worse than we.

After running about the whole of the next day to get help, we were obliged to sell everything we possessed, save the clothes we had on, for a Louis d'or. By the kind assistance of an Hanovarian Major, we were accommodated with a free carriage; nine of us in the mail cart to Bremen. It was my Father's intention, however, to stop at Nuremberg hearing that a Mr. Duncan was British Commissary there. We were dreadfully insulted by the driver on account of our free passage & the other passengers, particularly a soldier, behaved brutally.

We reached Nuremberg [Nienberg] at 12 at night & my Father, being determined to stop there, allowed the carriage to proceed to the Post House before we had properly made it understood that we had no friends in the place. We were, at first, refused admittance into the

Post House & it was only the Postmaster's humanity, on seeing the young Children, that we were, at length, allowed to sleep on the floor.

My Father had been in the Street quarrelling with the Servants of the Prince of Orange saying that as the English supported him as an Englishman he had a right to be attended to. The Servants behaved very gently on this occasion & brought him to the Posthouse. Next day we could only get Charity from Mr. Duncan, who gave a guinea, & we proceeded to Bremen but where we arrived with only a half a crown in our Pockets.

Bremen – Destitute again.

It rained all the way and we were in an open Cart, We were wet thro but had no change. My Father & the rest of the family immediately walked away from the Carriage leaving me with the Cartman. When I looked round & saw no one of my Family, I did not know what to do. I dared not move lest I should lose them, for I naturally thought they would return to enquire for me. I was all the day without eating. This was the second time I had been left since we took our departure from Frankford.

At length, tired of waiting, I set off to look for the rest of my family & after some time, I saw my Brother at the door of an Eating House, wherein was my Mother & the rest of the family. My Father had left them there & they knew no more about him than I did. In about half an hour he returned & said that he had been inquiring for Ships sailing to England & that he had found one & he expected that we should soon now be at home but he never considered that he had not a farthing to pay for the dinner his family had eaten indeed it now appeared that he had left me & the Cart, on our arrival, to avoid the Driver's application for a Present. I had not eaten all day & when I mentioned it to him he said that he could not help it indeed he appeared quite desperate for I afterwards found out that he had been to most of the Merchants in Bremen & had been refused assistance. Seeing him so low, I proposed to my Mother that we should go to the English Consul. We did so but we found him from Home. We saw his brother who declined assisting us saying that he himself was poor. He said that there was a benevolent English Lady in Town, to whom we might apply. He would not introduce us to her but he would shew us the house, which he did. My Mother knocked at the door & went in. I remained in the Street. It seemed that my Mother found great difficulty in making her Story believed, but after producing letters etc. she so far succeeded in interesting Lady Irvine that she promised that she would, on the following day, speak to several Officers of the English Army who were expected at a Ball in Bremen. She gave my Mother sufficient to support us a couple of days. She desired her to return at the end of that time. She said that she knew that no ships would sail to England for some time.

We immediately looked out for Some Lodgings & found One Room over a Stable to which we entered by a Ladder from the Stable. The dung hill was just under the Window & I should be glad to be able to say that was the dirtiest part about it. We were happy in being able to pass the greatest part of the day on the Ramparts. I slept on the Straw in the Hayloft. We passed a whole week here when Count A. De Harcourt brought seven guineas which he had collected among the Officers of the Army, but we already owed nearly as much.

A Captain of a Ship said that he would sail in a day or two & that he would take us but I do not know how it happened but my Father & the Captain quarrelled as the family were getting into the Boat & our voyage for that time all was at an end. I was absent when that happened buying Sea Stock for our passage was only to be trusted for. On my return I found my Father in charge of a Guard for fighting with the Captain. I soon prevailed on the Guard to release him. My Father appeared beside himself for although dark we advanced to the gate, & being Challenged by the Sentry, he cried out Deliver up your Town to the King of England. The Sentry was very angry about it & it required some time before I could quiet him.

Finding a Ship.

We went back to our old Lodging & in the morning my Father went off & hired a Boat to take us to Brock a village on the river Weser 20 miles below Bremen where we heard there were several English Ships at Anchor. We embarked & reached Brock at one oclock in the morning. The only Inn in the Village refused to admit us from our Shabby appearance. My Father found a little Boy who undertook to lead him to a Publick House. He left my youngest brother & myself on the Warf to look after what few things we had left. We had provisions with us, being our Sea Stock which we had laid in at Bremen & there was of course more than we could carry. My Brother soon fell asleep & I covered him up as well as I could. Here we remained about two hours, at length my eldest brother James came running towards us. It rained hard & he was advised not to come for fear of losing his way but, knowing we were exposed to the rain on the beach he would not stay in the house. We had some difficulty in awakening our youngest Brother & when we did rouse him our distress was great for we knew not how to convey our goods. At length finding some old cords in the boat used to bring up our provisions we tied them together & loaded myself & Brothers like little Horses. It was slippery from the rain & we fell down at every step but at length at daylight we reached the Publick House & I soon fell asleep on the ground, there being no floor.

This was Sunday & the House was so filled with drunken Sailors making such a disturbance we were glad to get into the fields. I went over the Village & Hamlets near in hopes of finding a better place to Lodge in but I believe from the Shabbiness I could not procure one till dusk in the Evening when I was returning in despair & about two miles above the River I found a House wherein was an old woman who spoke English. She agreed to let us have One Room but this would not do for me. I agreed to sleep in the Hayloft. Having made this agreement I was so much overjoyed that I ran the whole way to my Father. I found the family still in the fields not having been able to return to the Publick House on account of the drunken Sailors.

One of my Sisters had lost her shoe in the Mud & I was obliged to carry her, when I reached the Lodgings I had taken I was really so exhausted & could scarcely mount the Ladder to my Hayloft. It was now the warmest time of the year & I awoke in the night with a kind of irritation all over me, like the Pricking of Pins. I also found that I had a companion in my loft, a Danish Sailor who had been Shipwrecked.

In the morning we learnt that there was but one ship likely to sail very soon to England & upon applying to the Captain he required to be paid for our passage before hand & he demanded sixteen guineas. To comply with this was litterally impossible. My Father desired me to go to Delmenhorst, where the English Army lay. He said that I might apply to Count de Harcourt, the Officer my Mother had met at Bremen & to enable me to get there, a horse was hired.

It was always a foible of my Fathers to expect too much from Persons & I believe from seeing the disappointment he met with I have probably taken the opposite turn. He thought that being an Englishman that An Englishman would immediately assist him & probably from a long absence from his Country & being confined in dangerous times in France, he thought that an Englishman Abroad was a Brother to an Englishman but I did not succeed, Count de Harcourt did indeed behave kindly but in the first place he was not an Englishman & we had no right to expect much. He gave me a guinea & I returned. My horse cost me nearly that Sum as I returned along the dyke in doleful dumps with a French Bonnet de Police on my Head & a long Black Coat one skirt torn off. My Horse with only three Legs, I must have cut a conspicuous Figure. The dyke being elevated above the common Horizon shewed me off. Towards sun set in style & the Haymakers observing my unequal gait, cried, Sneider, sneider, myn coup. I do not quite know the meaning but the word Taylor was easily understood & I took it to myself in dudgeon

On my Return I found an English Dragoon come down on some business to Brock. I believe he was sent to look after an English Transport by Sir Robert Laurie. I met with him on the dyke & as a Countryman addressed him not expecting any thing from a Private Soldier. He said that He came from Birmingham & spoke of himself as of a good family, but that he had been wild. He certainly had some education.

My Father, who was very fond of telling every one who he was & that he was of some consequence at home, soon gave this Man to understand that he was somebody & a Warwickshire Man. The Young Soldier seemed to enter into our feelings & exerted himself with the English Captains of Transports in the Harbour who were fond of meeting in the only Inn at Brock to Drink. This Poor Soldier whose name was Thornton exerted himself much in our favor. I have since enquired about him at Birmingham but could never learn who he was.

A Sergt Robenson of the 11th Dragoons with a Farrier of the same

Regiment arrived from England but it seems that they had landed after their Regiment was embarked & they were ordered to return in the Same Ship.

A Passage to Hull and a Difficult Journey to Coventry.
To this Sergt, Thornton applied & Robenson said He would get us to England if he should lose all that he should expend & He did so, paid our Passage to Hull & the money due to our Lodgings & we went with him to Hull where he had a Sister. On our Arrival at Hull there were letters for us with Money, & I hope my Father recompensed him. I know he repaid him.

I was so anxious to reach my Guardian, for I had a small independency, that I left Hull the next day, but from my sufferings I had a disease on me which now broke out, an inflamatory sore throat. I reached Lincoln & would have proceeded but there was no Coach till the next day to Nottingham. I therefore remained that day, my throat was so painful I could scarcely bear it. The Landlady of I believe The Hart shewed me great kindness & would have persuaded me to remain but I would proceed & I advanced towards Nottingham in the coach.

I was become very ill indeed before we reached Newark & a Gentleman in the Coach going to Buxton, himself very ill, lent me his coat & was very kind. While the Horses were changing I ran to the Apothecary & told my distress. The Young Man in the Shop said that I ought to Stop but that I would not listen to. He gave me a gargle for my throat & would not be paid for it.

I reached Nottingham that night but here again I was unfortunate for no Coach left that place for Leicester the next day, however, I heard of one which would come into the Road about 3 or 4 miles from Nottingham & I advanced on foot for why should I find a difficulty in England walking a few miles by myself who had met with such greater difficulties but without health what can be done. I fell on the Road at some distance from Nottingham & with the greatest difficulty could drag myself to a little Inn but it seemed that the small inn was situated on the Junction of the two Roads by which the Coach was to come. I had a good rest & got myself some peppermint drops which were recommended & thought myself strong by the time the

Coach came. The inside was full & I mounted on top. The Weather was fine but a sudden shower came on & wet me to the skin.

I reached Leicester & the next morning as usual no coach to Coventry. I moved off on foot & quite exhausted reached Hinckley. Here new troubles awaited me (because) the Assises were at Coventry & the troops moved out. All the Inns at Hinkley were full. My appearance was not in my favor & going from House to House to procure a bed, in one Inn some soldiers drunkenly pretended to take me for a deserter. I had been in Arbitrary Governments & I was not aware of my safety. I felt alarm & began relating my History. The soldiers I believe thought it a good joke and, finding they had got a hold on me, one said, hah, hah You have been fighting against your Country among the French for I see you are a Soldier. I felt a dread come over me & I rushed out of the house making my way across the field, in the direction towards Coventry. At some distance, I daresay a mile, I got into the Road by a small Publick house. It was Sunday & every one dressed in their Sunday cloths. I had my one skirted Coat with a pair of Provencal Pantaloons called Catalans on. I had a French Bonnet de Police on my Head & no stockings. In this attire, it was not wonderful that they would not accommodate me in the House. The Landlord said he had no bed. I felt faint & heart broken, not more than 10 or 11 miles from home. I thought myself most cruelly used & weary with my Way & weak from my illness I fell down faint at the door. When I recovered, I found myself in the house & now I was kindly treated. Only some Sunday loiterers seemed to think my illness was brought on by my own fault. They spoke indeed in guarded terms & I could not quite understand them but I knew enough to be angry & hurt.

In the morning I advanced towards Coventry, within a Mile or two, I was ill, sick leaning over a Mile- stone vomiting, a Chaise passed by, in which were two Ladies & a Gentleman. One of the Ladies looked out & laughed at me saying to the other something against idle drunkards. That Lady I met the next Sunday at my Grandmother's & was by her congratulated on my return my distresses sympathised with but she did not know I was the person she had seen on the Monday before.

My Father had made me believe that I should be disgraced if I entered Coventry in such a ragged state & even cautioned me against seeing my Relations without proper Cloths but I had not wherewithal to equip myself. I bought a pair of stockings at Nuneaton & advanced to Coventry. When I arrived there I had forgotten the houses & I was fearful of going to a Stranger. I walked along the street looking in at the Windows & at length I recognised my Aunt. I knocked at the door. A Servant who had nursed me as a child opened it & seeing my appearance said "Go to the Mayor, go." I said I am Henry Sherwood.

—This happened in October 1795. I was then eighteen years old & being under age I could not make use of my property until the 1st of January 1798 when I became of age & with the Advice of my Friends determined on entering the Army which I succeeded in doing having purchased an Ensigncy in the 45th Regiment of Foot & soon afterwards a Lieutenancy in the 53rd Foot then stationed in the Island of Saint Vincents in the West Indies.

The ending in *The Value of Bread* is very different from the one that appears in Henry's extant account above:

…I knocked very lightly and humbly at the door. It was opened & there stood Susan Sukey, as they always called her. She had been in the family before I was born. (!). She did not know me & was shutting the door with "Go to the Mayor, go". "I. . I. . I am Henry Sherwood" I said. Of course, I was at once admitted & at once taken to bed. The Surgeon was summoned & he pronounced my disease, Scarlet Fever. I lost all recollection for days. During this time, my clothes were destroyed & unfortunately (so was) some part of the memorandum in my pocket which I much regretted.

Now all my troubles were over & here follows the ridiculous. My Great Aunt knew nothing of gentleman's attire & I knew little more of what was suitable to my situation; but I was to order new clothes & have my own way with unlimited means. Well, I would have blue & buff Fox's colours. I had admired it some years before when at Merchant Taylor's School. I had a recollection of a barge passing under Blackfriars Bridge, with a large party of gentlemen, thus dressed. I thought them very fine, so I would have blue & buff & nothing else.

In those days we were used to buying cloth at the woollen drapers & having it made up. So the draper was sent for with his pattern board & I chose blue, and, as I thought, buff also. Now this buff turned out to be a very fine yellow. Next, in ordering my boots, I must have a pair up to my knees. & now all things were sent home, I myself was restored to health & was to make my first appearance in public. An assistant in a ribbon manufactory was to take me under his protection, for my dear old Aunt engaged him on this account, half as a companion, half as an attendant.

This man was himself an oddity. He wore a crimson coat with hair fully powdered, a thick club knocker at the back of his neck & white cotton ribbed stockings with long quartered shoes. He carried, also, an immensely thick, short, club-like stick in his hand & he wore his hat cocked rather jauntily on one side. So I attired myself in my blue coat, yellow waistcoat & yellow knee breeches, which had immense bundles of ribbons at the knees & to which my ill-made boots joined. Away we two strutted into Coventry Park, on Sunday, & everybody stared at us. However, I was soon told of the out of the way (unsuitable) colours of parts of my dress & they were shortly put aside.

I remained idling the remainder of the year at Coventry. My Grandfather's Executor advancing money for me, but sadly puzzled to know what to do with me. All my education had been acquired before I was twelve years old and, in the intervening years, most had been forgotten again.

My Great Aunt, Mrs Patterson, was old, blind & quite incapable of directing me & thus I was placed in the most dangerous situation of having plenty of money at my disposal & no one to direct me how to spend it. I had, however, one steady & efficient friend, the Rev'd Gerard Andrews, [sic] Dean of Canterbury, who had married a Miss Ball, a first cousin of my Father's. This kind relative's attention & fatherly care of me was of vital importance. Whilst thus waiting to be decidedly my own Master, my cousin Mary came to London & I was, in consequence, induced to visit my Aunt at Bridgenorth as soon as I came of age, which happened on the 1st of January 1798.

'I have sent you a Little Protector in the 53rd uniform'

In 1796, when Mary left London, she went to Arley parsonage where her mother and sister had been staying with her Uncle Thomas who had been so kind to the family since Dr. Butt's death. At the end of May the three women left for a new life in Bridgnorth. Unfortunately the contrast with the parsonage was extreme and Mary found it a depressing, cold house. She missed the beautiful views of hills and secret woods which she had loved so much at Stanford. The tedium of life at Bridgnorth for Lucy and Mary was relieved by the kindness of two families. Their good friends the Hawkins Brownes invited them to stay at Badger in June. Mrs Hawkins Browne introduced Mary into local society by taking her to balls and the races. It was at the races that Mary first saw the two eldest daughters of Mr and Mrs Whitmore who lived at Dudmaston. Mrs Whitmore also acted as a chaperone and welcomed both Mary and Lucy to her home. When their brother, Marten, arrived for the long vacation he enlivened the atmosphere at Bridgnorth. The three of them would go for long walks in the countryside where they shared their love of botany and collected specimens to draw later. Marten also encouraged Mary and Lucy to begin learning ancient Greek. They made good progress and read the first six books of Homer.

After his departure, to prepare for ordination in April 1797, a miasma of gloom once more descended. Mary and Lucy missed Marten's genial company. After his ordination he became curate of Great Witley which was close to Stanford. For the two sisters there was little to occupy their minds so, when the curate of St. Mary Magdelene in Bridgnorth invited them to take charge of his Sunday school, they were delighted and embarked enthusiastically on teaching the girls who flocked to the school. However both young women were inexperienced in the classroom. Lucy describes their first day:

> … well do I remember our first introduction to that school; it was on a fine Sunday afternoon. We were taken into a small room in the back of the old castle, where a number of children were being taught, seemingly without plan or order; the room hot, crowded, and noisy, and we little alive to the vast importance of the work we had undertaken, knew not how to properly manage it …[62]

The sisters were responsible for two classes which were limited to thirty-five girls in each. A retired schoolmaster taught the boys. Mary and Lucy took their responsibilities seriously and thrived with this new interest occupying much of their time. The Sunday school movement[63] was growing rapidly at this time. Its purpose was to offer basic education to the illiterate working class children whose only free day from working long hours, often in appalling conditions, was Sunday. Teachers used the Bible to teach both reading and writing. Prizes were given to encourage regular attendance and picnics were held to reward the pupils. Copious cheap religious tracts by such authors as Hannah More were available. These inculcated the leading of a good Christian life. When Mary met Hannah More in Bath in 1798 she was not 'fascinated' by her. This was due to the fact that she was ignored by the great lady. Mary reported that Mrs More spoke 'oracularly' to her brother, Marten, and their friend, Mrs King, who had taken them both to visit her. However, Lucy, who was taken to meet her by the same friend three years later, was much more impressed. She described her as: 'plain, but had a holy, resigned, and benevolent countenance, and lovely manners, but I thought she sometimes used needlessly strong expressions. She was kind to me and took my hand when we parted.'[64]

~

House parties continued at Arley with the fun-loving Lord Valentia dressing up on one occasion as a Cherokee chief complete with war paint. But for Mary the most important and far-reaching event was Henry Sherwood's arrival to stay with her family at Bridgnorth. Mrs Butt and Lucy hadn't seen him since Kidderminster when he was a shy young boy. His experiences in France had made him independent and resource-ful. He was a handsome young man and an amusing companion for the two sisters, singing snatches from army and navy songs as they walked in the countryside and no doubt regaling them with some of his adventures in France. Henry was on the cusp of adulthood, having turned twenty-one on January 1, 1798, and come into his inheritance. and was trying to decide what he should do with his life. The most attractive option was to join the army. The 53rd Regiment of Foot was stationed at Bridgnorth and Henry was encouraged in this ambition by a friend of Mrs Butt, Major Buckland, of that regiment. Henry and Mary, who was then aged twenty-three, grew increasingly close and when he left in the early spring of that year Mary confessed to being 'very sorry.'

Henry was preoccupied with paying for a commission in the 53rd and wrote to Mrs Butt from London on March 19, 1798 that although the agents had received the money the necessary papers had not yet been received. He asked Mrs Butt:

> Pray give my Love to my Cousins. Their kindness to me shall never be forgotten. They have, I hope cured me of the worst of my faults and have been the Chief cause that I do not look upon the world in the same light that I did before. If I had not seen your family I should in all probability have become a selfish Character. I had learnt that every one for himself was a common maxim, but I hope that I am cured & it is to you & them that I owe it.
> Yr Dutiful Nephew Henry Sherwood.[65]

For Henry the maxim he refers to was essential for his survival during his wilderness years in France but now with the love and compassion shown to him by Mrs Butt and her daughters there is a gentler side to the young man's character emerging: he and Mary have fallen in love. Henry's next letter is from London, dated April 3, 1798, in response to a letter from his aunt.

> In obedience to your last Letter I called on Lord Valentia he leaves town today & will convey this. On the day that I wrote last I was informed that the Chancery Officers refused to allow my Name to be taken out of the bill filed against Mr Smith[66] except I gave security £400 for paying the expences already incurred. Mr Reynolds[67] & Mr Maskall[68] have kindly stood my Friends.
> ...I have with some difficulty found my Father. He is suffering seriously from the Chancery[69] & can get no money but he says that he is determined to go on if he should lose his Liberty. I soothed him as well as I could & we parted good Friends
> I am this day told that I am appointed to the 53rd Regt & ordered to join it with Capn Hobson therefore all is settled. I saw Mr Thomas Butt. Mr Smith says that he cannot advance me the Money for my Lieutenancy, this is hard but probably as well as it is. I had intended giving my Father what money I could

spare, but when I heard him speak so strongly about Law, I thought I might as well keep the Money as give it to the Lawyers. I expect to leave London on the 20th as I hear a fleet is appointed to sail. I have only to say that I shall never forget your kindness & I hope on my return "covered with Laurels" to thank you in person ...[70]

In a letter to Mrs Butt dated April 18, 1798 Henry kept his aunt apprised of his situation. He writes that he is studying Virgil, and has almost finished the first part of the Aeneid

...which considering my employment is I think a proof of my obedience to my Cousin Mary's commands & no less so to the Commands of Lucy for I have already drawn Nine Flowers better than those I sent you & I think I can say that I improve. I learn Military Mathematics, Field Fortification & the Rules & Legislation of the Army so my time is filled up, drawing I am told will be very useful in the Army....

My father is just as determined as ever to go on with the Chancery Suit. Just as well he thinks me gone which is quite as well. Mr Smith I think uses me ill. He has received a letter from the Lord Chancellor to settle with me & he acknowledges that he has £400 in hand of mine yet he says Money is scarce I have written to Mr Bishton about him. Pray give my love to my Cousins.[71]

Henry remains optimistic about procuring his commission in spite of complications. In his letter to Mrs Butt on April 23 he writes:

I am now going to inform you that I am not going to get my commission in the 53rd but in the 45th. I think the Agents did not behave well, it seems that after all our Trouble & expence there was no Ensigncy for sale in the 53rd Regt. Col Thornton has been most kind & attentive, he has lent me as much as £37 in this Purchase. I think I have prevailed on Mr Smith to let me have the money for a Lieutenancy. If I can get this settled what do you advise me. Shall I remain in the 45th or exchange into the 53rd. There will be no difficulty in either. I have sent you a miniature of myself in the 53rd Uniform. I therefore think that I need to go into the 53rd after all, when I return I shall be so altered I think I must leave my likeness behind me. As you are my best Friend I send it you in the Above to my dear Cousins.

Yr Dutiful Nephew HS.[72]

Under cover of the same letter he encloses a teasing letter to Mary and reveals that the miniature is for her in his absence:

To Miss Butt

You have most delightful weather "I suppose" for we have it to here & you have your Brother to protect you from the Cows, & other dangerous Animals, & you have me still between you and the French, you might be extremely easy.

Henry Sherwood (1777–1849), a miniature in the uniform of the 53rd Regiment of Foot

We have been in Alarm here, a plot has been discovered & we ought to have been burnt to death eer this by a Set of Republicans, I have been much frightened & have abandoned the City in consequence, I now reside in the Strand, but this is dangerous from the vicinity of the River the French may surprize us, do you know that the very day that I removed the Rascally republicans we caught close to my new Residence, Subterraneous passages, Barrels of Gunpowder, 1000 stands of Arms, French Colors, Guilioteens &c, beware, when I am gone. I have sent you a Little Protector in the 53rd Uniform he will fight perhaps as well as the Original.

Yr affect Cousin HS.[73]

This letter alarmed Mary's mother who thought Henry was 'unsteady' but for Mary it was an indication with the gift of his miniature that their budding romance would continue. Had there been some agreement between them before he left? Henry, with all the impetuosity of youth, had already purchased the uniform of the 53rd as well as swords and other necessary military equipment. Matters were resolved: on April 25 he bought his ensigncy and on April 28 he became a lieutenant in the 53rd. On May 3 he travelled to Portsmouth to await embarkation with the 53rd to the West Indies where the British army was engaged in the war with the French. Mary was prepared to wait for Henry until he returned from the West Indies.

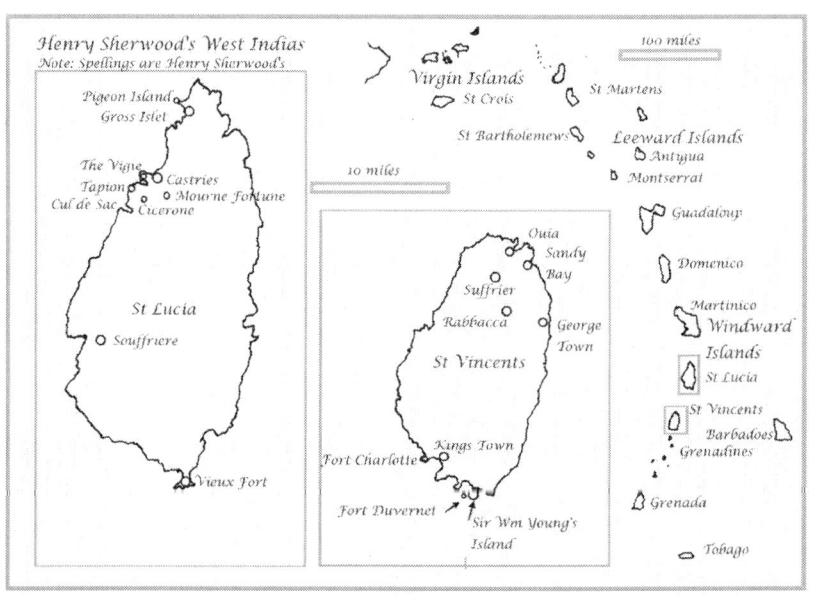

Henry Sherwood's West Indies 1798–1803

The West Indies, 1798–1803

Henry kept diaries of his time in the West Indies. He set sail from Portsmouth on June 10, 1798 for Bridgetown, Barbados. He recounts his hasty departure which left him short of rations:

May 2nd 3rd & 4th
Collected in all bills, paid all Debts called on all Friends & on 4th left London at 5 in the Morning for Portsmouth. Captain Hobson had arrived before me he was at the Bleu Posts Inn where I joined him after having my Hair well powdered. …

10th June
Mr Webb late Surgeon of the 53rd Regt but now a Surgeon on the Staff arrived from the West Indies & came to Breakfast with us, after Breakfast we passed over to Portsmouth & walked on the Parade at Guard Mounting observed the Signal for the Fleet to sail for the West Indies. Hobson said suppose you go to Captain Patton & ask if he has heard of any conveyance for us, It was eleven oclock before I reached Capn Patton's door, on seeing me he said you are just in time there is a Victualler unexpectedly come round & she will now be able to go with the fleet, you cannot have a better opportunity if you can get there in time, at any rate I will write an order for the Captain to receive you & if you are too late it cannot be helped. I ran with my order to Hobson he was extremely anxious to join as he had been absent very long. We therefore did not hesitate, but we made the best of our Way to a Boat. He ran over to Gosport & threw our trunks into the Boat dirty cloths and all huddled together while I ran to a Shop in hopes of getting some Stores, but it was Sunday & I could not get an ounce of any thing. I had a Pound of Tea & with this small stock we

pushed off & before half after twelve o clock we were under weigh for the West Indies on board the *Prince of Wales* Victualling Transport, Captn Codd. Before 9 o clock & consequently before dark we passed thro the Needles with a fine North Easterly wind & proceeded down Channel.

11th June

On rising this morning we were out of sight of land with a pleasant Breeze. We had leisure to put up & Trunks & look about us. The *Prince of Wales* was a fine Ship of 300 tons with a Poop and Deck. The Main Cabin below was given the officers who were few in Number, Captain Hobson Commanding, Lieut Fleming, Myself, Ensign Shackerly brother of Mrs A 14th Regt & a Volunteer Boothby for the 53rd Regt. Fleming had some sugar I had a Pound of Tea. This was all our stock, we were therefore to trust to our Sea Rations. There was a detachment of Soldiers on board for different Regiments. The Captain could spare us a few Potatoes & a few Bottles of Port Wine we must therefore make the best of it. Our duty was to see the Men Parade twice a day to see them clean and orderly. One Officer was on duty for the day whose business it was to see all the Hammocks on Deck & the Horlop Deck scrubbed& cleaned & once a week washed with Vinager.[74]
[The orlop was the lowest deck, at bilge level]

The fleet arrives in Funchal, Madeira and from there Henry sends a letter to Mrs Butt on June 30, 1798. He has taken to heart her reprimand for writing to Mary and all his letters are now addressed to her mother. Social rules needed to be maintained to protect Mary's good name. He has no wish to be regarded as 'unsteady' by his aunt.

I sent you a letter from Falmouth by a fishing Boat in a great hurry & confusion, informing you of my embarkation in greater confusion still. I embarked on board the *Prince of Wales* Transport on Sunday in such a hurry that I had neither Bed or Provisions, you may suppose me being uncomfortable for 18 days but to balance this, we have a fine ship, good Cabin, & fine delightful Weather. The disagreeable part is that we are loaded with Deserters & Thieves who are bad

Off Madeira. *Thomas Daniell, 1810*

Companions & there is some Danger. We arrived here on Wednesday last, As we have provisions to buy & the Men to watch I have had but little time to myself, what I have had, has been spent walking about the Island, but never more than 5 miles inland. The Country is all Rock & Mountain, in comparison of which the Morf[75] is a Molehill, the Hill is covered with Vines, Oranges, Lemons, Mulberries & by the Hedges of Cactus & Aloes. We have here the Plantain Tree & Cocoa Nut. The quantity of Wine exported from this small place is incredible, it is worth about 1/- per Bottle. Fruit is in great abundance we bought a very good desert for 8 which cost us 1/-. Mr Grant is well, I saw him yesterday Stewart has been with me every day since our arrival, the Sea sickness has had a greater effect on him than I ever knew on any one, he was sick the whole way, & much reduced, he is now better. We walked together the day before yesterday, about a Mile, we gathered Apricoes & Mulberries & Grapes & made the Portugese understand in a fashion. The Poor are very different from the lower Classes in England, they are Lazily basking in the Sun, covered with filth & Virmin. Red Faces Red Coats & activity, curiosity &c quite astonish them. The Women ran away, so I can say nothing of the Fair Sex only that they were brown. The Men have such villainous looks, indeed they say that it is dangerous to be on

Shore after Sun set. Captain Hobhouse behaves very kindly, he comes from Yorkshire. Yapp is well, My Cousins will probably be kind enough to tell his Mother so. I wish I could send you some Madeira, it costs only 1/- per Bottle. The Nuns here are famous for their preserves & Marmalade, they say that it is better at Martinico. I hope that you or my Cousins will write for me with a Letter to St. Vincents, there is nobody I delight to hear from so much as yourself, & that you should think me unsteady as you hinted in your last Letter would make me very uneasy. If I wrote thoughtlessly to my Cousin Mary it was because I had just received your letter by Mr Grant & I was in high Spirits but I forgot what I said. We sail tomorrow. I hope this Letter will reach you. I will write as soon as I arrive at St. Vincents, give my best Love to my Cousins, I often think of our quarrels in our Walks & I hope the time will come when we may renew them & I send a Defiance to the Cow.

Your dutiful Nephew HS[76]

After a brief spell in Barbados Henry records in his diary the regiment moving to Martinique on August 10, 1798 and then St. Vincent on August 19. Both France and Britain had plantations in St. Vincent worked by African slaves. Britain had gained control of St. Vincent from the French by the Treaty of Paris in 1763. The British development of colonial plantations met with resistance from the indigenous Caribs. France recaptured St. Vincent in 1779 but the British once again gained control of the island under the Treaty of Versailles in 1783. However, conflict continued between the black Caribs (the offspring of Carib women with the physically stronger and dominant escaped black slaves of the French) and the British. The 53rd Regiment had seen action in capturing St. Lucia from the French in 1796 and in the following year put down an insurrection by the black Caribs of St. Vincent who were supported by French revolutionaries against plantation owners. Over 5000 black Caribs were expelled to Roatán, off Honduras. The 53rd used St. Vincent as a base for expeditionary battles in the West Indies. Their numbers were greatly reduced by yellow fever.

Henry gives details of his appalling living conditions in Martinique:

My Memorandums are now missing but I find my letters that having left Barbadoes for Martinico, we landed at Fort Royal where the Men were placed in an old Barrack but the accommodation for Officers was so bad that neither Lieut Stewart or myself would go into them. Stewart hired a small room in the Town & I took up my abode in the Tavern. Boothby a Volunteer & poor Grant went to the Barracks. Grant died on the 15th & Boothby on the 17th. I believe we landed on the 10th. This as may naturally be expected alarmed us not a little we were only nine days in Martinico & in that short time we lost half our Officers & one third of our men.

Martinico is more mountainous than Barbadoes & the Vegetation more rapid owing to the soil being more moist. Fort Royal is situated at the Bottom of a Deep & Large Bay. Fort Bourbon a Strong Fort being immediately above it commanding it & Fort Edward which latter commands the Anchorage & inner harbour called the Carenage. I was much disappointed in the fruit which did not seem equal to what I had expected, the Pine Apple not appearing much better than Turnips. The expence at the Tavern was very heavy my dinner cost me a Guinea. I found the Climate much more bearable than I had expected.

~

St. Vincent

On the 19th we were embarked on the *Favourite*, Sloop of War & we landed on St. Vincents on the 21st. On joining the 53rd Regt in Fort Charlotte St. Vincents I found a great relief but the Novelty of the Scene altogether precluded any thought. Before I had been 4 days in the Island I made the acquaintance with Doctor Anderson of the Botanic Garden & was much delighted with him ...

In a letter to Mrs Butt from St. Vincent about November 1798 Henry describes:

When I wrote my last I was in low Spirits from the loss of Poor Grant but I have now recovered my Spirits & I think I can bear the climate for some time longer. It is true that I do think of home with fond delight but I am aware that at my time of life & with my prospects I must exert myself. The day before yesterday I rode about 20 miles into the Country & I thought within myself how delighted Martha would be to see hills piled on Hills with most delightful barrenness, some indeed covered with trees to the very top, in some places rugged rocks overhanging narrow paths & threatening to fall with every agitation. Sometimes our road lay by the Sea & then again ascending a Mountain overhanging the Coast the height thereof making my head giddy to look over. My Cousins would have laughed to see my companion & myself mounted on two Asses in full uniform. These animals retain their Character even in the New World & my poor Arm now aches from the frequent & unavoidable use of my Stick in beating my companion Bucephalus for we were obliged to assist each other in beating our Beasts. This Country at first sight is most beautiful, the heat however is very great & I cannot say that enjoy rest at night, what with the heat, Musquitoes & rats. The latter are my bedfellows & seem to live on the powder licked from my hair. I have often heard of a Mans Pig Tail being gnawed by the Rats but I always thought it a figure of speech I now find that it may be litterally true. When this letter reaches you I daresay you will be warming yourselves by a good fire in a close pent up room whilst I if I am alive shall be in a room with all my windows open, I shall be unable to bear my Coat on

In front of my room we have a long gallery or Balcony called a Verandah, which being covered from the Sun & Weather & running the whole length of Nine Rooms forms a pleasant walk. The Officers Rooms form the Ridge of the Hill & look out on both sides to the Sea, down a precipice of about 300 Feet altho we are so immediately above the Sea that a Ball thrown by the hand will in all probability roll to the level of the Sea yet we may at least calculate the distance by the winding path at Two Miles or while a Dutchman could smoke a Pipe of Tobacco.

In front of these Rooms, across a Valley is another ridge like a Back of an Animal of much the same height. About half way up are the Houses of the Negroes, appearing at a distance like a small Camp but on going to them like Pig Sties. We have also in view many Cascades but the most beautiful appearance is a heavy shower of rain falling in large drops between us and the opposite ridge & sometimes driven before the wind like a thick cloud. Behind our Rooms is a stone Terrace about 100 Yards long on which we walk after sun sett & from which we see the Town of Kingston, its Bay with the Shipping under us.

On the opposite side of the bay a ridge over which we see, the Fort Duvernet standing in the Sea & on the Sea side of the Islands called the Grenadines. The Principal & nearest is Bequa, the whole making a most beautiful appearance for the Grass is greener, the Sea is more darkly green & the Sky is of a deeper blue than you have it in Europe.

Mr Stewart is quite well and not a little proud of being appointed to the light Company which he has got thro the interest of his Brother for the Men justly observe that neither his figure or fashion would have entitled him to it, excuse my illnatured remark, I have been taking two Views from this spot but also they might do for any other place as well, I only want to return home to see you, otherwise all Countries are alike.

I am ordered into Banishment next Month, that is to go with a party to Fort Duvernet about 3 Miles from this to pass my time for one month with nothing to do but fire on Ships passing who do not hoist their Colors. I shall gain rank as the Officer Commanding this Island is always stiled <u>Governor, Commander in Chief, Chief Judge</u> Civil & Military of the Rock. Sir Wm Young's Island & its dependencies &c &c &c

Henry is delighted to receive a letter from his aunt and replies promptly on December 17, 1798:

I was not a little pleased my Dear Aunt at receiving your Letter the first I have received from England. There were other Letters by the same Packet but I broke the Seal of yours first. I had a Letter from Mr Maskall at the same time, he informs me that he has arranged a plan for getting My Sister[77] home & I hope that he will have succeeded. Stewart is well & desires his respects to you. Hobson is stationed at Ouie & Yapp with him. Hobson came in yesterday & I saw him, looking quite as well as ever he did in England.

I am writing this on Town Guard & I cannot well speak in favour of the Hospitality of the Island for I am dinnerless. I am too far from the

Mess to get any thing from thence & I cannot put my head into a Tavern for less than four Dollars. Lieut Palmer of the 53rd Regt takes this letter home. He has promised to call on you on his way to Ireland. He is the Son to the Bishop of Killala.

Pray give my best respects to Lord Valentia & tell him that Doctor Anderson has promised me some seeds & when I am to come home he will provide me with the Orphris, Orchis & Epidendrum,[78] but he says the Seapea[79] does not grow here. I can easily send any thing either to London or Bristol, from the latter place the expence of Carriage will not be much. I find from My Aunt that you are still great Botanists. I shall therefore study it more than ever. I am however sorry that I have not proper books. Doctor Anderson who has charge of the Botanic Garden here is very kind. The Distance from Fort Charlotte is too great for a pleasant walk. I continue drawing flowers & I have finished 28 & I have as good a collection of dried plants as Miss Rhodes herself. I have met with five very curious Trees here, one called Pawpaw which is said to have the property of making Meat tender, the other the Manchinel[80] which has a fruit like an apple with an Aromatic smell yet it is so deadly a poison that an Officer of ours was almost killed by only using some branches to make himself a hut, he was dreadfully swelled, he was cured by a Negroe. A Carraib Chief has made me Bow & Arrows.

In his diary Henry describes being continually plagued by:

Rats which get into my Bed & run over me. I wake & find them pulling my hair to get at the Powder when I move they leap on the floor. They Grawed the Rope by which I had suspended a Ham to a beam & it fell in the Night. I trod among them & could scarcely recover my Property. 5th January 1799 … here follows a list of my companions: Rats, Mice, Cockroaches, Fleas, Flies, Mosquitoes, Sandflies, Grasshoppers, Beetles, Snakes. Crabs, Centipedes, Scorpions, Green Lizards, Guanas [Iguana], Woodslaves, Black Ants, small & Large, Red Ants & White Ants & a Large Owl. These friends are very troublesome. I have procured a Hamock to sleep in which is suspended from the sides of my room & by this means covering myself over with the folds of the cloth of the Hamock I am pretty secure but the Mosquitoes bite thro'

& the Woodslaves[81] fall from the ceiling. I keep a Pistol loaded with shot on the table while I am drawing to fire at the Rats for they are seen running in the dunghill below my window like Pigs. … Killed a large Woodslave & on falling its tail immediately came off as if he relinquished it voluntarily, the tail kept moving for two hours after the body was dead. They say that this animal falling on your flesh will raise a wele on your hand like the cut of a whip, … The Men cook the Rats. One fine one was cooked & I preserved the skin. I had intended eating it but I could not muster resolution.

Meanwhile he writes to Mrs Butt on January 14, 1799 from Fort Duvernet, St. Vincent.

I am now at Fort Duvernet or the Rock a description of which I have given in a former Letter. It is a worse station than I can describe. It is an absolute Prison & to be compared to the Eddistone Light house near Plymouth. I have a Party of Men who are chosen as the worst men in the whole Regt. I have now given you some of the bad qualities of my present position. Now for its advantages. Imprimis, plenty of Fat Rats or the Cattle Kind they are as Edgar expresses it small deer. Plenty of Fish, Plenty of Herbs & Trees. I care not for the Fruit, My pursuit is the blossom, health as much as you could wish & plenty of exercise for I cannot move 5 Yards without ascending Steps & the Cheapness can only be compared with that of a Prisoner in one of our Jails where if you live on the Jail allowance you will not have much to pay & I do live on my Jail allowance by which I save my Mess Bill an Established Charge of Sixteen Dollars per Month or £4- besides One Dinner per week when on guard which may be reckoned as much more & I wear what cloths I like. I endeavour to avoid expence & I think that I succeed. In time I may expect promotion & then I shall do better. Our Regt both Officers & men is in perfect health, they could not be better in England. It is now Xmas & I am overpowered with heat while you I daresay are shivering. The Quarters I occupy are only seperated from those of the Privates by a deal partition, they are all in good spirits singing Night & Day, sometimes rather to my Annoyance. The Ratts & Cockroaches & Lizards are sporting around me.

I am sometimes attracted from my Studies by observing the latter moving along the Roof with their backs downward & appearing to walk as easily attached to the underpart of the Beam as the fly itself. You have no doubt often observed that the candle throws a shadow on the Ceiling like a Glory round the head of the Saints towards this light the flies seem inclined to collect & here you see the lizard watching his opportunity lies like a Crocadile ready to snap up his victim as it approaches his Jaws. My Bed stands in a Corner with curtains made of Gauze which are tucked up with the greatest care least the Musquitoes should enter, but every precaution is sometimes taken in vain & I am delightfully serenaded all Night with a song as loud almost as the humming of a May bee & I am sorry feelingly to say that their music is not the only inconvenience. I leave off that I may go to fish by moonlight Pray excuse the Paper. Yapp is well. I have a Servant from Kidderminster Named Yapp—I am &c H Sherwood Governor of the Island of Fort Duvernet, Commander in Chief of the Forces on the Island of the Rock & Sir Wm Young &c &c &c &c

∽

Henry enjoys going fishing for Parrott fish which he describes cooking with limes and chillie pepper, eating yams, grenadilla (passion fruit), plantains and sea eggs (sea urchins) but reports shooting 'a Sea Bird called Admiral immensely large in feather but not good to eat.' He draws the line at eating the rats which the men cook but did shoot and cook an iguana which he reports as tasting like chicken. In order to save on his mess bills which troubled him he kept goats, chickens and pigs. Punch was easily made as limes grew wild and rum and sugar were supplied by the plantation owners, 'my time passed away very quickly.' He and his brother officers were given hospitality by the estate owners which included balls at which 'all the Ladies of the Island were present.'

Later in his diary he admits that he would have been happy to stay on St. Vincent were it not for friends in England. He writes to Mrs Butt again from St. Vincent on April 23, 1799:

As the fleet is to Sail in a few days & an opportunity occurring of sending my collection of drawings & dryed Plants etc to England free of expence I am induced to avail myself of the opportunity as a heavy load of Baggage is a great hindrance in a Subalterns Haversack. I have therefore sent all my Collection in a Box addressed to Mr Maskell in London. If you do not think it worthwhile to send for them they will remain until I return. I do not think that you will find them worth seeing, but the very sight will prove that I have not been neglectful of your commands and any rate you must flatter me by saying that they are beautiful. The Shells & Jumble beads I hope will please you, as I have been 50 miles to Collect them to Ouia The very extreme point of the Island. My road led thro a most delightful Country far superior to the part of the Island in our possession. It was until this few months cultivated by the Charraibs. It is now wild but I dare say Government will allot it in a Short time. It will be then cleared for it is astonishing how soon a Country in this part of the World is overrun with wood & consequently affording a secure retreat for Slaves running from their Masters & others who prefer a life of depredation to a settled state. It is computed that there are 1000 outlaws now roaming thro this Country who commit every act of atrocity on unfortunate people of any Color who fall into their hands, it is therefore necessary to have an Escort in passing thro this part of the Island.

To give you any account of the beauty of the Scenery is far above my Powers, how Marten would rejoice to wander from one view to another. The only cultivated spots being the ground by the sides of Mountain Torrents. The Ridge of Mountains which like the back of a Whale runs the whole length of the Island is for the most part covered with clouds & there are not more than 2 or 3 Passages across them, in general it is adviseable to coast the island rather than attempt to cross even when directly opposite or as at St. Ouia to return all round rather than attempt to go 7 miles.

One of the remarkable facts is that the Island produces no venomous reptiles while the neighbouring Islands as St. Lucia & Martinique abound with them, so much so as to be a terror to the inhabitants. I am now quite fond of the Country & I should be sorry to leave it even for England at least at present. Stewart is well, Poor Yapp has drunk too much new Rum & lost his health. He is invalided & gone home. If you were here I should never wish to leave the Country.

21st May 1799 ... I forwarded to England a Box of dried specimens

of flowers & drawings. I sent them by Captain Wells of the sloop
St. Vincents who kindly undertook to deliver them to Mr Maskell to
be by him sent to Mrs Butt.

He eagerly waits for Mary's letters as this one dated June 2, 1799 shows.

All your kind Letters have arrived safe, the pleasure which I receive in
seeing the Bridgenorth postmark can only be expressed by bringing
to your remembrance my high spirits which you no doubt remember.
I can no longer eat, drink or sleep after hearing that a Mail is arrived
at Barbadoes until it reaches this Island & then we see the Signal for
the Packet, how I watch our Drum major as he goes to the Post Office
& count his steps along the side of the Hill as he returns, with my Spye
Glass in my hand. You are indeed in league with some thing you
ought to be ashamed of or how could you what was become of Virgil.
I acknowledge that he is very dusty but not out of respect, but Captain
Hobson declared war against him on Ship board & now I really have
no time to attend to him, I am even afraid to look on my Shelf where
he lays for fear of his reproaches. Your Account of Poor Mr Grant's
Pereginations is truly laughable tho I suppose disagreeable to himself.
[This must be a different Grant from the one who died in the West
Indies.] I wish I could see him here as the Climate would no doubt
agree with him, having been accustomed to a hot climate in his
Youth. Will you be kind enough to tell Mrs Grant that the 53 Rgt still
keeps its good Character. In this Island the inhabitants have voted
£200 to the Privates for a dinner on the 4th of June accompanied by a
Little expressive of their approbation. Stewart is in possession of my
late Government where he has been for a Month. I feel very proud of
the remembrance of the Ladies of Bridgenorth, pray thank them all
for me.

Henry records in his diary for August 21, 1799:

…On leaving England I had not £20 with me & I was put to great
expence more indeed than was necessary from my openness of
character, I advanced small sums to Officers & was not repaid, the
sums that I advanced were very trifling not amounting to much over

ten pounds but the expences incurred at Martinique and Barbados were much more and I therefore drew on Mr Bishton for £100 of the 200 which I had left in his hands. It however appeared that the £200 was invested in the Coventry Streets and therefore not immediately saleable there was therefore a demur on paying my Bill which was got over by the kindness of Mrs Butt.

Clearly Mrs Butt has bailed Henry out of debt. His interest in botany was shared by Mary and Lucy and would remain a life-long hobby. The descriptions he gives of flora and fauna in both his diary and his letters to Mary under cover of writing to Mrs Butt reflect this.

~

St. Lucia

By April 1800 news comes that the regiment is to leave St. Vincent for St. Lucia. This necessitates a hasty round up of Henry's livestock. Henry is once again in debt.

April 18th 1800

St. Vincents A Schooner arrived with orders for our immediately sending in all our Baggage as we are to leave St. Vincents. We are to be received by the 4th West India Regt but we do not know where we are going. I got my Baggage & 5 goats on board immediately & we who had expected to remain Months longer quietly, in the course of a few hours had embarked every thing we could. My Fowls 50 of which were running about my House & my House itself valued at £14 pounds were abandoned & we marched for Kingston in the morning leaving our Post absolutely abandoned.

... on the 3rd day to Fort Charlotte. The Schooner had reached before us & had landed My Goats & they were missing. As we are going off they will not again appear. My total loss in House, Fowls & Goats is 17 Joes - £31–17–6. This sum was more than all my Debts in St. Vincents & I reckoned it quite as good as ready money. I was therefore obliged to draw a Bill for £20 before I could leave the Island which I had hopes never to have done again.

On Saturday 19th we embarked on board the Regular Transport

the *Coromandel*, An old East Indiaman, the whole Regiment in that &
the Ocean, for St. Lucia.

... St. Lucia altho separated from our old Post of Ouia by a narrow
Channel of less than 20 Miles is as dissimilar as if it belonged to
another Hemisphere. The Soil is totally different. The productions
different. St. Lucia abounds with Venomous Reptiles as Serpents,
Tarantulas, Scorpions. St. Vincents has not one of these that is
reckoned dangerous. Here are large Parrotts as large as Makaws, Wild
Pigeons & the Sea is full of fish but it is very unhealthy.

To windward of Mount Fortune is a Mountain, much Higher, over
this Hill every Morning rises a thick black Vapour which brings a
damp unwholesome feel around, it is called the Black Vomit alluding
to the Fever which it is supposed to induce ...

May

Captain Elwin who arrived in good Health on the 27th April is dead
& the men dye very fast.

... The War which raged in this Island was not carried on as
formerly, but became a War of extermination by the rage of Royalists
or more properly speaking People of some Property against the
Republicans, or those of no Property, whether the first should keep
what they had or whether the Second should get into their places. The
Latter succeeded but unfortunately the instant that they had so, they
became the very persons with whom they had been contending &
another set arose in their Names who in their turn took their places &
contended against others, sometimes against the same who had been
driven out by themselves. In this State the Invasion of the Island by
the English was a real Blessing but they found half the Estates in the
Island Abandoned & the Negroes either living free in the Woods or
entered into different Corps as Soldiers, very few White dare live on
their Estates but all huddle into Castries[82] at Night or get under the
protection of some Fort. The Land is over run with weeds & little is
produced except Coffee & Cotton. The English are certainly better
Masters than the French & this may be in part be proved by the
different way in which the Slaves behaved in St. Vincents & St. Lucia.
In the Former when the Masters were overpowered by the French &
Charraibs, the Slaves followed them & surrounded Kingston in a

State of Starvation and even fought in their behalf. In the Latter the Slaves were in Arms & Murdered every European who fell into their hands. Still as a stronger proof. The Negroes belonging to the French Planters in St. Vincents, for St. Vincents was called a neutral Island, forsook their Masters & joined the Carraibs.

While on St. Lucia there were problems sending and receiving mail.

St. Lucia No Letters found till July 1800 it was not lost [margin note]

To Mrs Butt

My letters have been regularly unfortunate lately two have been taken to my knowledge & one sunk. I had complained of the great expence, but I am happy now to say that our Mess expences are now much reduced, it was indeed so great that our pay was scarcely sufficient to pay our Mess Bill it was indeed so bad that all the subalterns but one left the Mess, this brought our Seniors to reason & we are now in a fair way of getting it reduced. The Regiment is now much divided 5 Companies being at Martinique & 5 at St. Lucia, of the latter one Company is at Pigeon Island.

We are in great uncertainty whether we are to join the 5 Companies at Martinico or whether they will return to us, one or the other we expect will soon happen. This state of uncertainty is not very pleasant & we are longing to be united again. It is thought that we will go to them. We think that there is little doubt of our returning to Europe as we are very sickly & few in numbers we lose on average 1 Man each day & one third of our Men are incapable of doing duty & who will be invalided & go home by the first fleet. I am sorry that I did not write to you by the last fleet but I did not then know that the former letter I had written had been lost. We have a Packett to come here but none to go away, or any post office we therefore trust to Martinique should we send letters to Martinique they run then the risk of being lost at some Merchants Shop. (I, by pardon, Store). I intend keeping this letter until some opportunity should occur which is generally without any notice given, probably when we are in Town & the Vessel ready to sail.

The regiment is suffering high loss through deaths from yellow fever. He writes to his aunt from St. Lucia on August 7, 1800:

We have lost in the Regt since by death since the 24th April one Captain, 4 Sergts, 3 Corporals 51 Privates 1 Woman & 8 Children. Captain Hobson goes to Martinique Tomorrow, who will take charge of this letter, since the 7th viz 3 days we have lost Ten Men among the rest poor Cheek who was Hobson's Servant at Bridgenorth. We have now only 470 Men in the West Indias of which only 320 are capable of duty, we cannot therefore be long here. I have been walking about much & I think this Island will be most valuable when it is a little more cleared being a far better soil than St. Vincents & full of Fruit, but it is dreadfully unhealthy & it is distressing to think how many poor Men have been lost in this small Fort by disease. Stewart is well & sends his best respects.

Henry's diary records more deaths:

15th August We have lost 1 Officer & 16 men in 15 days out of 150.

Later he encounters 'serpents' which were a danger to life. On August 18, 1800, he describes the tragic consequences when the 10 year-old only son of his close friend, Weston, disobeys his mother:

I dined on the 18th Regiment with Weston, while we were sitting after dinner his only Son of Ten Years old ran out to Gather Guavas his Mother called him back & desired him not to go into the bushes for fear of Serpents. She seemed particularly alarmed about them & made the Boy sit down but he contrived to slip out while we were talking & we heard a scream. The Mother instantly cried out Alex is bit by a Serpent I knew it, it was true he had been gathering Guavas & was seized by a Serpent & died before 12 oclock at Night. He said that he saw the Serpents Eyes & tried to run away but could not, indeed he described the Serpent as having fascinated him & that altho he wished to run away he was obliged to advance but he was evidently in such alarm that we could not trust to what he said, every thing was done the part was so far as possible cut out & he was rubbed with

Mercurial Ointment until he died. The Serpent was killed & was Eleven foot long, it had taken the small of the leg intirely into its mouth. In the height of the distress Weston was called upon to Mount Guard I ran out & took his Guard for him but as soon as I had relieved the old Guard I ran down again & staid until 9 o clock when it was necessary to be with my Guard. The poor Boy did not seem in any Pain, he complained of a Numbness in his leg & it swelled very much & became black but we were not sure whether this was occasion by the Venom of the Serpent or the friction with Mercury.

As soon as the drawbridge was let down in the Morning I ran down again but found the Child dead. Weston finding himself unhappy was sent to join the Detachment at Martinico.

Martinique

Henry has noted the deaths of fellow officers and men from yellow fever.[83] When he next writes to Mrs Butt it is with the news that he has been desperately ill and that yellow fever continues to decimate the regiment. The letter from Martinique dated December 4, 1800 to Mrs Butt contains the alarming news of Henry's near death:

I write you this short note to say I am now recovering from a most severe fever called a Yellow Fever. My Life has been dispaired of & it has been reported from one Island to another that I was dead. You may conceive that in our retired corner of the World reports spread fast & it may be that they have even reached home. I was seized on the 13th Nov & I must say that I have received the most kind attention from all my Brother Officers. On the 28th I was so far recovered from the Fever as to be able to move & I was sent to Martinique. In England where diseases are protracted it may appear strange that in so short a time I should be able to talk of death & recovery but if you were aware of the effects of the diseases in these climates you would know that 36 Hours is quite sufficient to decide on the Effect of a disease.

I am now as yellow as Gold & the Surgeons recommend my immediate return to England but I am afraid of the expence & of being obliged to return, for I fear that all hope of our return to England as a Regiment is at an end. Hobson has been very kind &

attentive to me, he has a set of rooms attached to his situation & he
has given them to me. We do not expect to remain stationary long but
where our next Station is to be we know not.

Report which is very busy sometimes sends these 5 Companies to
St. Lucia & at other times brings the other 5 Companies here. We have
lost 5 Officers & 120 Men in 6 months.

He writes again from Martinique on December 29, 1800:

[Margin note] The order for our removal to St. Lucia arrived that day
I suppose you have heard by this time of the loss in Officers & Men
that we have now sustained. I am higher by Six than I was on leaving
St. Vincents & I now stand as the oldest Supernumerary Lieutenant &
I hope safe from being put on half pay should Peace happen
tomorrow. During my illness I received a letter from My Brother
James but being very delirious I tore it to pieces. I have since been able
to shake out most of it & I am much pleased with it. The 67th Regt are
now entering the Bay & we shall soon leave here for St. Lucia. Coll
Bradburn our Senior Major died yesterday.

St. Lucia.

On a happier note during February Henry and a friend go on a shooting
trip on their way to a Ball given by the French General and are invited to
dinner by a French planter. He is highly critical of the women's behaviour
in his journal.

Mr Nasaburre a planter came to us & invited us to dinner at his Estate,
but here again we were unfortunate for from some accident our
Cloths did not arrive & we were obliged to dine with the Ladies in our
Shooting dress. We however found that delicacy was not the order of
the day. The Gross indelicate language made use of both by Ladies &
Gentlemen exceeded belief. I was glad to get away. & I got down to the
beach & hired a fishing boat to take me to the Island. At Eight I
returned and supped on Lamb larded with Garlick & then to the Ball.
The indelicacy here was even worse than at dinner. Songs sung by the
French Ladies would scarcely have been tolerated at a Inn at
Portsmouth I hope these people are the outcasts of French Society

indeed I understand that many of the unmarried Ladies are Mothers & some of them have colored Children. This is the fruit of the French Equality preached in these islands. One Woman we met, a Niece of Monr De Longville one of the First Landholders, a fine Woman who has a large Family all born while the Mother is a Pucella & every Child differing in Color from his Brother.

The next letter to Mrs Butt from St. Lucia is on March 16, 1801:

We are now full of business. Expeditions are fitting out against the Danish Islands. The first sailed on the 11th Inst supported by 10 St. Croix, our hopes of our now returning home are now for the present at an end. When the bustle is over we may probably get away, but a larger extent of possession naturally requires a larger force. I am completely recovered from my late illness that I think myself well as ever I was in my life. We are now building new barracks not before they were wanted for we were before exposed to the Rain & like Mr Elwes glad to find a dry corner, the Dripping of Water has often kept me awake for hours.

His diary entry for March 25 starts:

I went to Town to see Buckland & Batty off for England. We hear that there is great News from Home, a Change in the Ministry. Mr Addington succeeds Mr Pitt as prime Minister. We are now all for Peace & it is said that Lord St. Helens is gone over to negotiate, some think the French will not treat thinking that we are afraid. Most people here are angry with Mr Pitt for resigning & say it will not do. I feel a Great loss at not having some Botanical Work to guide me in describing plants. I went in a Boat to a point under the Vigie in persuit of some Vincas (Periwinkles). I found two species of the Madagascar Perriwinkle, the Pink & the White. I killed a very large venomous scorpion which I preserved I am glad of it for McCaskell killed my present specimen & he threatened to take it away.

≈

The Caribs.

On April 20 Henry gives an interesting and very detailed ethnographic account of the native Caribs:

The Carraibs are Short & thickset of a Copper Complexion with long black hair & very active, their countenance very pleasing, the General height of the men is under 5 feet 6 inches the women are much shorter & more inclined to Corpulency, both sexes go almost Naked, in the Water they appear amphibious. They depend on the Sea in a great measure for subsistence. Like the American Indian they are very slothful or very active, no medium. The principle game on Shore is a small kind of half Rat half Rabitt called Agootie & the Manicou or Opossum. These they sometimes hunt with Dogs & sometimes shoot with arrows. They often shoot fish in the Transparent Sea with arrows but always by judging of distances, they shoot in Air & the Arrow falls on the fish. When tired or having sufficient food they sit in doors swinging in a hamock & pushing it with their feet one side & by some post in the Room to another. They sometimes plait a kind of reed to make basketts, they weave them so neatly that they will hold water & consequently will keep out water in any weather & being light are much used by the English to carry cloths in. Among these Yellow or Red Carraibs have arisen a Black Carraib supposed to be a mixed Race between the Negroe & Carraib women, they are more bold & robust & have almost destroyed their Copper Colored Brethren. When the Equalizing system of French was first promulgated in the West Indias the Blacks & People of Colour very naturally thought that the liberal system extended to themselves & for some little time united all Ranks in their favour. The Carraibs felt as others & not being so nearly allied as the Inhabitants of Martinique & Guadaloup, they continued to cherish the hope of universal equality after the hope was given up in the latter Islands. The consequence was that the Carraibs thought the french their real friends & being buoyed up they undertook a War against the English, on the first rising of these people the horrible cruelties committed are scarcely credible, but the most remarkable circumstance is the fidelity of the English Slaves who fought for their Masters & altho obliged to retreat they followed their Masters to Kingston & remained faithful even to starvation. The end as might naturally have been expected was that the English brought fresh Troops & having conquered the Carraibs, transported the Black part of the Community to Honduras & I believe to Sierra Leona.

The Yellow or original inhabitants are left, but the destruction of this formerly populous community was brought about by the Black Carraibs & not the Europeans.

The Carraibs formerly used bows & arrows & they now have them & are very expert in the use of them, yet they are given up as an offensive weapon.

The Chiefs have a plurality of Wives & seem to part with them on very slight grounds, the woman is a compleat Slave & is made to cultivate the Land & carry water which latter is no easy job for the Hutts are generally placed on a Ridge of a Hill every drop of Water must be carried from the Vale below. Their principal food is a paste made of Cassada or Manioc which like the Potatoe cannot be used without destroying the Crudity of its juice, the Juice is a very powerful poison. I have seen a Hog killed by drinking a small quantity of it. The Machine by means of which they express it is very ingenious, it is a loosely woven wicker basket which being filled is compressed by weights & alongated as may be seen in the Margin. [sketch] They afterwards bake farina on this plater of Iron like frying pans. They also make the Plantain into a food called tum tum. They pound the Plantain in a Mortar with Chillie Pepper. Their houses are very light being a very light frame of Reed on each layer of which they double down a plantain leaf the upper ridge covering the lower one & these huts soon constructed last a sufficient time for an hour. They are fond of keeping a fire at all times in their houses & when the weather is damp they have one under every hamock. They tye bandages pretty tight round the legs of their children & indeed round those of all the People both Men & Women, one above the Knee one immediately below & one round the ankle. This is generally [?] & fashioned on the Part, this bandage or Garter being put upon the legs of growing children causes a swelling in the joints above, they have unnatural Knees & Calves of the legs. Their way of counting is in french & indeed more than half of their present Language which of course arises from the new Wants which Europeans gave them.

A House	Baatee	A sheep	mutton
Husband	Teriete	A Plate	assietteè
A Fowl	Cuterac	Wife	Leane
A hammock	Eyran	A Blackman	Megoro
The sea	Ballowah	A Calabash	Commodee
A European	Balencè Comba	A Dress	Coolee Habit
A Bottle	Botteil	A Caraib	Califourna
A Hat	Bonnettee	a Goat	Cabra
A Man	Abene eera	A Tree	Waiee
A Horse	Caballo	A Woman	Eniero
Cassava	Elleva	A Cow	Vacasso
A Child	Erriaraux	To eat	Stega
A Hog	Piero	Rum	Binoo or Vinoo
To drink	Stanta	Water	Louna
Wine	Duvin	A Ship	Ocoona
How do you do	Ma bouy ca		
Very well	E Nay		

They reckon only to Twenty in French & then begin 20 and 5 or 6 or 15 & then two twenties.

From this short vocabulary it seems that all their furniture Cattle &c is derived from France or spain. The Carraibs have two names vz one French & one Carraib, Michel, Baptiste, Philip & to which is added Yarrowby, Amouraby.

The quickness of their sight is great they point out objects long before a white man can perceive them. I can make nothing of their Religion but they certainly believe in a resurrection, Angel & Spirit, the latter is called Zoombie & is sometimes a Sylvan god & at other times a more revenant. They are full of superstition & dread fishing if they have had unpleasant dreams. They will not allow a man to lay a net in the Sea if his wife has been brought to bed within the Moon. Sometimes they appear to be predestinarians for on remonstrating with them on their endeavouring to go to Sea in a small Canoe during a Gale they said "If our friends (meaning departed) want us we shall not return, if they do not we shall."

They are all very fond of Rum & they can scarcely refrain from drinking while any remains. One day they caught a very large Snapper (a Fish) & brought it up to sell for Rum. They bargained with me for a calabash of Rum, when the bargain was made they went down & brought a Calabash which contained four Gallons. I could not have supposed there was one so large however the bargain having been made they got it filled & after dinner I went down to their Hutts to see what they were about. I found them standing in a Circle & crying from intoxication, Men, Women & Children holding each others hand singing an old French Song which they called Chanson de Misere, The words were so barbarous as not to be understood, the burthen was O' Rochambeau! Rochambeau! Oh! Oh! The purport was that Rochambeau had enticed them to make War on the English which was the cause of their ruin, it is however to be observed that the black Carraibs were the Poets, they kept curtseying to this tune until they could stand no longer.

They generally in their songs take a child by the hand & curtseying without moving the feet cause the Child to do the same, it has much the appearance of begging. I believe they either never knew the whole purport of their french songs or have forgot it.

Their music consists of a hollowed tree or a small Barrel both ends covered with Goat Skin. The Musician seats himself astride on the instrument & beats with his Fists. When they once commence dancing they do not cease while they have liquor as long as they can stand. I never saw them dance while sober.

At this time they will sell any thing they have & send up deputations to the Officers offering to make Basketts or catch fish or do any thing the next day, if they will give them Rum but they invariably forget their promises if you lend them any thing. At certain Seasons they make an intoxicating drink of Cassada & they also ferment the Maize or Indian Corn & make a spirit of it. The Old women are employed to chew the Corn & throw it into a Vessel with water from which the Liquor is drawn off fermented & kept for use being of a very intoxicating nature. They complain of the destruction brought on themselves by the intermixture with Negroes yet so careless are they of the future that they have given their daughters as wives to the only 3 Black Carraibs remaining. When the Men are inclined to be Idle, which generally happens when they are not hungry or fearing to become so they sit down & make the women eradicate every hair from their Chin Eyebrows & other parts of the Body, they do indeed have a very very narrow single row of hair on their eyebrows. They acknowledge that in former times they put to death superannuated People & those who were useless to the community. The Murders & destruction of these poor Yellow Carraibs by the more ferocious Blacks must have been dreadful, they are now so few in Number & if you ask after their ancestors or even the Father of any Individual the Answer is he was killed by the Black Carraibs.

The Women have a singular Pincushion viz a hole in the upper lip thro which their always appear a Bundle of Pin points bristling out like a number of Eaveline's. *[tent guy-ropes]* This is a very formidable defence for their Mouths. These Pins they are able to remove singly with their tongue & can even pick out any one you may require without using the fingers. This is indeed but a poor description of these People but may serve to remind me of a race with whom I may say I was very intimate, having passed many hours of almost every day for 10 months in their Company. The Black Carraibs are stouter bodied Men. They are in all probability descended from run away Slaves who wishing to distinguish their descendents from the Negroes, contrived to flatten the Heads of their Infants by compressing them between boards.

When their Numbers increased they made war on the Yellow Carraibs & having destroyed the greater part drove the remainder into the Mountains & most barren part of the Island in 1796. The Black Carraibs, encouraged by the French rose suddenly on the English & such was the surprize that no resistance was offered, the poor Whites were murdered in the most shocking and horrible manner. The Carraibs gained possession of all the Island & even of Dorsetshire Hill which overlooks Kingston. I have mentioned before that the Negroe slaves were almost to a Man faithful to their Masters. They covered the Ground between Kingston & Fort Charlotte & were in a state of starvation. Some of the Planters who had lived on the road between Kingston & the Carraib Country & with whom the Carraibs had been accustomed to lodge on their Journeys, thought themselves secure from former friendship, but those who remained trusting to these savages were all murdered. At length St. Lucia being conquered some troops arrived the 53rd among the rest & soon recovered the Island, took all the Black Carraibs & transported them to an island called Rattan.*[Roatán]* It is said that the Spanish took them from their to work in the Mines. Others say that they were sent to Sierra Leone. I do not know which of the two stories is correct. The Yellow Carraibs having been less turbulent remain, but there are but few of them, residing at Masarica & Ouia. There are still some few Carraibs in the Woods, or it is supposed so far there are doubts, Several Person have been murdered but more particularly a Mr Clapham, a Gentleman of consequence, who was fishing near Mount Young. I must own that I have my doubts for I never heard of any appearance while I was among the Yellow Carraibs & I think I must have heard of these if any, indeed Negroes might have killed Mr Clapham & attributed his death to the Carraibs since the Rising of the Carraibs & the destruction of the Estates the Planters of St. Vincents.

∾

When he next writes to Mrs Butt, from St. Lucia on May 20, 1801, he is again in debt and seems to have decided that he does not wish to remain in England once the regiment returns.

Statement of my monthly expences

in messing	£1 – 8 –
washing 4 –	£8
breakfast	4 – 8
	£1 –17 – 4

My pay for 1 Week is £1- 18 - 21/2. My whole remaining receipt is 1/101⁄2. [sic] Can I with this provide Cloths, Servant & a Thousand other articles. I have really half starved myself yet I am now £22 in debt but I have something of a Soldiers economic turn & I will do if I can do. My Taylor must suffer, not by my non payment but the lack of orders, or as the old Joke has it when speaking of my Short Jacket It will be long enough before I have a new one. Should you see Major Buckland which I hope you will he will tell you how I get on. I should like much to see you but I do not wish to remain in England.

We are now again in expectation of seeing England but I only wish to see you for a short time & then go abroad again.

His diary continues with news of important military gains in 1801 for the British.

July 1st

A Vessel arrived from Martinique brings a paper with the following notification by Marshall Augereau to Holland, that Holland was no longer to consider itself a seperate State but that it was to form part of the great Empire. The Paper went on to state that the Dutch had revolted, that the fleet had sailed from Holland & given themselves up to the English in the Name of the Prince of Orange. The Paper further states that the English had defeated the french in Egypt & taken Cairo but with the loss of their General Abercromby.

1802 St. Lucia

The 1st of January being my Birthday I observed that I seldom get a dinner on this day. 1799 I went to the Rock in St. Vincents & got no dinner—1800 at Ouia, St. Vincents no dinner, 1801 St. Pieres Martinique no dinner 1802 no dinner having only a bit of Cold Salt Beef & a Yam which I eat & write that I hope for better times. I cannot however say that I feel much uneasiness on the occasion. Next Year probably I may have a Plum Pudding in England. It is true that I could easily get a good dinner at the Morne,[84] to which I have an invitation but my Men would all get drunk & quarrel & fight in honor of the New Year. In the Evening a Lobster fell in my way of which I am very fond. I therefore made a tumbler of Punch & sat down to enjoy myself but my soldiers were not altogether so sober as I flattered myself my presence would have induced & I was much disturbed. The room which I inhabit is only parted from that of the Men to about 7 Foot high, above that it is all open, it may easily be conceived that I lose none of their Jokes which are sometimes rather coarse.

... Feby

A letter from Mr Maskell says my Brother will get £500 prize money for a Danish East Indiaman taken near St. Helena on the 5th ...

16

A General order directing the 53rd Regt to be sent home immediately so that the Peace has in reality detained us. We now expect to sail by 19th April.

18

Our heavy luggage is ordered to Town which seems as if it was intended immediately to send us away. Weston gave me a Matress, I had never possessed one before, having slept in a hamoc. or in my Cloths this 4 years

21

A Report that 13 Transports are arrived from England to take home the [Regt] ...

17 April 1802

My Sore Throat becomes in a very Alarming state with ulcers in the roof of my mouth & around my Gums. I have no pain with it which the Surgeon says is more alarming.

News from Dominico, the Mutineers 8th West India[85] killed 1 Captain, 1 Lieut, 1 Ensign, 2 Commisssaries, 1 Artillery Officer. We do not know the reason for their Mutiny but it is said that Governor Johnson or Major Gordon made the Soldiers work on Private Estates (their own) & paid them nothing.

May 2

Two Ships appeared off. One full of Troops, we were in hopes that they were the French but they went off—we afterwards heard that the Ships had the Mutineers of the 8th West India on board with a detachment of the 11th Regt guarding them. The Commanding Officer says that upwards of 200 Mutineers were killed in the Action. 65 were buried in one hole & 60 in another. The Reasons given for the Revolt are 1st a Fatigue Party being employed by the Colonel to drain a Marsh his own Property without any extra Pay 2nd A Report raised by some incendiary that at the Peace they would be sold as slaves.

5

A large Frigate passed down, we hope she brings the Difinitive Treaty.[86] We hear from Martinique that ... the Treaty of Peace was signed on the 27th March. An official Report of the Mutiny of the 8th W India arrived. The number of Officers killed is not as great as we

had heard, there were 1 Capn 2 Lieuts + 1 Commissary 1 Sergt Major,
1 Sergt 1 Drummer 1 Artilleryman …

17th June
We had Parrots for dinner today. I have omitted to mention this
before the bird is very good food & so esteemed by the French but it is
not eaten in the English Islands.

The next month Henry receives news which will affect his pay and his
prospects of returning to England. He also uncovers the duplicity of his
immediate superior, Major Stewart

21 [July]
A General order is received for the reduction of Supernumary
Officers by this order every regiment on the Home Establishment is
entitled to Eleven Lieutenants. I stand 12th therefore liable to be
placed on half Pay & of course I shall go on half pay should no change
occur immediately which I have no reason to expect. An opportunity
is offered to all Supernumeraries to accept of vacancies in Regts not
ordered home & Major Stewart sent to me to say that he can procure
for me the choice of Vacancies in any Regt remaining in the Islands. I
feel a great loss how to act. I do not like to remain, & I do not like to be
placed on half Pay.

22
After taking some time to consider I determined to go to St. Vincents
& see what chance I might have of settling myself there. I therefore
went to my Friend Major Stewart & asked for leave of absence. My
Great Friend finding that this would not benefit his Countryman (for
the resignation must be immediately given in or the vacancies would
be filled up) told me that he knew I was the Eleventh Lieutenant by the
Adjutant's being considered a Supernumerary officer & when orders
came out that day I found that one order could not have been known
without the other. I afterwards found that he had played the same trick
with Lieutt Hughes in hopes of succeeding with one of us that he
might bring in a Junior Lieutt. Lieut McCaskell merely because he was
a Scotsman, I must however do justice to McCaskell & say that he was

totally ignorant of the Scheme & would not, I am convinced, have been concerned in such a business. I must also say that the Major's Brother was very indignant & told both Hughes & myself of the Scheme as soon as he found it out, & that in an open Manner. I was sent for to translate a Letter received from General Richpanse[87] the Governor of Guadaloupe to our Governor. The purport of it is this, that should the Negroes under the Idea of being free on the arrival of the French shew any synptoms of insubordination, he begs that the Governor will let him know & that he will immediately send a force & reduce them to order! Mirabile! We do not want French assistance neither do the Negroes want to learn Gallic Subordination.

On August 11, 1802 Henry again succumbed to yellow fever: this time more seriously. It had killed many of his regiment. He was confined to bed until September 28.

1 Sepr 1802
I had just written the above [on 10th August] when I was taken again with the Yellow Fever & did not leave my bed till 28th I cannot describe what I suffered for the very thing I had been looking for so long a time was now to me an object of the greatest dread, viz. Should the French come & relieve the Regiment while I am confined to my bed, I did indeed suffer most dreadfully. I now begin to eat soaked bread in tea & sit in a Chair, with my head shaved, my gums sore, & a Night Cap on. I hear the news & hope for a few days respite before I go on board Ship & eat Salt Pork & hard biscuit with Gums softened by Calomel. report has killed General Richpanse the French General & General Greenfield the English General & raised rebellion in all the French Islands. I am appointed to the Major's Company. This is my first Independent Step (I mean) having a Company from which I cannot be removed except to another. I am now high enough to have the Command of a Company.

4
I feel rheumatism in my Legs & cannot yet walk, my ankles are swelled & the otherwise small of my leg is larger than the Calf. We are informed that our Transports are coming.

6

The Doctor sent me to Pigeon Island for Change of Air…[88]

16

A Frigate & Two Large Vessels entered the Carenage[89] our hearts beat & our Chairs would not hold us. The Spy Glass was constantly at our Eyes surely it must be that the French are arrived, we have no boat large enough to carry us away & we are not able to walk for News. We are Prisoners—At 3 o clock the General's Canoe came.

It is true we are going home, we embarked in the Canoe & returned to the Morne. The French are not actually arrived in St. Lucia they are at Martinique, the Ships are our Transports to take us home. My State of Health is such that I feel very weak & not fit to go into the bustle, now going forward, our Baggage is embarking, all is fermentation, no regular food, nobody cares for it 18th 19th 20th all confusion. Hurry, bustle I cannot stand it & I feel overpowered & evidently becoming ill my strength is going. The Surgeon says I must embark immediately.

~

Return to England. September 29 – December 13, 1802

21st

I have been ordered on Board the Endeavour lying in the Carrenage, on embarking I immediately perceived a change for the better but why nobody can say. The Mind probably was satisfied at being embarked for England & I really think I should have refused to go on Shore again at any risk. The French arrived this Evening in Ships of War, full of Troops, low in the water, Dirty & hung round with Cabbages all singing Republican Songs. Poor fools they know not what they have to go thro. The Frigate broke from her moorings & ran foul of us, we lost our Main Top Gallant Mast & the Frigate (The *Castor*) was damaged. I felt alarmed being Nervous & sick. All the 21st was passed in waiting for two Transports to take the 9th West India Regt away. …

29th

We sailed this morning at daybreak with a light breeze, our Men were becoming very unhealthy in the Carrenage, there being no current, & a Swamp directly to windward, two Men died during the Night.

30

We passed close under Martinique yesterday Evening & this day we are becalmed under Dominique, which we see very plainly. A Man & a Child on board died today.

∾

Many died during the voyage. Henry's account of the final part of the voyage is very dramatic. He was lucky to survive.

15 [October]

Ensign Sutherland died of the Yellow Fever, he was a stout Young Man aged 18, a native of the West Indies, it has been truly alarming the number of deaths, since we sailed, the total number 28 in 16 days

…

17 [November]

Becalmed all day but at night a strong Breeze from the S. S. E. with which it was impossible to weather Scilly. The wind soon became a Gale, when we found it necessary to run before it, the Coast of Ireland being directly under our Lee we expected to make the Cove of Cork. We took in all Sail except the Fore Top sail yet we ran before the Gale 8 Miles an hour. The Captain had marked our situation at 12 oclock & calculating at the Rate we were going McCaskell & myself were afraid of being on the Shore before daylight & from our knowledge of the Captain we had no confidence in him, & so convinced were we of the danger that on relieving watch at 12 oclock we could not conceal our anxiety from the Commanding Officer Major Stewart we therefore awoke him & told him our ideas. He got up & called for the Captain, Spread the Map on the Table & McCaskell & myself pointed out the evident danger of what we were doing. Yet the Captain out of opposition still said we had plenty of room, As a Sailor he probably

thought it right to despise our knowledge. At length to quiet the
Major he promised to lay to at 4 o clock & we went to our Cabin as I
got into my Berth I said to McCaskell four oclock will be the time, he
must not delay. Having had the first watch I soon fell asleep & was
awoke by a most dreadful Cry. I ran on deck in my Shirt & saw a Head
Land of a great height overhanging the Ship, the Sea was beating
against it & the foam of the Ships way seemed to join the foam of the
Breakers, it was ½ past four. The Captain threw himself on the deck &
roared out like a Boy when beaten & when spoke to cryed out we are
lost we are lost, the first Mate was below, the Second Mate cried out
put up the Helm. He did not say which way, we were running before
the wind as direct as it could blow, the Helm was put up but not I
believe as he intended for we now stood to the Eastward. The Wind
now blew exactly on Shore & we saw the Rocky Shore as it appeared
close, to us, the Foam seemed all round us, there was no light, & at ½
past 4 on the 17th Novr it was quite dark after some time anxious
watching we cleared the Land & saw no more of it in half an hour it
appeared again as in the Margin [sketch map] our course being as the
Arrow there was now to all appearance no hope the wind blew on
Shore a perfect hurricane no one on board knew the Coast, The
Captain lay crying on the deck, the Chief Mate never came up, the
2nd Mate was the only active Man, (it afterwards appeared that the
Captain & Chief Mate had been drinking all Night & laughing at the
Landsmen's fears & supporting each other in a foolhardy daring) & he
joined himself to the Major & our officers & took the Command, in
which he took great responsibility in himself but acted like a good
Sailor. When he saw the land ahead he evidently saw that we could
not weather it & it became a question whether we should wear Ship,
[jibe to an opposite tack] for tack we could not, or run the Ship on
Shore in the hopes of finding a Spot in the Bottom of the Bay. We
found we could not get the Ship round, & our last resort was to run
the Ship on Shore, the place chose was the nearest place to the Bluff
head as it appeared, we thought it was higher land than the rest, &
judging from what we were in the habit of seeing aboard expected a
Sandy Beach within it, we therefore hoisted more sail & stood as near
to the wind as we could to give ourselves another chance of clearing
the point but we drifted inwards & all hope of saving the Ship was

over when instead of finding a beach we passed on thro a Channel narrow & seemingly full of rock yet we passed thro, & so rapidly that we had not time to think of getting an anchor out or in all probability we should have let go the Anchor under the Lee of the Island. On clearing this Channel we found ourselves in another Bay & by this time day began to break, we saw the Shore & two Rocks a head & just under our Lee another rock with the sea beating against it sometimes it was covered at other times stood a Mountain, we now saw our danger & determined on tacking to recover the Shelter of the Island & Providence befriending us, the Ship answered her helm & we tacked but it was a very anxious moment, we soon got under our Island & seeing a Bay to Leeward ran in, in doing this we seemed to slide down the side of the rock as a Cork would do in an agitated bason of water we anchored. The band began to play & we scarcely knew whether we were drowned or not, the Bay turned out to be Squince bay.[90]

I must again repeat from a better knowledge of the Land our situation & what we have escaped. The Head Land which we made at ½ past 4 o clock was called Dundiddy Head & having at the time cleared the head land we found ourselves in the Bay of Ross, the next Head land was Ragged Island & having passed between it & the Shore the Piramid Rocks a head were the Stag's the Rock under our Lee was called Black Rock near Castle Haven, & on our return we could not weather Caracanamen Rock & ran into Squince Bay, we are now as completely land locked as in the Carenage at St. Lucia but our exit seems doubtful as the entrance is extremely narrow & the Island closely opposite. Many gentlemen came on board & said that they had never seen a Ship in the Bay before. A Ship called the *Plymouth* had once anchored in the passage between Ragged Island & the Main but lost the anchor & was nearly on Shore in getting clear.

We have taken a wild Irishman on board as a Pilot to get us out & Pilot us to Cork, his name is Tim Haggerty & a funny fellow he is, he says that God must have been before the Ship, behind the Ship above the Ship, beneath the Ship & must have stood at the Helm. The Gentlemen of the Neighbourhood say much the same, we have received many civilities from them particularly from a Mr Townsend of Castle Townsend & a Mr Matthews.

Note added Jan 1803:

I was seized with a Yellow Fever which I never properly recovered until the Island was given up to the French in September, during my extreme illness my great fear was that the French would come before I was able to move but it pleased God to give me strength to get on board a Ship near a Month before the arrival of our New Friends. We reached England in December after being in the greatest danger off the Coast of Ireland & driven into a Bay called Squince near the Staggs & Castle haven on the North Eastern extremity of the Island, we were again driven into the Cove of Cork & again into Plymouth where we performed quarantine. I quitted my journal during this time, first on Acct of illness afterwards for want of opportunity for most of our Men being dead or Transferred we were stowed seven Officers, 2 Ladies & 3 Children in the small Cabin of a 300 Ton Ship & had not room to move. No one can conceive the Distress of Gentlemen on board a Transport under such circumstances at times it is bad enough but when the full strength of Officers for a Regt is quartered with 20 Privates the accommodation must be bad indeed. On Parade at Portsmouth I had on Parade of my Company 2 Officers, 2 Sergts, 1 Corporal & 1 Private. ...

On November 22, 1802 the *Endeavour* moored at Cork. Henry includes this sobering list:

53rd Regiment of Foot I examined the returns of the Regt found that the Regt		
Landed at St. Lucia in 1796 –		*857*
Men joined between 1796 & 1802		*824*
		1681
died	*805*	
deserted	*39*	
Invalided	*306*	
Discharged	*9*	
Transferred	*194*	*–1353*
		328
But we have only		*–307*
		21

25

A Circumstance has happened on this Coast within a few days which shews the Savage State of the Inhabitants, it appears that a Lieut Lapsley of the 17th Regt was on board the *Mary* of Liverpool lost on the 18th & that he had reached the Shore in safety but was murdered by the Natives near Clomkelty two men of the Neighbourhood of Clonkelty are taken up on suspicion.

∾

England once more.
On December 2, 1802 *Endeavour*, having weathered another severe storm, anchored off Plymouth and was put under quarantine until the 11th. On December 13, 1802 *Endeavour* arrived at Spithead after 12 weeks' voyage home.

13th December 1802 England Spithead
At day break a boat came off with Vegetables for Sail & I obtained leave to go on Shore to see Capn Park at Haslar.[91] I found then all well & kind I was pressed to stay but could not as I had promised to return. My Cousin Elize was in Nottinghamshire My Brother James is I find on Board the Hussar, at Sheerness serving out his time as Midshipman. On my return to Portsmouth I found the *Endeavour* had entered the Harbour with the Tide & we were ordered to Land tomorrow Morning & occupy Hilsea Barracks.

14

The pleasure of walking on Shore after being at Sea 12 weeks is delightful & we could scarcely any of us keep quiet on board this Evening.

15

We landed & marched to Hilsea where we found the other 5 Companies

16

Our Rout is for Shrewsbury after remaining here for cloathing & rest.

I asked leave for 3 days to go to London & received it.

17

Left Portsmouth at 5. Breakfasted with Mr Reynolds who seemed pleased to see me, went to Mr Maskell. I stated to him that I was much in want of Money being £25 behind hand & having a compleat new equipment to provide.

I have a reversion of a Considerable Sum on my Fathers death, he advized that I should apply to my Father & between us dispose of the Principal & he undertook to communicate with him, he has reason to suppose that there will be no difficulty, as my Sister has already done the same & received £430.

18th

I called on Mr Andrews [Andrewes] at the Rectory St. James's & found that Mrs Butts family were well at Bridgenorth which much delighted me, as I had not heard from them for some time.

19

My Brother John called & conducted me to my Father's. My Father did not behave well to me, but I refrained from answering & gladly escaped from his house, before we parted he became more calm & kind, but insisted on having half of the amount for which the Property might sell. He offered to Lend me Money.

20

Mr Maskall strongly advised me to Borrow £50 of my Father but I refused but on Mr M- begging me to do so & thinking it right to attend to his advise I wrote to my Father. My Uncle had a Large Party to dinner.

21

Called on Mr Reynolds who most kindly enquired into my Affairs & hearing what I was about to do remonstrated & even offered to Lend me what Money I might require & he pointed out the great loss that I should have that I thankfully accepted his offer & he lent me £70. My Father never answered my Letter & I left London most highly gratified by the great kindness I had met with from my friends particularly from Mr Reynolds.

22

On arriving at Hilsea I found myself attached to the Light Company[92] an honor I had not expected but not the less pleasing as it had been called for by my Seniors.

23

My Honor is but of Short duration but I had it which is sufficient. I am wanted to Command a Company & for which I am to receive £20 Pr Annum Extra. I leave the Light Company to take the permanent Command of the Majors Company. I am promised the Command of the Light Company the 1st Vacancy & I am allowed to retain my Green Feather & Wings, honors are showered upon me. ...

17 January 1803

Marched towards Shrewsbury At half after 8 This Morning marched from Portsmouth for Bridgenorth, the Weather was frosty. The road quite hard.

26th Heavy snow causes a few days' halt at Cirencester.

On Saturday 29 there was a Ball. The excuse was a Compliment to the Regt the real reason can be easily guessed. I did not like the Compliment but our Big Wigs pretended that it was a compliment & as in duty bound I went. The Gentlemen were almost all composed of Officers 53t Regt & there was no lack of Ladies. A Clergyman was the Master of Ceremonies who required that we should break up at 12 it being Sunday but as he had notified this early in the Evening the Ladies & Gentlemen contrived to put the clock back. The Gentlemen must have gone half way towards the deception or it would not have passed.

31

Marched at daylight, The Weather being frosty & pleasant we reached Tewksbury by 10 o clock. I now became anxious to have a few days at

Bridgenorth. I asked the Colonels leave to go on & it being granted I engaged a return Chaise to Worcester

1 Feby
I slept all the way to Worcester & I slept again there & at 6 oclock 1st Feby proceeded by Coach to Kidderminster where I was at School in 1789. The Town seemed to have shrunk into nothing since my Time, I could not I thought jump thro the Town hall in a hop Step & Jump, formerly it was a building of great consequence in my Eyes.

Henry is almost at Bridgnorth where he expects to be reunited with Mary but his hopes were to be cruelly dashed.

Meanwhile, Life at Bridgnorth

I nitially Henry's departure for the West Indies had been softened for Mary by a visit to Great Witley to stay with Marten. As curate he had taken lodgings in part of a building overlooking a pleasant garden. The other part was a shop and Mary enjoyed sitting in the parlour and watching the villagers come and go with their purchases. It was a very happy time for her. Here she began seriously to study botany with her brother and, during their rambles in the wooded hills, would collect specimens for identification later. That summer Lord Valentia held a ball and *fête champêtre*[93] at Arley. The two days of celebration began with a ball at which the military band of the 85th Regiment played. Mary described herself as being 'at the very pinnacle of enjoyment.' After breakfast on the following day the revellers walked down to the Teme where two large boats with sails waited; the second boat took the band and as soon as the party set sail down river it struck up. Crowds had gathered on the bridge at Bewdley to watch their progress before the passengers disembarked at Winterdyne. There they climbed up to the woods and enjoyed a picnic before setting back for Arley by river. That night there was a second ball for Mary to enjoy

Both Mary and Lucy continued to write. In 1799 Mary sold, for £40, her novel *Margarita* on which she had been working over the past five years. Mary describes the process of writing the novel as enabling her to 'acquire much command of the language.' Mary had also started writing *Estelle* which in time evolved into *The Lady of the Manor* after much revision. It would be published between 1823 and 1829 in seven volumes. She also began writing what she termed a modern novel. This was never published. The sisters' life revolved around writing, visiting their brother and going to balls in the surrounding area. It was while staying that July with her brother in Great Witley that Lucy met her future husband, the

Reverend Charles Cameron. He was one of Marten's friends from Oxford 'all of a reading and serious turn' who was also staying with Marten.

In 1800 Lucy was invited to go to London to stay with Dr. and Mrs Andrewes with the purpose of studying the Bible in greater depth. Lucy regretted her lack of education and, after some hesitation, she accepted the invitation the following year when she was twenty and, under Dr. Andrewes' tutelage, became a devout Evangelical Christian. She was also introduced into London society by the Andrewes and observed the courtesy and elegance of manners of her hosts. However, the theatre, Ranelagh (public pleasure gardens in Chelsea) and the opera met with her strong disapproval:

> What a foolish, sinful place is a theatre;…Went to Ranelagh; did not like it.
> I remember going to the opera, and being exceedingly disgusted. I thought it looked like a heathen temple; and the music not such as went to the heart, and the style of singing altogether artificial.[94]

In contrast, long walks, deep in conversation with her host, in the London parks and Westminster Abbey met with her approval.

Both young women found their home in Bridgnorth depressing. Matters were made even worse when in 1801, after Lucy had returned, a hard winter enveloped the country leading to food shortages. Although both Mary and Lucy had been left £400 with interest at four per cent in their grandfather's will, which made them financially independent of their mother, Mrs Butt extended her economy by limiting the amount of bread in the household to quarter of a loaf per week for each person. Not only this but the dinner they ate was frugal and no supper was available to ease the pangs of hunger. The sisters, influenced by their work in the Sunday school and the shortage of food for the poor, began to question the other aspect of their life: the frippery of much of their social life in which going off to balls and other entertainments was in stark contrast to the social conditions and hardships they observed around them. Infant mortality was a very present and all too familiar event as was the risk of maternal death in childbirth: the threat of the workhouse loomed for the poor and orphaned; diseases such as typhus and smallpox could threaten the whole community. The two sisters turned more and more to their religion. Mary drew up a list of seven rules for her conduct, which she believed would set her on the path to righteousness:

1. To rise as early as I can awake. 2. To spend my time in prayer till my mother is up. 3. To devote certain hours to my mother. 4. To read my Bible after breakfast. 5. Never to walk in the streets but when sent by my mother, or when any poor people require. 6. To go to church every Wednesday or Friday. 7. Never to indulge a worldly thought.[95]

For Mary a dissonance was growing between enjoying the gaiety of the fun-loving society into which she had been drawn and her increasing commitment to leading a good and committed Christian life in which such frivolity must, she felt, be eschewed. Her contact with the socially disadvantaged through Sunday school, and the poverty and hardship she witnessed, found expression in writing tracts. She and Lucy embarked on writing highly moralistic didactic tales in which the good and Christian life, however hard this may be, is rewarded by salvation. Mary began writing *The History of Susan Gray* for the edification of the senior girls in her Sunday school class. In it she draws on her background of rural Stanford and her witnessing the effects of poverty in Bridgnorth.

The book relates the tragic story of an orphan, the eponymous Susan Gray. Her parents had brought her up to know her place in society, to be Christian in her outlook, to attend Church, neatly dressed, every Sunday and to be hard working, honest and without vanity as to her appearance. The message would ring true to Mary's eager Sunday school pupils. All seems to be going well for the young Susan as she is brought up in the countryside mirroring that around Stanford. But at the age of six Susan is orphaned when both her parents die from a fever ravaging the neighbourhood. Their death is portrayed as a welcome relief 'from this world of sorrow and labour to that happy place where men are made "equal unto angels, and are the children of God."' Susan is placed in the parish poor house from where she is rescued by her father's aunt, who lives in Ludlow, in return for the parish's paying her twelve-pence a week for looking after the little girl. Mary now drives home her Evangelical message that children who fall into bad ways, as Susan does while living in abject poverty with her aunt, can be redeemed by attending Sunday school and going to church regularly. Her saviour is a rich benefactor called Mrs Neale who takes Susan into her household and sends her to school. She learns that she must lead a virtuous life if she wishes to go to heaven. Mrs Neale dies but has arranged for Susan to go into service with a Mrs Bennet.

Here she meets Charlotte Owen who has forsaken the church. Charlotte is vain and is intent upon enjoying herself in Ludlow and tries to persuade Susan to join her. Now Mary introduces the wicked Captain whom Charlotte sets out to attract by decking herself out in fine clothes and ribbons. But Mrs Bennet has other plans! Susan is sent by her to take linen to the Captain who then sets out to seduce her rather than falling for the wiles of Charlotte. Susan is about to suffer the same fate as Clarissa in the eponymous novel by Richardson which Mary had read when younger.

Mrs Bennet is in cahoots with the Captain and leaves Susan alone one night in the cottage. The Captain arrives and proposes that she should run away with him. Susan withstands his blandishments, goes to her room where she seizes the chance to escape his evil intentions by escaping through the window. Destitute, she has to find work and is taken on by a farmer. She is ostracised by the other farm-workers as gossip has it that she has encouraged the Captain and has lost her virginity. Desperately lonely and ill she turns to her religion, believing in her salvation at the hands of God. She grows weaker and dies in the presence of an old clergyman to whom she has told her story. Susan's death is described: 'never did any one prepare for death with so much joy, such holy hope, and humble confidence in God, as did this excellent young woman!' She even asks God to bestow forgiveness on the Captain, Charlotte and Mrs Bennet before she dies. And Charlotte? She dies in a garret abandoned by the Captain who, she discovers, has a wife in Ireland. As for Mrs Bennet, she dies in the workhouse in Ludlow. One event from Mary's experience is included: the Captain goes abroad to the West Indies where he later dies unrepentant. Henry is of course at this time in that country and facing both the dangers of war and of dying from yellow fever. Mary quotes the Bible throughout the harrowing tale to emphasise to her young audience the horrors awaiting those who do not repent their life of wickedness and the dangers of being seduced by a soldier—a real danger in Bridgnorth with its barracks. The dramatic plot with all its pitfalls would have been only too familiar to these young and poor girls. They would have been aware of the dangers of following a soldier and, in doing so, losing their good name. Mary ends the tale:

> Remember Susan Gray, and let her example be ever in your mind; and let it not be your wish to be rich and great, to seek for distinction and pleasure in

this world, but to do your duty in that humble state in which God has placed
you. And, however lowly and poor that state may be, yet fear not that you will
fail of your reward: God is no respecter of persons, but he will reward every
man according to his deeds.[96]

One imagines her captive audience listening to this tale as it unfolded in
all its highly moralistic detail. Mary has drawn on all her talent for a
compelling narrative into which she brings fire and eternal damnation
and her highly emotive death-bed scenes which she uses in many of her
later books. This tract novel is a foretaste of Mary Sherwood's prolific
period of writing Evangelical books for children. Later she will become a
household name.

Mary completed the manuscript on March 5, 1801 and while in Bath
at the end of the year she corrected the proofs. The book was published
anonymously, by Mr Hazard of Bath. Mary received £10. The book
became a favourite and went through many editions, many pirated, until
in 1816 Mary made some alterations before it was reissued under her
copyright.

~

Mrs Butt had been in a poor state of health exacerbated by the death of
her close friend Henrietta Hawkins Browne in April 1802. However, her
health had improved sufficiently for the family to accept an invitation in
August from Thomas Butt, Mary's cousin, who had succeeded his father
as vicar of Arley. Lord Valentia was absent preparing for his expedition to
India with Henry Salt,[97] Mary's cousin, who would accompany him as
artist and cartographer. While staying at Arley it was announced that
Lord Valentia was to pay a visit prior to leaving. Mary's feelings for Henry
Sherwood were no longer purely platonic at this time but whether Lord
Valentia and she had romantic feelings towards each other in the past is
pure conjecture although she does write: 'nothing ever passed among us
which was not strictly correct. Lord Valentia never seemed to forget that
I was the daughter of his beloved tutor.' Mary thought it necessary to
absent herself from Arley and return to Bridgnorth stating: 'By a singular
effort of discretion on our part, it was discovered that it might be quite as
well that my sister and I should not be at the Hall when the young lord
and his friend arrived ... So accordingly we walked off to Dudmaston[98]

and from thence to Bridgnorth, leaving my dear mother to receive her beloved Lord Valentia, of whom I may truly say that he was ever like a son to her.'[99]

However, Lord Valentia could not resist the opportunity to play a practical joke on Mary. At Bridgnorth while Lucy was out a Colonel Coburn was announced. The purpose of his visit was to bring her a letter from her mother. Mary was irritated by the seeming familiarity of the young man who she thought was impudent in his manner. She then discovered the true identity of her disguised visitor: it was Henry Salt! Mary and Henry repeated the charade when Lucy returned. She was angered by Mary's overfamiliar behaviour with the young man until he was unmasked once more.

It was while staying at Arley that Mary was approached by a friend in Bath to take care of an orphaned six year old girl from India. With Mrs Butt's agreement the child, Harriet, was brought by chaise to Arley. Mary had agreed to take the little girl as she thought a child's presence would amuse her mother. Harriet was small, very quiet and underweight for her age and not in the best of health. Having spent the first few years of her life in India 'her habits were completely East Indian, and her complexion too …' Mrs Butt was charmed by the little girl who was to be the first of many children whom Mary either adopted or took care of. Soon after Harriet's arrival the Butts left Arley which would be let while Lord Valentia and Henry Salt were abroad. The Butts' social circle was now depleted: Lord Valentia was abroad; Mrs Hawkins Browne had died as had Lady Winnington and Mary's uncle, Thomas Butt.

Mary and her cousin, named Thomas Butt after his father, were invited to visit his uncle and aunt, the Congreves, in October 1802. The Congreve family lived at Peter Hall near Coventry. On the journey Mary became ill with scarlet fever. Prior to setting out on this trip she and Lucy had visited a family whose children had caught it. So ill did Mary become that she and Thomas were forced to stop at an inn where the kind landlady, Mrs Bury, looked after her. Scarlet fever was a serious infection and the two servants who looked after Mary and two of Mrs Bury's ten children caught it: they all recovered, Mary, however, was seriously ill and it was some time before she could be taken to Peter Hall. It was there, while she was still recuperating, that she received a letter dated January 8, 1803 from Hilsea Barracks. It was from Henry who had just returned with his regiment from the West Indies. He had been away for almost five years and had 'twice been near death with yellow fever.' Naturally Henry was impatient to see Mary again as there was a very important question weighing on his mind. Mary by this time was feeling stronger so she went back to Bridgnorth with Mary Anne Congreve, known as Anne. In his diary Henry reports his reception:

1 Feb
I reached Bridgenorth at 2 it being nearly 5 Years since I quitted it. I ran to my Aunts House full of pleasing thoughts but was met at the door by the old Servant Keeping the door in her hand half shut as if fearing a Thief. She knew me but said she would call somebody down, at length I was admitted into the Hall when a Young Lady Miss Congreve came down and told me that My Aunt & Cousin Lucy had a dangerous Typhous Fever & that one Servant was dead. I own that I felt much hurt at my reception & I said that having served so long on the West Indias where the Yellow Fever carried off so many I did not feel the Dread of the fever, after some time my Cousin Mary came down with a formal Courtesy & after staying a few minutes I took my leave wishing that the Regiment would arrive that I might proceed to Shrewsbury, all my fond hopes of meeting my friends seemed in a Moment at an end. ...

26
Mr Marten Butt my Cousin came & I find he is shut out of his own house as well as myself which in some degree reconciles me.[100]

The longed for reunion had to be postponed due to typhus raging in the household. Both Mrs Butt and Lucy were seriously ill, as was the Indian orphan, Harriet. One of their much-loved servants, Mary Bailis, died from it. It fell to Mary, still weak from scarlet fever, and Miss Congreve to nurse the invalids with the help of a doctor.

On March 22 Henry visited both Bridgnorth and Arley to visit the Butts and recorded 'passing time with my Cousins in the most pleasant manner.' But much more importantly he came to ask Mrs Butt's permission to marry her eldest daughter. She gave the couple her blessing but refused to be drawn into any of their future plans. At the same time Anne

Congreve became engaged to Marten Butt. It was decided that the convalescents should travel to Arley, accompanied by Mary, Anne and Henry. Mrs Butt, after further recuperation, would take up the newly widowed Mr Hawkins Browne's invitation to go to Badger where Mary would stay with her for a week before leaving her mother with Mrs Gumm, the nurse who had looked after her at Bridgnorth during her illness. Once back at Bridgnorth Mary was joined a day later by Dr. Salt who was dying. He raised the question as to what would happen to an estate held in the names of himself, Marten and Mrs Butt if both he and Mrs Butt died at the same time. Marten and Mary substituted Salt's name with that of Mary without consulting him. When he discovered what they had done he agreed that he would in all probability pre-decease Mrs Butt.

On April 1 Henry received a letter which contained the news that his father had died on March 25. Henry's relationship with his father had been a difficult one because of Henry's grandfather's will which had bypassed Henry's father in Henry and his siblings' favour. He would realise that his late mother's property entailed in her marriage settlement would be released to him and his sister, Margaret. On April 22 he went to London and received £735. His financial worries were over. He immediately left London for Coventry and Bridgnorth but Mary was at Badger. However he dined with Anne Congreve and Lucy and noted in his diary: 'Tis hard to be parted from those with whom we could for ever dwell.'

After a short peace following the 1802 Treaty of Amiens, Britain had again declared war on France on May 18, 1803: a series of wars would last until 1815. Henry's regiment was ordered to Ipswich because the regiment was being reorganised.[101] There was unsettling uncertainty as to where the regiment would be next posted. On May 19 a ball was held for the officers and their guests. The officers had marched to Wolverhampton and had to return for the ball at Dudmaston which was organised by Mrs Whitmore a friend of the Butts. Mary describes it:

> The evening was externally gay, though inwardly, no doubt, sad to many. The war had broken out again after the short peace, and all the feelings which the English ladies had experienced before the short peace were, with increased force, revived. These feelings consisted in the close connection between gaiety and death, in the fearful apprehension that the blooming young man, in his goldlaced coat and emplumed cap, who last month, perchance, was the gayest member of the circle of the little country town, might, perchance, in the next month's Gazette be reported as a breathless corpse.[102]

Henry reluctantly returned to Ipswich:

June 1
To Ipswich, I have no eyes, Ears, tongue or Pen to see, hear, speak or record, all being left at Bridgenorth.

Henry and Mary wanted to be together and with war having been declared there was added impetus for them to marry. Events now moved rapidly. Henry's diary records his marriage in June in the briefest of terms:

… 24th at Ipswich was mustered & then got a fortnights leave to Bridgenorth. I was married on the 30th & passed the night at Hagley. My uneasiness now is the idea of going away for my leave expires on the 7th but I obtained leave til the 24th. The 20th I was obliged to leave Mrs Sherwood & return to Camp at Bromswell near Ipswich here I was only allowed to remain 3 days when an order was received to send 3 Captains 3 Subalterns 10 Sergts 10 Corporals & 10 Privates to York. I was the first for duty & not sorry to go for I found the Camp Cold & unpleasant.

The couple remained in Bridgnorth until he returned in July to his regiment in Ipswich:

When I found myself in orders for York & a Party of Men going to March I immediately conceived that I might spend a week at Bridgenorth & overtake the Party before it arrived at York. …As I am not the Subaltern for Duty I interpret the order to mean "go by Bridgenorth." I therefore set off immediately & stopped at Woodbridge for the London Coach in which I proceeded & from London to Coventry Birmingham and Bridgenorth. I Met Dr. Salt in the Church Yard who was astonished to see me. Mary was at Badger but expected to night & I had the pleasure of seeing her at Ten oclock. I passed the day at Oldbury with Mrs Butt & Mary & I fancy that I am formed for retirement & wish for a Cottage, no Duties, no Promotion—on Monday I was again put to it for I dare not remain longer. I passed thro' Wolverhampton, Litchfield, Derby, Sheffield to

York & on my arrival found that I could as well have waited a week longer as there were no orders for us.

The sisters found lodgings for their mother at Oldbury, near Bridgnorth and they moved her there on July 28.

Following the 53rd Regiment

T he regiment was quartered in Sunderland. Mary remained at Bridgnorth, visiting her mother regularly at Oldbury. When she left at the beginning of October she had only seen Henry once since he left in July. She set off from Lichfield on a journey which took from two o'clock on the first day until midnight on the second day and was not without incident. When the coach with its six passengers arrived at Durham where she would spend the night at a coaching inn, one of the other passengers, a young officer, had noted that Mary was alone and proposed they should eat together. This over-familiarity alarmed Mary who promptly changed her plans. She explained her predicament to two elderly Quaker gentlemen who were travelling on to Sunderland by chaise and they welcomed her aboard. Henry was on guard duty when she arrived at the lodgings which he had taken so she was greeted by his servant, Luke Parker, who would remain with the Sherwoods until 1816. For Mary it was a lonely introduction to being an army wife. Henry was heavily involved with army duties. Mary, who had expected life to be stimulating, found that she was bored. Instead of absorbing herself in writing fiction she set down another list of rules by which she was to lead her day. There were twenty-one daily tasks to be performed: six were prayers; three were Bible readings and the other eleven involved secular tasks. She became so bound up in her reading of the Bible that she wanted Henry to follow suit.

> It was then, for the first time, whilst still at Sunderland, he very quietly and calmly let me know he was not quite convinced that the whole of the Bible was true, although he thought parts of it might be so. It was on a Sunday evening, I well remember, that he made this startling observation, on which I became excessively angry, and

asked him, if such were his opinions, wherefore had he not told them me before we were married; for during the days of our courtship, which had not been very long, he had made no objections whatever to hearing the Bible read, or to any religious observances whatever. He replied that he did not mean to interfere with me, and that I might do just what I pleased, in reading the Bible, going to church, or anything else in a religious way.[103]

This was a bombshell for Mary. Had they married in too much haste before they had discussed something so fundamental as her religion and his scepticism? Mary's first few months of married life away from her family were proving to be more of a trial than she had imagined. Moreover, she was pregnant. The baby was due in April but the uncertainty of where the regiment would be posted hung over the couple. By December the weather had turned bitterly cold, the coast was dreary and there was little to amuse Mary. But the regiment was on the move again: this time to Carlisle and then to Ireland. Boxing Day saw Mary following the regiment by post-chaise in the company of the surgeon's wife, while Henry marched in the fog and melting snow, before the regiment stopped at Newcastle. The following day they set off for Carlisle at four in the morning. The orders for Ireland were changed so the regiment remained in Carlisle. The Sherwoods took lodgings with Lieutenant and Mrs Andrewes: 'a plan which tended rather to economy than comfort.' Caesar Andrewes was in his forties, had been a gambler, was irreligious and loved his food. His wife was deemed by Mary 'to be the most idle woman I ever saw.' Their daughter did not escape Mary's harsh criticism: 'a spoilt, wasteful, ignorant, chattering, and not a very bright child.' To make matters worse their landlady by the name of Mrs McClarty was not overfamiliar with cleanliness in the household so it fell to the faithful Parker to instil order in the Sherwood's quarters.

The next move was to Hexham in February 1804. Here Henry's health suffered from exposure to the cold climate and he was ill for some time. In March the regiment was on the move again; this time to Morpeth. It was here that Mary received news of her mother and Lucy: Lucy had become engaged to the Reverend Charles Cameron; she and Mrs Butt had moved to Stockton on Teme where they remained for two years and where 'amid orchards and hop-yards' Mrs Butt's health improved.

However, Dr. Salt had died. Marten was a regular visitor as was Thomas Butt. Lucy was fully occupied writing tracts and chapbooks. In 1803 she had written *The Two Lambs* which became a popular tract and sold for threepence. She was also busy organising the Sunday school which was held in their large kitchen and had forty pupils.

Mary was preparing for the birth of her first child and was delighted to receive a box from her mother with baby clothes. On April 1 Henry travelled down to London to put in for the 53rd Regiment of Foot position of paymaster from which the present incumbent, Mr Todd, wished to retire. On April 20, 1804 Mary Henrietta Sherwood was born in the afternoon. Henry had returned from London the previous morning. The baby was christened but without any close family being present. Then on May 9 Henry was ordered to join his Company in Tynemouth leaving Mary and the baby at Morpeth. June brought good news: Henry was now paymaster of the 53rd Regiment of Foot and promoted to Captain which brought with it 'a very great increase in pay.' Soon they were on the move again, this time to North Shields. Mary was much happier there. She had Mary Henrietta to look after with the help of Luke Parker who had turned out to be an excellent nurse. He would happily push Mary Henrietta in her pram: she was an extremely pretty baby and much admired. Mary had started writing again but found that with a small baby she had little time to get very far with *The History of Lucy Clare*: she would not finish the book until 1810. It would first be published in Calcutta in 1814 and was published in England in 1815 when it received good reviews. By 1835 it was in its 22nd edition and had become a mainstay of teaching in Sunday schools.

July saw the Sherwoods on the move once more. This time to Ramsgate. This necessitated a short sea voyage for Mary and her baby. Mary was a poor sailor and was taken aback to find her passage was booked on a ship carrying coal. However, she was pleasantly surprised to find that the dust and dirt had been swabbed away. Her cabin, which she shared with the captain's wife and daughter, was large with two separate small cabins for sleeping. Mary was seasick until the *Peggy* reached the mouth of the Thames. The journey had taken eight days. On the last day a press gang came aboard. One of the sailors rushed into Mary's cabin and hid under her bed concealed by the curtains. Mary remained lying on the bed and after a cursory check the press gang departed much to the sailor and Mary's delight at having tricked them. In London Mary and her little daughter stayed with William Maskall, Henry's maternal uncle. He was a merchant who lived at Grove Place, Hackney. One day the Maskall family took her to Walthamstow where Henry's mother, Margaret, was buried. They recounted how Henry had chanced on her grave one day when he was a small boy and living in the area. Having tired himself out running around he rested on a tomb. To his amazement the inscription read: *Sacred to the Memory of Margaret Sherwood*.

Naturally Mary wanted to show her new baby to her mother so travelled to Stockton where her mother, whose sight was dimming, now lived. Mary was shocked by how old her mother now looked. She was fifty but relished being pushed in her Bath-chair with the baby on her lap. When the visit ended in September Mary was aware that she might not see her mother for some time depending upon where the regiment, which was now at Canterbury, might be posted overseas. Rumours were rife as to where this might be, the East Indies being one possibility. The next couple of months until the beginning of December were contented ones. Mr Hawkins Browne had given her several introductions into Canterbury society, which was a lively one. There she met the great but aged Elizabeth Carter,[104] a renowned bluestocking, whom Mary later met at dinner in South Audley Street in London; and Mrs Duncombe who had been a correspondent of Samuel Richardson in her youth. Both women had been close friends of Mrs Chapone who had furthered women's education with her best selling book *Letters on the Improvement of the Mind*,[105] published in 1773.

Lucy had joined Mary in Canterbury and the two sisters started teaching children from the barracks, something which Mary would continue to do throughout Henry's army career. Lucy returned to London: 'I had several objects in view during this visit to London. One was to help my dear sister to forward her missionary plans abroad. Of these we had very indistinct ideas as to the manner of accomplishing them; but the object was very dear, and I got what books I could from the Society for Promoting Christian Knowledge, and with that society is connected my first missionary taste.'[106]

Prior to 1813, when Parliament passed the Charter Act – sometimes called The East India Company Act – the government did not encourage missionary activity in British territories in East India. It did not want to jeopardise trading interests by interference with established religions or to threaten religious beliefs. However, with the growth of the Evangelical movement in England attitudes began to change. William Carey, a Baptist minister, had sailed for India in 1793 and by the turn of the century leading Evangelicals: Charles Simeon, David Brown, Charles Grant and William Wilberforce were powerful advocates: by 1806 they were actively seeking, training and sending out missionaries to India. The eleventh resolution of the Charter Act of 1813 affirmed that 'it was expedient that the Church establishment in British territories in the East Indies should be placed under the superintendence of a bishop and three archdeacons, and that adequate provision should be made from the territorial revenues of India for their maintenance.'[107] This was recognition and encouragement for establishing Christianity which would, with time, lead to active missionary work among the natives.

Part Three

Bengal

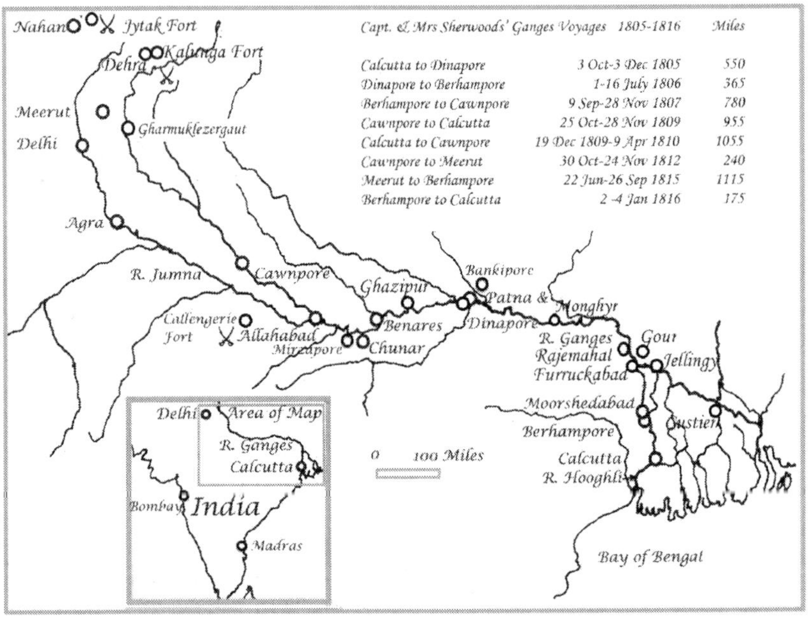

Capt. & Mrs Sherwoods' Ganges Voyages 1805-1816 Miles
Calcutta to Dinapore 3 Oct-3 Dec 1805 550
Dinapore to Berhampore 1-16 July 1806 365
Berhampore to Cawnpore 9 Sep-28 Nov 1807 780
Cawnpore to Calcutta 25 Oct-28 Nov 1809 955
Calcutta to Cawnpore 19 Dec 1809-9 Apr 1810 1055
Cawnpore to Meerut 30 Oct-24 Nov 1812 240
Meerut to Berhampore 22 Jun-26 Sep 1815 1115
Berhampore to Calcutta 2 -4 Jan 1816 175
Nahan
Jytak Fort
Kalunga Fort
Dehra
Meerut
Delhi
Gharmuklezergaut
Agra
R. Jumna
Cawnpore
Ghazipur
Bankipore
Patna &
Monghyr
Dinapore
Benares
Callengerie Fort
Allahabad
Mirzapore
Chunar
R. Ganges
Gour
Rajemahal
Jellingy
Furruckabad
Moorshedabad
Berhampore
Custien
Calcutta
R. Hooghli
Bay of Bengal
0 100 Miles
Delhi
Area of Map
R. Ganges
Calcutta
Bombay
India
Madras

The Sherwoods' India 1805–1816

Farewell to England

Mary's worst fears were confirmed when at the beginning of March the order came for the regiment to march for Tenterden, a Cinque Port on the Kent coast. Mary and Lucy had little time to enjoy the rural setting of Tenterden before orders came for the regiment to march to Portsmouth. Mary guessed correctly that it was to await embarkation there for Bengal in the East Indies. The Sherwoods had already made the decision that should the regiment be posted overseas then they would leave their darling baby with Lucy and Mrs Butt. Henry accompanied his wife and sister-in-law to London where they stayed with friends but in spite of being entertained Mary was naturally preoccupied with the forthcoming separation from her daughter who was almost one year old and beginning to speak. Mary knew that Lucy and her mother would love the little girl but she would miss her daughter dearly.

> I took leave of my sister and the fairest, sweetest baby. The last time I saw my lovely Mary she was sitting on her nurse's lap. She was eleven months and eighteen days old. She could then walk a few paces alone, could call Mama, and tell me what the lambs said. At the sound of lively music she loved to spring and caper. Her skin was soft as the finest velvet; she was tall and slender, and very fair, and had hair of the finest light auburn; her eyes were large and blue and very bright. My sister and mother took her under their care, and I left her to be brought up among lambs and flowers, among sweet woods and hills, near where her mother was brought up.[108]

The decision to leave Mary Henrietta in England was a wise but heartbreaking one for her parents especially in view of their destination. Not only was the voyage to India a long and potentially dangerous one but, once in India, European children ran a high risk of dying in infancy: diseases, poor hygiene on the part of ayas, and the climate all contributed to the high mortality rate. However, these risks would be tested as Mary was now pregnant with her second child.

On April 9 Mary travelled by coach overnight to Portsmouth where she stayed in lodgings before moving to Hilsea Barracks where she met the wives of other officers in the regiment. Expecting to join Henry on board one of the ships of the fleet she found that when the regiment embarked on April 20 Henry had not been allotted a cabin. However, unbeknown to Mary, Major Buckland, their old friend from Bridgnorth, held the special position of being able to invite the lady of his choice to join him on the same ship. The other officers' wives had all been allocated berths before Buckland took his place on the *Devonshire* when he announced that Mary and Henry were to have passage on the ship. The number of women allowed passage was limited to ten for each company so Luke Parker's wife, Betty, was fortunate that Mary selected her as her servant on the voyage. Others were not so lucky and had to return, weeping, to the shore. Unfortunately all the cabins were already taken except for that of the carpenter. However, in return for a down payment of thirty guineas[109] he was happy to relinquish it to the Sherwoods. The cabin, made of canvas, so as to be demountable for gunnery action, was as far forward as the main mast and extremely cramped. In order to enter the cabin the Sherwoods had to climb under the suspended cot and over a fixed cannon. Foul water from the bilge pump ran through the cabin in which there was only room for a single chair. The porthole would not open and once inside there was darkness. The sailors' language was crude and because they were separated only by canvas walls it was audible: not a salubrious setting in which to spend the next four months.

The fleet of East Indiamen sailed for India on April 24, 1805 under escort of *HMS Blenheim*, 74 guns, with a miserable Mary facing a journey of considerable hardship and danger. The voyage on the *Devonshire* was not for the fainthearted. There was the threat of French attack, pirates, storms and shipwreck, and when they reached the tropics, the heat was stifling in their cramped cabin. Adding to all these discomforts Mary also had to contend initially with severe seasickness although by May 13 she was getting a 'good sea appetite.' Little washing could be done so enough clothes and linen had to be packed for access on the voyage. Fresh food was limited, as was privacy. Mary took to getting up

A Fleet of EastIndiamen at Sea. *Nicholas Pocock, 1803*

early and sitting on deck in the company of some of the officers who treated her with great respect. They read aloud to her to alleviate the boredom.

Luke Parker did his best to make sure that Mary got reasonable rations of food for breakfast; any that she left she gave to Maria, the Parker's six month old daughter. Mary soon spotted a little ten year-old boy, a soldier's son, and set about teaching him to read after breakfast every day. The day was punctuated by meals: breakfast was followed by two sittings for dinner; the cadets ate at one o'clock followed by the officers and ladies at three o'clock. This was followed by tea at six and then supper at nine which the Sherwoods did not take. There was a cow on board and fresh bread was made daily, although not in sufficient quantity. Later in the voyage when the ship was in warmer latitudes there was music and dancing on deck most evenings, although Mary did not dance. She and Henry would go down to their cabin early so that they were already in bed by the time the sailors descended. There in the privacy of their cramped and damp, dark cabin Henry would read the Bible to his wife by lamplight

The voyage was not without incident. Henry kept a detailed diary during the voyage recording wind, weather and sea conditions, latitude and longitude.

Sunday May 5th:

The wind rose in the Evening & at 12 at night it blew so strong that we lost our Topmast & Main Top Gallant Mast. This disabled us so much that at Daylight the fleet was nearly out of sight. The *Greyhound* Frigate however missed us & came to our assistance & sent six men on Board but the Sea was so rough & we rolled so much nothing could be done except clearing the broken Masts that lay in the way until near One o'clock, when a strange sail appeared which we soon made out to be a Ship of War much larger than the *Greyhound*. We were rather alarmed & the *Greyhound* sent for her men back. The Frigate still approaching under easy sail, we found she was the *Immortalité* Capt. Owen on a cruize but intending immediately to proceed to England Capt. Owen offered to stay by us until we could repair our damage. The *Greyhound* proceeded after the Fleet. I wrote Letters to all my Friends to send by the *Immortalité*. The Sea became calmer Towards the Evening. 7th During the night we had much lightning & there was every appearance of Bad weather. At Day light it cleared up. We saw the Fleet about Twelve miles a head Laying to, we had no observation today but we suppose we must have drifted to the North.[110]

The opportunity to send letters home while at sea was seized whenever possible. In June, as the weather grew hotter some of the passengers became ill. Matters were made worse by the smell of bilge water and the tainted drinking water which, combined with the heat, added to the general discomfort felt by the female passengers. Mary tried to remain pragmatic although she was missing Mary Henrietta and at times was still extremely seasick when the sea became rough.

The ceremony of Crossing the Line was celebrated a day late, on June 4, George III's birthday. The event was viewed with some trepidation by the female passengers. King Neptune and Amphitrite, his wife – two of the crew in heavy disguise – came alongside and boarded the ship where Queen Neptune embraced the gentlemen. King Neptune was banned from doing likewise to the assembled ladies. In order to avoid the customary baptism by ducking, the passengers gave Neptune and his consort presents. Strong superstitions were observed by the crew: whistling, dancing and the wearing of spurs were all outlawed that day.

Gentlemen had to take off their hats when going on the quarter-deck. Every landlubber had to pay a fine to be released from the shrouds when he passed the main-top sail. This prevented over-adventurous young male passengers from climbing too high in the rigging and falling to their certain death. For the crew there was plum pudding and extra grog. Grog – rum diluted with small beer or water – had been introduced into the Royal Navy in 1740 by Vice Admiral Edward 'Old Grog' Vernon, whose nickname derived from his grogram coats. On long voyages, lime or lemon juice was mixed in which helped prevent scurvy.

Communication with family during the voyage depended on the ship's being able to manoeuvre alongside other ships which were returning home. Two months after leaving Portsmouth Mary was able to send letters via the *Admiral Gardiner*. When she reached India letters home would take four to six months in transit with a long wait for the recipient's reply. As this was the only method of contact with home the importance of mail arriving from England was a major preoccupation. Safe despatch was not guaranteed: many ships were wrecked in storms and letters could be lost when pirates or the French intercepted ships so often duplicate copies were sent in the hope that at least one would make it home.

Among the other passengers were: two colonels inhabiting two state cabins with their wives, one of whom had a small child; eleven officers of the 53rd and nineteen cadets; and several civil servants going to Madras as well as three unmarried women, the Misses Layard, daughters of the Dean of Bristol, 'on Matrimonial Expeditions consigned to their Brothers on Ceylon.'[111] East India Company policy, having once banned women on its posts now encouraged unmarried European women, known as 'the fishing fleet' to travel out to India in the hope of catching an officer either on the voyage or when they arrived in India. Few of them could have known the kind of life they would lead if successful in a country which was so alien to their Eurocentric world. If they were not successful they were sent home labelled 'returned empty.' Women passengers were under the authority of ships' captains who, for the most part, treated them well. Captain Murray, in command of the *Devonshire*, treated the women passengers with respect and kindness. When they appeared on deck he would offer his arm and walk with them. One of the unmarried sisters mistook his attention for deeper feelings on his part much to everyone's amusement.

Rounding the Cape of Good Hope on July 10 albatross and pintado (cape petrel) were sighted but then the weather began to grow colder and stormier. Mary began to be very unwell again with seasickness. The fleet now split with the ships going to Bombay via the Mozambique Channel leaving the main fleet. The storms the main fleet then encountered were nothing compared with the unwelcome appearance of three ships approaching on August 6. They hoisted French colours and began to fire at the English fleet. Three shots went through the rigging of the *Devonshire*. One of the French ships, commanded by Admiral Lenois, carried upwards of seventy guns while another was a large frigate. The third French ship did not engage. Niceties were forgotten! The women were 'tumbled into the hold' and all the cabin partitions were cleared for action: furniture and possessions were tumbled in too. For the women and the children it was a terrifying experience. They were in pitch darkness, under the water line, with no means of escape should anything drastic happen to the *Devonshire*. The deafening noise of guns added to their fear. They had no way of knowing which way the gun battle was going. All the women could do was wait and hope that the ship survived. At last, late at night, silence came. The hold was opened and the women were hoisted up on deck. The French had backed off. The success of the surprise encounter with the French was toasted in negus (port mixed with hot water, spiced and sugared) and biscuits. However, the French did not accept defeat quite so easily and the next day made threatening approaches to the fleet but remained out of reach of the guns. When dawn lightened the sea on the morning of the 8th the French had gone. The fleet had suffered some damage; two men had been killed and another terribly wounded, losing both his legs.

Ten days later Ceylon was sighted and on August 21, India. The town of Pondicherry was clearly visible from the ship. Britain and France had each claimed the town over the years but in 1805 it was under British sovereignty having been taken from the French in 1793. It would revert to France once more in 1814 before being reclaimed by Britain in the 1850s. The sense of excitement grew among the passengers as the fleet sailed for the port of Madras where for Europeans the climate was relatively benign. In the bay were the massed masts of ships waiting to be loaded with cargo. As the ship drew closer to the shore an exotic scene opened: native fishermen aboard their catamarans on the calm blue-washed sea floated near them; by the shore were palaces set among palm trees. Through binoculars, palanquins were visible with the bearers making their way to Fort St. George where the East India Company had its administrative and military headquarters of the Madras Presidency. Madras had been ceded by treaty to the East India Company in 1639 and the heavily fortified Fort St. George started in 1640. It was finally completed one hundred and fifty years later.

At ten o'clock on August 23 the ship anchored a mile offshore with the Fort and the magnificent Custom House dominating the shore. Mary was fascinated when local Indians paddled out to the *Devonshire*. At first she thought the people on board were women as they were wearing muslin but as the boats came closer she realised that they were male:

> We lady passengers all went out on deck to look at these visitors, who were ascending the side of the vessel, not by any means understanding what sort of person they were, or why they had come. Could we have doubted before that we were in a new world, we could now have doubted it no longer. These were a description of persons hitherto represented to my fancy only in Arabian or Persian tales. The men were arrayed in long muslin dresses, bound about the waist with ample bands of muslin. They wore large turbans and gold earrings and chains, their beards being trimmed and cut with great nicety, and their faces, in many instances, marked with yellow or white streaks or spots.[112]

The men were looking for employment as head servants or sircars with the newly arrived Europeans. Soon they were followed by boats laden with fresh fruit, meat, vegetables, flowers, bread and palm fans. After four long months at sea the sight of so much fresh food filled their senses with delight while the noise of Indians bartering battered their ears.

For passengers arriving by ship there was a major obstacle: there was no natural harbour so they were forced to face a terrifying transfer from ship to land through crashing surf. All looked calm from the ship but when Henry went ashore the following morning he was in for a shock. He set off for shore on board a flat-bottomed, high-sided boat, without a keel. On either side two catamarans accompanied the boat. As they approached the shore a tremendous roaring from the hungry surf filled the air; the near naked boatmen began to row furiously as the boat rose

Madras Landing. *Charles Hunt*

to the top of the huge waves before crashing down into the valley of the angry sea, a pause and then the boat rose again to almost perpendicular as the boatmen gave voice to the rhythm of the oars. On the third mountainous wave the boat was carried onto the shore with great force where it was seized by a hundred men and pulled clear of the surf. Henry, somewhat shaken, made his way by unaccustomed palanquin, in which he had difficulty balancing, from the Custom House, through Black Town to Fort St. George, a distance of about a mile. There he reported to the Paymaster's office and received orders that the regiment was to disembark without further delay. Having revived himself with a cup of coffee he then braced himself to face the return through the crashing surf. Going back to the ship was even more terrifying as the boat was going into the surf rather than with it. When Mary faced the journey with Henry to the shore from the ship the next day not surprisingly she was seasick. She describes:

> Never shall I forget the yells of the boatmen when preparing to meet the fury
> of a wave. Amidst the wild howlings of the men, all of whom were almost
> naked, the roar of the surf, and the agitation of the whole fabric of the boat,
> there was not time to analyse a single feeling. All appeared to me one wild

scene of terror and confusion, until I felt the shock of the vessel against terra firma, and heard the cry of the multitude whose business it was to seize hold of her and pull her up on the shore. I was instantly assisted to get out, and I found myself standing on solid ground thousands and thousands of miles removed from my native land.[113]

The sights and sounds of India crowded her senses on landing in Madras: the smells of spice; the heat; the noise of a foreign tongue she could not understand; dark-skinned men wearing only loincloths and the dirt and squalor made her feel like a child seeing the world for the first time. Mary would not see England for eleven years during which her life would be far different from the safe, known and comfortable world which she had inhabited for the past thirty years. The Sherwoods rented a barrack apartment of two rooms

but without any Furniture it had more the appearance of a Small Church we immediately got the Room furnished with a bed and made ourselves as comfortable as we could hoping for a Little enjoyment but on the next day 25th we received an order to embark again & on board the same Ship for Calcutta as soon as possible.[114]

While in Madras Henry ordered suitable clothing for the climate:

I was obliged to make up a great many white Jackets & Pantaloons which are worn in India & I paid Three Rupees per Piece for nankeen, [a yellow cloth used for trousers] the Taylor worked fast but he could not get on without a pattern & I was told they can imitate very well but they have no invention, the Story goes so far as to say that an Officer sent an Old Coat as a Pattern to make a new One & that the old one was patched at the Elbow, the Taylor thought it necessary to put a patch upon the new one.[115]

Before leaving Madras Mary visited the Black Town, the Indian quarter. All her Eurocentric feelings as to the superiority of Christian belief over what she termed the superstitions of the heathen came out. She was further affronted by the official line of non-interference with native religion which she maintained led to degradation especially for women.

Soon they were on the move again and left Madras on September 2 to sail to Calcutta, the administrative centre for Bengal. Before setting sail in the *Devonshire* Mary, much to her relief, had time to get all the laundry washed, something that was impossible to do during the four-month voyage. Mary was now eight months pregnant and far from well so it was with some relief when, having endured the terrors of the surf once more, she discovered that she and Henry had been allotted a pleasant cabin on the quarter-deck, starboard side. Thirty-three officers and seven ladies re-embarked. A pilot navigated and recounted how it was customary for parents to offer the seventh child of the seventh son to the sharks at Sangor island as thanks to their god for being blessed by so many children. What Mary made of this she does not say but it doubtless added to her growing Evangelical zeal to save the souls of the heathen. When the ship arrived at the mouth of the Hooghli river it anchored off Sangor Island to wait for the tide to make safe passage past treacherous sand banks to Diamond Harbour, the head of navigation for large vessels and some fifty miles from Calcutta.

> In this island Mr Munroe was seized by a Tiger, he was on Shore sitting with Another Gentn with Guns in their hands when a tiger sprung on Mr Munroe & seized him by the Head was carrying him off as a Fox does a Goose, the other Gentn fired on the Tiger who let Mr Munroe fall but he had died almost immediately.[116]

Henry hired one of the many boats plying for trade and the couple disembarked finally from the *Devonshire*.

By this time Mary was very unwell and, having got into the boat, lay down in the shade on a mattress made of palm leaves covered with canvas. The boat was rowed by six oarsmen with a steersman standing at the stern holding a long oar. When the tide turned they stopped at a small European hotel at Falta. Mary was nervous on shore and mistook a buffalo's bellow for a tiger about to attack. They enjoyed a good dinner with two bottles of wine, 'the Remains of which we put into the boat to comfort us on our passage'[117] before resuming the journey upriver at ten o'clock that night with the incoming tide. Finally after another stop they were within sight of Fort William, the magnificent symbol of British Imperial power, begun after the Battle of Plassey in 1758 by Lord Clive.

Old Fort Gaut, Calcutta. *Thomas Daniell, 1810*

The boatmen and Henry were unable to communicate as to where the Sherwoods wished to be landed. After spending an hour in the fierce noon-day sun, they were rescued by a European man in a passing boat, who explained to the boatmen where Henry wanted to land. Once formalities at the Custom House were cleared Henry joined the weak and sick Mary at The Crown and Anchor, a reassuringly named tavern for English passengers. There they spent the night contending with the mosquitoes whose bites added to Mary's woes.

Culture Shock

lthough Mary was still far from well this new and exotic world fascinated her. Henry had taken two vast rooms in the Fort where they would remain for the next month before travelling up country on the Hooghli and Ganges to the regiment's posting to the Dinapore cantonment near Patna. Mary was pleasantly taken by her new lodgings: gazelle grazed under the walls of the heavily fortified Fort; tree-shaded walks and green squares refreshed her eye while the buildings, faced with chunam (a highly polished plaster) were on a grand scale. Their apartment in the officers' quarters opened off an upstairs veranda. Servants were housed on the ground floor.

Henry now had a highly responsible and respected position as paymaster in the regiment. He held the strong box and because of this had to employ a sircar. The man appointed was Brahmin (high caste) and he had already found servants for the Sherwoods' temporary home. Both Henry and Mary list them in their diaries. Henry notes in his diary on September 30 the servants' wages:

> *1 Sircar: 16 rupees.*[118] [He took care of the money.]
> *1 Kitmutgar: 9 rupees per month.* [His function was to oversee the cook and go to market to select produce. Mary comments that he would not carry anything home from market. He also waited at table.]
> *1 Mussaulchee: 4 rupees.* [He looked after the lamps and washed dishes. He was directly responsible to the Kitmutgar.]
> *1 Bheesty, (meaning Heavenly): 4 rupees.* [His task was to carry water on his shoulder often in a goatskin.]
> *1 Sirdar—bearer: 6 rupees.* [He was in charge of the palanquin bearers. He also took care of books.]
> *1 Mate 5 rupees* [He assists Sirdar, cleans boots and clothes and assists bearers.]
> *5 Bearers: 20 rupees.* [They carried the palanquin, a new mode of transport for the Sherwoods.]

1 Matranee: 4 rupees. [Female member on the staff. Dressed ' in full chintz or silver petticoat, a white muslin jacket and veil, and a quantity of silver ornaments.' She swept the rooms and took her orders from Mary during the day as to anything which needed doing or getting.]

1 Dhoby: 7 rupees. [The clothes washer was responsible for household linen and clothes.]

1 Bauwerchie: 7 rupees. [The cook.] The grand total for the month being 82 rupees or £10/17s/2d.

The Sherwoods found the religious obligations of their Muslim and Hindoo servants puzzling. The Hindu caste system into which Hindus were born, and must remain, also puzzled them. The sircar could clean boots but could not touch meat while the Mussaulchee could wash plates but not clean boots.

Each Sunday the Brahmin sircar would sit on the floor and weigh out the rupees to pay officers, soldiers and servants. This meant that far from being a day of quiet rest for Mary the apartment was busy with the comings and goings of the regimental officers and soldiers, their wives, ayahs[119] with children, and letter bearers. She would retreat to the inner room which overlooked the main square. The heat and mosquitoes were proving to be an incessant annoyance to her and she suffered from prickly heat. How she must have wished for cooler, less European clothes. During their time in Calcutta Henry was extremely busy. Mary rarely ventured out preferring to spend her time watching the Indian crows, and the large adjutant birds whose stupidity amused her. Reading and sewing occupied her and she took on teaching two boys from the regiment, one of them being the boy she had taught on the sea voyage. She also took this opportunity to continue with *The History of Lucy Clare* which she had started writing three years earlier in 1802, a companion piece to *The History of Susan Gray*.

The Sherwoods were soon on the move again after just four weeks at Fort William but not before the regiment had been seriously depleted by illness: a fever which also took the life of Luke Parker's little daughter Maria. On Saturday, October 13 the regiment set off, in a fleet of about 100 boats, upriver on the Hooghli for the cantonment at Dinapore (now Danapur). Henry and Mary set off a day later, travelling on a large private pinnace, (a light boat, propelled by oars or sails) with a baggage boat on which the dhobie lived with his family, and a cooking boat carrying the cook and servants as well as goats, chickens and ducks which could be slaughtered for the table en route. The cost of hiring the three boats was £60 for the five hundred mile journey, which would take almost eight weeks, first up the Hooghli and then the Ganges. The boats were hauled on shallow sections of the rivers or rowed by sixteen oarsmen. When conditions were suitable they could sail. The boat was well-stocked with food: hams, tongues, tamarind fish, flour and salted European butter in casks, wine, spices and other cooking essentials. Whatever discomforts faced the Sherwoods, lack of food would appear not to have been one of them. Travelling by day in the main pinnace with the Sherwoods were Luke and Mrs Parker, who slept in the servants' boat, and Lieutenant and Mrs Andrewes. Mary disliked the Andrewes because of the Lieutenant's lack of respect for religion. She had shared lodgings in Carlisle with them and their daughter but had found their behaviour unpleasing.

Mary settled herself happily on board where the accommodation comprised two rooms: one five metres by three and a half metres wide which was used for sitting and dining, where the Andrewes also slept; the other a three and a half metres square bedroom for the Sherwoods. Both had shutters to keep out the heat and insects. Outside was a small veranda. To the fore of the two cabins was a small deck where the 'dandies' (boatmen) rowed and on the prow was another boatman whose job it was to test the depth of the river. At the stern stood the helmsman with a long steering oar. The palanquin was stowed on the roof of the two cabins where the bearers and other servants sat and slept.

With everyone on board and provisions stowed the boat tacked up river ahead of the fleet carrying the regiment. For Mary, now heavily pregnant, it was a welcome scene of ever-changing sights. Passing boats carried women in their brightly coloured saris like exotic birds. Mary with her ever-observant eye was much taken by the young women's beauty and the simplicity of their clothes. At sunset the boats moored up for the night. Everyone got off and the servants set about their allotted tasks on the river bank: the dhobie set to with washing for the day; the cook set up his fire and ingredients for the evening meal, while the other servants lit their own small fires. Meanwhile the Sherwoods would enjoy a gentle stroll along the bank on which by this time their goats were grazing. The Sherwoods, on returning aboard, were served their dinner, complete with tablecloth, glass and china. In the cool evening air the smell of spicy cooking drifted into the cabin. This attracted packs of jackals in the night, scavenging for any food – the goats having been safely tethered aboard once more. The disadvantage of the crew sleeping above the cabins soon became apparent: the crew did not sleep at night but sat up talking and moving about over the Sherwoods' heads.

Some of the passing sights shocked them. Henry records:

> As soon as you get clear of Calcutta the banks are frequented by the Brahmins burning Dead Bodies, and every few Yards is the remains of Funeral Piles or Bedsteads in which the Body has been brought to the River side but the unburnt Bodies floating down is still worse some of them are stranded, and the Wild Dogs and Vultures eating them, thus the whole Bank is covered with human bones, sometimes we see them floating, with Crows resting upon them and eating them. We anchored this evening close to a Dead Body which was very offensive, but we cannot get it removed, nor can we find a place free from them.[120]

Apart from the distractions of the passing scene, which included Mary's first sight of monkeys, Indian rubber trees and two fakirs, whom she thought disgusting, Mary found time to complete *The History of Lucy Clare* and catch up on her reading. Henry settled down in the evenings and read the Bible to his wife. Mary read it to Mrs Parker as she sat sewing during the day. Evening walks were hampered by the crowds of Indians who were intrigued to see a white woman walking among them.

On October 18 the fleet caught up with them and the relative peace of travelling independently was lost. The boats were now to travel in set formation of about a hundred regimental boats, with Colonel Mawby leading, then officers, while the soldiers brought up the rear and finally by a large number of camp followers. The whole fleet stretched for two miles. Each morning a gun sounded and the fleet would set off at daylight. It proceeded upriver reaching Berhampore on October 31 where there was an unoccupied barracks for 1400 Europeans. Here they stayed a few days and enjoyed walks on the riverbank in the cooler evenings. Continuing up river they reached Moorshedabad, the residence of the Nabobs of Bengal. In the evening the Sherwoods crossed the river in a small boat with the Andrewes and entered:

Near Gangwaugh Colly on the River Hoogly. *Thomas Daniell, 1810*

> ... a pagoda in which was an Idol with an Elephant's head a big Belly
> & Number of hands. The blacks threw themselves on the ground
> before him & struck their foreheads against the Ground. It appeared
> that the Inhabitants were much frightened at us as we were followed
> by at least 500 People who vanished in an Instant when we turned
> towards them & appeared again in our rear.[121]

Having spent the previous day on the shallow reaches of the Hooghli
they entered the much wider Ganges on November 10. For the officers
there was the added amusement of shooting wild fowl and jackals but
although the print of a tiger was seen in the sand, tigers eluded them.
Mary comments:

> The English, however, have turned the tide against the tigers within the last
> few years by promising a reward of ten rupees for every tiger's head brought to
> a collector, and it is wonderful how many are now killed.[122]

The Sherwoods caused consternation among their Hindu boatmen, who
would have been vegetarian, when, having bought a suckling pig from a
village, they insisted on taking it on board. At times their lack of understanding and respect for local sensibilities reflected the European innate

sense of superiority. As they were approaching the end of their journey on December 2 Henry observes:

> … we anchored at a distance from a village and the boatmen told us we must be on our guard all night. We therefore placed a guard, Andrewes, myself and my servant Parker: we loaded our fowling pieces & pistols but we were not disturbed.[123]

Life on the Cantonment

On December 3 the regiment reached Patna having travelled twenty miles in the day. Late the next evening they finally reached the cantonment at Dinapore which had capacity for two thousand men. The following day Andrewes and Henry found suitable quarters. Having an allowance of ninety rupees per quarter for accommodation Henry paid sixty rupees a quarter for eight rooms, a house for servants and a house for cooks:

> Our quarters were in the large square in the line which formed an angle with the barracks. Our apartments were the last in the line, at the farthest end from the barracks, and we had the advantage of a long verandah at one end opening to the country. The quarters consisted of three large centre rooms, one of which was glazed and had a fire. Three corner rooms, one of which was a bath, another a dressing room, and a third looking to the yard, was given to Parker and his wife. There were also three vast galleries, one opening to the square, another to the country, and the one behind to the yard. I can compare the buildings at Dinapore to nothing but churches; all but the old Government House were of a single floor, though lofty, with large windows, double and closed with green lattice work. We looked over a green, neatly kept, to a row of officers' quarters, built nearly like our own, and we could catch a glimpse of the lesser square beyond, in which our colonel had taken a quarter. Beyond the second square was a wide plain, the hospital, and the burying-ground, and behind us and our servants' houses was the native bazaar and the road to Patna. The river ran at some distance across our corner of the cantonment but not within our view. [124]

It proved to be a very cheap area of India. For Mary now nearing the end of her second pregnancy it was a relief to have at last arrived after the long journey from Portsmouth from where they had sailed on April 24. She had endured terrible seasickness on the sea journey; faced the demands of living in an uncomfortable and cramped cabin; met the storms and skirmishes with the French with calm resolve; been both enchanted and horrified by the sights and culture of India in both Madras and Calcutta and then on the long river journey. But she was with the man she loved and whose second child she would soon bear.

The Sherwoods settled happily into their new environment. Mary had the use of a ton-jon (open palanquin)in which she and Mrs Mawby, the Colonel's wife, would go out to enjoy the sights in the bazaars where they were shocked by the dirty appearance of many of the people. Henry had a pony for which he employed a syce (groom). Mary soon realised that her clothing was unsuitable for the climate and quickly had a tailor make up white dresses for herself. She bought white kid shoes, and now wore a light lace cap with ribbons, cooler than the bonnet which was de rigeur when going out in England. Thus clad she fitted in with the sartorial style of the other European wives in the cantonment.

On Christmas day 1805 her first son was born. He was named Henry after his father, grandfather and great-grandfather. Mary recounts how on the night of his birth, once Mrs Parker had retired, a native nurse took the baby to lie on a couch in the room while Mary slept. She was woken by the cries of the baby. The nurse was cradling a pillow which she was soothing instead of the newborn. To Mary's horror she realised that the nurse was drunk. No one came to her call so she got out of bed and retrieved the baby, taking him into the safety of her own bed. The nurse was dismissed the next day. Mary did not recover quickly from the birth nor was the baby strong, adding to her anxieties. Infant mortality was high among European babies and in June the baby fell seriously ill. Yet in spite of both her own and her baby's precarious state of health, after a conversation at a dinner party in the cantonment about the lack of schools for which there was no government provision, Mary set about starting a school for children of the regiment. With the help of her husband and his clerk, Sergeant Clarke, a large verandah at the northern end of their quarters was set aside as a school. The children, attended from eight till midday. Soon the thirteen pupils grew to fifty including local Indian children. For Mary it was a demanding task especially when the weather grew hotter in May.

> I refused none who came to ask me to receive and instruct their little ones, not even when the children were coloured; but I was speedily brought to see that many of my pupils were extremely wicked, and complaints of very bad language and very bad conduct were brought to me.

> In my first indignation I used to get Sergeant Clarke to exercise his cane on
> the children's backs ... We always dismissed the girls before the boys, in order
> to let them get home quietly. [125]

Mary was, at this time, wholly convinced that salvation for herself and
others lay in performing good works: educating children fitted her belief.

As there was no church at Dinapore the service on Sundays was held
in a large room with a high ceiling. Here the regiment gathered with their
wives, dressed in white and carrying painted umbrellas against the glare
of the sun. Seating was in the form of benches or, for those of higher
rank, chairs brought in by their servants. The chaplain, whom Mary
dismissed as a 'most easy, careless and ignorant person,' stood at a table
to conduct the service; his sermons offered little benefit to his congregation but at least it was a time when the wives came together and there was
a feeling of Christian solidarity in a heathen land far from England.

∼

Mary's life was not devoted entirely to good works and caring for her
baby son. There was a stimulating social life within the cantonment. The
Sherwoods paid visits to both European and Indian households. Mary
enjoyed these visits on which the baby and their retinue of servants
accompanied them. They were invited to spend a week at a large house
owned by Mr Ricketts, a nabob, the Collector for Bihar, who lived in
great luxury and style at Bankipore near Patna. The Sherwoods set off
with about forty servants.

> Our train was little Master Henry in his bullock-cart, with his nurse; Mr
> Sherwood and myself in a garden chair (we had only a few miles to go); the
> palquin and bearers, unoccupied; the child's crib and his little wardrobe,
> carried on the heads of porters, called coolies; the waterman, his wife and
> children, on foot, with their baskets and their irons on their heads; the tailor
> walking like a gentleman, with no apparent burthen (caleefa is the title
> generally given to this person), the mate and matranee, each with their short
> broom in their hands; the kitmutgar and mussaulchee; six or eight bearers,
> with their sirdar; the bullock driver, and a saïs or two with the horses. Add to
> these bangy wallahs, or persons carrying baskets of the lady's and the
> gentleman's clothes, and you have a view of our party as we set out to proceed
> from Dinapore to Bankipore. [126]

They were met half way to Bankipore by an elephant sent by their host. Mary was ecstatic about the views from the howdah as they progressed at a stately pace through the countryside: the baby remained closer to *terra ferma* in the bullock cart. Having set off at dawn they arrived in time for breakfast, served by highly attentive servants, towards whom many of the European women acted in a haughty way which embarrassed Mary.

Here life was pleasant for Mary with every luxury provided and, most importantly, no demands on her time apart from meals and meeting other visitors. The quiet time, from three till five, after tiffin (dinner), gave Mary the peace and tranquillity which she needed to try to rebuild her strength. At five she would bathe and change into clean white linen before appearing at six on the verandah where a choice of transport awaited the guests: the elephant, horses and several types of carriage were all drawn up ready to take the guests on an 'evening airing.' Supper followed once the rapid twilight had died into the Indian night: great quantities of freshly cooked veal or mutton, chicken, ortolans (small buntings 16 cm. in length, weighing 20 to 25 grams) wrapped in vine leaves and roasted, and curries were served.

Hygiene in the kitchen was of key importance as food went off so quickly. One problem lay in meat becoming tainted very quickly which led to well-fed crows enjoying a feast when it was jettisoned. European salted butter became liquid because of the heat. Mary recounts one amusing incident of how a kitchen servant boy in their household had only ever seen European butter in the liquid state so was alarmed when a cold night in winter had frozen it solid. Memsahibs rarely ventured into the kitchen. They gave their orders to the cook for meals and he was left to his own devices. Servants could not always be trusted: food was often stolen by the servants for their own use. For young children, once weaned, milk could be the carrier of disease. Mary was still breastfeeding Henry but was being urged by both the ayah and European women in the cantonment to wean him.

In June when the baby was six months old the regiment was ordered down river to Berhampore, 308 miles away. The solicitous Mr Ricketts hired the Sherwoods a sixteen-oared budgerow (a lumbering, keelless barge, much used by Europeans travelling on the Gangetic rivers.) The monsoon rains made the river dangerous to navigate in such a flat boat. Two-thirds of the length aft was occupied by cabins which had Venetian

A Budgerow

windows. [127] At this time of year the temperature was fiercely high. The family set off on July 1 and arrived eight days later. The climate at Berhampore was an unhealthy one for Europeans, causing languor and headaches: it was known as a 'place of graves.' In August severe floods hit Berhampore causing the embankment about two miles below the cantonment to collapse.

> The Water flowed like a River & inundated the Country so much that we had scarcely time to embank our own Cantonement & we are now like an Island in the midst of the Sea, fortunately where it burst there were no Inhabitants & the Noise frightened the Neighbours so that they all escaped & ran far Inland or towards the Cantonements they however lost every thing except their live stock. I walked down the Bank & saw the Poor creatures collecting their goods & carrying them on Rafts from one height to another. We fortunately had no Wind and the Furniture of a Native is not worth much. We saw Curios fishing today, at One of the openings through which the Water was rushing violently several Persons held Nets who caught the fish as they were hurried through & sometimes the Fish in attempting to avoid the extreme rapidity of the current leapt on Shore & were knocked down by persons who waited for them with sticks. The Instant the Fish found themselves drawn into the violent stream they attempted to leap out. When the Nets were instantly thrown under them or a good Blow of a Stick knocked them down, great Numbers

were killed in this Manner.

The Water kept increasing around us & we began to fear that our Cantonements would be soon overflowed we are now considerably under the Level of the Water and the Road from Cantonements is two feet at least flooded, every thing is damp in our House. But we suffer little in comparison.[128]

Damp pervaded everything including their quarters. Undeterred Mary started a school for the children of soldiers on her verandah with the help of Sergeant Clarke who had only one or two days' work a month with the regiment.

> The school began with thirteen pupils, but gradually increased to forty or fifty. It consisted of children from barracks, a few officers' children (in general even worse brought up, because more pampered, than the soldiers' children) and children of merchants and other people in the neighbourhood of the cantonments. I refused none who came to ask me to receive and instruct their little ones, not even when the children were coloured.[129]

Mary finished writing *Margery* about a little girl aged four. It consisted of three stories which were designed to teach young children obedience to their parents, good behaviour, love of nature and church attendance.[130] She then began writing *The Infant's Progress*. The idea for the book had come from a request from Marten, her brother.

In September 1806 all the Europeans above a certain rank were invited to attend the annual celebrations given by the Nawab of Bengal at his palace upriver at Moorshedabad. The invitation was written in Persian, on paper 'sprinkled with gold.' It was for dinner and to view the splendid annual illuminations. Travelling upriver by boat and accompanied by their little son and his two nurses the Sherwoods passed throngs of Indians making their way to the celebrations in gaily painted boats with their prows carved in the shapes of peacocks, horses, dragons and other beasts. Some had colourful silk awnings under which the male passengers reclined smoking hookahs. Lower castes were making their way on foot along the river bank. After finding a mooring and eating tiffin the Sherwoods set off to explore the town which was famous for silver and gold embroidered shoes with curled up toes. Henry could not resist buying a scarlet and gold pair for two rupees. As the sun went to sleep the river was transformed by the lower caste Indians who set afloat paper boats, bearing lights, many in the form of peacocks, which floated down the river. Then at eight o'clock the Europeans set out for the palace and an evening which was one of matchless opulence. They processed through two courtyards accompanied by a 'fearful screeching and skirling' from the Indian band before arriving at a large pavilion in which the Nawab was sitting surrounded by his court. He greeted his European guests courteously although he spoke no English. Seated on sofas under English chandeliers and cooled by fans of palm leaves they were offered wine and water. The nautch (singing and dancing by attractive young women) had already started. This was followed by jesters performing plays which the Nawab, smoking his hookah, watched without any outward sign of enjoyment. He was apparently addicted to strong spirits although under twentyfive years old. He had an income of only £190,000 a year to support his family and retainers under British rule. His father had had £875,000.

The highlight of the evening was the illuminations which were viewed from a balcony overlooking the river. On the opposite shore bamboo frameworks were set alight revealing buildings of great magnificence in the form of palaces and forts. Guns blazed, the crowds roared their approval and the band played. Dinner was served at two tables at ten o'clock. Two young boys who sat at the Sherwoods' table wore necklaces of huge precious stones 'some as large as pigeons' eggs'. The European guests remained seated for an hour after dinner and then were 'dismissed by having a drop or two of attar of roses thrown upon us, and by every person receiving a collar of the flowers of the jasmine. We also received a little betel-nut wrapped in leaves; this last I found to be an acceptable present to Henry's nurse.' [131] When they returned to their boat Mary was amazed to learn that her son had slept through all the noise. She later learnt a possible reason for this: ayahs were in the habit of dosing their small charges with opium to make them sleep and Mary was later to see at first hand the effect on her darling baby. The party slept contentedly as the boat made its way downriver once again to Berhampore where they arrived in the morning.

On Good Friday, March 25, 1807 Lucy Martha, their third child, was born. Lucy was an exceptionally beautiful child with gold hair, large deep blue eyes and pink cheeks, the latter being uncommon among European children in India. They are usually described as having a deathly pallor.

Her brother, Henry, meanwhile had contracted whooping cough a potentially fatal disease. Fortunately the ayah Mary employed for the first month of Lucy's life looked after both mother and baby with competent quiet care. It was during this period that Mary's strong religious views began to dominate her life. She became reluctant to participate in the balls and dinner parties held in the cantonment. However, she was persuaded to attend a dinner and ball thrown by the regiment for Lord Lake, the Commander in Chief, who was en route to England.

To Mary's delight in May she had received a letter forwarded from Madras telling her that in June 1806 her sister, Lucy, had married the Reverend Charles Cameron, their brother Marten's closest friend. Marten had been engaged to Miss Winnington, the eldest daughter at Stanford Court in 1800 but tragically she had died shortly before the Sherwoods left England. However, later in 1807 Mary received a letter telling her of her brother's marriage to her close friend, Anne Congreve.

Death and Religion

Mary was finally persuaded that Henry should be weaned not only because he was failing to thrive but also because she continued to be weak and was now also nursing Lucy. At this time there was a ready supply of wet nurses as local girls were married as early as ten and they did not wean their children until the next child was born. As was customary, Henry's daye or wet nurse, Ameena, was given fifty rupees as a present to mark the event. All the developmental stages of a baby's life, walking and cutting the first tooth, were rewarded with money given to the daye. Ameena also received new clothes: a wide silk or chintz petticoat, a muslin jacket and a veil. After bathing, doing her hair and dressing in the new clothes, Ameena was presented with Henry. It was a few weeks later that Mary discovered why her beloved son was sleeping so deeply when she saw opium being crammed into his mouth. The wet nurse was sacked. Another nurse, a former nautch girl took her place. She had a lovely singing voice and would lull him to sleep in her arms as she sang Hindustani lullabies.

Weakened by the whooping cough Henry failed to regain his strength and lost weight and by July 1807 was a dying child. Mary spent hours walking on the river bank and on the verandah with him in her arms. Her pain at witnessing her dying son struggling for life at little more than eighteen months is deeply moving. To make the situation worse the servants were quarrelsome, arguing over who should change the linen on his bed. Finally the station surgeon, Dr. Penny came and, having seen how the baby was struggling, took him from Mary and placed her in a room where she could not witness his death. But when she glimpsed him through a window she ran to him.

> Someone said to him "Henry, kiss your mama." We supposed he had passed all knowledge of present things, but he turned his lovely eyes to me, and smiled.

Oh! what a smile! I kissed his lips; they were quite cold and clammy. I was again drawn from him, but soon after, returning, I sat down and took him on my lap, stretched as he was on his mattress. He was breathing hard; his breath became slower and slower. He suddenly raised his eyes as if to heaven, and they became fixed. He fetched his breath at longer and longer intervals, and soon it ceased for ever.

Oh! My baby! Oh my Henry! I saw the remains of my precious baby for a few minutes that same night; he was laid out on the sofa of the parlour. They would not suffer me to stay with him. They tore me from him.[132]

The next day his body, lying on the knees of his wet nurse, was taken in the Sherwood's carriage to be buried in the cantonment graveyard, the scene of many such burials. Mary had taken refuge with Lucy in another officer's quarters. That night Mary could not bear to return to their quarters but spent the night on the budgerow with Lucy. The next day Mr Parson, the chaplain, took them to stay at his house where Mary spent the day trimming Lucy's cap with mourning black love-ribbons and tying a black love-sash round the baby's waist. Such harrowing scenes may have been commonplace but for each family who lost a child it was a deeply personal tragedy. Mary's distress at the death of Henry continued and she spent most of her time in her room with Lucy. Henry left each day after an early breakfast to return to their former quarters to carry out his paymaster's duties. Mary had given up her school as orders had come for the regiment to move up river to Cawnpore. Henry understood his wife's grief and one day suggested to her that perhaps they could adopt an orphan from the barracks. However, on making enquiries Henry found that at that time there were no orphans needing new families.

It was during this very distressing period that Mary turned even more deeply to religion and found a willing and sympathetic teacher in Mr Parson, a young Evangelical. Mary seized on the doctrine that redemption did not alone lie in doing good works:

In my daily life, until I accepted Mr Parson's teaching, there always came in my false views of what God required of me, or of what I was to effect by my exertions. I was, I thought, either to work or to suffer severe punishment, or, if I escaped through the Redeemer, others, I thought might perish through my neglect. I therefore did work at all risks.[133]

In her acute grief Mr Parson brought comfort with the doctrine of divine love which altered her religious views: these would dominate her later books. He also brought other leading Evangelicals to Mary's notice, many of whom she would meet later and who would further influence her.

Cawnpore

The regiment was on the move again. It left Berhampore on September 8, 1807 to move upriver to Dinapore and then on to Cawnpore. The Sherwoods departed on September 9. Mary left Henry, her beloved son, in the graveyard where a moving memorial marked his grave and so many other European children lay. She said goodbye to the Evangelical chaplain, Mr Parson, who had offered her such comfort during her grief. Prior to the journey there was an initial problem with their servants some of whom refused to accompany them to their new posting and others who demanded prepayment for provisions on the journey but then deserted them. Once on board the vessel the Sherwoods discovered that the servants who had refused to go were in fact already aboard, including the rather ugly dwarf, Babouk, the kitmutgar, who served their meals. Mary describes him: 'a certain hideous kitmutgar, with a huge head and shrivelled limbs … the name of this monstrous dwarf was Babouk.' Unfortunately the cook had absented himself, so, for the first twenty-four hours, no cooking was available. Pragmatic as ever Mary made do with bread, cheese, a leg of mutton, a few vegetables, wine, beer, brandy, coffee and sugar which were already on the budgerow. Clearly they were in no danger of starving! The cook and baggage boat joined them later. After the first twenty-four hours the Sherwoods caught up with the fleet and sailed upriver in convoy, setting off each day at four o'clock when a gun was fired. The journey upriver was not without incident. At the end of September Henry recounts a major mishap:

> The Bank under which we anchored during the night was falling & very dangerous which I presume caused our moving on the 29th altho it blew a Gale of Wind, about half an hour after we sailed my

Cookery Boat overset in the Middle of the River, it was with some difficulty we saved the People and not before I threatened to fire at a Boat which was passing to make them stop & assist me. I did not lose above 100 Rupees but we were just to great inconvenience. The wind increased so much that we were obliged to Anchor on a Sand bank & we passed the night very uncomfortably and on the 30th It was so bad and the waves rising our Boats struck on the Shore I expected to go down every instant. Towards midday Lieutt Groombridges Budgerow which lay between us and the Shore beat the Bottom out & sank & Seven Soldiers Boats were dashed to Pieces at four oclock it was so bad we were obliged to trust to the river & we got under sail with difficulty however we found an entrance of a small Nulla[134] into which we all ran & found shelter for a night during which the wind fell.

Conditions continued to be difficult with high winds making progress hazardous and necessitated the married officers and their families walking in intense heat for two miles along a marshy jungle bank until smooth water was reached. In spite of these hazards, Mary was continuing to write *The Infant's Progress*. She decided to rewrite the sections she had completed while in Berhampore, and incorporate and personify original sin as a child called 'Inbred Sin' who accompanies and tempts the children on their pilgrimage to the Celestial City (Heaven). While she rewrote the book on thin Indian paper Henry was busy with regimental accounts, maps and keeping his own diary.

It was on this river journey that Mary resolved she would never dance again for such gaiety and pleasure, which she had once enjoyed so much, now seemed frivolous. However, on a visit to an Anglo-Indian family, a wealthy doctor whose Indian wife observed purdah, Mary found herself trapped in a social situation. The couple had seven daughters. Unmarried girls in India could not dance unless a married woman opened the ball. Mary reluctantly agreed to do so if her host, who was in his seventies, would be her partner. To her surprise he gamely agreed. Mary opened the ball in some style, amidst the excited young women with their partners, and to her astonishment, young men partnering each other holding fans. It was the last ball she would attend.

∼

When they were nearing Dinapore the Sherwoods had a chance meeting with the man who would further influence Mary's religious belief and commitment. His name was Henry Martyn.[135] Martyn was a Cornishman, born in Truro in 1781. The son of a self-educated, Non-Conformist father who had shares in Wheal Unity, a local mine, Henry was a bright child and attended the grammar school in Truro where the headmaster, the Reverend Cornelius Cardew, encouraged the young boy who, by the age of fourteen, was showing great academic ability. In 1797 Henry Martyn went up to St. John's College, Cambridge to read mathematics, which at first he found extremely difficult as he had received a classical education. However, with perseverance he triumphed; graduating in 1801 with the highest marks in the first class division of the Mathematical Tripos and thereby was awarded the title of Senior Wrangler. The previous year his father had died suddenly and Henry turned to religion for solace. He came under the influence of Charles Simeon, a member of the Clapham Sect and a charismatic Evangelical preacher. On Friday evenings Simeon held gatherings or Conversation Parties in his rooms at King's College. Henry was drawn into Simeon's set of young men who burnt with Evangelical righteousness to spread the word and save the heathen in Africa and India. The young brilliant Cornishman decided to abandon academia and to follow in the footsteps of missionaries like William Carey. Henry was ordained at Ely cathedral in 1802.

Simeon had been approached in 1788 by a group of Evangelicals, among whom were the Reverend David Brown, who was based in Calcutta, and Charles Grant, the Chairman of the Board of Governors of the East India Company, to send two missionaries to Bengal. However, at the beginning of 1804, following his father's unexpected death, Henry's hopes of becoming a missionary were dashed when he received the shattering news that his patrimony had been appropriated and it would prove almost legally impossible to reclaim it. Unfortunately he could no longer afford to go out as a missionary as he had intended. Instead, in July 1805, just three months after the Sherwoods had embarked on the same dangerous journey, he sailed for India as a chaplain in the East India Company aboard the *Union*, in a fleet of fifteen East Indiamen

The Sherwoods accepted Martyn's invitation to stay with them but for Mary it was an uncomfortable two nights. She was suffering from a painful face and at night there was only a very hard bolster in Martyn's sparsely furnished bachelor quarters which she describes as 'destitute of every comfort.' Further upriver the Sherwoods went ashore at Benares, (the holy city, now Varanasi) where the living conditions and appearance of the inhabitants shocked and alarmed Mary. In her account she reveals her growing antagonism towards the beliefs and practices of both Hindus and Muslims with the yogis coming in for damning condemnation. Henry recounts:

> The Town of Benares and all Indian Towns are so different from those in Europe that no comparison can be made, the Streets are narrow, the houses very high with dead walls almost touching at the Top and the only openings outwards are more like loop holes in Towers than Doors or Windows, in these uncomfortable Streets you see Hogs, Sacred Bulls, Naked Fakeers, Pariah Dogs, disgusting objects of deformed men women & Children, processions howlings in fact you may suppose yourself in the Devils House. The Naked Fakeers are Horrid they walk about the Streets without a rag on, both Men & women & Glory in their Nakedness. We were insulted by one who came down to the Boat side & we were obliged to shut our windows I took my Horsewhip to one but I was afterwards told it was very dangerous.[136]

At Chunar the Sherwoods met another Evangelical, Daniel Corrie, who became a good friend.[137] Mary describes him as 'a tall man, nearly six feet high. His features were not good from the length of his face, but the expression of his countenance was as full of love as my father, and more I cannot say. With a simplicity all his own, he never departed from the most perfect rules of politeness; he never said a rude or unkind thing, and never seemed to have any consciousness of the rank of the person with whom he was conversing, being equally courteous to every individual ... He met us not as strangers but as a dear brother and sister, opening out his plans for instructing the people, and urging us to make every exertion for advancing the cause of Christianity.' Like Martyn he sought to spread Christianity to save the heathen from what he saw as depravity.

However, Evangelicals had to be circumspect at this time in their activities because of government policy.

At Allahabad, passing the junction of the Jumna and the Ganges, the water was particularly fast and turbulent so Henry had to hire twenty extra men to haul the boat. The regiment lost several boats, but no lives were lost. In spite of some of the shocking sights which Mary encountered on the journey to Cawnpore, and put down to the depravity of the natives, she enjoyed the beautiful countryside. At the end of November the fleet arrived at Cawnpore where Henry purchased a pleasant house from the paymaster of the 17th Regiment which was vacating the cantonment. Henry was pleased with his purchase: he paid £500 for the house, which he would be able to sell when they left. Although they found the wind and dust disagreeable, their quarters were far better than either those at Dinapore or Berhampore.

The building was thatched, single storey, with a large verandah shaded by trees in which doves nested. There was a pleasant garden with apple trees, a vine and native Indian fruit trees. The Sherwoods employed four gardeners for the upkeep of the garden. Inside there was a large front room measuring seventeen by three and a half metres. This opened onto the garden. There was a large hall, off which there were two small rooms. Beyond the hall was a room with a fireplace for winter months. The climate was much colder in winter than in their previous postings. Bedrooms and bathrooms lay in two wings opening off the winter room. The carpets came with the house and moving in was quickly completed. Apart from an abortive trip to Calcutta this would be their home for the next five years until 1812.

As had become her habit Mary wasted no time in setting up a school, which in the cooler months was housed on the verandah. There were four classes: one each for older boys and girls of the regiment and two for the younger children. Mary set about producing books for their instruction as there were no suitable books available. At Cawnpore she set up a fund to support the orphans of the regiment and organised working parties to make them clothes.

Her wish to adopt a companion for Lucy was fulfilled at the end of 1807 when she adopted Annie Childe, an orphan then aged three, whose health had been compromised by being fed gin while in the care of a soldier's wife. At the beginning of 1808 she heard of another child being terribly maltreated: she was being starved by a woman who was meant to have been taking care of her since the death of her mother. Mary, with her husband's backing, sent for the woman and child:

> The woman was brought in. She was young and coarse, and a disagreeable person. In her arms she carried the child which was then little more than two years old, but attenuated to a degree that was fearful. The skin about the mouth was stretched until the mouth and teeth were quite prominent. The cheeks were fallen in, the eyes staring, and the whole physiognomy that of the most eager famine. The little creature was naturally fair, and had very light and soft but straggling hair. The head was covered in a muslin cap. The child wore a muslin frock which had been hastily put on, and there were little long sleeves rudely attached to the short ones. The frock was clean. The child had no other garments than the frock, and its legs and feet were merely covered in skin; every bone was prominent.[138]

Mary asked the woman if the child was ill. When the woman replied that she was very ill, Mary approached the child who held out her arms to her. Picking her up, Mary dismissed the woman who at first refused to go without the child. The bearers were called and they firmly saw her off the premises. The cruelly neglected child was Sally Pownall whose father gave his permission for the Sherwoods to adopt her. Gradually with the loving care from the ayahs she blossomed. Now Mary had three little girls to care for as well as her teaching commitments which meant a busy life. In May 1808 Mary heard that the previous August Marten has had a son and that her mother has taken Mary, their daughter, to live at Worcester. But grief stalked the Sherwoods once again. Their daughter, Lucy, became ill in July and died from dysentery on September 2, 1808. Mary's grief at losing a second child plunged her into depression.

The climate in the early months of 1809 proved to be very cold. A fire was lit in the evenings and the family snuggled under 'pellises wadded with cotton' to keep warm. To add to their discomfort rumour was rife that wars with Marathas, Sikhs and Goorkhas threatened which seemed to be confirmed by the arrival of the Eighth Light Dragoons and six companies of artillery to strengthen the fighting force. This caused Mary some anxiety and she was highly disapproving of any levity concerning war among the ladies of the cantonment.

By the beginning of 1809 Mary was pregnant once more and spent most of her time in the house and garden with her two adopted daughters. Annie was turning into a bright and attractive child under the care and guidance of Mary. This led to a shift in opinion in the cantonment about 'motherless white girls of low degree in India' and their future prospects. Annie became a model for how nurture could transform a life which had started so inauspiciously. The death of Lucy and the fact that she was pregnant once more would later lead Mary and Henry to make a momentous decision. The regimental surgeon, Mr Millar, advised them that death was almost inevitable for European children in India: Mary should return to England with her baby and place her in the care of her sister and mother. The thought of leaving Henry, resettling Annie and Sally, and the long voyage, were daunting prospects but needed to be endured if their next child was to survive. Mary settled down to wait for the birth in August 1809 occupying her time with her two little adopted girls and writing. Teaching was on hold.

In March 1809 the Sherwoods were concerned to receive a letter from Marten's wife, Anne, telling them that Mrs Butt and Lucy Cameron:

> had sent our poor Little Mary at <u>Four Years & a Half Old to an</u>
> <u>expensive Boarding School</u> against a positive bargain made by Mrs
> Cameron and also agreed by Mr Cameron before his Marriage that
> they never would abandon the Child. They also knew both my (&
> Mrs Sherwoods) rooted dislike to a Girls Boarding School. Both Mrs
> S & myself wrote home as strong as we could requesting that she
> might be taken from School & this will be an additional reason for
> Mrs Sherwoods return to England in this Autumn.[139]

The weather was now extremely hot. Mary describes their typical day:

> I generally sat on a sofa, with a table before me, with my pen and ink and books; for I used to write as long as I could bear the exertion, and then I rested on the sofa, and read. I read an immense deal in India, the very scarcity of books making me more anxious for them. A new book, or one I had not often read before, was then to me like cold water to the thirsty soul. I shall never forget the delight which I had when somebody lent me "Robinson Crusoe," and when Mr Sherwood picked up an old copy of "Sir Charles Grandison."
> But to proceed with my picture. In another part of this hall sat Mr Sherwood during most part of the morning, either engaged with his accounts, his journal, or his books. He, of course, did not like the confinement so well as I did, and often contrived to get out to a neighbour's bungalow in his palanquin, during some part of the long morning. In one of the side rooms sat

Sergeant Clarke, with his books and accounts. This worthy and most methodical personage used to fill up his time in copying my manuscripts in a very neat hand, and in giving lessons in reading and spelling, &c, to Annie. He always dined at our tiffin time. In the other room was the orphan Sally, with her toys. Beside her sat her attendant, chewing her paun, and enjoying a state of perfect apathy.

Thus did our mornings pass, whilst we sat in what the lovers of broad daylight would call almost darkness. During these mornings we heard no sounds but the monotonous click click of the punkah,* or the melancholy moaning of the burning blast without, with the splash and dripping of the water thrown over the tatties.+ At one o'clock, or dinner, in fact, consisting always of curry and variety of vegetables. We often dined at this hour, the children at a little table in the room, after which we all lay down, the adults on sofas, and the children on the floor, under the punkah in the hall. At four, or later perhaps, we had coffee brought, from which we all derived much refreshment. We then bathed and dressed, and at six, or thereabouts, the wind generally falling, the tatties were removed, the doors and windows of the house were opened, and we either took an airing in carriages, or sat in the verandah but the evenings and nights of the hot winds brought no refreshment.

* The punkah is a piece of mechanism attached to large houses in India, which, being worked, acts as a monstrous fan to the whole house. – Ed.
+ The Tatta is a screen of moss-like grass, which is constantly kept wet by the water-carriers. – Ed.140

Henry Martyn

A major change in Mary's life took place in April 1809 with the arrival of Henry Martyn at Cawnpore. Martyn had come up from Dinapore by palanquin, travelling in the cool of the night, until he reached Allahabad some one hundred and thirty miles from Cawnpore. He then travelled without stopping to rest for the next two days. The heat and the fierce winds across the plains during the day were brutal and the twenty-eight year old Henry, who was not a strong young man, arrived in Cawnpore with a dangerous fever. The Sherwoods took him into their home where Mary nursed him with great tenderness. The temperature inside the bungalow reached 90°F during the day in spite of the punkah fan being wafted at full speed. Henry's already delicate health was further compromised by the long journey and it is highly probable that he was already suffering from the tuberculosis which was rife in his family. Not only was his physical health suffering, he was recovering from the tragedy which beset his personal life and happiness.

When he set out from England in 1805 he had left behind Lydia Grenfell, the woman he had fallen in love with. He had fully expected that Lydia would join him in India as his wife. However, Lydia's mother had other ideas for her youngest daughter and refused to let her go. Correspondence could take several months to reach the recipient and when Henry proposed to Lydia by letter dated July 30 1806 he was confident that she would come. So confident, in fact, that he purchased a dinner service. Although she responded on March 5 by return of post he did not receive her reply until October 24, 1807, turning down his proposal. He was heartbroken. However Henry did not accept her refusal and persisted in trying to persuade her to marry him. Finally, when she broke off all correspondence with him on the advice of her family, and in spite of Charles Simeon's intervention to plead Henry's case, he accepted

Reverend Henry Martyn (1781–1812)

that she would not be coming out to help him in his mission to save the heathen.

This broken young man found some comfort in the domestic life of the Sherwoods. He loved the children and played with them allowing Annie to sit by him as he studied Hebrew. By the end of May when he was stronger, he took up his role as chaplain and moved into one of the two least attractive bungalows in the cantonment. In the other bungalow he lodged Nathanial Sabat, a fiery Arab who had converted to Christianity from Islam, and his seventh wife Ameena. Mary was shocked by Ameena's indolent life: she spent the day sitting on cushions under mosquito nets, having her hands and eyelids stained with henna, her hair combed and arranged, while she gossiped. The ever-industrious Mary felt she should have been more gainfully employed. Ameena had remained Muslim when Sabat had converted to Christianity. The marriage was not a happy one. When Ameena asked her husband where Christians go after death he replied 'to heaven.' She then asked 'where do Mahometans go?' Sabat replied 'to hell and the devil.' Ameena responded, 'Well then, I will continue to be a Musselman, because I should prefer hell and the devil without you, to heaven itself in your presence.' [141]

Henry Martyn had been tasked with the translation of the New Testament by the Baptist missionaries, led by the Reverend David Brown, at Serampore, close to Calcutta. To assist him he employed Murza Muhammad Fitra from Benares for the Urdu translation, and Sabat for the translation into Farsi and Arabic. Unfortunately the two translators were jealous of each other and both could be devious. Sabat's translation into Farsi employed a style and vocabulary which Henry felt was too high and flowery to appeal to possible converts and he was proved right when the completed translation was sent to Calcutta in 1810.

In June Daniel Corrie and his sister, Mary, arrived from Chunar, near Benares, en route to Agra. Mary stayed with the Sherwoods and her brother with Henry Martyn. The Corries and Sherwoods would go for gentle walks along the Ganges or sit on a budgerow and enjoy the breeze off the river. When the baby, their fourth child, was born on August 10, 1809 Henry Martyn baptised her Lucy Elizabeth but always called her Serena. It was now that the Sherwoods began planning Mary's return to England to safeguard the newborn baby's health but first, arrangements needed to be made for her two adopted girls, Annie and Sally. The Corries agreed to take Annie. Sally was to go to a Mrs Robinson in Benares. Henry Sherwood got leave of absence to accompany his wife and daughter on the long river journey to Calcutta. The bungalow was sold and having put their plans in place they left Cawnpore on October 25, 1809, having paid three hundred rupees for a large sixteen-oared budgerow and seventy rupees for a small cooking boat.

At Allahabad the budgerow was swept against a pile. Water began to pour in. As the boat filled with water the family managed to scramble up the bank, the terrified children clinging to Mary. Repairs were made and they set off once more. En route they were entertained by Mr Ricketts who now lived at Mirzapore. Conversation centred round a low caste woman who had committed suttee two days earlier. Mary, although shocked by the practice, accepted that life for a low caste widow was hard – all her jewels would pass to her children to whom she now would become a slave. Mary comments with some asperity:

> There are reasons and motives for Hindu women burning themselves, independently of any wish they may have of joining their husbands (and of the existence of such a wish there may in many cases be some doubt, as Hindu husbands and wives are by no means renowned for their conjugal affection).[142]

Both Annie and Sally were left at Chunar under the care of the Corries. Sally would remain with them until Mrs Robinson, who was heavily pregnant, had given birth to her own baby. Mary Corrie promised that she would keep Sally too if Mrs Robinson changed her mind. Annie, the older child, understood that she was to be left at Chunar but Sally was too young to understand. Mary took the two little girls to the Corrie's home. She kissed both children goodbye and left two dolls, dressed in European clothes, to be given to them when they woke the next morning. Although it was a bitter decision to have to make it proved to be the catalyst to involving influential Europeans in India in making provision for the welfare of motherless white girls.

Mr Robinson arranged for the Sherwoods to call at Bankipore where Dr. McNabb vaccinated Lucy. They reached the Hooghli on the 17th of November and Calcutta on the 28th.

Having said goodbye to Annie and Sally, Mary faced the even more painful parting: that from Henry. Arrangements moved rapidly. Four ships were to leave in the next two days. Henry was recommended by an agent to take passages on the *Ocean* for Mary and a Mrs Wiley, who had travelled down with them and was to accompany Mary and the baby on the voyage. Henry had bargained with the captain's brother for half a roundhouse cabin on the quarterdeck but was asked for 7,000 rupees which he could not afford. They were then offered a cabin under the roundhouse for which Henry offered 4,000 rupees. The rate was 5,000 but Henry was assured that if they went downriver to where the *Ocean* lay at anchor the captain would accept the lower price and take Mary, with the baby and Mrs Wiley. However, when Henry returned to the boat, Mary told him that Mrs Wiley had announced that she could not leave her husband and refused to go which left Mary in a distressed and vulnerable position.

That evening Mary was in tears wracked with indecision over what to do. Henry pointed out 'the great inconvenience she [Mrs Wiley] had put us too [sic] & the difficulty in procuring a Servant by morning.' They went to bed but could not sleep, becoming increasingly agitated at the prospect of parting: 'I lay and fancied it in every way til at length I could bear it no longer.' [143]

They agreed to postpone the journey until the next fleet on December 15. After a sleepless night they decided to seek medical advice while in Calcutta. After a 'happy breakfast' Mary wrote to Mr Shoolbred, the leading authority on child health in Calcutta. While they were waiting for him to arrive they received a note from the captain of the *Ocean* offering Mary passage. Mary declined. Mr Shoolbred arrived with an eminent doctor, Dr. Russell. Both medical men advised her to remain in India for several more years. The Sherwoods accepted this advice and decided to return to Cawnpore together. To the Sherwoods' surprise both doctors refused any payment. The stress of the situation caused Mary's hair to fall out. Thankfully it regrew after a few weeks.

❧

Henry hired a pinnace for the journey back to Cawnpore. They moored downriver for two days: 'Let not anyone assert that there is not such a thing as happiness in this world. It would be impossible to give an idea of our peace, joy, our delight during the two days we passed on that solitary shore, we who had so long anticipated a fearful separation. I remember even now our walks upon that quiet beach, our baby being carried by a black nurse at our side, our little fair and smiling Lucy.' [144] Before setting off on their long journey Henry called on Thomas Thomason, a missionary and a friend of Henry Martyn from Cambridge days when both had been assistant curates to Charles Simeon. Mary was invited to his house where she talked to other guests about the plight of motherless white orphaned girls in India, describing her own experience in the cantonments.

On December 19, 1809 the Sherwoods set off back to Cawnpore. Much to their surprise, while on the Hooghli on January 4 they saw a budgerow coming downstream with a European family on board. It was the Robinsons with Sally. Henry went back downstream in a small boat to enquire about Sally in the hope that the Robinsons would relinquish their charge. Mrs Robinson's baby had died soon after birth and they were going to Calcutta to help her recuperate. Mary was saddened to learn that Sally had pined for her but was even more upset by the Robinsons' treatment of her. The Robinsons had had forebodings as to how a child who was of lower rank would be regarded socially. Sally was now dressed in a loose chintz wrapper with long loose sleeves instead of the white muslin dresses she had worn when with the Sherwoods. Her hair was cut short and she had an expression of deep unhappiness. Mercifully, the Robinsons agreed to Sally's returning there and then with the Sherwoods to the benefit of all concerned.

Entering the Ganges from the Hooghli Henry takes the opportunity to explore the archaeological site at Gour on January 18 before continuing upstream. By February 13 they reach Patna. On the 15th Mary sends the manuscript of *Little Henry and his Bearer* to Mrs Hawkins, the wife of the Judge of the Court of Appeal at Patna, who will translate it into Hindustani. Mrs Hawkins has just returned from England and presses them to stay for two days. However, they decide to take Mr Hawkins's carriage and rejoin their boat at Dinapore that evening only to find that the boatmen refuse to continue until the 19th. When they reached Chunar on March 9, they stayed with the Corries until the 11th. They were looking forward to being reunited with Annie. She had been much loved by the Corries and had become a good companion for Mary Corrie. Annie had pined for Sally and was delighted to see her. When the children had been taken to another room after dinner the subject of her returning to the Sherwoods was uppermost in everyone's minds. Daniel Corrie felt that another uprooting for Annie would not be good for her. Moreover, both he and his sister, Mary, were now extremely fond of her:

> We would gladly keep her, though we must not insist upon it; though she would like to go with you, she would be grieved to part with us; you have other children and many other calls for your compassion.[145]

The Sherwoods saw the wisdom of this argument and put the welfare of

Annie first rather than their own desire to reclaim her. They again stopped on March 14 at Mr Ricketts's at Mirzapore where they stayed for two days. Mary was shocked to learn that native wet nurses' babies commonly died due to lack of milk whereas the white babies thrived. She was strongly advised to keep a wet nurse until all Lucy's teeth had been cut. Between Mirzapore and Allahabad, which they reached on the 21st, Henry employed himself copying *The Infant Pilgrim* to send to England. When they finally reached Cawnpore on April 8, sixteen weeks after leaving Calcutta, they stayed with Assistant Surgeon Miller while Henry set about finding a bungalow again. This proved to be difficult. On the 19th they moved into a former shop on the river bank. From there they sent the first four chapters of *The Infant Pilgrim* home.

Good Works

The Sherwoods settled back into their former life in Cawnpore. Henry Martyn, now a very sick man, welcomed their return and under his guidance Mary began to study Hebrew and to study the Bible closely. During their absence Martyn had negotiated the use of another bungalow next to his as a place set aside for worship. He had also established a school for Indian boys where they could be taught the rudiments of reading. In spite of his frail health he preached on Sunday evenings to a large motley crowd of Hindu and Muslim holy men and women whose appearance – some covered in mud, some with withered limbs, some almost naked – revolted Mary. The East India Company had been obliged to ban any overt missionary activity until 1813 which meant that Evangelical chaplains like Martyn had to be very careful not to overstep the rules prior to this date. Martyn restricted his preaching to the Ten Commandments in the hope that his audience would see the error of their ways and accept that they needed to be saved by conversion to Christianity. These Sunday evening gatherings, sometimes numbering five hundred, became a source of entertainment for the local youth and a source of baksheesh for the holy men and women who would be rewarded for attendance by Henry with a pice[146] each.

When the Corries arrived in Cawnpore in June 1810, en route to Agra, Annie and Mary Corrie stayed with the Sherwoods and Daniel Corrie stayed with Martyn. The weather in Cawnpore was very hot. Henry describes it:

> The weather exceedingly hot, the wind not being steady to the West, we could not keep our house at a less heat than 92 at Night & 97 in the day. This lasted all the Month. The bed at night when you went to lie down seemed like an Ironing blanket & Mrs S and Miss Corrie walked about the greater part of a night, it is impossible to describe it, heat alone will not, for I have often felt it hotter.

THE

Indian Pilgrim;

OR, THE

PROGRESS

OF THE

PILGRIM NAZAREENEE,

(Formerly called Goonah Purist, or the Slave of Sin,)

From the City of the Wrath of God to the City of Mount Zion.

Delivered under the Similitude of a Dream.

"In a dream, in a vision of the night, when deep sleep falleth upon men, in slumberings upon the bed, then God openeth the ears of men, and sealeth their instruction."——*Job xxxiii. 15, 16.*

BY MRS. SHERWOOD,

Author of " Little Henry and his Bearer," &c. &c.

WELLINGTON, SALOP:
PRINTED BY AND FOR F. HOULSTON AND SON.
And sold by
Scatcherd and Letterman, Ave-Maria Lane, London.

1818.

The Indian Pilgrim, *1818. Title page*

The missionaries in Serampore were embarking on a project to translate English religious books into Hindustani. However, when they had begun to translate Bunyan's *Pilgrim's Progress* the direct style and references were incompatible with Indian taste for a more flamboyant style. Corrie and Henry Martyn persuaded Mary to become part of the project, which they would oversee, to rewrite Bunyan in a more approachable style adapted to Indian taste. It was not published in English until 1815 as *The Indian Pilgrim or the Progress of the Pilgrim Nazareenee from the City of the Wrath of God to the City of Mount Zion, delivered under the Similitude of a Dream Formerly Goonah Purist or the Slave of Sin.*[147]

The publisher's 1818 advertisement at the beginning of the book explains the background:

ADVERTISEMENT

IT will readily appear to the most cursory reader of the following pages, that they were primarily intended for publication in a very remote land. In the year 1810, during the author's residence in that far country, a plan was formed by certain pious persons in Calcutta for translating Bunyan's *Pilgrim's Progress* into Hindoostannee, for the use of such of the natives as were beginning to shew an interest in religious subjects. But upon making the attempt, the style of that celebrated work and the manners therein displayed were found so entirely repugnant to the Oriental taste, as to render the prosecution of such design no longer desirable. A proposal was then made to the author to write an Indian *Pilgrim's Progress*, adapted to the taste, the manners, and the peculiar prejudices of Hindoostann:– in consequence of which, this little work was immediately composed with a sincere desire to assist in preparing the way of the Lord among a people, who have contributed, in no ordinary degree, to the extension of our national affluence and renown. Certain circumstances, however, occurring to prevent the printing of this volume abroad, the writer has been prevailed with to lead forth her *Indian Pilgrim* upon English ground; where, she trusts, if he make an *unusual*, it may not be altogether an *uninteresting* spectacle. And though this humble traveller to Zion presents himself in the garb of a stranger among his fellow-subjects in this kingdom; it is nevertheless presumed, that he bears about him the marks of our common Lord and Master, exhibiting the most unequivocal proofs of his belonging to that sacred brotherhood, in which there is *neither Greek nor Jew, circumcision nor uncircumcision, Barbarian, Scythian, bond nor free.* It has not been thought necessary, on this occasion, to alter those foreign appellations, which were indispensable to the original design of this under-taking: nor was it judged advisable to omit those allusions to Indian customs and usages, with which it abounds; since if they add nothing to its embellishment, they will at least afford the European pilgrim an opportunity of comparing the reasonable services of Christianity with the superstitious vanities of Heathenism.

It may be proper here to state, that the story of the Pilgrim Bartholomew, as far as related by himself, presents the real history of a certain schoolmaster employed by the author and her friends in the instruction of native boys. Nor may it be amiss to add, that many of the facts and conversations introduced with relation to the Indian Pilgrim *himself*, were taken from real life. February, 1818.[148]

In the summer of 1810 the church which Martyn had laboured to establish was opened on August 30. His health was causing grave concern; so much so that Daniel Corrie had got permission for Martyn to have extended leave in order to travel back to England. Corrie would take his place in Cawnpore. Martyn left Cawnpore in September 1810 but instead of returning to England by sea he set out overland for Persia where he would do more work on translating the New Testament into Farsi and Arabic. Mary thought that Martyn's idea of Persia was too romantic: 'a land of roses and nightingales, of fresh flowing streams, of sparkling fountains and of breezes laden with perfume.'[149] Some of these sights he did enjoy but for the most part he met resistance to Christian belief.[150] He would finally set off from Tabriz in north-west Persia in 1812 and would die near Tokat, in eastern Turkey, en route to England, aged thirty-one. The Sherwoods did not hear of his death until March 1813 when they were stationed in Meerut.

The Sherwoods' fifth child was born on July 20, 1811. They intended to call her Martha, after Mary's mother. When the day of the christening arrived Daniel Corrie took the baby in his arms and asked for her name. When told it was Martha he put the baby down refusing to christen her.[151] ' "What, then, will you please to have her called?" we asked. He answered, "Emily." "Then Emily it shall be," we replied, and he took her up again and gave her that name.'[152]

Mary had reopened her school which was thriving and was writing a Church Catechism which native children could more easily understand as English references were alien to them. Her husband had also started instructing young soldiers with their reading and writing as well as providing religious instruction. It was now that Mary put into practice her plan for setting up an orphanage for motherless Anglo-Indian girls. She placed Sergeant Parker from the regiment and his wife in a house within the church compound. To offset some of the expenses in caring for the orphans she made a collection from the officers and settled the first of many orphans, Maria Clarke and Mary Parson into their new home where they were well looked after by Mrs Parker. Sadly Maria Clarke died later that year. Mary took a great interest in the orphans' welfare and visited them every day in addition to teaching them at the school.

> This orphan-school is an asylum which was provided for the destitute children of European soldiers, without any respect to the colour of the mother, or her character as wife or otherwise. It was just and right that such a refuge should be provided, but it was not right, and an offence to propriety, to class the daughters of English women, of good character, with children which had been nurtured by Hindoo or Musselman mothers of the lowest description.[153]

The social stigma of being born to an Indian woman of low cast marked a child out for different treatment. Soon more girls were taken into the orphanage and the model flourished.

In a long letter to her sister, Lucy Cameron, Mary describes her happy memories of their shared childhood before giving Lucy some insight into her life in India and the deep impression that Henry Martyn has made with his Evangelical fervour to convert the natives:

> We have got the print of Bridgnorth hanging up in our room, bought for me by Captain Andrews & I often try to trace the places on the hill where we used to separate & meet again when we went to visit the poor & pennyworths of tea—God has been so good to me that I cannot say I was happier then than I am now, yet there is a sweetness in the remembrance of those days which words cannot describe.
>
> Oh sister, beloved of my heart, it was my earnest wish that our daughter & dear Marten's might be brought up to live together & feel for each other as you & I felt for each other. If we return to England, whilst we are in England in a few years this may still be the case. Young people must have companions, & to provide for them holy and chearful ones will be the chief care of mine—please God I live to rear my children.
>
> Our children are beginning to suffer, at least in their looks from the heat. They first in the coming on of the heat lose their bloom & then break out in a kind of rash looking something like the measles which continues all the hot season. With many persons all kinds of food becomes unpleasant in the hot season. I have sometimes myself been a week or a fortnight without taking

any food whatever & yet not ill nor getting much thinner. Children when weaned too early not uncommonly starve themselves to death not having the sense to force their appetites. On this account being unable to carry on the nursing so long as is requisite I am almost forced to get a native nurse for my babes when they are about eight or nine months old.

In the year 1807 we first became acquainted with the Reverend Henry Martyn. We were at the time going on boats on the river Ganges from Berhampore to Cawnpore & our boats came to an anchor about two miles below Dinapore. Mr Martyn came walking down to see us & would insist on our going the next day (as the regiment was to halt a few days near Dinapore) to his quarters in the Cantonments. His first appearance was particularly agreeable to me as I saw in him a strong resemblance to my Father, his features were not naturally handsome & he was pale and thin, but his countenance was in general remarkably serene denoting that the peace of God was with him, & at times his whole face was lighted up with a degree of holy fervour such as I seldom if ever witnessed & which showing the power of mind above matter make a face naturally plain appear beautiful…

Mr Martyn preached every Sunday evening from a terrace in the midst of his garden. I have been sometimes present on these occasions when the atmosphere has been as oppressive as cannot be felt in a house in England. I have seen the perspiration pour down Mr Martyn's face as he has been speaking & when he came into the house after having finished he has thrown himself on a couch ready to faint.

Mr Martyn made the Ten Commandments the subject of his exhortation to these poor people-no doubt intending had he lived long enough in that place to have used the Law as a Schoolmaster to bring them with God's help to Christ.

After he had finished his lecture he gave to each a piece of money of about the value of two thirds of a penny, I have known him distribute 800. Besides the Fakeers there were several natives of some respectability who used to come to hear Mr Martyn.[154]

Among this group was Sheikh Saleh who was from a good family in Lucknow. He had been engaged by Sabat to translate the New Testament into Persian. When the translation was finished but not yet bound Saleh read it and became converted to Christianity taking the name Abdool Massee'h. He then preached the Gospel in Upper Bengal. Mary continues:

> …Among the lovely traits in Mr Martyn's character none appeared to me more remarkable than his kindness to children. With what earnestness he blessed them-how patiently he endured their attention-how he bore the little ones in his arms. Every parent could not but feel grateful for his Christian tenderness & courtesy towards their children. I remember once seeing him

studying Hebrew Etymologies with a large collection of books round him on a couch—my little girl, then very young climbed upon his couch & laced herself upon his knee, from which station he would on no account allow her to be removed but went on with his labours with the infant in his arms. Every one too must have observed his extreme politeness & even elegance of manners, his were the manners of the most finished gentleman. He was an uncommon instance of extreme chearfulness without levity, therein I think we have proof of the very great purity & holiness of his mind in that his mirthful thoughts & words never seemed in the least degree to verge towards unholiness.

Mary continues heaping praise on Martyn and extolling his virtues. She then reports on the visit by Lady Nugent, the wife of the Commander-in-Chief. She had inspected the school and given Sally a present for reading Hindustani. Mary reports that Lady Nugent later sent 200 rupees towards the running of the native school. The letter ends with comments from Mary: 'our time has been pretty well occupied' and references to having received letters from England – always an eagerly anticipated event.

~

In December 1811 five companies of the regiment were ordered to Bundelcund to the south, where there was unrest and fighting among the local rajahs. As was their custom the Sherwoods gave their friends and the orphans a Christmas dinner before the regiment's departure on December 24.

Five Companies of the Regiment order to take the Field again some Forts to the Westward. The Commanding Officer Colonel Mawby goes & the Staff are to go. I am preparing. On the 24 We marched to Cultrah where we halted the 25 & 26th. As I am not obliged to conform to the Line of March I had an excellent opportunity of seeing the proceedings of an Indian Army & I can say that from the Ground on which we halted one day to the Ground we were to occupy the next was one chain of followers Hacknies. Men & Women on Bullocks, on foot, on Tatoos, carrying spears, Swords, Shields, Bird Cages, Puppy dogs & parrots of the Latter I observed an Old Woman riding a Tattoo (a Pony) on a Pillion was a Puppy peeping from under the Old womans cloak, a Man carrying a Parrot on his finger &

teaching it to speak all the way he went, to calculate what number of followers an Army must have I can only relate my own, I have 5 Camels, 2 Drivers, 2 Tent Pitchers, Carry Basketts, Water Carrier, 1 Link Boy, 1 Sweeper, 4 Coolies, 1 Ketmedgar (Footman) 1 Horstler, 3 Grasscutts every one of whom has a wife or something like it & some have Children – of Publick Servants it is impossible to speak & of Market People a person not having seen the thing cannot form a conception as far as the Eye can reach all round it is an Ant Hill in Motion, we have 25 Publick Elephants besides many Private ones & several Thousand Bullocks, Xerxes Army is easily accounted for. I found my Canvas Bag (Tent) very cold & uncomfortable.[155]

Henry writes to Mary with descriptions of the taking of the fort of Callingerie (Kalinjar, about 100 miles west of Allahabad):

With immense labour two 18 pound guns were got up to the top of the hill. All our regiment was employed, and they actually forced the guns up nearly perpendicular roads. Some parts of these roads are said to have an angle of 75 degrees. No opposition whatever is made to anything we do. This sort of conduct is usual in Indian warfare; we do not expect a severe contest. The fort-keeper is aware that the fort must fall, but he will make a determined stand. He seems to wish to affect a show of justice, as much as to say " I do not begin the war; he wishes to pass for an innocent, injured man, but we know him better. He is a robber by profession, as are almost all the governors of these small forts and the heads of these inferior principalities.[156]

The fort held out for three days before the final assault. Henry, as paymaster, did not take an active role in the fighting. On February 2 the regiment marched before sunrise to make a final attack on the hill fort. So steep was the rock that the soldiers could not use ladders and had to cling to the perpendicular rock as huge boulders were rolled down on them from above. Officers and soldiers perished in the assault. Henry reports a large number of casualties. The next day the fort surrendered.

Mary found time during Henry's absence to start on her next book, *The Ayah and her Lady* which was translated into Hindustani by a moonshee [secretary] while she wrote. *Little Henry and his Bearer*, which

Little Henry and his Bearer, *1814. Title page*

she had completed in 1810 and was translated into Hindustani by a friend, Mrs Hawkins, from Mary's manuscript. Her pupils now had two of her books with familiar Indian settings and references that could either be read aloud to them or they could read for themselves. Both books taught the Evangelical message that the non-believing sinner could be saved through divine love.

By 1812 Daniel Corrie's health was deteriorating and it was decided that he and his sister should leave Cawnpore. Henry returned from the battle of Kalinjar to Cawnpore in time to say goodbye to the Corries who left on February 12 to make an excursion down country by river, in the hope of improving his health, before taking up his post at Agra.

In 1812, Henry sent the manuscript of *Little Henry and His Bearer* in a letter to Lucy Cameron. It is a highly Evangelical story in which a small orphaned English boy, born in Dinapore, whose father 'was an officer in the Company's service, and was killed in attacking a mud fort belonging to a zeemaeender' is adopted by a wealthy and vain European lady who lives in a 'large puckah house near the river between Patna and Dinapore.' Little Henry's Christian education is neglected and he is brought up initially as a Hindu and speaks Hindustani: European values are alien to him. The major influence in his life is his faithful Hindu servant, Boosy: 'He used to sit on the verandah between his bearer's knees, chew paun, and eat bazaar sweetmeats. He wore no shoes nor stockings, but was dressed in panjammas and had silver bangles on his ankles.' Footnotes explain the Hindustani vocabulary with which Mary sprinkles the text. Little Henry is saved by an Evangelical young woman who converts the little heathen to Christianity but not before a struggle by him to continue in the worship of Hindu idols. After a trip down to Calcutta the young boy falls seriously ill. In a death-bed scene of high drama Boosy realises that his pantheistic religion cannot bring him salvation: it is the pious dying boy who brings his faithful servant, Boosy, to salvation. Not only does he save Boosy he also saves his selfish adoptive mother. She repents her sins and both she and Boosy convert to Christianity.

The book, which is only fifty-nine pages in length and illustrated with woodcuts, became a huge bestseller when it was published anonymously in 1814 and by 1816 was in its seventh edition. It ran to thirty editions by 1840 and was translated into Hindustani, French, German, Chinese and Singhalese. Mary drew on her first-hand experience of living in India: the scenes she draws of Indian life; the Eurocentric view of India; the Evangelical mission to convert the heathen; the early death of many European children; and the problem facing orphaned children in the regiment are all portrayed in this little book which displays Mary's narrative and descriptive powers which would grip any child's imagination. She drew on her experiences in India for other books: *The Memoirs of Sergeant Dale, his Daughter and the Orphan Mary* (1815) which is set in the Cawnpore cantonment and has detailed descriptions of life, army duties and the care of young children; *The History of Little Lucy and her Dhaye* (1823), and *The Last Days of Boosy, the Bearer of Little Henry* (1842).

~

The family had been suffering with inflamed eyes during the intense heat and dust in August 1812. The heat continued into September:

Sepr
1.2.3 extremely hot, no rain. The Opthalmia [sic] very painful, Mrs Sherwood had it to such a degree that she could not rest, in the course of the Night I gave her 25 drops of Laudanum yet she could not rest, no rain till 5th & the hot wind blew. This is very uncommon, the 5th we had a violent wind which did damage to our thatch at length Rain came on. Mrs Sherwoods Eyes were very bad until the 10th when the pain abated after having had 13 Leeches & two blisters. Sir George Nugents Commander in Chief arrived & we are reviewed on the 26th. The Heat at the Review was very great, a Man died there.

Meerut

The Sherwoods were on the move once more at the end of October: this time to Meerut, about 50 miles north-east of Delhi. Before leaving, a parcel of New Testaments, translated into Hindustani, arrived from the Calcutta Press: the Evangelical message could now be promoted to the heathen in their native language, with due circumspection. The government would ease restrictions on missionary activity in 1813 and then the Evangelical message could be preached openly. The Sherwoods set off by river on October 31, 1812. 'Near Shahjehanpoor they arranged themselves for the night in their tents as usual, but they had scarcely fallen asleep before they were awakened by the howling of wolves and wild dogs, and the dogs several times actually made their way into them.' [157] On November 24 Henry left the boat and his family to travel by a relay of palanquin bearers 60 miles to Meerut where he purchased a bungalow. He borrowed tents and draught cattle to convey the family from Garhmaktesar Gaut, 30 miles to Meerut. 'Mrs Sherwood was pleased with the House, 3 large Rooms with a verandah all round & two Baths on the North end … the Verandahs all divided into small rooms, it must be noted that the Servants rooms are all at a distance from the House forming separate Hutts at the Bottom of the Garden.'

After reaching Meerut on December 2, Mary employed herself by starting on what would be her most famous book, *The History of the Fairchild Family*. Mary initially titled it *The Child's Manual*. She would finish writing the first volume in October 1813. The book met with huge success when it was published in 1818 by Hatchards, Piccadilly. Parts II and III would follow later in 1842 and 1847. The title makes reference to the fair complexions of European children in India. The three children in the book bear the names of her own children: Lucy, Emily and Henry.

Soon after they arrived in Meerut the Sherwoods followed their

Infidels Barbarians! we are come to convert you to the european faith. by Order of the great Authority whose Image I bear on this shield. the benignant beams of whose countenance enliven the ignorant inhabitants of this country. therefore destroy your Gods burn your books, be converted and be saved.

Master, you very fine Gentleman got very fine Topy[158] – but not speak too much good sense – Master I'm poor people all black fellow poor Man, all master slave – What for burra Sahib behauden Send Master for black man not become Christian; … got one God already – What can I say more? Wah! Wah! Topywalla

Missionary Influence or How to Make Converts

custom of founding a school for local children. At first they were ridiculed for the idea but through a chance meeting with a thread seller they were put in contact with an elderly man who was willing to act as schoolmaster. When he arrived he brought thirteen boys who were given two annas[159] each for attendance. By the end of the month the roll had risen to nineteen. The school was housed in a disused stable. Mary commented that all of the pupils smelt of garlic and were smeared with oil. The school flourished with twenty-eight enrolled by 1814 but the schoolmaster overstepped the mark by becoming impertinent and had to be dismissed. He departed taking many of the pupils with him. Numbers were swelled by 'eight big half-caste drummer boys from the 3rd Native Infantry.' In spite of reservations on Mary's part about teaching them she got on well with them. In December 1812 Lord Moira, the Governor-General, came to Meerut and inspected the school.

Henry Sherwood had converted a stable building into the school but on hearing that Lord Moira was to visit, Mr Parson, the chaplain, who had arrived from Berhampore, cleared everything out so Moira inspected a building devoid of tables and chairs. Mary suspected jealousy on the part of her old mentor, Mr Parson, of what Henry had achieved. Henry was not put off by Parson's actions and the following year opened up another building for native children with one room acting as a nursery and the other as a classroom. Henry also refurbished another building for worship where services conducted in both English and Hindustani could be held on Sundays. During the week it was utilised as a schoolroom for the regiment. Mary's time was fully occupied with teaching, writing and looking after her own children and running a Gospel class for seventeen native boys who were examined by Henry once a week.

While at Meerut Mary and Mrs Thomason realised that in order to establish an orphanage for European white girls they needed the support of an influential person in government circles. That person was Lady Loudon, Lord Moira's wife. Mary entered into correspondence with her supplying information about the current situation in the Calcutta Presidency.

During their time in Meerut Mary describes three visits which reflect the clash of cultural backgrounds and sensibilities. The first took place early in 1813 when she visited the Begum of Somru. Mary had received a bottle of rose-water from the Begum. The gift indicated that if Mary paid her a visit she would be received.[160] The Begum had come to Meerut to meet the Commander-in-Chief, Sir George Nugent. She was the widow of a European who had spent his time in India in the service of various local nabobs. He had been rewarded with the district of Sirdhana which had passed to his haughty wife on his death. Nominally Christian, she ruled with absolute power over an area some twenty miles long and twelve wide. Any misdemeanour was met by torture, with thumbscrews being used as her favourite method of punishment. Rumour also suggested that on one occasion she had two unfortunate women buried alive. Allegedly she would take pleasure in dining above the spot where they lay entombed. Mary decided to take a beautifully bound copy of Henry Martyn's translation of the New Testament in Farsi and present it to her. She found the Begum sitting in the hall of a bungalow surrounded by a motley collection of servants. Mary was not impressed. The Begum was old, 'very short, very yellow, and very wrinkled.' She accepted Mary's gift with good grace.

Mary's sixth child, a much longed for son, was born on July 1, 1813. He was 'the tallest, thinnest baby I ever saw.' He was named Henry Martyn after the Sherwoods' friend who had died on October 16 the previous year. Thankfully he thrived. The following year, in March 1814, Mary was invited to attend a nautch which was to be held in the cantonment. Mary brought the servants and children into a long room where the performance could take place. Mary, with her disapproval of entertainment and dancing, was highly unlikely to approve of the nautch girls:

> These nautch girls are regularly brought up to the profession; some of them as slaves, often sold by their parents for the purpose. The most beautiful girls are selected, and those who have fine voices. There is generally an old female at the head of the company—one who lives on the wages obtained in various ways by these unhappy girls. Oh, who would desire to investigate the secrets of such families! When these girls travel they are generally hidden by crimson curtains in a rut, or car, (a native carriage) drawn by bullocks. Their education consists of singing, dancing, and playing on a small harp or guitar. Some of the higher ranks of them are taught to read, on which account it is considered disgraceful for respectable women of the East to learn. The influence of these nautch girls over the other sex, even over men who have been brought up in England, and who have known, admired, and respected their own country-women, is not to be accounted for. It is not only obtained in a very peculiar way, but often kept up even when beauty is passed. It steals upon those who come within its charmed circle in a way not unlike that of an intoxicating drug, being the more dangerous to young Europeans because they seldom fear it; for perhaps these very men who are so intoxicated remember some lovely face in their native land and fancy they are wholly unapproachable by any attraction which can be used by a tawny beauty.[161]

The experience was not wasted. The nautch girls appear in *The History of Henry Desmond*, which was published, anonymously initially, in 1829. In it Mary included many details of life in India which she had been exposed to during her time there. India proved to be a rich source of material – both narrative and descriptive. To European readers who, unlike Mary, had no first hand experience of India, it brought an exotic world into their imagination

∿

On October 12, 1814 the fighting force of the 53rd regiment was ordered to march north to Dehra in the Himalayan foothills to fight the 'Goorkhas' of Nepal because of border disputes. The regiment left Meerut on October 14 and encamped nine miles north. Mary would not see Henry for three months. In his diary Henry writes of his anxiety in leaving Mary and his children.

> These are the severe tryals of a Military Life, when the husband is suddenly ordered to leave his family uncertain whether he will be able to return to the same place. The Private Soldier has fewer anxieties for the Government provide for his family. (I speak of India.) [162]

The regiment waited for the camels and elephants to arrive at their camp before marching again on October 21. Henry was forced to dismount from his horse in the crowded procession of baggage animals, bullock carts and native-bred ponies when they set off in the early morning. At dawn he remounted and galloped away. Henry rode alone preferring the relative peace and solitude as the regiment made its way towards the mighty Himalayas which rose from the Gangetic plain. Secrecy surrounded the route ahead. There were two alternative high passes to cross – Timli or Kiri.

Orders came on October 28 to march via the Kiri Pass in order to join Colonel Mawby. When they camped the following evening, in a letter to Mary, Henry describes the scene almost lyrically in spite of the hard marching conditions:

> We moved at one oclock to day the Sun was not so oppressive as I had expected but still it was bad enough & made our backs pretty hot, for we were marching North Eastwards, dreadfully hot, for the first four Miles we travelled over a waste of long grass with here & there a small field which had been planted with Badgera or some grain of that kind

but now cut & carried we saw several Men's nests in the trees & at the
end of the distance (vz 4 Miles) we came to a Dhawk Station & the
Hircarrahs explained to us that the nests which we had seen in the
Trees were Stations for watchmen & Hircarrahs to be out of the reach
of Wild Beasts, particularly Tigers & Elephants which are very
common so that they dare not sleep on the Ground but at Sun Set
retire to their nests, from this we entered a kind of Forest of high
Trees with very little brush wood, the Grass beneath being beautifully
green & fine, about a foot in height, we here perceived a great change
in the species of Trees most beautiful Trees covered with fruit. One
like a small Apple but we dare not taste it, the Natives say it is only fit
for horse medicine & I think it is used as a strong astringent in
Blacking like Galls. Another very Elegant Tree with a Transparent
fruit like a plumb. The Tree itself like a fir. We travelled in this Forest
for 4 Miles delightfully shaded from the Sun. I could almost have
fancied myself in the Dingle at Badger when suddenly a most
enchanting Scene opened to us at a turn we saw a Mountain in front
as if on the other side of a River, not abruptly rising but apparently a
gentle swelling, but to a great height green with grass & Clumps of
Trees as if formed artificially. The beauty of it struck us the more as it
reminded us of Europe. The River between us and the Mountain was
dry but its bed was so different from the green Banks that it
resembled a large River. We entered the Bed of the Torrent & almost
immediately found ourselves shut out from the plain by the
Mountains so high as to intercept the Beams of the Sun, the walking
was now very painful as we could not leave the Bed of the Torrent
which was composed of large round smooth stones about the size of a
Mellon, just large enough to tempt you to place your foot on the edge
& then rolling over upon you & breaking your Shews, in the Middle
was a beautifully clear moving stream filtering as it were among the
stones but tempting you to walk in it stepping from Stone to Stone &
invariable wetting your feet every 20 Yards. Here we saw the Fir Tree
& I gathered a Cone with the greatest delight, here also we saw the
Willow & the Fern. The Mountain is worn away by the passage of the
Mountain Torrent and formed a wall on each side generally
perpendicular always inaccessible so that should a sudden storm
arise I doubt whether we could get out of the way. It reminds me of

the Ravines in the West Indies, particularly Rabbacca River in St.
Vincents. I dismounted on entering the pass & preferred falling my
own height to the greater fall from my Horse, after proceeding at a
very slow pace about 4 Miles I came to Millers buggy abandoned in
the Road, but uninjured, he could not get it further. Nothing can be
greater than the change it reminds me of Mount Jura, but my feet tell
me that it is much more difficult My feet are so sore I can scarcely
crawl & what is worse there is not a level piece of ground in our
encampment, or any means of fixing our Tent Pins, should a Storm of
wind come we shall be all blown away. We are employed picking out
the softest stones & Harrington is employed boiling them hoping that
they will become softer like the Pilgrims peas. We are all in good
health, not one officer sick but all their feet are dreadfully sore which
we expect will be well with a Nights rest.

It is a fine Moonlight Night & the beautiful appearance of our place
of encampment exceeds all description, the lofty Mountains on each
side, with waving woods. The Men cooking with the fires spread
along the valley. The shewing of the Sentries Firelocks in the Moon
light is like but very far superior to a Scene I remember in Blue Beard.
I allowed my fancy to work until I expected Blue Beard to come out &
sing a Song. We are now about 3 Miles from the Top of the pass & the
Guides say the road becomes more difficult as we are to advance we
expect to march Tomorrow afternoon for we cannot go before
Colonel Mawby is said to be only Eleven Miles in advance & we shall
join him in one march, thank Lucy for her message thro Mrs Mawby.
I am afraid that dolls are not to be procured in the Dhoon I must
catch her a Monkey or buy her a young Ghorkalee or a Young
Dhoonee for here we find that Parents sell their Children as a
common trade. She should be thankful that she is born to a different
lot. I am much obliged to Mrs Mawby for her letter, but the Colonel
writes me word that he shall call me to account for corresponding
with his Wife in his absence. I saw Howarth completely knocked up
laying by the road side Yesterday, but it is entirely fatigue he was well
enough after dinner. The less you say about our movements the
better, this marching in the heat of the sun has lengthened Polloks
face a Yard. I do not think that he will ever smile again.[163]

During the campaign Henry wrote to Mary with vivid descriptions of their progress. When the Nalapani Fort, near Kalanga on the outskirts of modern Dehra Dun, was reached, Henry was critical at the lack of clear command. The defenders of the fort rushed out to attack, killing General Gillespie, the commanding officer. He had misjudged the situation and, angered by the losses incurred, had acted impetuously before the time he had set for his surrounding forces to attack the enemy. Henry records:

Another letter dated 3 Miles from Dehrah in the Dhoon 1st Novr 1814
Yesterday I wrote you a short & hurried note to prevent if possible exaggerated reports reaching you without your having any certain intelligence. The death of a General sometimes occasions the loss of an Army but in our case it seems the contrary, I mean not to take from General Gillespie what he really deserves vz the praise of Courage but he had risen too high in the Service. He was a good partisan but should never have had the command of an Army. His last words we must stand, we will never retreat, Death or Victory & as long as he had lived the Men would have remained to be killed I mean the Europeans. He was shot thro the heart & was dead in a moment. He had advanced with a small Gun, close up to the Stoccade of a Fort & stood like a Boy shooting peas against a high wall exposed to the Fire of the Enemy without the smallest possibility of hurting them in return we have many wounded men of the Regt but only 8 killed, but the wounded are severely hurt, we had only two Companies engaged & the Members as belonging to them will of course be much talked of & what is exterordinary they are almost all of your acquaintance, being the religious Men of the Regiment. Lieutenants Young & Anstree are severely wounded & dear as the experience is bought we hope it may be eventually of service in restrain such foolish self confidence as our English Generals have when attacking the Natives whom they have foolishly been taught to consider as wanting in every energy, but I will begin from our termination of my last letter, which was written from Toombarrah in the Kenie Pass. We lay there to recruit our Men until 12 o clock on the next day indeed it was necessary for many stragglers & particularly the sick did not arrive much before it was notified that we should march the same Evening,

the Instant this was known notwithstanding orders to the contrary all the baggage was in motion every one anxious to get his Tent over the Pass before it should be choked up by the Column & altho I was inclined to attend to orders I found myself insensibly drawn to leave my Tent to be struck & tacitly to authorize the removal of it when the Tent was once removed the next thought was to advance myself intending to go slowly, for why might I not sit down by the road side as well as run about the bed of the River where I was, & I therefore set off. I had not proceeded far on foot & looking into every bush for plants before I was overtaken by Colonel Buckland & Lieutt Emery (now acting Quarter Master) They were on horseback & as the Stones were rather hard to my feet I mounted & joined them, Bucklands Horse being larger than mine contrived by taking longer steps to get over the Ground quicker than mine & would have left me behind had I not trotted after every practicable part of the pass like a dog running after his Master this kept my mind fully occupied in watching my opportunities as we advanced the Ravine grew narrower & the number of camels being gradually confined in a narrower space that we were obliged to dismount, & now we had a scene of the most delightful confusion. I was soon separated from my Companions & holding my horse by the bridle I crept under one camel & over another for some were fallen in the Road & literally stopped up the passage which was not 9 Feet wide with a wall like hill on each side & the ascent itself as steep as the Ridge of a House, such swearing & beating of Camels & hallowing & Echo's it was enough to stun me. I could only compare it to the Kings going to the Theater, supposing Camels & Horses were to be the Auditors, this part of the Road was about 100 Yards & after having surmounted it & being joined by Buckland & Emery we stood on the Top professedly to give advice & no doubt added to the noise by our own Shouting. The Apex of the Hill was not 5 feet wide & I could not help laughing at the Colonel who was drowned in perspiration as white as a sheet dragged up by Emery. One Native Camel chose to fall in the narrow passage & nothing could make him rise, we were under the necessity of turning him on his back & putting a rope round him, to drag him backwards partly by his Tail till we had cleared the Road as it grew dark I outwalked my Companions & getting down the Hill which was not so

steep, I seated myself under a Tree & got a fire lighted prepared some
dinner, when Buckland & Emery came they were delighted at finding
me so comfortable & we drank a bottle of wine in expectation of the
Moon rising, which it delayed much in doing which gave me occasion
to sing "Rise Guthrie Rise" in my best stile which did not a little anoy
the Colonel as he felt the Cold & would much rather have been in
Ibbotsons Hotel, indeed I would almost have agreed with him we
thought it not prudent to advance further we therefore covered
ourselves with our great Coats & lay under a Tree. The distance which
I had marched could not get the Quicksilver out of my feet so that I
was up & down every moment, at length about Ten o clock the
Regiment arrived & we proceeded, it became very cold & a most
heavy dew fell. It was twelve o clock before we reached Deyrah where
Colonel Mawby had been encamped but on coming to the Ground
we could see by the light of the Moon, the round marker made on the
Ground by the Tents now removed but no sign whatever of Man or
beast, we were of course astonished, but I quietly lay Myself down to
sleep while others rode about in search of our Army.

The Camp is as found about 3 Miles off, but it was three o clock
before we reached it, we found the Camp opposite & apparently three
or 4 Miles from a Fort called Kalunga [Kalanga] situated on the Top
of a Mountain no body appeared until day light & as it became light
we anxiously looked out for the fort which appeared in front of us, it
had no appearance of size or strength but stood on the highest part of
a Ridge [sketch] which had no very imposing appearance for it was
only the foreground to a very high range called the Second Range &
which from our Station seemed to join to it. We heard that the forces
under Colonel Mawby had attacked on the 24th but found its Natural
defences so strong that he was obliged to desist after losing & one or
two Men, after this he had drawn up his 2 sixpound Gallopers half
way up the Ridge & formed a small Battery. Now we find this Battery
occupied by some Men of the 8th Dragoons & the Two Companies of
ours which left us at Seharanpore. Soon after day light Three other
Companies of ours were ordered to the Battery, but the provisions
had not arrived & some instructions were waiting they paraded in
front of our Camp & did not march immediately I was with them
with my Glass in my 242 hand, when suddenly I observed a large fire

near the Fort & heard a heavy firing, on looking thro my Glass I
observed numbers of Men jumping over the walls of the Fort. It
immediately struck me that some fire had broken out within the Fort
& that the Garrison were making their escape from a fear of being
blown up, but I soon perceived that whatever might be the reason of
their leaving the Fort it was soon over for they returned to it again & I
perceived that a very heavy fire was kept up from the Fort, altho I
could not see what it was directed against. We all agreed that it could
not be an attempt at Storm for no Person was seen advancing towards
the Wall, indeed there did not seem any break, or apparent way in &
the firing continued very long, but what grieved us was that we found
that our 3 Companies were expected up the Hill for some duty even
before they had marched from our ground. The firing of small Arms
at length ceased, but a great Gun from one of the Angles of the Fort
occasionally fired being pointed outward, a plain proof that whatever
had caused the firing, the Enemy had still possession of the Fort.
After cessation of all firing for about half an hour it again commenced
& we now plainly saw the Enemy coming out of the fort & defending
themselves in great numbers behind a Stockade, here the firing was
very brisk, but the smoke became dense, I forget to mention that
about the time that the first firing had finished two other Companies
of ours had marched, & as the first two which marched this Morning
must have been too late for the first firing, so the two last must have
been too late for the present. While we were in anxiety about these
two firings an Officer of the Native Cavalry came galloping down &
said General Gillespie is killed "& the attack has failed" soon after this
we saw the wounded carried into Camp both the Officers of our first
Companies vz Lieutenants Young & Anstie were brought in wounded
& many Men, we soon learned that three Serjeants and 8 Men were
killed & that the 8th Dragoons had lost more, these attacks are
described as having been conducted in a most rash manner &
unworthy of a General. Just a few Dragoons were sent (a most unfit
body for a Storm, they were followed but not near enough to support
the Two Companies 53rd Regt. The Dragoons were unencumbered
by knapsacks or firelocks & soon outran the Infantry, they were eager
to enter on Action, but having only Sabres were altogether unfit for
such an Attack they were fired on as they stood (as I may say)

unarmed, but the Enemy gaining courage jumped over the wall & rushed down on them with Sword & Shield but they soon found that they had made a mistake for they were not equal to the Dragoons hand to hand & were glad to excape back again into their fort from which they could fire down while themselves were entirely covered. When the Two Companies 53rd Regt advanced they could find no means of getting into the fort which had no breach or opening & they had no ladders. The Seapoys refused to advance so that several of their Officers left them & joined the European Troops & several were Killed. The first attack was no sooner abandoned than the Second Two Companies of the 53rd Reached the Top of the Hill & they were sent, had there been only one attack with the 4 Companies in all probability it would have succeeded. Contradictory orders had been given & the Signal for Attack having been most clearly pointed out in general orders, was so completely unattended to by the General himself that he headed an attack at least two hours before he had appointed & what was more extraordinary his own orders of the day before clearly pointed out what would be the result of such disobedience of orders. The 7th Native Infantry had received instructions to advance on a certain signal & the Officers of that Corps had their watches in their hands waiting for the time & dare not advance for fear of disobeying positive orders & at length one division under Captain Campbell who thinking he might be mistaken advanced & was the Means of saving the Gun which the General unGenerallike had been serving with his own hands. The General was in the act of abusing & calling the Seapoys "Cowards": when he was struck by a ball in the heart & never moved after. He repeatedly said that he would never return & when he was struck he had few except Officers near him & was within a few paces of the wall. Major Ludlow the Senior Officer ordered a retreat after the loss of nearly 500 Men Killed or wounded the 53rd Regt lost 107 of these, Officer killed, General Gillespie, Lieutts Ellis, Fothergill, Goselin, O Harah, Broughton. The Wounded are in great numbers & many with little hope of recovery. The events of today have thrown a damp on all, but it is the general opinion here that Gillespie's death has saved the Army.[164]

Left without protection in Meerut, there was high anxiety among the women for their own and their children's security which was threatened by warring local tribes. The Begum came to the rescue by sending guards for each family although Mary did not feel great confidence in their ability to repulse an attack. The insecurity of the women left behind was illustrated when one night there was a terrifying disturbance: it was said that a band of armed thieves had entered the cantonment. Mary gathered her children together and prepared for the worst. Terrified, they could hear shots being fired, shouting and men running around. However, by morning all was quiet. The ladies of the cantonment decided that the Begum's guards had set the whole thing up to 'increase their own importance.' After this unsettling event the Begum sent some sepoys to guard the compound.

Henry writes to reassure Mary in his letter, dated November 5, 1814:

I suppose you know the itch of lying to be so great among us that you will not be frightened by reports.[165]

This did not allay Mary's anxiety. Henry writes on November 18:

I heard of you from the Colonel yesterday, and I find that you are still alarmed by reports...

I sent yesterday three bottles of honey, and I think you had better open them all and see if they are fermented; and if you find it good and useful, I can send you more.[166]

Capturing the fort was proving difficult. Reinforcements arrived on November 25 in the form of a battering train to attempt to break the stockades surrounding the fort. An eighteen pound gun was dragged up the hill but once more the Gurkhas repulsed an attack. Henry received orders to move up and join the army with his treasure (money). The next day a fresh attack was made on the fort and, as Henry lay in his tent, he heard drums and shouts. The Gurkhas had made a rush to abandon the fort at two o'clock in the morning but were driven back. A second desperate attempt to escape was made. This time it resulted in the fort being taken. The hillside was covered in dead and dying Gurkhas. The scene Henry describes in his diary is one of carnage. The wounded begged for water as they lay dying. Henry sent his family a chukoor (hill partridge) which had been abandoned when the regiment took the fort after fierce fighting and heavy losses. It arrived in its enclosed wicker basket and became a family pet. They christened it 'our prisoner of war.' Mary incorporated the chukoor in *Juliana Oakeley*, first published in 1823 in *The Youth's Magazine*.

In December the regiment marched to camp 14 miles from Dehra from where he writes to Mary on December 9 with news of his illness:

> ... My dearest love, a letter from you though ever so small, is the greatest of pleasures. I used to think when we were first married that when a few years had passed we should not be so uneasy at every little separation but I find quite the contrary. I feel quite a solitary being. You have the sweet babes. I hope this business will not last long. I am interrupted by officers coming into my tent. They are all well. Kiss the children for me.
>
> We marched at seven o'clock on the 10th through fine level country to Sainsipore. Afterwards we gradually got on higher ground advancing towards Timli, and encamped on the ascent of the first range in a grass jungle. I find myself very unwell and cold, and being often obliged to go out among the wet grass during the night, and in the morning I felt seriously ill. On the morning of the 11th I could scarcely sit on my horse, and I could not walk, I was so weak. [167]

Henry continued to suffer from illness during the march to Nahan which was reached on December 20. From there Henry again wrote to his wife describing how the Gurkhas had deserted the town and retreated into Jeytuk Fort, situated at eighteen hundred metres and about four miles from Nahan. The ruler, Ranjor Singh, was alarmed having heard the fate at Kalanga. Henry deemed the mission to capture the fort as 'one of the most ill-judged, illconducted enterprises ever heard of.' He was of the opinion that the fort would fall because of a shortage of water, not through guns and mortar fire. The lack of a suitable road made transportation of heavy armaments dangerous and difficult. On the 27th the attack began. It was repulsed. 6,000 rounds of ammunition were lost when the coolies deserted and ran off. A further attack ended in retreat with heavy losses. Several men were taken prisoner by the Gurkhas but later released except for a drummer boy.

Battle Scene during the Anglo-Nepalese War
(Gurkha War) 1814–1816

For Mary it was an increasingly anxious time. Her pregnancy was nearing its end, she would give birth in February; and now she had news of her husband's ill health. Mary wrote to her mother on December 27, 1814.

My Dearest Mother,

I fear you will begin to think that it is very long since I have written to you; but you, no doubt, have heard of us through my dear cousin Butt, at Trentham, to whom I have addressed two letters lately. You will have heard that Henry is not with me, but with our regiment, and other considerable force, attacking the country of the Ghoorkas, which lies in the valleys among the mountains which divide Hindostan from Thibet, and extend from the Caspian Sea to China. The regiment has been absent almost two months, nor can we guess when it is likely to return. Dear Henry, from whom I often hear, is well, and I hope doing good wherever he goes. His tent is a place of worship to all devoutly disposed…As to myself, I am at Meerut, and have much upon my hands, having three dear babes of my own, the two orphans, and Henry's nurse's child in the house, besides the care of two infants, whose nurses I have to overlook. I have also an English and an Hindostanee school to see to, the latter daily, besides giving attention to the Hindostanee service, which, without care, would have dropped through on Mr Sherwood's going to the camp; but … it has suddenly revived, and become more flourishing than ever. …

I am in expectation of an addition to my little family in the beginning of February; I am afraid before I see dear Henry … You can form no idea, my beloved mother, of the spirit which is required in the management of a family in India, particularly when the master is not at home, or rather gone out in dangerous warfare. The natives have no respect for females. Four or five men walk into your parlour, and quarrel altogether before your face, using the lowest and most abusive language, and trying in the night to frighten you with cries of alarm of thieves and fire …

The hooping [sic] cough is so prevalent just round us that I have resolved to move, and go into a small house which Mr Parson, our chaplain, possesses within the walls of his grounds, where I hope to remain quiet, so please God, till Mr Sherwood's return, of which I have as yet no distinct hope.[168]

Mrs Mawby, the Colonel's wife, was extremely kind to Mary during Henry's absence. She understood only too clearly the problems facing wives when their husbands were absent on active duty.

When Henry applied to Colonel Mawby for leave because of ill health it was granted. In a letter to his wife, Mawby writes:

Mr Buxi [from 'bakhshi' a military paymaster] came up the hill this morning at breakfast time, and I asked him what he wished for. He said, "I wish for many things." "Well! what are they?" "Why, Sir, I wish I was off this hill." "And what more, Mr Buxi?" "I wish, Sir, I could be allowed to go to Meerut to Mrs Sherwood, after mustering and paying the regiment on the 4th." I left him of course, in suspense, but on going away he said, "Well, Sir, may I write to the Collector to lay bearers for me to Meerut?" so that, I suppose, he will be with his family about the end of this month.[169]

Henry returned from Jeytuk to Meerut on January 3, 1815 having covered the last 74 miles in 24 hours. He arrived in the early morning as dawn was climbing over the horizon. He was as 'dark as a mulatto, and he with the rest of the officers had let their hair and moustaches grow, to protect them from the cold winds of the mountains.'[170] Sophia, their fifth daughter and seventh child, was born on February 20. It was predicted that she would not survive, however, she was in fact a healthy baby. Mary later admitted that she had wanted another son as a companion for Henry who by then was eighteen months old. His father remained in Meerut until April 19 when he returned to the regiment which had continued to fight at Jeytuk.

On Easter Sunday, 1815, Mary paid the old Begum a second visit when the Begum and her retinue were encamped on the plain near the Sherwoods' house. This time she took Mary Parson, Sally Pownall, Lucy and Emily. Once again the Begum was wrapped in cashmere shawls with only her face showing. Female slaves stood around the walls of the tent in dirty white cotton saris. The Begum greeted the children who all responded except Emily. The Begum threatened to have the child's tongue cut out and fed to the crows. Emily flared up at this and stamping her foot called her a naughty wicked bebee, (a lady and title of distinction to Muslim women.) Much to Mary's relief the Begum was amused at the temerity of Emily who was almost four years old.

The Gurkha campaign ended in May. Henry got private leave and travelled back to Meerut by palanquin arriving on May 27. The regiment then spent a short time in Nahan before receiving orders to march on June 5 back to Meerut, arriving on June 20, en route for Calcutta where they would remain until December before embarking for Madras. For the past year it had been in the Sherwoods' minds to leave India and return to England with their young family:

> Mr Sherwood was beginning to be tired of India, … the children were coming to an age in which they required to go to a cooler climate; we had a child in England, and I had a tender mother who was growing infirm … Yet I had a dread of leaving India; I had long loved the country.[171]

Henry, having paid the regiment, left Meerut on June 21 with his family at three in the morning for Ghurmucklezer Ghaut, from which the regiment would embark on the Ganges for Calcutta.[172]

> The day had been uncommonly over clouded for the season with occasional Showers & it seemed so dark that we ventured forth at three o clock in the following order, Bullock Carriage, Mrs Clarke, Lucy & Emily, Mr Darby's palenkeen Carriage Mary & Sally, Palenkeen Mrs S. Sophia, Palenkeen Dhye & Henry, Rhut, Ayah & Dhye's Child & lastly H S. P M & ASS on Horseback, behind were 17 Coolies Carrying provisions & Cloaths our procession advanced for about 2 Miles as far as Gwatken Lodge where the Rain began to pour not a Storm but a dead Solemn Calm. The whole Horizon being dark heavy Cloud & soon the whole plain was one continued sheet of Water. The bearers & Cattle, sliding at every step, for the Earth about Meerut being a Soapy nature, under these circumstances & knowing that the kali Nuddy lay in our Rout we judged it right to return which we accomplished with some difficulty to Mr Parson's slipping & Sliding all the way, myself wet thro & thro. It rained a good deal

during the Night but about one o clock it stopped. The wind began to blow away the Clouds which passed Rapidly before the full Moon. I arose & collecting the Family moved off. The Roads were wet & slippery & we advanced with difficulty. The day broke before we reached Mow & I was glad it did for a little further on the water was between 3 & 4 feet deep. I was now very glad that we had returned last night & almost afraid that the Cattle would be knocked up. We however all got safe & Breakfast Ready in less than an hour the rain again fell in Torrents & we congratulated ourselves on being snug. Fish actually fell from the Clouds, as we saw.[173]

The family eventually arrived at the river on June 23 where they dried out and were given breakfast by the quartermaster. The following day the regiment arrived, soaked to the skin, complaining that they had not been dry since the 20th. The Sherwoods, with the regiment, then moved to Cawnpore where, on July 15, Henry received a year's furlough to visit England but not permission to leave the regiment. The Sherwoods sailed down the Ganges with the fleet. For part of the journey Henry rode beside the river on horseback. Sophia, then only five months old, fell seriously ill just before Berhampore. Her life was saved by the care she received from Jevan, an Indian bearer.

∾

The Sherwoods left the fleet on September 24 to make preparations for their passage to England. Henry records:

I mustered the Regt (as I suppose for the last time) & on the 25th I took my departure with some feelings of regret (for I had never left any Corps before for any length of time for 17 years & a half.

They arrived at Chowringee, a suburb of Calcutta, where they were met by carriages sent by Mr Sherer, who was now married to their old friend, Mary Corrie. Sherer held an important government position as the East India Company's accountant-general. The Sherers lived in some style in a European enclave for the Sahibs. There the Sherwoods were reunited with Annie, who was now living with the Sherers but who was already suffering from the disease which would kill her. They met Mary Sherer's two young daughters, Mary Anne and Lucy, a baby of less than two months. Sadly she would die in infancy. The Sherwoods had their own four children with them, and their adopted daughters, Mary Parson and Sally Pownal, who would travel to England with them. Their fathers had said their final farewells to their daughters in the hope that they would lead a better life in England.

Life was pleasant, but busy for Mary. The Reverend and Mrs Thomason visited the Sherwoods most days. Socially, Mary was in great demand from newly arrived members of the church. *Little Henry and his Bearer*[174] had been published in England in 1814 causing a sensation. Published anonymously, the general opinion was that it had been written by a man. A newly arrived wife of a Baptist missionary had brought a copy out to India. It was being circulated among those in the missionary and religious circles in Calcutta. Mary was delighted when, having been lent the copy, she saw it in 'its new and elegant dress.' But now that the identity of the author had been established as Mrs Sherwood, she was in great demand:

> I began to pay the penalty for my greatness by finding myself sought after and being obliged to endure much talking to. Let it not be supposed for one instant that people seek a lion in order to have the pleasure of hearing the lion roar, or of contemplating his fine countenance and beautiful skin. No, a regular lion-hunter seeks his object that he may prove to the animal that he can roar as well as he does...[175]

Mary's philanthropy towards children who had lost their mothers, been abandoned by both parents or been cruelly neglected is recorded in her detailed diaries. Her work at Dinapore, Berhampore, Cawnpore and Meerut was brought to the notice of the then Governor General, Lord Moira[176] when in December 1814 he had visited Meerut in the company of the Reverend and Mrs Thomason and had the opportunity to witness Mary and Henry's work. Mrs Thomason was then very involved in the day-to-day running of the orphanage. Most importantly, she had valuable connections in Calcutta and knew Lady Loudon, the wife of the Governor General.

Annie's plight and rescue by Mary was well known in religious circles in Calcutta. Lady Loudon got to hear of the story. Annie was physical proof that a wickedly ill-treated, motherless European white child could, through loving nurture and given an education based on Christian principles, become part of European society in India – though some did have reservations about children from such lowly backgrounds mixing in high social circles. For them birth was all-important not loving nurture.

Before she left India, Mary received great pleasure from a visit to the European Female Orphan Asylum, of which she had been pivotal in the conception. This had been opened in 1815.[177] Although Mary paid tribute to Lady Loudon, Daniel Corrie, Henry Martyn and the Thomasons, much of the credit for its establishment lay in her own pioneering work in Upper Bengal where she had taken care of orphans and in her recognition that little provision had then been made for white European girls. Two orphanages already existed near Calcutta but one was mixed and the other was for orphans from low-ranking soldiers. Most of the children were the offspring of native women and white men. The government permitted men in barracks to take a native woman as a 'temporary wife' or 'bibi' while they were serving in India. Mary felt that there should be a separate orphanage for white girls born to European mothers who had died either through childbirth or from one of the many diseases which scythed down so many. Motherless European girls were open to abuse in barracks as borne out in the treatment of both Annie and Mary: one being fed gin and the other severely malnourished.

On her visit to the orphanage Mary was impressed by the progress that had been made:

> The house first appointed for the Orphan Assylum, at Calcutta, was in the Circular Road. This situation was more airy and open than most others in the neighbourhood, and there were shrubs and grass, and a few palm trees, within the domain. The rooms of the house were arranged, as they most commonly were in Indian houses, one large hall in the centre, and the other apartments round it. Each little girl had a cot to herself, with green gauze musquitto curtains, a good wardrobe, either of white cotton or muslin, and a complete suit allowed every day. Already had the hours of study, meals, recreation, and rest been arranged by Mrs Thomason; and a most respectable governess, an English lady, had been appointed. But probably without the powerful sanction of Lady Loudon, this Christian work would never have been brought to bear; and the reason for this conjecture is plain, because the first declared principle whereon this asylum was to be formed, was that it should receive only white orphans … There were about eleven little girls in the white Orphan Asylum when we visited it.; amongst these were two of the 53rd, Mary and the infant Elizabeth, a nice little smiling, unconscious baby. Mrs Thomason kindly showed us all her arrangements, and explained all her plans. The children

were to receive a thoroughly good English education—writing, needlework, and accounts. They were never to have any intercourse with native servants, even to speak to them. Cleanliness and order were to prevail everywhere, and Scripture instruction to take the lead of all others.[178]

The visit moved Mary to tears. She continued to stay in touch with orphans in India once she had returned to England and raised money for their welfare.[179] However, in Calcutta feelings had run high on the opening of the orphanage which had prescriptively prevented girls of mixed race being admitted.[180] Thomason had seen his effigy burnt in public and had received letters purportedly from an orphan of mixed race pointing out the injustice meted out to girls from the same background.

~

Six of the Sherwoods' children had been born in India. Two were buried there; her first son, Henry, in the cantonment at Berhampore, and Lucy Martha in the cantonment at Cawnpore. The Sherwood's surviving children were loathe to leave India. The older ones spoke little English: Hindustani was their language. All had been looked after by ayahs, who sang and talked to them in their native language. Leaving India, their home since birth, meant they were leaving a familiar and loved environment behind them, to travel to England, an alien land, known to them only through their parents, books and the European friends in India. The children would also meet their eldest sister, Mary Henrietta, for the first time. Their parents had not seen their eldest daughter for eleven years. While in Calcutta Lucy's former daye, Piaree, came to see her. She was now working for Lady Loudon's niece. Lucy never forgot her nurse and sent regular gifts to her until her own death. Mary recognised the debt that European mothers owed to these devoted and loving Indian servants. In 1823 she published *Little Lucy and her Dhaye*.[181] Much of it was based on her experiences of dayes in India and their relationship with their European charges.

Part Four

England Once More

Homeward Bound

On October 25, 1815 Henry booked the family's passage on board the 750 ton *Robarts* for 6,000 rupees (then about £750). The ship had been built in Bengal and this was her maiden voyage. Mary busied herself with the packing arrangements for seven children and two adults. As laundry facilities were non-existent during the voyage enough clean linen and clothes needed to be packed but packed separately in order that dirty linen could be replaced by clean at regular intervals. This was no easy task for a voyage which would last several months. According to Darton, though it appears unlikely, Mary set up a system that gave each child one change of clothes per day and linen for a week. She did include a double allowance for the two youngest children, Henry and Sophia. Then each collection of bundles was sewn up into a separate bundle and put into six camel trunks. The trunks could then be brought up in turn from the hold. Thus prepared they sailed down river from Calcutta on January 2, travelling with only one servant, a six foot tall injured soldier, by the name of Robinson. They had said goodbye to Babouk, their kitmutgar, who had been with them since 1806. He took 'an old goat which had been with us in all our travels.' The Sherwood family joined the *Robarts* downstream and set sail for England on January 11. 'The children cried bitterly when they saw the shores receding, and truly we were all very sad.' The voyage would last twenty weeks.

The cabin they were allotted was small, measuring ten by eight feet, and, although cramped, was much more comfortable than the one the Sherwoods had had on the outward voyage. But now there were seven somewhat bewildered children travelling with them. It was fitted up like a pigeon house with two tiers of holes for sleeping in. Mary and Sophia slept in a standing cot; Captain Sherwood had a cot swung across the door on the outside;[182] Lucy, Emily and Henry had pigeon-holes; Mary

Parson and Sally Pownall had beds made up on two flat trunks, and Mary Howarth, another orphan who was travelling with them, had a fourth pigeon-hole. Henry was no sooner in his pigeon-hole than he would call out to Sally in Hindustani to come to him. There she would cuddle him and soothe him to sleep with lullabies. Robinson proved to be an excellent nurse to Sophia and also kept an eye on the older children. The children ate their meals in the cuddy. Mary preferred to eat in the cabin but soon was struck by her old enemy – seasickness. This she cured by drinking a goblet of claret.

Temperatures were in the mid eighties Fahrenheit which made sleeping in the hot and stuffy cabin uncomfortable. During the day the hatch over the cabin was kept open. In February the heat at night became intolerable for the children. Mary sat up fanning Sophia. One victim of the heat was the cow the Sherwoods had brought on board to provide fresh milk for the children. It died from heatstroke barely a month after they left. The children continued with their lessons under the guidance of Mary or Sally. Every evening Captain Sherwood would read the Bible aloud, followed by prayers and then hymns.

This voyage, although there was the welcome absence of French warships, was not without incidents. The ship lost its main top-gallant mast on March 7 and four days later had almost run ashore at Cape Aguilas at the tip of Africa where the Indian Ocean and the Atlantic meet. Reaching the Cape of Good Hope on March 13, Mary took the children ashore, including Sophia, who had been unwell, and it was here that Sophia learnt to walk. Mary comments on the Africans – hottentots – who had been slaves under the Dutch but were now servants under British rule. She was anxious to return to the ship because by eleven each morning clouds would roll in covering Table Mountain presaging high winds.

After the Cape the ship was heading for colder climes with rainy weather which made life on board depressing for the passengers:

> What in a small way, can be more annoying than being on board ship in rainy weather? A washhouse is nothing to it. Slop, slop, drip, drip – one is thankful if one can find a dry corner of the nautical cage to perch on, with one's feet off the ground, and fixed on a box or a bed or a ledge of a chair. Everybody looks dirty and forlorn, and then comes the drying afterwards, and the process of rubbing the decks with the holystone before one is up.[183]

On May 26 there was an eclipse of the sun and that evening as Henry began prayers a violent storm swept in creating a heavy swell. The terrified family huddled below. Suddenly a huge wave crashed over the deck and poured down the hatchway flooding their cabin. The children were hastily hoisted into their beds to relative safety from where they watched loose items in the cabin bobbing about in the water, with the ship's creaking and groaning adding to the family's fear of drowning. The next day by three o'clock in the afternoon the weather was abating leaving in its wake exhausted and frightened passengers who had prepared to meet King Neptune in the deep and turbulent ocean.

~

The voyage was nearing its end when, on May 30, a foggy morning, the ship entered Caernarvon Bay. A pilot boat brought fresh bread, meat, potatoes and butter to the ship. The Sherwoods roasted their share of the potatoes in their cabin, much to the delight of the children. The following day the *Robarts* anchored in Hoyle Lake outside the port of Liverpool which had just been opened to East Indiamen. The journey of some 1500 miles from Meerut by river and 11,500 by sea was at an end. Henry gives this account in his diary:

31st May

Now all was confusion and bustle on board, I hired a boat to take us on shore in the morning. We could get no sleep during the night the noise was so great, and when I arose in the morning not a white face was to be seen. The Lascars even were all drunk. I was of course anxious to get on shore, but the Boat which I had hired last night to carry me on Shore was gone, I asked the Tindal what was become of it, but found him drunk & told him so. This man repeated to the officer what I had said a plain proof that he & the officer understood each other for such a thing is never done in India. The fact turned out that all the officers had been smuggling, & of course in the power of the Sailors. Some time after this a letter came on board, but there was not an officer sober enough to read it, and I was obliged to speak sharply before one could be brought up, but as they were aware of their own bad conduct, I had no incivility shewn, all that appeared was an anxious whish [sic] to get rid of me, but now a more curious fact appeared which was that the Pilot was absent. The officer was quite drunk, the Custom House Waiters[184] were so too, and after a short time I was let into a Secret, for my boat returned with the Steward on board, and I found they had been smuggling all night & either trusted to my not rising so early, or else they themselves were detained. I was glad to get away for from the Chief mate to the lowest Laskar there was not one Sober, the Custom House Waiters as bad as any. & they were very insubordinate for before we left we had two or three Battles between the Chief mate and the private Sailors! we got off as soon as we could & reached Liverpool by 12 & soon our Baggage got quietly to the Inn and we had a good fresh Dinner. The children being delighted with the Fresh vegetables.[185]

It is Mary who describes their party's landing in Liverpool on Saturday June 1, 1816:

> The bells were set to ring, and we the largest and most remarkable party from the ship, were followed wherever we appeared by thousands. We were remarkable for the number of children with us, for their exceeding transparent fairness, and also for their dresses. There was not a bonnet among the party. We all wore caps trimmed with lace, white dresses and Indian shawls. When we landed at the quay there were thousands of spectators, waving welcome and looking kindly at the fair babes.[186]

Each passenger was permitted to bring in free of duty, an Indian shawl, then highly fashionable, so each of the girls wore one. For the children it was an overwhelming and rather intimidating introduction to England. Still followed by the crowd, they walked up to the Talbot Inn with Robinson, their servant, accompanying them. Captain Henry Sherwood had gone to the Custom House with all their baggage. He despatched heavy items to Worcester by water. At breakfast their children were excited to see fresh English food causing their son, Henry, to shout in Hindustani, 'rooty, muchun, cheenee' (bread, butter, sugar). Emily had never seen a white female servant and asked Mary if the chambermaid who showed them their bedrooms was a woman. The children were amazed by the feather beds and the wallpaper. It being Sunday, Mary took three of her girls, all still bonnetless, to a nearby church where they caused a stir with their unusual attire. The rest of the family joined them for a walk in the town and once again they were followed by crowds. The Sherwoods were now contemplating, with some anxiety, a far less affluent lifestyle.

> My mind was made up not to persuade him to return to India, and therefore I had nothing before me but the reduction to a very small income. My dear mother was still living, and I had only as yet an annual income of £50 a year, which had hitherto been spent on Henrietta, who was at this time at school at Gloucester. I had therefore nothing to look forward to but a retired and humble life, for which my own habits for the last eleven years and all the habits of my little ones had ill prepared us. I had never even combed my own hair during that time; my first attempt of the kind was on the ship. Certainly a few months' residence on board ship is a fine set-down to one too much accustomed to high habits.[187]

Although Henry had resigned as paymaster he had not resigned his commission. If he decided to return to India then either he would go alone leaving behind Mary and his family, or they would both go but leave the children in England. Clearly they would need to find a way of supplementing their income.

The following day they set off for Trentham Parsonage, near Stoke on Trent, where Mary's cousin, the Reverend Thomas Butt, lived. Their plan was to go from there to Snedshill and stay with her sister, Lucy Cameron, and her family for a few days before continuing on to Worcester where her mother lived and where they would be reunited with their eldest daughter, Mary Henrietta. Beyond that they had no fixed plans. Mary was consumed by regrets that her husband had left a highly paid position in the army but still could not bear the thought of his leaving her and the family, so she refrained from advising him that returning to India would be the best option to avoid straitened circumstances. Having said their goodbyes to the kindly Robinson, who had taken such good care of Sophia on the voyage, the family set off in two post chaises for the first leg of their journey. Henry travelled with Henry, Sally and Mary Howarth while Mary had Sophia, Lucy, Emily and Mary Parson travelling with her.

That evening they arrived at Trentham where they were welcomed warmly. The welcome contrasted with the temperature which was chilly for them especially as the children were still dressed in muslin clothes. After a week's stay they set off again this time for Newport, Shropshire, where Charles Cameron would meet them and accompany them back to Snedshill. While waiting for her brother-in-law Mary was approached by a man who, much to her surprise, greeted her as the author of *Little Henry and his Bearer*. It was Mr Houlston, the publisher from Wellington a nearby town, to whom Lucy had sold the manuscript for five pounds.[188] Houlston would become one of the main publishers of her work.

Like her more famous sister, Lucy had continued to write tracts and stories with a strong didactic message for children although her pen was not as prolific as Mary's so her financial rewards were not so great, nor did she achieve such widespread popularity. It was Lucy who had in 1805 shared with Mrs Butt the role of guardian for Mary's eldest daughter, Mary Henrietta, when the Sherwoods left England. By the time they returned Lucy was a married woman and Mary Henrietta was twelve. Lucy had married the Reverend Charles Cameron, on June 12, 1806. Charles was the eldest son of Dr. Cameron and his wife, Anne, who lived at the White Ladies Aston, near Worcester where Mary's son, Henry would much later become vicar. Soon after their marriage Charles accepted the living of Donnington Wood, close to Telford, in Shropshire. The church was built 'for the benefit of the colliers and miners in that part of the Marquis of Stafford's estate...' The Camerons settled at Snedshill, two miles from Donnington Wood, to 'begin our missionary work, among the dark-faced, but warm-hearted and affectionate colliers.'[189] Lucy was soon made aware of the dangers faced by miners when she had to accustom herself to the distress at their deaths from fire-damp in the pits. Accidents were frequent. On one occasion, as several miners were being pulled up in the lift out of the mine, the rope broke. All the miners were killed. But when the bodies were brought to the surface one was missing. The pit was searched for several days yet the missing body was not found. It was the body of a cock-fighter who had confessed that he had sold himself, body and soul, to the devil. The body was never found.

For Lucy it had not been an easy start to married life: '... I had many difficulties in my house and my family, for I was young and inexperienced...'[190] The Camerons would remain at Snedshill for thirty years and it was there that all her twelve children were born. After the birth of her first son, Charles, in 1807 she had written:

> I used to think of myself clever in education, but now I find I know nothing about it, and what need I have to pray fervently for direction respecting the management of my little boy. I shall correct him with a rod when he is naughty, and have him with me as much as I can. I cannot agree with the modern notions, so opposed, in my opinion, to the Word of God, nor can I forget the sad end of Eli's sons,—had he whipped them when boys, they might have proved a blessing instead of a curse...[191]

Lucy was convinced before each child's birth that she would die; a not surprising anxiety when so many women did indeed die in childbirth. After the birth of each child she was not happy until the baby had been baptised. She was fortunate in that only Archibald, who was born in 1814, died when a baby of only five weeks old.

> It was on 3rd September, 1814, that death first crossed our threshold, and took away my beloved little baby, Archibald, whom God lent to me five weeks—it was on a Saturday night. I did not hear of the event till Sunday, for being worn down with fatigue, after kissing him on my knees and involuntary saying to myself, "Farewell, sweet baby." When our servant came into the room in the morning, I begged Mr Cameron to ask after the babe, for I dared not. I remember well her answer, "He is better, sir—he is happy." Mr Cameron came up to me, and asked if I had heard the reply. "Yes," I said. "Did you understand it?" "Yes; I expected it." I remember weeping, for my heart was very sad, but I felt such calmness of spirit as I cannot describe ... When I was up, and had breakfasted, I begged to see the baby. He lay in his little basket where he used to sleep—his poor little body was shrunk almost to a skeleton. I burst into tears when I looked at him, but thought how much sweeter a sight that was than to see him grow up to a wicked life.[192]

～

Snedshill being in a mining area, blackness pervaded everything. For Mary's children it was a dark and alien landscape. Lucy had by then six surviving children: Charles, Lucy, Mary Anne, Eliza, Ewen and Emma. However, the cousins were from such different backgrounds that they did not find it easy to play together. Mary's children were very polite and found the rough and tumble in Lucy's home unsettling. Henry spoke little English and Mary's other children were more fluent in Hindustani than English, as were the two orphans, Mary and Sally. Cultural readjustments were having to be made. Lucy was surprised when in the evening she went up to the children's room and found them all sitting in a circle on the floor while Mary and Sally sang lullabies: not English lullabies but Indian ones where the references were to the land they had loved so much. With Lucy's help Mary and the children were fitted out in warmer clothes more suitable for the English climate. Bonnets replaced their white caps. After a week at Snedshill the family set off for Worcester where the reunion which Mary longed for, yet was apprehensive about, would take place.

Mrs Butt, who had been expecting the family, had become over-agitated and had decided to postpone seeing her daughter and family until the following day. She had sent her companion, Miss Yate, to greet them on their arrival. However, one reunion could not be delayed. Mary found her daughter, Mary Henrietta waiting in the parlour.

> I cannot describe the effect of seeing her again. The intense interest, the strangeness at finding myself the mother of an almost grown-up girl, the close connection and the strange disunion of habits, the shyness and yet strong affection on one side, and maybe almost fear of these new-found parents…She stood near the parlour window when I came down. We ran into each other's arms, and it was not until she became occupied with her sisters that I had leisure to look at her and try to trace the lovely baby I had left. She was greatly changed, and one moment's glance convinced me she had missed her mother. The great misfortune of her education had been that she had had too many masters; my mother had not been left to use her own judgement with her; probably the dear lady had too old a mind and too formal habits for managing a lively, restless, healthy child.[193]

When Mary was reunited with her mother the next day she was taken aback by the old lady's aged appearance. She was now an invalid in her sixties and had been widowed for twenty years. Mary resolved not to leave her ailing mother so it was decided that the Sherwoods would take a small house behind her mother's lodgings. The accommodation was cramped for the family yet Mary was unperturbed: they camped in it using their camel trunks for storage. Mary and Henry were still anxious about their reduced financial situation and were undecided whether Henry should return to India with or without his wife. They had resolved that if Mary accompanied him then they would take Mary Henrietta but leave the other children in England – a somewhat surprising decision given that the younger children would suffer the same separation from their parents as Mary Henrietta had suffered. The Sherwoods now learnt that their daughter, whom they had known as Mary, had become known as Henrietta during their absence.

~

Mary's brother Marten, his wife Anne, Mary's great friend, and his family were living at Oddingley, six miles from Worcester, where he was vicar. The name Oddingley was famous. In 1806 the rector, the Reverend Parker, who was not popular with the villagers due to his over enthusiastic collection of tythes, had been murdered. His assailant was pursued but when the pursuer too was shot at he abandoned the chase. However, the pursuer had recognised the man and named him as Richard Hemming, a carpenter from nearby Droitwich. In spite of a fifty guineas' reward being offered for his capture the crime remained unsolved. This much was known when Marten and his family lived at Oddingley. Years passed until in 1830 a local farmer, Thomas Clewes, sold his farm. The new farmer discovered a skeleton under a barn floor. Mrs Hemmings identified the remains as those of her husband by the clothes and a carpenter's rule. Thomas Clewes was arrested. He confessed that Hemming had been hired by six farmers to despatch Parker and was paid for his trouble. Hemming then decided to blackmail the farmers for more money and the six took retribution into their own hands: Hemming was murdered. When Clewes was brought to court at the Guildhall in Worcester, large crowds gathered to hear the verdict. This came after thirteen hours' deliberation by the jury which found him guilty as accessory after the fact but as this was not the charge against him the judge refused to accept the verdict. Clewes was then acquitted.[194]

Marten and his wife had six children; the youngest, George, was just over a year old. When Mary took her son, Henry, to visit he was shocked by his cousins' boisterous behaviour, calling it to the attention of their governess. In contrast to Marten's children Henry was extremely polite and well-behaved. He was beginning to speak some English and had become a favourite with Mrs Butt's servant. She was alarmed by his thin appearance and fed him up in the kitchen on bread, butter and cheese. That August when the Corries paid a visit they knew they had found the right house when they heard Henry calling to the servant in Hindustani for his favourite food.

Lucy visited Mary and Marten at Oddingley. Mary had strong views on bringing up children and she was critical of Lucy who records:

> My dear sister,—she has greater powers of commanding than I have, and she says I ought to govern like a king, from whom there is no appeal. She also thinks that I do not make my children do enough, and that I should make my instruction less hard work than it is....
>
> My sister says, 'never give your child a bad character;' what sweet things she says about courtesy and respect! How very much may a mother do for her sons. Their habits greatly depend upon the mother: my sons are very fond of my company. They walk with me after tea, and learn a lesson for me before breakfast. I would make children, according to my sister's plan, learn every lesson twice over, and read a story to them whenever they sew or draw etc. in the evening.[195]

Lucy's views on the education of her daughters centred on 'the knowledge of all needful household business, and of such things as are likely to be useful for their situation in life. Next attend to dress and carriage, and train them up as brothers and sisters; also neglect not the education and working for the poor.'[196] Lucy was a disciplinarian when it came to behaviour. On Saturday or Sunday she made each child sit in a separate corner for five minutes and reflect on their behaviour over the past week. Then they would each confess their faults in a whisper to their mother who would note them down without commenting on them.

In September Mary's mother took new lodgings at Henwick Hill just outside Worcester and Henrietta went with her. The Sherwoods found a small house there so they could be near Mrs Butt. It stood on a bank overlooking the River Severn. Mary Parson managed the children while Sally Pownall and a servant helped in the house. Henry was desperate to get half-pay from his regiment so travelled to London to put his case. The situation did not look promising which depressed Mary, who could not now bear the thought of his returning to India, and decided that she must do something to avoid this. It was then that she hatched a plan to take pupils for she knew that many parents in India were aware of the dangers posed by the climate and illness in keeping their children with them. With Marten's wife's support Mary began to think how this could be realised. In 1817, before she could take her plan further, Lord Mountnorris, their old friend, offered his help to secure Henry half-pay, if he did not rejoin his regiment after his two-year leave of absence. The Sherwoods were fully aware that half-pay in England would not solve their financial problems. Daniel Corrie and other friends suggested that Henry should try for ordination so he started to prepare himself by learning Latin and Greek. Corrie wrote a letter of recommendation addressed to Henry dated January 13, 1817.

> My Dear Sir,
> I shall be very happy if any testimony I can bear will be of use in promoting your wishes to obtain holy orders. I recollect full well the labour you and dear Mrs Sherwood bestowed on the children of the 53rd at Cawnpore, before the regimental school was formed, and the exemplary conduct of several of those children, now grown to riper years, is the best proof of the care you took of them…I recollect full well, also, the excellent fruits of your adult soldiers' school, at that period, in the good conduct of some of the men, ignorant before of letters, and in some instances of morals, and now useful non-commissioned officers in the regiment…
> I am happy, also, to bear testimony to the exemplary Christian conduct which you have manifested in all our intercourse since 1808.[197]

The letter was signed with Corrie's position as 'Chaplain to the Honourable East India Company's Bengal Establishment.' However, before Henry could progress his plan to become ordained, events changed their plans.

Mrs Butt's health was deteriorating rapidly and by that January she was confined to her room though she was still able to walk up and down. Mary described her disease as 'an inward one' that caused her much pain although by the beginning of March the pain had gone. However, on March 19, 1817 she remained in her bed where she died later in the day. She was sixty-six and was buried at Stanford church where her husband lay. After spending a short time at her brother's parsonage at Oddingley where she completed work on 'correcting' and evangelizing Sarah Fielding's *The Governess or The Little Female Academy*[198] Mary returned to Henwick. There she finished *The Indian Pilgrim*[199] which she had begun at the behest of Corrie and Henry Martyn at Cawnpore. Financially the Sherwoods' situation improved with the death of her mother for Mary now inherited her patrimony. The same year Henry's sister Margaret reappeared on the scene. Margaret, who had remained in France after her release from prison in 1794, had married a number of times, was anxious about her inheritance. Mary found her sister-in-law's

French mannerisms somewhat trying but agreed that Margaret's daughter Catherine Elize Boujonnier, whom Mary refers to as Eliza, should come to live with them. Not yet nine, the little girl was duly despatched by coach from London and arrived to live in this busy household with only ten words of English. It seemed Mary was constitutionally unable to refuse taking in children who were less fortunate than her own and giving them her love coupled with a strong sense of Christian morality. Also at Henwick studying under Mary's tutelage was her sister's eldest daughter, Lucy, whose mother comments:

> I think my daughter improved in activity and habits of industry; and herein I think lies my sister's grand forte. She has a bold and noble imagination, much method, great activity, fine affections, ardent zeal, and is besides a great disciplinarian, with little fear of men. But her system of education seems to me to want correctness. The reason is not cultivated, and those soft and delicate touches which are needful to complete the female character are neglected. I think, however, of pursuing my sister's method of instruction, making some additions or alterations according to my own views.[200]

Having decided to set herself up as a schoolmistress Mary needed textbooks to teach her pupils. She duly set about writing them and laid down the methodology by which the children were to be taught. In the *Advertisement* at the beginning of *An Introduction to Astronomy* (1817) she explains:

> accompanying Lessons are the first of a course of lessons intended to give young persons an introductory view of Astronomy, Geography and Ancient and Modern History.
>
> In the astronomical lessons, every thing difficult and abstruse has been omitted, as far as it was possible to do so; and such parts of the Scripture as have been found to be applicable, have been introduced, in order that in every day's lesson, some portion of the Scripture might be impressed on the mind of the learner.
>
> The manner of using these lessons is as follows: the head of each section, with the beginning of the accompanying verse, should be written on a card, and put in a bag, and drawn out indiscriminately. Those who are not able to repeat the section, the head of which is written on the card, are to lose their places, and go to the bottom of the class.
>
> If changing place is found to excite an evil spirit among children, it is

recommended merely to give the child the lesson which has been forgotten after school hours.

The children for whom these lessons were first prepared, learn a section, or part of one, every day; and, also, when they are a little advanced, they are accustomed to repeat, every morning, one of the old lessons or sections, constantly going through the same. This repetition of an old lesson every day, becomes shortly so easy to the child, that it only occupies a few minutes a day, and yet prevents the child from forgetting as it goes on what it has previously learnt.

A teacher, when hearing the class, should use globes, or plates, such as may be found in most elementary books of astronomy, to assist the children in what they learn.

Underneath is printed a specimen of the recommended card with ASTRONOMY as its heading. Below that is the methodological scheme of work 'And God said,' is printed, followed by a quotation from the Bible. The text book opens with: 'Astronomy is that science which teaches us the names and natures of heavenly bodies' followed by a quotation:

> Let there be lights in the firmament of heaven, to divide the day from the night; and let there be signs, and for seasons, and for days, and years: and let them be for lights in the firmament of heaven, to give light upon the earth: and it was so. Gen.I.14,15.

In her lessons on the Planets Mary covers Juno which had been relatively newly discovered in 1804 by Harding. Having described the planet, Mary selects a quotation from the Psalms: 'Such knowledge is too wonderful for me; it is high, I cannot attain it.' Was perhaps science threatening her belief in the God-ordered heavens? In her description of the Earth she dismisses the Torrid zones and their inhabitants while promoting the people of the Temperate zones with: 'It is within the Northern Temperate Zone, that all the nations known in history have flourished.'

In October the Sherwoods moved again. The house at Henwick was too small, and since 'in one way or another all our necessities were richly supplied,' a move was made to Wick near St. John's, where Captain Sherwood bought a house.[201] This time they were not in cramped lodgings but in their own home: the first they had been able to buy since returning to England. Mary was delighted. It was near the Teme, the river which had meant so much to her as a child growing up at Stanford. Adding to her delight were the orchards and a garden where her children could enjoy the freedom she herself had enjoyed.

In spite of the War Office's still not resolving Henry's pay they enjoyed more prosperity in 1818. In June the same year a legacy of £100 was paid to Mary. This had been left to Mary some years earlier by her godmother Mrs Hawkins Browne. Mr Hawkins Browne, who had been so kind to the family, had died that summer. In August Henry received the welcome news that finally, and after the intervention of Lord Mountnorris on his behalf, he was put on half-pay as captain: not with his old regiment but in the Brunswick Hussars.

Just as Henry and Mary were putting their financial anxiety behind them her brother, Marten was hit by tragedy which changed his life cruelly. Mary's dear friend, Anne Congreve, who had become his wife in 1806 and borne him seven children, died in childbirth with her eighth child, a son, christened Theophilus. Sadly the baby died soon afterwards. Marten became deeply depressed and unable to care for the surviving children, four sons and three daughters. Mary took in the four boys and Lucy, her sister, took the three girls. Gradually Marten recovered and the children returned to their home to be looked after by Jemima Hubbal who would become his second wife in 1821. She had doubts about committing herself to a man who had become so severely depressed. It was her attachment to his children which persuaded her to marry him. Her reservations about Marten were cruelly proved to be right some years later.

MRS. SHERWOOD,

Now residing in the Neighbourhood of

WORCESTER,

Wishes to undertake the Education of a Few

YOUNG LADIES.

———❧———

Her Terms are Eighty Guineas a Year when the young Ladies go Home for the Holidays, and One Hundred Guineas when they remain with her the whole Year.

The young Ladies are taught—

ENGLISH,	HISTORY,
FRENCH,	GRAMMAR,
ASTRONOMY,	WRITING,
GEOGRAPHY,	CIPHERING,

And the Learned Languages if required.

₊ A Quarter's Notice is expected before the Removal of any Pupil.

~~~~~~

Printed by Houlston and Son, Wellington, Salop.

Advertisement for Mrs Sherwood's School from her book An Introduction to Geography, *1818*

A Busy Life

It was after her mother's death and the move to Wick that Mary embarked on her plan to open a boarding school for girls. She was encouraged by both family and friends to advertise for pupils and they were not long in arriving. The fees were one hundred guineas a year. A large room was converted into the schoolroom and in 1818 she accepted her first pupil. In *An Introduction to Geography* (1818) published by Houlston, an advertisement for her school appears. It is interesting that Scripture is not included in the list of subjects to be studied. The reason might be that as quotations were included in her card methodology to underpin the lesson more instruction was unnecessary. Certainly time was set aside each day when the Bible was read to the children. In her lessons on Geography she covers a lot of ground and includes physical features separately from countries. Mary had at this point in her life travelled to India but had not yet visited any European countries. The section on India is headed HINDOOSTAUN:

> Hindoostaun extends from Cape Comorin in the south to the mountains called Hindoo Koh at the north of Cabul and Cashmire, being nearly 1,390 British miles; and from the river Araba on the west of the province of Sinde to the mountains which divide Bengal from the Birman empire, being about 1,600 British miles. This country is divided among various powers, the chief of which are, the English; the Nizam, or Soubah of the Deccan; the Mahrattas; and the Seiks. The original inhabitants of this country are as gross idolaters as any in the world…[202]

Mary is equally judgemental on France when it comes to religion which is given more space than the physical characteristics of the country.

> The religion of France has been for many ages Roman Catholic, but, of late years, strongly tinctured with infidelity. It is, however, remarkable, that the valleys and retired parts among the mountains of this country, have afforded,

for many centuries, a place of security to a small remnant of true Christians, who were thus kept, during the height of the power of the Pope, in peace and security; thus fulfilling the assurance which the holy psalmist gives us of the care of the Almighty for those he hath redeemed.[203]

Japan receives scant description of just five lines before Mary states: 'The Japanese are idolaters, and bitter enemies of Christianity.'[204] In contrast Persia is treated to an almost lyrical account:

Persia is a country of mountains, abounding with fruit and beautiful trees, flowers and shrubs growing wild, especially the jasmine, the tulip, and ranunculus, and the blue and scarlet anenome.[205]

There is no condemnation of Islam but she dismisses the Persian empire since Alexander the Great's time as having been 'of comparatively little importance.'

Not only was Mary accepting pupils in England but she was also taking in pupils from India. Added to which, she now had the care of her brother's sons, her own large family and, in September, her old friend Mrs Parson arrived from Meerut with six children for a visit: 'we were then twenty-five in family, and I complain I have no quiet.' An unsurprising observation! It was decided that Marten's three youngest boys should be sent to school locally. Marten, the eldest, was boarded out with a neighbour and returned for lessons with Henry Sherwood. Apart from her husband her only helpers in the school were Miss Yate, her mother's former companion, and her two adopted children. Added to all these responsibilities Mary was pregnant again.

George, named after his grandfather, was born on January 31, 1819 and was their eighth and last child. Mary was forty-three. 'My babe was fair as the fairest flower, with ever meandering vein visible through the transparent skin, with eyes of deep blue, and dove-like softness.' The Bishop of Calcutta attended his christening and a party afterwards, at which George charmed everyone with his smiles. Mary's ties with the Evangelical movement in India remained strong. Missionary activity had vastly expanded in India since the Sherwood's time. In October the great William Wilberforce[206] visited Worcester where the Sherwoods were introduced to him. Wilberforce was eager to hear of Mary's recollections of Henry Martyn and her experience of the heathen in India. Mary was impressed that he listened intently to her and was the perfect gentleman but was less impressed by his appearance describing him as 'peculiarly small and ill-formed, and illfeatured.' While in her company he toured the local china works. Mary used this experience to write a tract, *The China Manufactory*.[207]

Henry had not been idle. He had opened a school near Henwick and had bought another property at Powick, a nearby village. He had abandoned the plan to become ordained and instead, now that he was on half-pay, teaching and good works occupied his time. Mary, after her mother's death, produced a prodigious canon of chapbooks,[208] with their emphasis on religious duty and obedience. She wrote books, tracts and textbooks for children, although some Evangelicals disapproved of her use of narrative. She became the leading Evangelical writer for children and fame embraced her as her books were now produced under her own name by her publishers. Houlston had benefited from their association with her yet had paid her remarkably little for her early books. By 1818 Houlston had published the following works: *The History of Little Henry and his Bearer* (1814), *The History of Susan Gray* (1815), *The History of Lucy Clare* (1815), *The Memoirs of Sergeant Dale, his daughter and the Orphan Mary* (1815), *The Ayah and her Lady* (1816), *An Introduction to Astronomy* (1817), *Stories Explanatory of the Church Catechism* (1817) but printed in 1814 in Calcutta; *The History of Theophilus and Sophia* (1818), *The Indian Pilgrim* (1818), *An Introduction to Geography* (1818) and *The Little Woodman and his Dog Caesar* (1818).[209] The latter, a highly moralistic tale, with enchanting woodcuts, became hugely popular and was reprinted many times until 1901.

Her sister, Lucy, was also highly productive, writing tracts and stories. However, she did not achieve the same fame as her elder sister, a fact she commented somewhat bitterly about, writing: 'Had I not been ill-used about my books, and had I received what I ought to have done in common honesty, I should have been rich...'[210] Lucy was less Evangelical than Mary but, like her sister; wrote stories which held appeal for children. Both of them could produce a tract in a morning. Mary alone wrote about a hundred between 1818 and 1830.

Mary broke free of Houlston's monopoly[211] and sold her most famous book *The History of the Fairchild Family* (1818) to a different publisher of Evangelical literature – John Hatchard of Piccadilly, London. John Hatchard was the main publisher for the Clapham Evangelicals and

"The young men buried their father, the day after his death, in a dark corner of the forest. And when they had closed up the grave they returned to the hut, leaving William and Cæsar sitting by the grave."

The Little Woodman, *1860 Edition. Title page*

enjoyed the custom of the wealthy and influential as well as the reformers and Evangelicals. For Mary it meant an endorsement of her views on religious education and an endorsement of her position as a writer. In *The History of the Fairchild Family*, as in so many of her other books, Mary drew on her own upbringing in Stanford with its rural setting, her experience with teaching the poor in Sunday school, illness and death. The deathbed scene with the grieving family gathered round the bed of the dying child or adult is described in detail in many of her books. Mary, like so many mothers of the time, had suffered the agony of losing children and babies. She had written a moving first hand account of both

Henry's and Lucy's deaths in India. The Evangelical belief in original sin from which the child or adult finds redemption by embracing Christianity with fervour before accepting death with calm and happy certainty is a theme she used in many of her books. The deathbed scene of the eponymous Henry in *Little Henry and his Bearer*, although heavy with sentiment, is effective. *The Little Woodman and his Dog Caesar* has a deathbed scene where the father repents of his wicked ways, as both son and father, before he dies.

The most harrowing scenes of death are described in *The History of The Fairchild Family* which has several deathbed scenes, of both children and adults. If the child or adult is an unbeliever the deathbed scene as written by Mary is one of fear and darkness.

The structure of the book revolves around the Fairchild family. The children are taught a series of moral lessons which inculcate Christian principles within a fictional framework. Balancing the dark and often horrifying descriptions of death are captivating descriptions of family life, scenery and food and the stability provided by the morally strict but loving parents. The Fairchild parents are bringing up their three children, whose names are those of Mary's children: two daughters, Lucy and Emily, aged eight and seven, and a son called Henry, who is aged between five and six. The most famous scene is gruesome by modern standards.

It takes place after the children have been quarrelling over a doll and when the little girls say that they hate each other in their father's hearing he punishes them severely for the sin of envy and hatred to teach them a moral lesson:

> 'I will take the children this evening to Blackwood, and show them something there, which, I think, they will remember as long as they live: and I hope they will take warning from it, and pray more earnestly for new hearts, that they may love each other with perfect and heavenly love ...'
> 'What is there at Blackwood, Papa?' cried the children.
> 'Something very shocking,' said Mrs Fairchild. 'There is one there,' said Mr Fairchild, looking very grave, 'who hated his brother.'
> 'Will he hurt us, Papa?' said Henry.
> 'No,' said Mr Fairchild, 'he cannot hurt you now.'

They set off for the dark wood, representing the darkness of the soul, which contrasts with the light of the known, familiar, safe world in which the family lives. As the wood becomes thicker and darker the children become increasingly frightened. Near the end of the wood they see a disused house standing in an overgrown garden:

> Just between that and the wood stood a gibbet, on which the body of a man hung in irons: it had not yet fallen to pieces, although it had hung there for some years. The body had on a blue coat, a silk handkerchief round the neck, with shoes and stockings, and every other part of the dress entire: but the face of the corpse was so shocking, that the children could not look at it.
>   'Oh! Papa, Papa! what is that?' cried the children. 'That is a gibbet,' said Mr Fairchild; 'and the man who hangs upon it is a murderer! one who first hated, and afterwards killed his brother!'...[212]

Mary's ability to hold her readers with her description and suspense is terrific but strong stuff for a child who might well have suffered nightmares after having it read to them! The lesson is learnt by the Fairchild children that hatred must be banished from their hearts and replaced by love.

Later in the book the children are taken to view John Roberts's corpse:

> When they came to the door, they perceived a kind of disagreeable smell, such as they had never smelt before; this was the smell of the corpse, which, having been dead now for nearly two days, had begun to corrupt, and as the children went higher up the stairs, they perceived the smell more disagreeably... the whole appearance of the body was more ghastly and horrible than the children expected.[213]

Their father informs them: 'the soul which has sinned must be born again.' Some ten pages later Miss Augusta Noble dies in agony and fear when she disobeys her mother and plays with fire. She embodies all that is bad: lack of a Christian upbringing, disobedience to one's parents, lying, vanity, love of material things and a sense of superior social position. For her there is no salvation. In contrast the deathbed scene of Charles Trueman, a saintly child who has seen the light, epitomises the good death of the faithful believer. Mary ends each story concerning the three likeable but predictably naughty Fairchild children with a moral which is underpinned with a biblical quotation, a prayer and a hymn. With the publication of *The Fairchild Family* Mary brought the Evangelical doctrine into the homes of the upper classes. Her setting was not some distant land, although she had begun writing it while still in India in 1814 on the journey from Cawnpore to Meerut and read some of

Don't tease me Henry. The Fairchild Family,
4th Edition

it to her own children while there, but the domestic scene which was
familiar to both parents and children in England.

The book, with its strong Evangelical emphasis, became a household
essential and remained popular until the late eighteen eighties and in
some homes until the nineteen twenties. So successful was *The History of
the Fairchild Family* that John Hatchard requested a sequel. Despite
Hatchard's plea, Mary did not comply immediately: the second part was
not published until 1842 and the third, with the cooperation of her

daughter, Sophia, in 1847 when Mary was seventy-two. In the preface to Part III Mary writes:

> As during the last few years of my life, prolonged beyond the appointed age of man, I have been constantly aided by my daughter, [Sophia Streeten] in whom I find the same gift of interesting young readers, which it has pleased God to bestow upon me ! so renewed, that we can work together, as with one mind, ! I think it but due to her, and the public, to add her name to mine in this, the third volume of the Fairchild Family, in the composition of which she has been of especial service to me.

The History of Henry Milner,[214] which Hatchard published in 1822, met with huge success in both England and America. Mary attacks Rousseau's educational theories in *Emile*[215] in which he argues that 'man is a naturally good being' and any moral education of the child should be delayed until adolescence has been reached: in contrast Henry Milner's education begins at the tender age of four. Rousseau's views were not shared by Evangelicals who expounded original sin and Mary condemns Rousseau for being 'the well-spring of infidelity'. However, Mary was not above criticism herself. When, in 1820, Houlston had published *The Governess, or The Little Female Academy*, Mary was accused of plagiarism.

~

Mary's personal life was struck by tragedy in the spring of 1820. She suffered a bout of rheumatic fever in the late autumn of 1819 and when she had recovered she and Henry left home for a 'change of air.' They had only been gone for a few days when they received a letter with the alarming news that George and one of her Indian charges were ill. The Sherwoods returned to find both children a little better. Sadly they both died a few days later. Mary describes George as: 'my little Benjamin, my youngest born, my beautiful goldenhaired baby! My baby with dove's eyes.'

Mary's surviving children were growing up: Henrietta was now sixteen, Lucy was ten, Emily was eight, Henry seven and Sophia five years old. Mary Parson and Sally Pownall were older but still part of the family. Ever mindful of her financial responsibility for her many children, Mary decided to sell the Indian shawls they had brought back from India and put the funds thus raised into a Savings' Bank for their benefit. That summer Mrs Sherer brought her three children and Annie to stay. Annie appeared unhappy and was physically unwell although Mary does not elaborate. Four other visitors also came to stay so it is not surprising that Mary wrote: 'Our house was quite filled, and I was almost distracted by business.' Added to all her commitments of family, writing and teaching, she began to go into the 'dark districts' of Worcester to read to the 'gloveresses' and spread the Evangelical message. Worcester was at that time a centre for glove making: the industry in and around Worcester employed about 30,000 people but would decline by 1826 when the government lifted taxes on foreign gloves which brought mass unemployment.

A Holiday in France

After Mary's illness and the death of their son George, the Sherwoods decided to take a holiday. On June 12, 1821 Mary, her husband and Henrietta set out for France. The younger children were to remain in England, boarded out with friends and relations. The party set off by coach at four in the morning and were in Oxford by lunchtime. In London they took lodgings at the Castle and Falcon, an inn in Aldersgate – where the first public meeting of The Church Missionary Society had been held on April 12, 1799. It had been fifteen years since Mary had last been in London. She was disgusted by some of the newer monuments 'with figures of heathen deities as large as life.' While in London she took the opportunity to see John Hatchard who was again pressing her to write a sequel to the highly profitable *The Fairchild Family*.

The crossing from Dover to Boulogne cost ten shillings each. Mary, never a good sailor, was seasick throughout. They had to be landed in small boats because the tide was out. This reminded Mary of the rough landing she had endured many years earlier at Madras. Once on land they were surrounded by a jostling throng of people among whom were poissards:

> These latter, with their naked feet, short petticoats, and bronzed complexions, are the fish-women, and are the coarsest, most masculine, and fiercest of all the classes of the fair sex in all countries of the earth. They spoke in their loudest voices, mingling their notes with those of the men, and making such a clamour with their incomprehensible jargon, that it rendered me after my paroxysms of sickness so utterly stupid that I scarcely knew what was passing.[216]

Little had Mary expected that some grey balls of wool she had brought with her would be the cause of concern at the Custom House. The balls were examined closely and debated as to what their purpose was until, finally, the customs officials took the precaution of stabbing the balls repeatedly with Mary's knitting needles. When no sinister content was discovered they were returned to Mary with the comment: 'Madame est bien industrieuse.' After being frisked by female officers, Mary rejoined Henry and they walked to a hotel owned by an English woman. Cold and hungry they settled by the fire to wait for dinner. To Mary's surprise everything was served separately and by the time the last course had been served she was exhausted. Travelling by sea did not agree with her so she spent the remainder of the day in bed and breakfasted in bed the next day. The Sherwoods were required to register with the police before they were permitted to explore the town which was still a refuge for English debtors. Henry had spent time in Boulogne all those years ago when his father had taken his family to France so he knew the town well. Their next destination was Abbeville which held so many memories for Henry. En route in a barouche drawn by two horses, Mary was shocked by a large crucifix standing in the countryside: this confirmed her anti-papist[217] views which would grow stronger in the following years.

At Abbeville Mary was enchanted by the old houses and narrow streets enlivened by the bustling scene:

> Then the objects in the streets—Benares itself hardly presented more variety! There were Soeurs de la Charité, with their hoods and rosaries, hastening on their work of mercy, supplying the most pleasing form in which Popery ever appears; smart and spritely grisettes and femmes de chambres, running along with their short step and jaunty air; priests and beggars and marketwomen, and unwashed artificers, and bustling housewives, with their scissors dangling at their apron-strings, with persons crying their wares, and mere idlers of all sorts, who seemed to have nothing to do but to kill time. All these fill the streets and all moved to and fro and all looked different from anything we had ever seen before.

Here they took accommodation at the Tête de Boeuf, an old inn built round a court. Their next stop was Paris where they had arranged to stay with a Miss Rowden who had been a teacher at the St. Quintins' school. Mary was appalled by young English women aping the fashions of the French: 'In the name of common sense do not let any English girl conde-scend to an awkward affected imitation of a manner which can never sit naturally upon her – the manner of a French girl. Anything assumed is not only disgusting, but disgraceful.' A visit to a cemetery, Père la Chaise, brought back her grief, while looking at the graves of young children, at losing her son George so very recently and also her memories of the two children, Henry and Lucy who had died in India. The inscriptions she read on the graves inspired her to write two stories, the first with the name of the cemetery as the title[218] and *The Infant's Grave*; and a tract, *The Blessed Family*. It was with some relief that they left Paris and made their way in a leisurely fashion to Nantes, Rouen, Dieppe, St. Valéry, Abbeville, St. Omer and finally Calais. For Henry it was an opportunity to share with Mary many of the places of his youth except this time it was under very different circumstances. While at St. Valéry they stopped to look at the Abbey and the house which Henry's father had owned.

> It is an edifice of vast extent, partly of brick and partly of stone, having long ranges of windows, galleries of immense length, with arcades or cloisters in a ruinous state…We walked in, and to the left of the house, near where the church had once joined it, we were much surprised at the very handsome appearance of the building, and the extent of the garden, which was full of fruit trees in full bearing … Leaving the garden we returned to the road. My heart was full. I could have liked to have lingered longer there, for it was a place of immense interest to me, and if to me, how much more so to Mr Sherwood?[219]

They then visited the church where Henry's half-sister, Mercy, was buried.

 ∼

At the end of July, reunited with her children once more, Mary resumed her busy life. She was writing *The Guingette and The Noble Allamont*.[220] Former pupils were joined by new ones. Teaching occupied six hours of her day around which she also fitted writing tracts and books; reading and prayer; as well as writing and reading letters; telling a story in the early evening to her family and pupils, and receiving visitors every day. All this necessitated an early start to the day which she welcomed by drinking a cup of coffee. Mary notes: 'I am amazed in looking over the memoranda for this summer how I could possibly have done what I did.' But it was not all work. At the end of the Christmas term there was a concert for the pupils at which the children played: Lucy and Emily on guitar, Henrietta on harp and Marten, her brother's son, on flute. Pupils who lived in England went home for Christmas but children from India remained with the Sherwoods. During the holidays, classes were suspended which meant that Mary had more time for writing and other duties in the household. In 1822 the household was expanded once again by the arrival of the two orphaned youngest daughters of the Reverend and Mrs Brown. David Brown had died some years before but his wife had only recently died. She had requested that Mary should look after her daughters, Lydia and Sarah. In May, General and Mrs Mawby arrived to stay and enjoyed singing Indian hymns with the children. Mary welcomed other visitors from India during the summer months so the Indian connection remained strong.

Henry bought a boat for the family to use on the River Teme. Going on a small voyage by boat brought back happy memories of their much longer voyages on the Ganges. They limited themselves to taking only two children with them at one time. However, they stopped these river trips later because of possible danger to the children. Mary incorporated one of these little voyages into *Henry Milner*. They also had a little carriage and a pony in which they went on outings. Unfortunately this activity came to a sudden stop when the pony ran away with them! Amidst all these activities, from 1822 Mary also became a regular contributor to *The Youth's Magazine*.

Mary came up with the plan for starting a Penitentiary[221] in Worcester in 1822. 'It was immediately taken up by various parties, and I was established at once as the head of the Charity.' Money was raised in 1823 and 1824 through bazaars. Her involvement lasted until 1827, when, for some reason which she does not disclose, but probably because of her loosening ties with the Evangelical church and her attitude and outspoken views on political reform, she records: 'I found that my name had been erased as patroness of the Penitentiary. Thus was I bowed down from my seat of honour.'[222] She was also asked to stop visiting the gloveresses. Mary did admit that 1822 was a 'year of drudgery' and that she was short-tempered and irritated by all the demands on her time. Because of her growing fame and her involvement with penal reform she was invited in 1824 to meet Elizabeth Fry[223] who had done so much to improve conditions for women prisoners. Mary was invited with her daughter Emily to a public breakfast at a Quaker house in Worcester where she was introduced to Elizabeth whom she described as a 'fine, composed, majestic woman.' To Mary's surprise she and her daughter were invited by Elizabeth to accompany her in her carriage on the drive to Worcester Prison which had been built in 1813. En route the two women discussed the perils of being famous. Mary pointed out that she lived a retired life so was not a public figure like Elizabeth whose public profile was much greater. A large crowd awaited their arrival but it was Elizabeth the people wanted to see, not the famous author, so Mary and Emily 'followed in her train' and listened to her address in the chapel.

The School at Wick

The school was flourishing. Mary took great interest in her pupils' progress as is evidenced by the thirty-one Sunday notes[224] which she wrote, in 1824 to one of the older pupils, Lydia Ann Commins, from Bodmin, Cornwall. The notes start on January 25 and end on December 9, some are undated and others may be missing. Many of them are repetitious and I have included the most interesting in the order in which they appear in the handwritten copy. The use of capitals in the salutations varies and punctuation of sentences is often lacking. The notes give an insight into Mary's religious fervour and her care, both academic and pastoral, for her pupils. In an undated note in May she gives an insight into her relationship with her daughter Henrietta. Above all, the notes communicate a sense of maternal love towards her pupils and especially for Lydia.

> Jan 25th
> My Dear Child
> I have as yet seen nothing amiss in you & should I see what is wrong & should tell you. I trust you will have grace to receive it well. I know that you are in trouble about a dear friend I therefore am not surprised if I sometimes deem you low & attribute it to the real cause. be assured that all in this house will sympathize with your trouble.

> Undated.
> My Dear Child
> I am pleased at the effort which you have made to appear more chearful since I spoke to you. to some young people I should say you want feeling—you are hard hearted to others I should say do not yield to sensibility to the destruction of usefulness. This world is not our resting place this is not our home. we must not expect happiness here. tho we may enjoy many comforts—let us then try to be useful. I have myself very strong & quick feelings but I pray that my feelings may not be my Tyrants—remember that you have certain duties to perform whilst with us. strive to do these to your utmost for your

dear parents sake. & endeavour my dear child to throw all selfish considerations into the back ground, & to bring all your feelings under the control of religion.

Feb. 21st

My dear child

You have appeared more chearful the few last days. & more attentive to your improvement. when you feel melancholy you must consider that everyone round you has trials perhaps some more severe than yours. tho they do not speak of them the happy death of friends is that trial of all others which admits most of religious consolations. It is sin my dear child, which weighs most heavily on the feelings of a Christian. Oh that we could be free from sin then indeed we should be happy. & why should we lament that those we love are set free from this torment yet I know that there will be some natural sorrow in losing dear friends. to this day I can hardly speak of the parents & children I have lost without tears yet I would not have them back again if I could.

Undated.

My Dear Child

Why should you mourn because your friend & Sister is in heaven. what real affliction is there in the death of the righteous—I who am a parent would rather see my children in the grave, than growing up in sin. I would not have the babies back again whom I have lost. Oh let us hasten on in the heavenly way till we are united in glory with these beloved ones who are gone before.

Undated.

My beloved child

I have been much pleased with your conduct during this week which has been a week of trial. these are the times which try the characters of young people when the watchful eye of the parent is taken off for a short time & you are left to yourselves I am happy however to say that you have stood this trial & not been led to evil by your young & giddy companions. seek above all things with the divine blessing a uniform & consistent mode of acting—to which nothing so strongly contributes as a constant sense of the divine presence. My beloved child, our acquaintance has not been long—but I hope it may be blessed to us both.

March 20

My beloved Child

I have the pleasure to say I think you improved in many respects—some little outward things of no great consequence might be better—these are holding up your head being neat in your drawers & doing your hair rather more carefully. I hope my dear child that you will continue to be open & faithful in every respect & to reprove sin wherever you see it.

March 27th

My dear child

I have no fault whatever to find all you have done has been well & I am
pleased with all your improvements. I hope you do not talk in bed. Oh! that we
could devote the moments whilst we are waiting for sleep in bed to the service
of our God. in taking account of our past faults & visiting our God in our
hearts. how should we grow in grace by this practise, but our hearts are
deceitful above all things & desperately wicked—blessed be the time when we
are freed from sin.

April 18th

My beloved child

When I spoke of coldness & ingratitude I never thought of you. during the
short time we have been together I have met with every kindness &
consideration. but there are some young people which nothing seems to touch
whose hearts are wholly occupied by self & their own concerns. whose love
even to their parents seems altogether selfish. this is a character of which I
have an excessive horrour & which I thought right to speak of in public. If
youth is not tender & warm hearted when are we to expect warmth of feeling.
Of you I would not say that you want feeling—I would rather say pray that
your feelings may be controuled by religion. for I too well know what it is to
have strong feelings—

May 2nd

My beloved Child

I have no fault to find. on the contrary I think you much improved
especially in manners & attention to conversation. I am pleased also with your
sweet & affectionate manner & the interest you take in every ones feelings. I
have not yet recovered the loss of my Missy but in a few days I hope I shall but I
have comfort in the rest of you my dear children.

Undated.

My dear child

I have seen nothing amiss in you this week. I rejoice to see you trying to
improve yourself & making the best of your time, also trying to be attentive to
conversation & looking intelligent & not dull & stupid—at your time of life
intelligence is shewn by endeavouring to listen & by this means the habit of
conversing rationally & pleasantly will be acquired. There are many I am sorry
to say in this house who are very deficient in this respect.

Undated.

My Dear Child

I have this day recommended to Henrietta to seek your friendship. A thing

I have not often advised her to do with any young person but this proves my opinion of you more than any words can do She is naturally reserved, & does not come forward to form attachments with any one. In the holidays perhaps you will see more of her & it might do her good to associate with a pious young friend— you perhaps know that she was separated from me many years & from all her sisters & I do not think she ever feels at home with me as the others do. it is a sad thing for parents & children to be parted so many years. in the holidays I must be absent perhaps a week. I wish you could confirm to be absent at the same time as I do not wish to lose your company for you are become very dear to me.

May 21st
My dear child
    I feel with you that I had much rather you did not go from home, at midsummer for I know that you consider this as a home— but as soon as I know when I shall go out I will let you know & I hope it will be so arranged that you may be absent at the same time— My situation my dear is often an anxious one many children come to me out of pious families & with high characters, whom I find on close inspection are in a dreadful state of mind. it might perhaps be easier for me to pass over their private faults, but I can not be insincere & I have many unhappy moments in thinking of the sins of my children, however they all one & all thank me for my sincerity & many like poor Missy are ready to lay down their lives for me but I thank God that in you I have never seen any evil habits or bad tempers—you have always been tender affectionate & lovely & I trust your good conduct is the effect of true religion. When the time of your separation comes tho it will be to restore you to your parents we shall feel I well know but we may love each other tho far away.

May the 30th
My beloved child
    I am much pleased with your attention to your little pupil. & indeed with your whole conduct & I hope that during the holidays you will do all in your power to improve yourself. It is with pleasure I say, that your whole conduct has been lovely & blameless since you entered this house but forget not to give the glory to God.

Undated.
My dear child
    I shall keep your lovely little copy of verses & long I trust even for ever retain the remembrance of you my precious & blameless child. without the hope of our meeting in heaven I could not bear the thoughts of separation from so many of my beloved young people. but the hopes we have of endless joy in the world to come & of enjoyment in the presence of those we love [?] all things right. Your ever affect 2nd Mother

Sunday Aug 1st

I did not like to say as much to you on Friday but I meant that you were one of the two who have quite pleased me during the holidays. There was another at the same time in the room Miss Burns with whom I am perfectly satisfied—I am also satisfied with my Emily—Sophia—H Morgan & Mary whilst at home The others have all been giddy. but Sally being obliged to be with Miss Clewlow & hearing too much of dress there is some excuse to be made for her being unsettled—I wish you all to be neat my loves but I do not wish you to think of dress more than necessary. I pray that the next 6 months may be blessed to us & that when we part you may remember this house as a place of holy peace

Undated.

My beloved Child

It is good for young people to be sometimes separated from their dear Mothers, & those who watch & protect them because then they are led to know & feel their weakness & to humble themselves & to feel the need of help. My beloved child I hope that you will never be parted from me till you return to your own dear Mother. yet when we are parted I shall still remember my Lydia with tender love & look forward to our meeting in a happier world.

August 7th

My dear child

You have behaved as usually very well this week, I hope that you may always be enabled to continue in well doing & tho the more we advance in a holy life the more we are humbled with a sense of sin yet we ought to consider it as a great blessing when we are preserved from open & grievous fallings off—avoid much talking my dear child not only here but wherever you are. I have found by long experience that I never yield to talking without committing sin. & wounding my own conscience & I find most peace in an active life yet withdrawn from the world.

Aug 14th 1824

My dear child

I have seen nothing wrong in you this week tho I hope you have been sensible that all is not well with you in the sight of God for wretches so vile as we are offend continually—it is however a great blessing when we are enabled to maintain a steady & equal conduct in the eyes of our fellow creatures. the heart is that however to which we ought to look. if the heart is in a holy state all will be well. look to your private thoughts consider what they are & pray that they may be cleansed. the time when the thoughts are most busy in sin is when we are on our beds Oh pray that your bed may be blessed to you & that your best thoughts every night may be devoted to your God.

Aug 29th

My dear child

I being much tired to day I shall not write you a long note. I thank God I have no fault to find with you this week but we must all watch & pray for there seems to be a restless spirit got in amongst us & this will lead to sin. each of you my dear elder girls must endeavour to contend with the evil in the little ones more especially under your care. I am pleased with your behaviour to poor little Soffrona. you have never my dear child given me a moments pain.

Oct 2nd

My beloved Child

I was pleased with your reading The Hermit on Friday evening. you are certainly much improved in your French since you came here, Oh make a finish & strive to add improvement to improvement & continue so to do beloved one when we are parted. Oh happy world when we shall part no more. there will be no parting among the fair & fragrant regions of the Millenium. a little while & we shall all be united in everlasting Joy. Joy purchased for us Miserable Sinners by a bleeding Saviour. all who love their Lord will then…

Undated

My dear child

I have no fault to find. I thank you for your kindness to my little Sophia, tenderness to the young, to the old & the sick is one of the sweetest qualities of young women & I hope that you will ever endeavour to retain this quality. you are very quiet & give no trouble over your stream

Oct 23rd

My dear child

I have no fault to find this week I hope that before next Sunday you will try to finish your stream of time[225]—& then be able to give more time to your Music. If you like it some body shall go to call with you at General Is—It will be a sad hour when I part with you my child but you are going to dear parents & we shall hope to meet in a better world nay perhaps again in this but our hearts will meet often & when you advance in life you will point out perhaps to your children the stories that were written by one who once instructed you & who ever will love you.

Undated

My dear child—

I have been pleased with you this week which having been an unsettled week has been more trying. you are much improved in reading your French & understood you as you went on last night with the greatest of ease. if you ever see any thing like levity in your schoolfellows I depend on you my child to tell me if you love your Sisters in this house you will not suffer sin in any of them &

I should be really obliged to you if you see any thing amiss if you will say so in confidence to me. Lucy I know is giddy. have you ever seen any thing worse in her. I have no suspicions for I believe her to be strictly innocent I only fear her being led away by high spirits. I thank you for your tender kindness to all the little ones.

Nov 18th
My beloved child
    I can not write a long note—not being strong & having the history class to go thro but I must thank you for all your sweet & kind behaviour during my illness.

Dec 9th 1824
My beloved child
    I have said much I wish to say to you in your Conversation book. I have also spoken to your dear Mother in my letter of what I think of my beloved child & now that I am writing my last Sunday note I find that my heart will not let me write. Oh! my child it is a bitter thing to part from one so dear you are however going to a happy home & tender parents not like some poor orphans who have left this house to go they knew not whither or to whom. this is a sweet thought to me for you have the best of parents & the tender reception they will give you will presently dry your tears. Yet you will ever remember our Sunday Evenings they will afford you sweet recollections I am well assured thro life & you perhaps may talk of them to your childrens children & say how your poor old Instructress had to lead you in the way of holiness. Oh my child my child the time will come when all all my children will be gathered together in such regions of glory as eye hath not yet seen—where the palm Tree & the olive & the Willow of the Brook[226] shall all flourish together & we shall all be gathered together in the Tabernacles of our Shepherd.
    In this hope I can say adieu to my beloved Child but without such a hope how would the bitterness of parting be endured Your ever affectionate

In a letter, dated December 8, the previous day, to Mrs Commins of Bodmin, Cornwall, Mary reports on her daughter, Lydia Ann's progress at the school:

My Dear Madam,
    It is not without much pain that we part with your blameless and lovely child, indeed my dear Madam, you are blessed in your daughter, she is gentle without being weak, for she never allows anything wrong to pass without reproving it; her tenderness to little children is almost beyond example, in so much as my little Sophia and the orphan baby Soffrona hang about her as upon a tender Mother.
    I think her generally improved, particularly in French and Music, and I

have given her some very accurate directions respecting what she should do to carry on her improvement, for we must not consider her education finished though she may do all which is necessary under her parent's roof, nothing however would so thoroughly occupy her, and improve her, as much as teaching a little child and I think she would very much like to have a little pupil, in this case she would be compelled to go over all the old ground again, and as the early part of her Education was not so well arranged as we could wish, here will be the means of grounding her well and thoroughly without the drudgery of learning lessons.

Her chief defect is not a common one with young ladies, but it is a thing to be attended to, a little want of attention to her dress, hair etc. I have enforced this as a duty and you will perhaps think it right to do the same. Vanity is hateful but neatness desirable and young people require to be constantly reminded of these things. I have begged Miss Commins to write to me every half-year and I hope though so very distant that our children may meet again and renew that tender affection which has subsisted ever since they knew each other.

I thank God that Miss Commins has enjoyed invariably good health since I was so happy as to know her, and I trust she has been happy under our roof. How much she is loved I cannot say, but perhaps it will give her parents delight to hear that I never had a pupil whom I thought more worthy of my love and esteem. Thank you for your kind invitation to my children, it is not possible for them to accept at present but I still hope that it may be done at some future time.

With best Compliments to Mr Commins,

I remain Dear Madam, Most truly yours, M.M. Sherwood.[227]

Family and Financial Security

As Mary's fame as an author grew, so did her financial reward for her books. Her output was prolific. She seemed to be able to produce stories, tracts, pamphlets and articles while still running her school; as well as organising parties, charades and feasts, engaging in charitable work and looking after her family. She tapped into her own family and events for inspiration for her stories and she not only had Houlston and Hatchard, but also Darton, Melrose, and the Religious Tract Society among her publishers. She was writing for *The Youth's Magazine* and editing *The Child's Magazine*. The Sherwoods were now able to enjoy a financial security they had not known since leaving India. Henry invested the proceeds from his wife's writing into various properties in Worcestershire.

Their connection with Henry's former regiment had not been lost. In 1824 the 53rd regiment was stationed at Weedon Barracks in Northamptonshire and Mary and Henry, accompanied by Henrietta, Lucy and Emily, were invited to visit. The party stayed for a week and while there, Mrs Sherwood, much to her surprise and delight, was reunited with some of the band whom she had looked after and taught many years ago in India.

> The youths stood together, and as I went up to them they gathered round me, forming a circle, their eyes sparkling with pleasure. They were all full-grown, tall, and, as young military men might be expected to be, finely set up and well-acquainted with what was due from them to me.
>
> For an instant I knew none of them, but soon recognised in them the babes I had nursed, dressed and lulled to sleep, and the boys I had taught ...
>
> Henrietta and the two girls stood looking on. "Which of those ladies is Miss Lucy?" asked William Coleman, and she came forward among the group, while they all exclaimed, "Is that Miss Lucy?" but were too respectful to say more. Lucy smiled at them as if they had been so many brothers. I was relieved

The Sherwood children, *1825. From a painting based on* The Gower Family *by George Romney. Emily (13), Henry (11), Sophia (9), Lucy (15) and Mary Henrietta(20)*

> when this scene was over, and I could get away alone to weep and pray for my orphan boys.[228]

That Sunday the band positioned itself outside their windows and played *Auld Lang Syne*. It was a happy stay for the Sherwoods and their daughters. While Mary and Henry reminisced about Indian days with members of the regiment the three girls enjoyed the parties and dancing. Two days before Christmas 1824 the party left Weedon to travel home. There they found the younger children deep in preparation for an evening of charades.

Soon after their return the Sherwoods commissioned an artist in Worcester to paint a picture of their five children in a sylvan setting, closely based on George Romney's portrait *The Gower Family*.[229] It depicts the four younger children holding hands in a circle and dancing to a tambourine played by Henrietta in the background.

In 1826, family life was about to change. On a visit to Lichfield Mary met the Reverend Thomas Dawes after hearing him preach. He had translated *Little Henry and his Bearer* into Spanish. A month after their meeting he asked for the hand of Henrietta. She accepted him and on December 14, 1826 they were married. 'We had a large party at the breakfast, and all the young ladies dressed in white. They danced afterwards.' Mary adds a fascinating footnote: 'I did not foresee how closely I should be connected with a remarkably fine old gentleman who sat at the head of the table, nor was I aware how the unexpected appearance of Emily in her bridal array delighted his son, she being as utterly unconscious of this circumstance as I was myself.'[230] Emily at the time was not yet fourteen but was regarded as the beauty of the family and, like her sister Lucy, was sweet-tempered. The son was Dr. Robert Streeten. Henrietta's husband was of good birth and was gifted the living at Adbaston, near Eccleshall, by Dr. Chapel Woodhouse, a longstanding friend and now the Dean of Lichfield. The first of Mary's daughters had left home. The following month Sally Pownall became engaged to Thomas Bird, a glover in Worcester. After a long engagement they would be married on January 2, 1828. Mary commented:

> A cause of great anxiety opened to me at this time, namely, several of my young people, and indeed, more than I then knew of, had become objects of attention, and were likely soon to leave the paternal home. I shall say little on the subject of my own children's marriages, or on the marriages of the orphans under my care, nor even what I thought of them at the time; but as in the course of this life much good is mixed with evil, and much evil with good, to work out the wise arrangements of Providence, so the results of these marriages have proved a twisted thread of both.[231]

The Sherwoods' contact with India continued: there were visits from the Reverend Thomason, who was Sophia's godfather, and from Mr and Mrs Sherer. They brought the sad news that Annie, their adopted daughter, had died. Lucy Cameron's health was delicate. In May 1828, while visiting her mother-in-law, Mrs Cameron, she consulted Dr. Streeten about her symptoms. Much to Mary's surprise she learnt from her sister that Dr. Streeten 'had entreated her to make interest with us for my young and lovely Emily. My first enquiry was "Does she like him?" She has never mentioned his name at home to any one.'[232] According to Mrs Cameron, Emily was too naïve to comprehend what had been said the previous day and so had no idea of Robert Streeten's ardour. Mary had a meeting with Streeten the following day at which Henry was also present. It was decided that the whole matter must in the end be left to Emily but they would not object. Three days later Emily accepted his proposal: she would be seventeen in July. Lucy Sherwood was heartbroken at the prospect of her younger sister leaving home. However, just three weeks later, Dr. Battles, a friend of the Reverend Dawes, asked for Lucy's hand. Although he had been brought up in England he was of Spanish extraction and had been forced to flee Spain due to his violent opposition to the Inquisition. Lucy refused him. Mary comments: 'He was not only a foreigner, but an outlaw.'

Emily was married to Dr. Streeten on November 18, 1829. This left Lucy aged twenty, Henry, sixteen, and Sophia, fourteen, still at home. Sophia was shaping up to be strong and assertive in manner. She was fearless and loved physical challenge, riding bareback to Snedshill and back. On a visit to Newport where there was an exhibition of wild animals she put her hand through the bars of a sleeping lion's cage and came home triumphantly clutching some lion hair. The name of the sleeping lion was Wallace.

~

Mary's relationship with the Evangelical church had become strained. *Emancipation*,[233] published in 1829 was criticised:

> Her insidious writings, under the guise of friendship, have brought contempt upon religion, and diffused all the evils of novel-reading through numerous families where they could not, otherwise, have been introduced…[234]

She had argued that Evangelical societies encouraged young people to embrace religion when they in fact were too young to understand the full meaning of the message preached. *Emancipation* is an attack on liberal principle. A liberal father rues the upbringing he has given his two oldest children:

... for I have not only despised the Bible, but all those persons who drew their
wisdom from the Bible, and their authority from God; and I have ruined your
brother and sister...[235]

Those who believe in God and his mercy obtain:

... eternal happiness in the world to come, but also entitled them, in this world,
to the precious benefits conferred by the reaching of the Holy Spirit—that
sacred Person of the adorable Trinity who has, in his infinite mercy, taken
upon himself to call, to sanctify, and finally to glorify, all such as have been
predestined to salvation by God the Father.[236]

With the help of his youngest daughter, Sarah, the father is brought to see
that the Church is central to good governance within the family. The
book ends with his rejection of his liberal ideas:

... we are all set free from that absurd system of liberality by which every bond
of society is broken through, and every ancient and sacred obligation
dissolved; by which the wife is emancipated from the dominion of her
husband, the child from the parent, the servant from that of his master, and
the members of the Established Church from the authority of the legal ruler of
the empire.[237]

When the first volume of *Roxobel* (1830–31) was published Mary took a
further swipe at her Evangelical critics:

The writer is aware that an extended narrative, which if natural, must embrace
various stages and conditions of human life, is rejected by many worthy
persons, as not being a desirable mode of conveying instruction: and there can
be no question that this form of composition...has often been rendered an
exceedingly powerful engine in the hands of the evil one. But, because an
engine is powerful, should it merely on that account, be relinquished to the
foe? And if some have been busy in directing this engine against the bulwarks
of religion and morality, should others refuse to use it in the case of
godliness?[238]

In spite of some criticism, Mary's books had brought financial security so
in 1830 the Sherwoods could afford to stop running the school at Wick
House. A Mrs Tookey took on the school in June, bringing with her as
many pupils as she could. Lucy Butt, Marten's daughter, joined Mrs
Tookey in partnership. Only one of Mary's pupils chose to remain and
the school failed the following year. The Sherwoods moved only one field

away to a small house, Lower Wick, near the mill and the bridge on the road to Malvern. A sloping garden surrounded the house on three sides. Now they afforded a housemaid and manservant but the change from a hectic life to a much quieter one proved difficult for Mary. She missed the bustle and companionship of the children.

However, her new freedom from domestic demands meant the family could travel to Liverpool to witness an historic event: the opening on September 15, 1830 of the double track railway between Liverpool and Manchester. They had to walk across fields before arriving at the side of the railway where they purchased seats on forms for 3/6d each. Standing room opposite cost 6d. Huge crowds descended in time to see magnificent processions of open carriages drawn by steam engines, one from Liverpool and one from Manchester. Wellington, the hero of the Battle of Waterloo, was on board the latter. The procession went slowly past, amidst cheering, flag-waving and handkerchief waving. Further down the line one of the dignitaries, William Huskisson MP, dismounted from his carriage in order to pay his respects to Wellington and was run over by Stephenson's Rocket engine which was pulling the train from the opposite direction. He died later. This caused great alarm as to the safety of travelling by rail.

An Extended Holiday: August 1831–June 1832

The Sherwoods decided to let both houses and travel abroad, first to Paris, then to Geneva, Lyons, Nice and Italy before returning via Geneva and Paris:

> We had formed a resolution to give up our residence in Worcester, and travel abroad. It was the wish of our children, and we thought it might do their health good, for they showed too plainly by their delicate appearance that they were natives of a warmer climate than England.
>
> I have said it was only during the first year of our return from India, before my mother's death, that the taking of pupils, in a pecuniary point of view, was needful to us. But I liked it; my heart was in it, and it was one labour to educate my own children with others. The right and pleasure of educating my own children and my orphan girls I would not willingly have given up to any one whilst life and strength were spared me from on high. But now we gave up our pupils, as I was not as strong as before, and as our daughters missed their young companions, for they had been accustomed to a large and cheerful family circle, we looked on travelling as a resource.[239]

Before making any plans Henry needed to get permission for leave of absence from his regiment, the Brunswick Hussars. This necessitated a trip to London. Permission for Henry's leave of absence was granted. However, the holiday was delayed because Emily became seriously ill so the family did not depart for France until the end of August 1831.

Mary's views on the Catholic religion had hardened considerably since her previous holiday in 1821, when she and Henry had revisited the scenes of his childhood at Abbeville. The Popery Act (1698) had imposed a number of penalties and disabilities on Roman Catholics in England; the Papists Act (1778) eliminated some of these. The Roman Catholic Relief Act of 1829 established further Catholic emancipation throughout Britain. The passing of the Act caused alarm among

Protestants for now the Papists enjoyed the vote and the right to stand for Parliament. To many Protestants the symbols of the Catholic faith were viewed with disapproval and misgiving. Lucy Cameron shared Mary's antipathy towards Catholicism and writes:

> The probability of Roman Catholics entering Parliament has filled my mind. Oh England, my country, how wilt thou be lost, if thou again puttest thyself under the yoke of Rome! I have heavy thoughts on this subject.
> ... Good Friday. "It is finished." The voice from the throne has proclaimed, "It is done." Antichrist reigns over us once more, and the witnesses, the Protestants of this land, once more bear testimony in sackcloth.
> ... Lord clothe us with spiritual sackcloth, and make us abhor our lukewarmness, which has brought such evils upon us.[240]

In France Mary was once more confronted by a religion which she felt threatened her own religious belief. During this holiday Mary's anti-Catholic views and prejudices became more entrenched. She was shocked by the lack of Sabbath observance on her travels. Her diary records her outrage on finding people going about their ordinary business, enjoying themselves at the theatre and behaving in a manner which she felt was indecorous and disrespectful on the Sabbath.

In Geneva the Sherwoods lodged next door to Monsieur Malan.[241] Born in Geneva he had come under the influence of the Evangelical church and later embraced the doctrines of Calvin.[242] Ordained in 1810, he later espoused the doctrine that salvation was through faith not through human righteousness. This led to open conflict with the established church in Geneva and he was asked to change his doctrine 'because of the danger that would come from preaching that good works are not necessary to salvation. Malan refused.'[243] In 1818 the authorities in Geneva banned Malan from preaching in the city and in the cantons. Malan maintained that he was upholding the old church of Geneva, the church of Calvin. On October 7, 1818 an advertisement for one of his services at Ferney was placed in the *Feuille d'Avis* by his opponents:

> On the following Sunday there will be in Ferney-Voltaire a troop of Momiers [mountebanks or mummers] under the direction of the master Regentin. They will continue their fantastic performance, juggling and sleight of hand. The black clown will amuse the crowd with his drolleries. Tickets can be had at the lottery office.[244]

Malan recounts how he became aware of this derogatory label which was devised to heap ridicule on him.

> At first he was not aware that he was meant; but supposed that as the habits of the places and time encouraged Sabbath day exhibitions of all kinds,—it was a real juggler who had availed himself of the crowd and would actually exhibit his mountebank tricks. "When I found out the truth" said he, with his dark eyes beaming light—"I was full of joy. Then I knew this was a great thing. I did not see it so plain before. They had given it a name; it is a great work; they have so treated great works before: I saw that God intended great things!"[245]

Malan was not defeated: in 1820 he built a chapel in the grounds of his home at Pré l'Évêque. For him this was the true church, the church of Calvin. The family attended a service in the chapel and heard Malan preach. Mary was much taken by Malan and when he took her to task in a kindly way on her *Church Catechism Stories*: 'in which I had asserted that Christ instead of acting according to the will of the Father, had, as it were, by interposing himself between the Father and the sinner, compelled, him to have mercy.' Mary spent many hours listening to the teaching of Malan and as a result her views on salvation changed dramatically.

> In measure, as I see the non-conditionality of salvation to the child of God—a non-conditionality wholly built upon the fulfilment of all conditions by the second Adam, Christ, there is a cessation of my feelings, of what in former years had almost filled them. I find no longer any references to those weary and fruitless searchings for any good in myself, which are recorded in my old journals as accruing day after day, and year after year, almost from my youth, till I was far advanced in middle age, with occasional strong expressions of hopelessness because I found it not, or sometimes those of self-satisfaction when any flatterer told me that I had found what I was searching for. But when I was blessed by clearer views of the work of the Saviour, and of the demerits of man—which views were first conveyed to my mind with clearness through the ministry of M. Malan— all these expressions of self-seeking, harassing fear and doubts, suddenly disappeared from my diary. Though I know that human agency unassisted can do nothing, yet I must ever believe and say that M. Malan was, by divine blessing, made decidedly useful to me.[246]

Mary also met Lady Sophia Raffles while in Geneva. She was the second wife and widow of Sir Stamford Raffles. He began his career at 14 as a clerk in the British East India Company. In 1805 he was posted to Prince of Wales Island (now Penang). His first wife, Olivia, died in 1814 while

Raffles was Governor General of Java. Devastated by her death and in poor physical health himself he returned to England where he was knighted and married Sophia Hull three years later. He returned to the Far East with his wife and in 1819 founded modern Singapore. He and his family settled in Bencoolen, (now Sumatra). Here he could indulge his fascination with the local fauna and flora, collecting specimens that were then sent to England. To the delight of his children he kept some of the unusual animals as pets: one, a Sun Bear cub, was allowed to join him at dinner, eating mangoes and drinking champagne![247] Sadly three of his four children died in Bencoolen within six months of each other. The surviving child, Ella, was sent to England. On his return to England in 1825 he founded the Zoological Society and London Zoo becoming its first president in 1826. Many mammals and plants bear testimony to his discovery while in the Far East, a part of the world he loved. He learnt the Malay language and history. Both he and his wife were in poor health when they returned, impoverished, to England and, in 1826, he died, a day before his forty-fifth birthday. He was refused a burial inside his parish church because of his anti-slavery stance: the vicar came from a family that had made its money in Jamaica in the slave trade.

Lady Raffles was in Geneva with her daughter, Ella and a nephew, Charles Raffles. Ella would die at the tender age of nineteen. Lady Raffles was deputed to call on Mary by a group of religious English and Genevese ladies.

> We had desired to live unknown at Geneva, but it seems that some of the principal religious Genevese and English ladies, who were then residing there, had a little scheme in view, and so, contrary to the etiquette of the place, Lady Raffles, was put forward to call upon us as soon as our arrival was known. This scheme was, that I should write a book on a very curious custom existing in Geneva, which is fully detailed in the little work. The Christian ladies who wished this done, at my desire, sent me written documents on the subject, which being received, I wrote the story 'The Little Momiere'.[248]

This long holiday was proving to be a rich source of material to inspire Mary's writing which was becoming violently anti-papist in tone and reflected her increasingly hostile view of Catholicism.

~

The Sherwoods arrived in Lyons on October 22, 1831. There they found lodgings at the Hôtel du Parc, in the Place de Terraux, where they negotiated for a second sitting room and were given one with good views of the Hôtel de Ville. Each evening they were brought an 'English' dinner; the French way of serving meals was not to Mary's taste. Mary had complained about the bread since leaving Geneva and took to giving Sophia rice instead.

The silk weaving industry was a major source of employment in the Lyons district. Silk demand had declined in 1831 due to the economy so the silk price had dropped and, as a result, so had the silk workers' wages which created social unrest in Lyons at the time. This unrest would unleash itself in revolts by the silk workers against their masters: the Canut revolts. The Canuts numbered about 8,000. They were the silk weaving craftsmen, owned their looms and employed apprentices who lived with them. Most of their workshops were located in the Croix Rousse area of Lyons. They sought to impose a minimum fixed price on silk so that their standard of living would remain unaltered. When the manufacturers refused, anarchy broke out. The Sherwoods seemed to be blissfully unaware of the brewing violence. When the party went out for walks they were identified as 'les Anglais' which would have put them in grave danger as the English were not popular at the time: they were seen as being responsible for injuring trade. In spite of being followed the family went out to join the local populace in celebrating All Saints' Day. Mary found much to be critical about:

> We met multitudes of people, chiefly women, all dressed in their holiday garb. Much is said of the beauty of French women, but those who extol this beauty must have curious taste…Their countenances are never at rest; they are either forcing smiles or rolling their eyes, or wrinkling their brows, in consequence of which they lose their smoothness at a very early age.
>
> But to return to our walk on this fête day. Our young people insisted that the females looked like shuttlecocks, with the feathers of course uppermost. These holiday dames all wore immensely large fly-away caps, their lower limbs being tightened and finished off with well-fitting shoes, for they are certainly very neat about the feet.[249]

After dining they decided to go to the theatre where they sat in a box and caused much interest from the rest of the audience. Mary was horrified by the French style of acting:

I never saw anything worse; such ranting, raving, and exaggerating would not have passed in a barn in England. But this was not the worst; dancing was introduced in the regular opera style—a style about which I have ever wondered how it could be tolerated by respectable people, as it is in the English opera.[250]

The party swept out of the box 'having had enough of the French theatre for ever.' A few days later, on November 4 a mob gathered in the Place de Terraux but were driven back by the National Guard supported by dragoons. The Sherwoods appear to have enjoyed the spectacle not realising how serious the situation would become after they left the town on November 14. Their landlord, Monsieur Levrat, fully aware of the gravity of the situation, hit on the plan of sending his four-year old son, Paul, who was well known in the quarter, with them on a dummy run. They had all their luggage with them but passed the barricades without harm, both on leaving, and on returning, to their lodging. The next day they left, without incident, for Nice.

The Times newspaper dated November 24, 1831 reported that the 'scenes of riot and bloodshed originated in the distress of the workmen employed in the silk manufactures of that city, and had no political object.' News of the rioting continued to be reported by *The Times* from various sources including *La Gazette de France* and private letters from France.

On Monday the 21st at 7 o'clock in the morning, the silk weavers who inhabit the commune of the Croix Rousse rose in a rebellious manner, and barricaded the quarters which they occupied. They first assaulted several manufacturers; they disarmed some National Guards, and prepared to march against Lyons. This movement was announced only by loud menaces against persons and property.

The authorities being warned, immediately took measure, and sent troops against the rioters. All endeavours to disperse them by persuasion having failed, it was necessary to have recourse to force. The troops of the line and the National Guard prepared to repel their criminal aggression; the Prefect repaired to the spot. The workmen then desired to parley. The Prefect and General Ordonneau, desiring to stop the effusion of blood, in fact advanced towards them; but they had scarcely approached these madmen when they were seized and made prisoners.

The next report revealed the gravity of the situation:

Paris, November 25 at 4 o'clock in the morning P.S. The President of the Council has received at midnight an estafette, [dispatch rider] which a person in high office at Lyons succeeded in despatching to the government. His letter written on the 23rd, at 1 o'clock in the morning, announces that the revolt of workmen has recommenced, that they have made themselves masters of the bridges, and intercepted all communications. The troops were defending the Town-hall, the arsenal, and the powder-magazine. General Ordonneau has been given up by the rebels ...

The Times reports continued:

5 p.m. The cannon have been firing for these three hours on the people, and the people return the fire with advantage because they are masters of the heights...

7 p.m. 40 of our National Guard are killed, above 150 wounded: despondency filled every heart. When will the frightful carnage cease? The insurgents cry, 'Long live Napoleon, chief of the republic!' The General and the Prefect have been eight hours prisoners in the hands of the insurgents. They were not released till three canons belonging to the National Guard were employed.

Two of these cannons have fallen into the hands of the insurgents.

At the departure of the post they were masters of all the heights that surround Lyons.

The problem facing the government was the lack of force available to bring the rioters under control. It was not until December when 40,000 men – as reported in *The Times* – other sources gave 20,000, under the command of the Duke of Orleans and Marshal Nicholas Soult, Minister of War, brought a cessation to the fighting. Arrests were made among the workers, the fixed price was abolished and a large garrison put in place to maintain order.

The Sherwoods had had a lucky escape. The appearance in English papers of a report that Captain Sherwood and his family had all been brutally murdered caused their family and friends in England unimaginable grief. In fact the family which had been murdered were called Saunders. They had been living in Lyons for the past three years. Mr Saunders went out with the National Guard to try to drive back a group of rioters from the silk workers' Croix-Rousse district. Saunders, a hot tempered man shot one of the rioters dead. Immediately the cry went up: 'À bas les Anglais.' Saunders rushed back to his hotel arriving just ahead of the howling mob. He barricaded the top of the stairs with a chest of drawers behind which cowered his wife, three teenage daughters and his six-year old son. The mob rushed up the stairs. Three were shot and killed by Saunders which enraged the mob even more. He was shot dead, his three daughters raped and killed and his little son almost beheaded. The only survivor was the traumatised Mrs Saunders who had hidden in a closet.

∿

Having escaped the events in Lyons, the Sherwoods remained in Nice at Croix de Marbre in the English quarter until April, 1832. Here, shortly after their arrival, their manservant, Joseph, announced that two aides-de-camp to the King of Sardinia were waiting in the upper salon. Nice was at that time part of the Kingdom of Sardinia. Mary was alone in the house and received the news with great anxiety as to what she had done to merit this visit. She went upstairs muttering to herself, 'Courage! Courage!' As she entered the room three officers from the Brigade d'Acquis moved forward, bowing. Much to Mary's relief she learnt that the purpose of their visit was social: they were planning to throw a ball for the English in Nice and had hired the neighbouring houses on the left and right of the Sherwoods, whose house shared a splendid marble terrace onto which windows opened from all three houses. The question was, could the terrace be used to provide a link between the two houses: one for the ball and one where supper would be served at midnight. It seemed churlish to refuse so Mary gave her permission. At the weekend, preparations for the ball entailed erecting an awning over the terrace thus reducing the family 'to living in the light that owls do.' The colonel invited the ladies to attend the ball but Mary firmly refused saying 'there are many Protestant families who do not approve of public amusements for their daughters.' This did not deter the colonel and the entreaties from both him and his officers continued but Mary was adamant. Their mother does not record what Lucy and Sophia felt having seen the opulent decorations: garlands of roses, myrtle and swathes of muslin with little lights twinkling enticingly. The terrace was transformed into a card room and was the main thoroughfare between the ballroom and the house where the sumptuous supper was laid on. On Tuesday, the day after the ball, the colonel appeared and thanked Mary profusely and expressed his regret that none of the young ladies had come. He then presented a box edged with silver on which was an enamelled panel depicting a young girl at the altar of Cupid – much to Mary's amusement.

Inside, the box was filled with 'bon-bons, comfits, hearts and knots of ribbon.' Perhaps small comfort to her daughters who had missed out on all the gaiety.

~

In April the family set off for Italy, making short stays at Genoa, Pisa, Florence, Ferrara, Padua and Venice before returning via Milan, Turin, Geneva and Cologne to Rotterdam which they reached in June 1832. Here Mary encountered Sir Walter Scott who was waiting on the quayside at Rotterdam.[251] Scott was a very sick man when the Sherwoods met him: he was returning from a tour of Europe where he had been lionised. He was lying on a bed in a barouche, the horses having been uncoupled, before being transferred on to a packet boat to the *Batavier* on which the Sherwoods would also cross the Channel. Scott became ill once he had been transferred to a cabin where he was treated by a fellow passenger, a Russian doctor, who gave him a sedative. When he woke up he asked for a pen and paper. It was Mary's habit to always carry these so that she could note the passing scene and the people she encountered. She was approached to give him the pen and paper she was using at the time and records how honoured she felt in giving them to the dying author of such fame: he would die in September that year at his home near Melrose in the Scottish borders.

'We looked on travelling as a resource'

After her return from France in 1832 Catholicism was presented in her writing in a wholly negative way. *Victoria* and *The Little Momiere* were both published in 1833. *Victoria* portrays the dangers of entrusting a young ten-year old, nominally Protestant, English child, Victoria, to an Italian nurse, Teresa, who is Catholic. Set in Nice where the inhabitants were 'subject to a very severe discipline under the authority of the priests' the book describes the Rosebury family who have come to Nice, in the Kingdom of Sardinia, for the winter. Although Victoria's family is Protestant her parents lack any commitment to their religion and her mother is represented as worldly and vain. Worse still she neglects her daughter's religious education. Victoria has accepted Teresa's Catholic teaching and is unaware that her parents are Protestant. This revelation takes place in a dramatic scene between Mr Rosebury and his daughter after Teresa has left:

> '…You shall soon know what my religion is, Victoria—we will read the Bible and study it together.' …
>
> 'I had rather not hear about it,' answered Victoria. 'About what?' asked Mr Rosebury. 'About your religion,' replied the child; 'please, papa, let us talk of something else.'
>
> '…In one word, has Teresa set you against my religion? Look at me and speak candidly, and be quite sure that if you speak the truth I will forgive Teresa everything she may have said.'
>
> The shattering response comes with:
>
> 'Teresa did not know that you had any religion.'[252]

The plot takes many twists and turns before Mary resolves the family's religious predicament when a Mr Reynolds urges the family to leave Nice and return to a Protestant country where 'they were enabled to enjoy the society of persons professing the parent Christian principles and to attend a ministry as far as possible removed from the errors of Papacy, though not, I fear, in the established Church of Geneva … Victoria became teachable as a child ought to be; Mr Rosebury was confirmed and enlightened, and all the energies of Mrs Rosebury's character became directed into the right channel.'

~

The Little Momiere attacked the lax attitude to Sunday observance in Geneva. In the *Advertisement* at the beginning of *The Little Momiere* Mary explains the background to the book:

> The Little Momiere, having been written by the express desire of certain pious ladies of Geneva, and actually commenced in that place, it is hoped that it will be found to be a correct representation of the manners of the little territory, and a faithful picture of that singular custom, by which the daughters of the higher classes of Genevese are thus deprived of the blessings and privileges which children in other Christian countries derive from their leisure of the Lord's Day.

The Little Momiere tells the story of Sophie Levrat the daughter of a Geneva merchant. Her mother has died giving birth to Sophie who has been taken by Janet, her very pious Calvinist wet nurse, to live with her and her family outside Geneva. When the child is four she returns to Geneva to come under the influence of a governess from Paris: 'it was expedient that she should render Sophie as agreeable in the eyes of the world … . Perceiving that the little girl had acquired some ideas of religion which she did not approve …' Sophie's older sister, Pauline, has no interest in her young sister and is jealous of her beauty. Both girls marry, Sophie for love and Pauline for social position. Mary describes the Sunday Assemblies in Geneva. These are held in private homes and are limited to twelve or fifteen girls with a difference in age of four years between the youngest and oldest.

> You may understand from this that mothers are very scrupulous regarding the choice of the young girls who are admitted into the same Society with their daughters, and who are to form a friendship which may last for their lives, observing carefully that their rank in life be the same.[253]

When Sophie's husband is posted to London by his bank Sophie goes too:

'nor could Sophie hesitate for one moment between her country, however dear that country might be, and her husband.' A sentiment which Mary had experienced when Henry was posted to Bengal. London is a lonely place for Sophie and made worse when her father, Levrat, dies. However, Sophie is saved from her loneliness and despair by an Evangelical family, the Seymours, who happen to live next door. It is through the teaching of her friendly neighbour, the Reverend Seymour, that she is brought to the truth 'not that you will be saved but that you are saved, that you are a child of God.' Sophie brings her husband to see the light and the two families form a close-knit group. She has a daughter, also called Sophie and is blessed by a state of happiness. But happiness is fleeting. Her husband dies. Mother and daughter travel back to Geneva braving high mountain passes before they reach Pauline's home. By this time Sophie senior is dying. Mary describes the lingering death bed scene in the presence of Sophie's beloved nurse, Janet Keller.

The worldly aunt and her family depart for the delights of Paris and little Sophie is taken by Janet to her mountain village where her home 'was as a garden in a wilderness, being within the limits of Savoy, which is a Roman Catholic county.' When the bells ring on Sunday Sophie is firmly instructed 'that bell ... is not for us ... but we will pray for those of our poor neighbours who are summoned by it to their mistaken services.' Sophie is taught that the only true religion is Calvinism and that Roman Catholicism preaches the wrong doctrines for true salvation.

When her aunt and family return from Paris Sophie and Janet leave the mountain village for Geneva. Mary then introduces the momiere theme. Sophie is taken to a service 'to one of those places of worship in and near Geneva, which are so well-known, and so dear to those persons in that neighbourhood, who are attached to the old doctrines of the reformers.' On leaving, Sophie is attacked by a mob shouting: 'Ah une momiere de plus! Une momiere de bon ton!' When her aunt and family return from Paris Sophie is shocked to see her aunt and cousins dressed in the latest Paris fashion:

> They all wore trousers, ruffled at the heels, having short full white frocks, which scarcely reached below the knee, the bodies being long, and closely compressed round the waist, a pelerine or tippet being over the shoulders, with immense wide flaps hanging over the upper part of the arms; the hair forced up from the face á la chinôis, [sic] terminated by a huge tortoiseshell comb.

Her two cousins do not want Sophie to join their coterie and when Sophie asks to attend the chapel at Pré l'Évêque her angry aunt refuses saying: 'these momieres have poisoned the mind of a child, and rendered her wiser in her own eyes than all who went before her.'

Sophie lectures her aunt: 'people called momieres know the way, and they speak of that way in their churches, and sing it in their hymns, and talk of it in their common discourse, and I am happy with them, and in their company.' Her aunt then has a change of heart and decides that Sophie should be admitted into the select society on Sundays which she and her two daughters have been part of since young girls. Sophie is dressed up for her introduction into the society. She naively thinks that it will take the form of a Sunday School with hymns and Bible readings. When she enters the room she is bewildered by the scene and when cards are brought out she flees the room: 'I cannot, I will not stay. Let me go!' A few pages later she is found collapsed on the floor of her room; Janet is called for and another death-bed scene flows from Mary's pen. Sophie's final words being: 'Oh! Janet! I was not mistaken! I am redeemed—I know it now! ... He has taken my sins away...' Mary incorporated the theme of the lone child who, having seen the light, tries to bring others to redemption – a message that she uses in many of her works. Mary had clearly drawn much of this story from her observations in Geneva. Sophie Levrat's surname is taken from the Sherwoods' landlord who saved them in Lyons.

Mary finished writing the book in Lyons, and dated it November 5, 1831. In *The Little Momiere* Mary's skill at combining dramatic narrative with lyrical description of the Swiss scenery created a structure which her fictional characters inhabit with strong realism. Most importantly, Mary used the theme of religious persecution to promote her embrace of Calvinism

'all the evils of novel-reading'

The holiday had not only hardened Mary's views on the Papists but had provided anti-Papist material which she incorporated into several books of this period. Her ties with the Evangelical church were loosened further now that her understanding of salvation had been so radically changed by Malan. She was defiant over her strong use of narrative in spite of attacks by Evangelicals who had accused her of using the novel form to put across her moral message

Undeterred by her critics, including her former allies in belief – the Evangelicals – she produced two alarmingly anti-Papist novels: *The Nun, A Narrative*[254] (1833) and *The Monk of Cimiés*[255] (1834). The first recounts the horrifying fate of a nun who has apostatised from the Catholic doctrine and become Protestant in her views which leads to cruel psychological persecution when she is labelled a heretic. The second recounts the story of a young man who renounces the Church of England and joins the Catholic Church. In her Preface to *The Nun* Mary defends her position by justifying her views which she says are based on first-hand observation:

> The history of the Nun is founded on various facts which came to the knowledge of the writer during a residence of some months in Italy. The internal arrangements of the convent, and the mode of life of its inmates, having been carefully compared with an account given by the superior of a convent on the Continent, and proved to be correct by reference to books upon the subject, procured from a Jesuit's library, and other sources, in a city of Italy.
>
> The author is anxious to state that she has been particularly desirous to avoid exaggeration, and that whenever she has brought forward any very strong doctrine of the Papal Church, she has been careful to give her authorities: the book from which these are principally taken is the Catéchism Théologique, par le R.F.P. de la compagnie de Jésus, published at Avignon in 1775; which Catechism was composed by the R.P. François Porney, de la

compagnie de Jésus, at Lyons, in 1664, and published by the permission of l'Abbé de S. Just, Vicar-General. There are some points in the present narrative taken from a book also printed at Avignon—being the history of St. Patrick, and authorized and approved by Simon Ximenez, Vicar-General of Madrid. There are also many means which the Author had of obtaining information, which (as may be easily understood) she is not at liberty to particularize; but she is willing to refer, for the truth of her statements, to any persons, who, having been on the Continent, may have given themselves the trouble to investigate such subjects as are treated of in this little narrative.

If it is suggested that the Romish Church has not the power at the present time, to persecute to the extent stated in the history, the objector is requested to observe that the narrative is dated before the French Revolution, although most of the facts on which the story is founded are of a more recent date; and may it not be inferred, that as semper eadem is the motto of the Romish church, and that as the Jesuit asserts in his Catechism, "que depuis son établissement, elle a toujours été la même, et le sera jusqu'à la fin de siècle"— that if the persecution has ceased, it is only because the power is diminished; and that with any increase of power would come abundance of will to make this evil use of it.

The Author begs also to refer to Dr. Buchanan's '*Christian Researches in Asia*,' under the article of '*Goa*'—and to a vast number of modern writers, (some of whom have suffered in their own persons) who have published works on these subjects, many of whom have brought forward facts of a nature not to be admitted in a narrative intended for the instruction of young people in refined society.

Both *The Nun, A Narrative* and *The Monk of Cimiés* owe much to the fashion for the Gothic genre: a genre which enabled Mary to utilise her descriptive and narrative powers so successfully. The settings in Italy of mediaeval convents with secret subterranean passages, secret grottoes and chapels, create a minatory atmosphere. Mary does not disappoint:

> There was a part of the house, the passages to which were by doors at the end of a long gallery ... Here also was a tower, which had been resigned for years past to the owls and bats ... We believed that the sister Clarice slept in some of those chambers, and that she was under the special surveillance of Madame.[256]

Far from being a refuge, this enclosed world, which Mary creates, brings horror and isolation for the beautiful nun, Clarice, who is trapped in a nightmare world from which there appears to be no escape except through death. The power of evil, represented by the Papists, threatens the right-minded, good Protestant. Into this narrative structure Mary delivers a vehement anti-Papist polemic. *The Nun* ends:

... and thus I terminate my history, trusting that those things respecting the Roman Catholic church, which I have faithfully recorded, may tend to fill the inhabitants of this Protestant land with a sense of gratitude to that God, who has liberated their country from the slavery of that great apostacy whose name is MYSTERY.

The Monk of Cimiés is more extreme in its warnings against the Papists and the inherent danger should Roman Catholicism gain strength in England. There are lengthy passages devoted to debating the nature of the true church. Mary includes debate between dissenters, Jesuits and Catholics. The Abbé of the monastery argues:

The true church did not acknowledge the Church of England, as being any thing more than an assembly of heretics; "for, inasmuch as," continued he, " your church does not agree with ours in every article of faith, it has not the characters and proper qualities of the true church; for the proper qualities of the true church are, that it is one,—that it has the same faith, and the same chief—is universal and perpetual, and that it is holy. Now there is only the Roman Catholic church which has these qualities, from whence it follows, that this is the true church, and that all others are but synagogues of satan."[257]

When the narrator, Edmund Etherington, sees the error he has fallen into through the arguments of the Jesuits and the Catholics, he delivers a damning verdict:

The papacy,—that deepest conception, and mightiest achievement of Satan; into which he hath admitted the whole canon of truth, and yet contrived that it should teach only error; into which he hath admitted the whole revelation of light, and yet contrived that it should breed only foul and pestilent darkness. Oh! It is an ample net for catching men, a delusion and bondage made for the world.[258]

Her message, which at times is over-didactic and melodramatic in its condemnation, received this stern comment in 1837:

...unfair and unconvincing. The party to be praised is made all that is excellent; and the party to be reprobated all that is wicked; and the sympathy of the reader is gained by artificial colouring, instead of the judgement being guided by sober truth.[259]

Sabbaths on the Continent (1835)[260] is an autobiographical travel record of her observations in several cities which she had visited on her continental holidays. Mary goes into a full attack on the lack of religious

observance and the perils of embracing Roman Catholicism. She opens
the book in Boulogne which she had visited with Henry and Henrietta in
1821.

> I am a great observer of human manners, and especially as they are more or
> less affected by our religious feelings; and that it is my particular caprice in a
> journey I am making on the Continent to observe how the Lord's day is spent
> in the various towns in which I have happened to pass that day, for our party
> makes a point of never moving on a Sunday.[261]

In each town she stays on her travels she searches out the Protestant
chapel which she invariably finds difficulty in locating and then
discovers is closed. She complains about the noise and merriment taking
place in the streets. Catholic churches and graveyards with their large,
heavy marble statues and images are cause for strong censure by Mary.
After she arrives in Paris, she is directed on the Sunday to a theatre where
there is a political speech being delivered from the stage by an orator who
employs histrionics to illustrate his point. She begins to object and is
silenced by a member of the audience with the admonition: 'Listen ... be
silent and be instructed.' Mary and her party remove themselves from
'the manifold errors of popery.' She damns the fountains for playing at
Versailles and the statues in the Tuileries gardens as 'false taste.' She
observes men and women behaving like children at a funfair when they
should have been engaged in more sober and elevating pursuits.

At Dijon they stay at the best hotel in town, the Chapeau Rouge, and
Mary expounds on the transubstantiation:

> The poor misguided people believe that when they have been present at a
> ceremony of this kind, although they only look on while the priests perform it,
> they have done a meritorious work, which will weigh heavy in the balance
> against any sins.[262]

A celebration involving fireworks and prizes for shooting a pigeon and a
swan brings censure; not for cruelty to winged creatures but because it
takes place on the Sabbath. Dijon cathedral is full of 'tawdry ornaments,
artificial flowers, with which the Papists destroy the fine edifice.' Some
relief is provided by a walk on the ramparts where she can see the Jura
mountains in the distance but relief is short-lived on sighting people
playing shuttlecock and battledore in the streets below. The party retires

to the hotel. A little perspective on her critical view is brought by a conversation with a Frenchman who maintains that he has witnessed no less debauched scenes in Hyde Park and other parts of London on a Sunday adding:

> You, my good friends, no doubt, when at home, live in some very respectable street or retired county, and never dream of what you would see were you to become an inquiring traveller in your own country as you are in this … leaving us to look at one another as persons who have received a total discomfiture when they expected a brilliant victory.[263]

Mary reprimands herself stating she should be less proud. On they journey to Geneva and Mary reassures her companions:

> In a short time, my dear young people,…we enter into a Protestant country: we shall no more see emblems of idolatry set by the way, no gilded crosses or grated shrines…objects which have wounded our feelings so continually since we commenced our travels. But we shall see the towers where Calvin and Beza[264] preached.[265]

She has harsh words for Voltaire who had lived in Ferney: 'I had forgotten that the residence of this blasphemous man was so near Geneva! … Let us hope that Geneva has not admitted the venom of this serpent.' In Geneva Mary takes the opportunity to lay down the doctrine of Calvinism which is now close to her own in doctrinal beliefs. To her horror they meet an old man who announces that the church is now reformed due to the influence of Rousseau[266] and Voltaire.[267] Some relief is found from the evil effects of the Reformed Church in Geneva when the party attends a service at Malan's chapel.

In Lyons Mary is irate when, having retired to bed at nine o'clock, the family is disturbed by a fun fair near their hotel. A ride called the Montagne Russe causes great excitement among the younger members of her party. It consisted of little cars hurtling down an inclined plane and then being dragged up the opposite side. To everyone's horror a terrible accident happens involving a young man. But ten minutes later card playing and dancing resume. Poor Mary, her disapproval prevented her from enjoying the life and culture of the towns she visited.

At Aix she is able to spread the word when she is asked by a young man how Protestantism differs from Catholicism. She explains that his belief in the Virgin Mary being the mother of God is blasphemous: Mary is the mother of Christ, the man. Having corrected the young man on this point of doctrine and given him a Bible she notes that this is the 'happiest Sabbath.'

High drama awaits the group at Nice. They discover that a young Englishwoman is about to take the veil and enter a Catholic convent. Mary blames this event on the fact that the novitiate has been taught by a Catholic and perverted. Immediately Mary springs into action to prevent the young woman taking this terrible step. Joseph, from the hotel they are staying in, is deputed to take them to the church where the religious ceremony will take place. However, Joseph takes them on a circuitous route to the church and they arrive too late.

When they reach Cigliano, a small town on Lake Garda in Italy Mary writes:

> I am grieved, however, that my last paper should be filled with darkest views of human corruption which I have yet given ... I was anxious to see popery in its true colours such as it exhibits in the Italian States, in Spain, and in Portugal![268]

Cigliano lives up to her preconceptions and she is horrified and censorious at what she describes as idolatry.

Mary's views on Roman Catholicism are couched in strongly worded anti-Papist propaganda which found full expression in the three books written either while on her travels on the continent or shortly after she returned. She felt that an anti-Christian mood had swept through France and although she attacked popery there she felt it was losing its influence over the populace. No doubt her views had been influenced by the Roman Catholic Relief Act (1829), which was seen as a threat, and further by what she had observed first hand on the continent.

~

Mary did not take up the anti-Catholic message again until ten years later when *The History of John Marten* was published but, perhaps because of the criticism she had received about her earlier attacks on Catholicism, this book was less melodramatic and was set in England rather than the continent. It was published by Hatchard who had not published the two earlier virulent attacks on Catholicism. By this time her own views on the matter had somewhat mellowed. She did return to the Gothic novel again when in 1835 *Shanty the Blacksmith*[269] was published. Written for a young readership it is a gripping tale which has all the elements of a Gothic romance: the orphan, Tamar, abandoned by mysterious gipsies; a minatory atmosphere with ruined castle, prisoner and a lost heir. It is a powerful work of fiction which, no doubt, Mary knew that the Evangelicals would disapprove of in the strongest terms. The same year she published *Caroline Mordaunt*.[270] The novel depicts a young woman who is left an orphan as a child. Relatives pay for her education so that she can become a governess in various households. Mary incorporates both humour and satire in the novel reflecting the influence of Jane Austen in it.

Millenarianism and Hebrew Types

The long holiday in 1831–2 meant that Mary had put on hold a project which had fascinated her:

> I had long been convinced that the Scripture types, or emblems, or that figurative style which is used almost entirely in the prophetic books, is a complete language. We had found it impossible to make anything of this language without looking to the Hebrew; from this circumstance, that the Hebrew and English words do not, and cannot, exactly answer to each other. For example: there are six Hebrew words which are translated earth indiscriminately, whereas these words have all some difference, but necessarily of a very trifling description, to the simple reading of the Bible. These six Hebrew words would describe land or earth in different degrees of cultivation … As types, then, were the object in hand, and those who have once tasted of the extreme interest of the subject can never lose the sense of delight which they are calculated to impart, my daughters soon were deeply interested in the Hebrew.[271]

In order to research this further, Mary, Henry, Lucy and Sophia had begun to study Hebrew. Mary embarked on compiling a 'TYPE DICTIONARY' of Hebrew types or emblems.[272] It was a project which occupied much of her time and would continue until her death. Mary worked at her grandfather's desk which was moved with his bookcase to the little parlour, a low room at the front of the house at Lower Wick. From the window Mary looked out on the orchard: 'a quiet and shady scene, which I have always connected with my first ideas of the millennium.'[273] Lucy, Emily and Sophia were fascinated by the project. Henry also became involved and set about the task of compiling a Hebrew and English Concordance. In *The History of Henry Milner*, Part III, published in 1831, Mary had explained both the millennium and the Hebrew emblems or types. The key character in the book is the saintly Mr

Dalben, who is Mary's mouthpiece. Dalben is teaching the studious young Martyn, then only fifteen, in preparation for Oxford and ordination.

> "…In the language of types, one day, in the most extensive import of the type, stands for one thousand years and vice versa."
> "I know this, sir," replied Henry. "In consequence," returned Mr Dalben, " each day of creation is supposed to become a type of one thousand years of the world's duration. Do you understand me, my boy?"
> "I do, sir," replied Henry.
> "Thus," returned Mr Dalben, "we have a hint of the proposed duration of the world's existence…"
> "In the seventh, we look for the millennium, or Sabbath of a thousand years, which will far exceed the glories of the first Sabbath spent in paradise…"
> "This is very fine and pleasant, uncle," replied Henry, his eyes kindling at the thought of the millennium.[274]

Dalben has already urged his young pupil to embark on making a dictionary for types:

> … Take a blank book, and enter each word alphabetically, writing the meanings of those already received, and adding more as you find them, bringing your proofs from Scripture, and adding others from the classics as you meet with them.[275]

Some sixty pages later Mary again expounds the millennium and defines certain Types from Genesis:

> … The mighty ocean being their mass of the spiritually dead; the fowl, of spirits, or spiritual rulers; the fish, of those among the heathen to whom the spiritual life is imparted, or of such as are prepared to be drawn upon the dry land by the net of the spiritual Fisherman; and the whale or leviathan (for the word in Hebrew is similar, and hath the same import as that translated leviathan in other places of Scripture), is the western Antichrist…[276]

Lucy was still at home, much improved in her health, and on the verge of becoming engaged to William Bagnall, the son of a family friend. However, the gentle, sweet tempered, beautiful Emily, perhaps Mary's favourite daughter, who had suffered from much ill health, became ill once again in 1833. She appeared to be getting better and Mary did not at first realise how ill her daughter was as Emily remained cheerful and positive and continued to enjoy reading. She had remained close to her mother after her marriage and was clearly adored by Mary, who records her anguish as she sees her daughter, the inspiration for many drawings in her books, lose her fight that autumn:

> My Emily was for some time still able to read, and she seemed really to enjoy life. Her affliction was indeed short, and shrinks to nothing in comparison with the glory that was secured to her by her Saviour's death and resurrection.

On October 7, 1833:

> ... my Emily was dressed as usual, and laid on the sofa; she was easy and perfectly cheerful. She remarked on the chimney-piece of white marble and the alabaster ornaments upon it. She noticed the painting of the family group above it, and said, "It was the prettiest chimney-piece in the world." She spoke, too, how she had fallen away; but still I was not alarmed. Early, very early on Tuesday, a violent ringing of the bell in her room made me hasten to my child. I found her dying, flushed with the effort to draw her breath. I stood till her spirit had departed. I saw her last sweet, solemn smile. Then I remembered nothing more for some hours, but seeing all weeping through the house. "Eheu! Emily! My Emily!"[277]

Their beloved daughter, born in Cawnpore in 1811, so beautiful and loving to all who knew her, had died aged twenty-two. Emily was buried in St. John's churchyard, near Worcester, beside George, the Sherwood's last child, who had died in early infancy.

In 1834 both Lucy and her brother married. Henry married Mary Sleigh Barber. He was preparing to take orders and Lucy, married to William Bagnall, was living near Birmingham. Henrietta, Mary's eldest daughter, was settled with her husband, a vicar, in Staffordshire. Now the once busy household was much quieter:

> Then I was left with my youngest daughter; I who had been so rich in children. Yet still for awhile I had these beloved ones on earth. It was at this period that I instructed Sophia in the art of composition; for with a mother's partiality, I fancied she inherited a portion of that talent which I had got from my father. So I spent much time with her alone, teaching her as my own beloved father had taught me. Since then we have been often published together...[278]

Sophia started to write under the name 'Miss S. Sherwood'. After her first marriage she would write as Streeten Butt and Mrs Streeten and later as

Sophia Kelly. Sophia collaborated on several of Mary's later works.

Henry and Mary were delighted when Lucy announced her pregnancy. Their joy was short-lived when, in 1835, Lucy died as a result of childbirth, aged twenty-five, after only ten months of marriage. The baby was baptised immediately before the death of her mother. Lucy had wanted to call the child Emily but William, her husband, intervened, realising that his wife was dying, and announced that she was to be baptised Lucy. Her second name was Emily. Understandably, Mary was bereft having lost two daughters in so short a time.

After the death of Lucy, the Sherwoods decided to leave their home at Lower Wick which had been the setting for so many happy family memories but was now clouded with sadness and, with Sophia, they moved to a house in Britannia Square, Worcester. Mary was finding it difficult to adjust to a much quieter life:

> Most rapid were these arrangements of my children. A few, a very few years, and we, the parents of many, were left, as it were, alone with the youngest one. The only peculiar circumstances in our case were, the changes were more decided, and more quick one upon another, than they were in most families of our rank and station in England. I had not then learned to be alone: to sit often solitary—to miss the voices of my beloved children—to think of them scattered and changed, so that on earth they can never be again to me what they once were.[279]

The Sherwoods were now concerned about Sophia's health. Mary was of the opinion that like her sisters, 'her constitution had been affected by our residence in India.' Thankfully Sophia would prove to have a far more robust constitution than her sisters.

Cruel Reality

hen Mary returned to England from the Continent in June 1832 she had already learnt of her brother Marten's relapse into mental illness following the death of his oldest son, also called Marten. This time there would be no release from the black borders of that dark world which he would inhabit until his death. Mary recounts seeing her brother for the last time in March 1833. A reunion of Mary's Sunday school pupils had been arranged at Bridgnorth and Marten and Jemima were also there. Mary describes how shocked she was to see these once young girls now in middle-age. It was too much for Jemima who broke down in tears. For Mary it was difficult to try and place memories with the present.

> My hands were caught and kissed, whilst every eye ran down with tears. I could not let it pass, and, though some may blame me, I acknowledge that I kissed them all; though for me to recognize the individuals present was impossible, and I did not pretend to do it.
>
> At length we were seated, I with my pupils about me, though some of these, having lived lives of hardship, unquestionably looked older than I did; for age had then dealt gently by me, and I looked, as many told me, much younger than I really was. [She was then 57.] My first question was to ask "who was who?"[280]

Mary hears of the lives of some of her former pupils including one called Margaret who had fallen to the blandishments of a gentleman. He had taken her to London but she had returned home and died 'in deep repentance' – a fate which Mary had warned her pupils about so many years earlier. On that same visit a young boy was brought by his mother to meet Mary. He was called Henry Milner, named after the eponymous character in Mary's books.[281] He presented Mary with 'two ornamental pens wherewith to write another volume of the work from whence he

received his name.'[282] In the evening friends and family, including
Marten, gathered. A discussion took place as to the salvation of animals
who had suffered with man after his fall. Some were of the opinion that
animals, like man, would find salvation, while others disagreed. Mary
argued for the former but Marten became heated, arguing for the latter.

> I took an opportunity of moving next to him on the sofa, and whispered
> "Cæsar," the name of the poor, large, yellow dog which had been the
> companion of our childhood. He turned round and gave me a smile, which
> acknowledged he was conquered. I do not say this was a proof that I was really
> scripturally right; but if it silenced my adversary, for he did not say another
> word against me, it at least showed the tender affection of my brother to the
> companions of his boyhood...
>
> The next day I parted for ever, in this life, from my own and only brother;
> then and there all personal intercourse closed with him who had been my
> cradle-fellow. My beloved brother, I thank my God there was a light from on
> high resting on his head, and he is blessed for ever and ever. I looked back
> from the carriage to gaze on him as long as I could see him; he was walking
> under the rock, Mrs Butt holding his arm. He came quickly; as if to see me, too,
> as long as he could, his person was bent, and the wind agitated his thin white
> hair. The carriage turned a corner of the road, and then that thread of my
> existence, which consisted in intercourse with my Maker, snapped to be
> rejoined on earth no more...[283]

The fact that Mary never saw Marten again, her brother whom she
adored, reflects the stigma she attached to mental illness. Marten's illness
and removal to a private asylum in Staffordshire changed his wife's and
his childrens' lives. Marten's first episode of mental illness had occurred
in 1818 following the death of his first wife, Anne Congreve, after twelve
years of marriage. Their last child, Theophilus, a name which Mary used
in several books, died soon afterwards. When he had married Jemima in
1821 they and the seven surviving children had moved to East Garston,
near Reading where:

> It appears that Marten carried out his religious and pastoral duties most
> conscientiously, and was respected by East Garston, despite what Jemima later,
> rather endearingly, described as his "natural eccentricity of character."
>
> Unfortunately, the pressure of his work led to a complete and irreversible
> mental and physical breakdown after nine years in East Garston, and in 1833
> the family were forced to place Marten in a private lunatic asylum in
> Staffordshire. Marten was never to regain his sanity...[284]

Attitudes to what was then termed lunacy had undergone change in the previous century. The illness of King George III, who had suffered episodes of what was diagnosed as insanity, had affected public understanding and tolerance to some extent towards the insane. The care of the mentally ill was still open to abuse with many placed in private houses or private lunatic asylums. An Act in 1774 for the regulation of private madhouses within a seven mile radius of London did not cover provincial madhouses or public subscription asylums. Many lunatics were housed in the workhouse. In 1808 the County Asylums Act was passed:

> ... recommending that each county erect an asylum for the care of the insane. The asylums were to be supported by public funds. The Act was a permissive one, since it had no power to enforce its regulations. As a result few county asylums were built for the time being.
>
> The following years saw the growth of a 'free market in lunatics' and private madhouses multiplied to cope with increasing demands. Although some asylums provided a high standard of care, many kept lunatics in dreadful conditions. These were publicized in 1815 and 1828. In York Asylum a series of tiny cells was discovered each housing many filthy and incontinent patients ... In Bethlem Hospital this was particularly true ... 'the patients in this room were dreadful idiots, their nakedness and their mode of confinement gave this room the appearance of a dog-kennel.'[285]

Only twelve county asylums had been built by 1844, whereas the number of private madhouses had grown to meet demand. Thomas Bakewell, who was born in 1761, had spent much of his time with his grandfather, John Chadwick, who lived in Grindon in the Staffordshire Peak District. His sister had been committed twice to a madhouse but her mental health failed to improve. Chadwick decided to turn to an itinerate 'mad doctor' who would treat her at home in the hope she would be cured. After a year under the doctor's care her health improved and she recovered. The doctor, who had practised for fifty years, and Chadwick became friends. He passed on his knowledge of treating the mentally ill to Chadwick. After the elderly doctor died Chadwick opened a private madhouse at Grindon and it was here that Thomas Bakewell, his grandson, observed and learnt about treatments for those suffering from mental illness. After his grandfather's death, Thomas's uncle took over the running of the private madhouse, which was now located near Tamworth, where Thomas worked as an assistant to his uncle for three years. Then, about 1793, after a period working as a weaver, in which industry Thomas rose to be foreman, his uncle, by now ill and with his business in decline, called on Thomas to take over the business, exhorting him 'in the most feeling manner, to adhere strictly to the paths of honour and humanity, in all my conduct towards my patients; representing to me how much good I might live to do.'[286] Chadwick was not alone in his more enlightened treatment of the mentally ill. William Tuke, a Quaker, had founded The Retreat, at York, which was opened in 1796. Tuke had been deeply shocked and moved by the plight of the inmates of York Asylum who were kept and treated in inhumane conditions.

Thomas Bakewell had received no formal medical training but in 1805 his book *The Domestic Guide in Cases of Insanity* was published. This was a practical guide to caring for the insane at home with advice on their care and management:

> Humanity is an absolute requisite. By humanity is meant, that he who has the management of the insane, should be determined upon doing all the good possible, with the least possible suffering to the patient: it does not imply that he should be restrained from exercising due authority.[287]

Bakewell's methods included 'the occasional use of the whip, the forced acceptance of medicine, and the employment of physical restraint.' He also included an early form of shock therapy;

> I would then try the effect of sudden shocks, or violent motion; perhaps the first might be done by plunging the patient into water, and make them apprehend drowning; or the appearance of fire might answer the purpose: for the latter, the swing recommended by Dr. Cox might be useful; or, making a patient fast in a cart, and driving smartly over a rough road.[288]

However, Bakewell stressed that 'great patience and perseverance' must be shown and that whatever methods of his were employed 'the approach was to be gentle, promoting rest and comfort.'

In November 1808 Bakewell overcame local opposition and opened Spring Vale, a private asylum set in beautiful grounds in an idyllic setting near Stone in Staffordshire. In the advertisement for the asylum, he states that patients committed to the asylum would 'receive every comfort and consolation humanity can dictate.' Furthermore, for added reassurance to concerned and fearful relatives, 'no chains used nor would there be

Thomas Bakewell's Spring Vale Asylum. *T. Radclyffe, 1830*

any other severities.' The stigma attached to the insane would be avoided by the 'most profound secrecy.' It would have been expected that, with the resulting success which his more humane treatment brought, Bakewell would have enjoyed financial success too. Unfortunately his methods enabled the discharge of cured patients after only a short stay, which failed to bring the necessary profit. The publication of *Letter On the Treatment of The Insane* in 1815 with its highly polemic tone brought his views once more to public attention and he continued to promote his ideas both in articles and in lectures in the hope that his methods would be widely adopted. In 1818 the Staffordshire General Lunatic Asylum opened and some of the patients at Spring Vale were removed there which further caused a drop in the number of patients and income.

The supportive domestic atmosphere at Spring Vale for those patients who were well enough to interact with Bakewell's children was a further indication of Bakewell's attitude to mental illness. These patients were encouraged to play with the children, take meals with the family and converse and be treated as rational beings. One of Bakewell's children, Samuel Glover Bakewell, was influenced by this early interaction with patients and this led him to qualify as a doctor and join his father. It was into this atmosphere of humane support and hope of cure that Marten was committed in 1833. The rural surroundings and the beautiful grounds would have held familiar references for Marten who had always loved the countryside. Thomas Bakewell would die in 1835. Dr. Samuel Bakewell carried on his work at Spring Vale, before buying a large house at Oulton, a nearby village in 1838. He fitted it out as an asylum called Oulton Retreat, set in 80 acres of land, licensed for 20 male and 12 female patients. An advertisement for the asylum shows that it was to be run on the same lines as Spring Vale under Dr. Bakewell's supervision and women patients were under the immediate care of Thomas Bakewell's widow, Sarah. The terms were 'One to Five Guineas per Week, and upwards, according to the circumstances of the Patient and the accommodation required.' Marten would remain confined for the rest of his life, dying there in 1846, fourteen years after Mary had cut him from her life.

Jemima's plight

Marten had left the vicarage in 1829, apparently 'in some haste.' Mary makes no mention in her diary of Marten's illness or Jemima's plight. Jemima was responsible for the surviving children from her husband's first marriage to Anne Congreve, and the four surviving children from her own marriage to Marten. After Marten had been committed to Spring Vale, Jemima decided that the best course of action for the family would be to sell the contents of the vicarage at East Garston where a curate would stand in for Marten and would be paid from Marten's stipend.

The loss of income for Jemima and her children was a serious financial blow so in order to release capital, Jemima put the contents of the vicarage up for auction. Apparently she set about doing this without reference to other members of the Butt family. When Thomas Congreve, known by the family as Congreve, Marten's second son by his first marriage, who was training to be a surgeon, learnt of this he became alarmed.

The financial complications which ensued and the bitterness which was engendered by Jemima's actions is well documented in the exchange of letters by those who had a financial interest in the outcome. Congreve was extravagant by nature and was described by his aunt, Lucy Cameron, as 'the only wandering sheep in the family.' Congreve starts a correspondence[289] concerning the sale with: Jemima; his uncle J. F. Congreve (uncle of Marten Butt's children by his first marriage and later, most importantly, a trustee in the Commission in Lunacy of John Marten Butt); Elizabeth Congreve (aunt to the children of the first marriage); Henry Woodham, a solicitor; and Mr Wright, the auctioneer. Lucy's brother-in-law, A. Cameron, and Henry Sherwood are also referred to in the correspondence.

Congreve writes from Worcester on October 24, 1833 to his step-mother, Jemima, after Emily's death earlier that month.

> My Dear Mother,
>   I have just a few minutes to write & inform you that I have been here a few days, & that I start to-morrow for Snedshill [Lucy Cameron's home] where I hope to have the pleasure of seeing you when you return.
>   My Uncle & Aunt Sherwood are as well as you can expect them to be after the loss of Emily, and the Dr. [Streeten, Emily's husband] suffers most, but I hope that God will support him thro all his trials.
>   Lucy is looking very well. I dined with her at Malvern the other day …
>   I have heard from George [his younger brother by Anne; his father, Marten's first wife] that you are gone to East Garston. [Jemima was no longer living at East Garston] I am sorry that you find it necessary to be so much put out, but if I can be of any assistance to you, you must let me know… He mentions something about a sale being likely to take place. In this case as executor to my poor brother Marten, I must request you to let those books wch belong to him to be safely housed…
>   When at Snedshill I shall be at Head-quarters & shall know all about you, Geo & Henry, whom I hope to find prospering satisfactorily. [This suggests that Jemima and the family had been staying with Lucy].
>   With best love I am Dear Mother, your aft Son
>   Thos Congreve Butt.

His next letter is entirely different in tone and sentiment towards his step-mother, Jemima. Dated November 7 from Snedshill, it is to his uncle J. F. Congreve, the brother of Anne Congreve, Marten Butt's first wife. J. F. Congreve was a solicitor and registrar in Stoney Stratford.

> My Dear Uncle
>   Mrs Butt is gone to East Garston without taking the opinion of any of my father's relatives, to sell the furniture and has not told any one, of her intention of selling any thing else.
>   But by a letter from Trentham I hear that the sale is advertised by Mr C Wright of Newbury of my father's books furniture & effects together with ancient engravings by Eminent Masters—
>   In a letter to myself dated East Garston Oct 29 Mrs B says "I have seen the necessity of making a clearance here."
>   But she does not tell me that any heirlooms of the family— such as family books, pictures &c are to be sold. Such conduct speaks for itself.
>   My brother & myself will feel much hurt if such things are sold & will consider it a great favour of you to endeavour immediately to put a stop to these proceedings.
>   The sale is advertised for the 13th & 14th inst.

I know that I can legally do nothing but still it is my duty to my brothers and sisters & myself to acquaint <u>her</u> with the <u>legality</u> & consequences of such proceedings as throwing away things wch cannot be estimated by those to whom they are most endeared by family ties.

My father you know is confined at Spring Vale near Trentham.

I wanted to have written more but the post will not allow of it.

If you will write to Mrs Butt you will

Much oblige yr aft nephew T C Butt

Congreve is trying to protect family heirlooms from being sold and accordingly has also alerted his aunt, Elizabeth Congreve, to the situation. She writes a letter, also dated November 7, to her brother, J. F. Congreve, showing her concern and anger at the situation. The family is closing ranks on Jemima.

… but enough about my unworthy self. The business Congreve has written to you about Mrs Cameron & myself think if you would have the goodness to write a letter to her [Jemima] by tomorrow fridays post & inform her of the illegality of her proceedings it might put a stop to them! What possible right can she have to dispose of all her husbands effects now he is confirmed lunatic & in confinement. So the childrens property is squandered away. She is not fit to have the management of money. She sells any thing she can lay her hand on & is quite neglecting Georges education. While she lived at Bridgnorth he went to a capital school for several pds a year. Though she has meant to pay for the house another twelvemonth yet for some freak she chose to come to a small village near here & brought George with her who is thrown out of his school & is doing nothing this may show her character…

Jemima responds to J. F. Congreve on November 12:

Dear Sir

Your letter did not reach me till 3 o'clock yesterday when the sale which you wished me to forbid had commenced as you will see by the advertisement was to be the 11th & not 12th.

I cannot but suppose that you have had a statement made to you far different from the facts to induce you to write to me in the way in which your letter was indited as if I had any wish or motive contrary to the interest of the Butt family. I came to East Garston in consequence of hearing of the neglected & dilapidated state of the Vicarage House & its contents & the disinclination of any Curate to enter upon it in the state in which it remained.

When I had investigated the furniture & had found things were even worse than I had anticipated—though from the melancholy & distressing state of dear Mr Butt's health previous to his hasty departure things were left far from in a complete & orderly way four years ago. Added to which a great part of the furniture was the same Mr Butt's family has had in wear ever since his first marriage & from age not suitable to the use of a Clergyman's family without much replacing, money for which I had not at my command.

The house has been some months vacant owing to these [?] & was likely never to be inhabited unless they were improved.

The Curacy itself has been near to bought for & is now likely to be properly & desirably filled shortly.

Under these circumstances I considered I was doing my duty as surely as I have done & if I have done any thing contrary to law I am sure it was not intentional & I am perfectly willing to surrender the accounts & that my conduct should be investigated for I have no intention but to benefit & would on no account injure the family. You must be aware that a much more painful task to them that which in a sense of duty I have imposed upon myself should not have been undertaken. I am sure I would willingly have spared myself the pain I have undergone if only I had reconsidered it to my conscience let my husband's property gone to so that since myself & a woman & since have been employed for three weeks repairing things to make any of them saleable & nothing but the conscience of doing right could have sustained me & I shall feel obliged if you will kindly point out wherein I have done wrong & what under present circumstances you as trustee or in any other situation require of me & I trust you will find my actions answer my proficiency when I repeat that I never had or wished to have any private motive in any thing I did since I entered the family.

Till this day week I expect to be here & afterwards I shall be for a day or two at Bridgnorth & then Blythshill rectory near Shiffnal will find me.

I am dear sir yours sincerely

J Butt

It is at this point in the increasingly contentious correspondence that a solicitor becomes involved. J. F. Congreve had written to Henry Woodham, his solicitor in Newbury, on November 10 apprising him of the situation, before he had received Jemima's letter. Woodhams replies on November 12:

Sir

re The Rev J M Butt

I beg to acknowledge the Receipt of your Letter of ye 10th Instt by this Morning's Post. Upon calling at Mr Wright's House I learnt from his Wife that he was at East Garston, and that this was the Second Day of the Sale. I acquainted her to my Errand and she readily told me that her Husband had received your Letter on Sunday Morning and considering it to be a Matter of Importance he immediately rode to East Garston and communicated it to Mrs Butt, but that the first Day of the Sale being Yesterday, it was deemed altogether impracticable to stop it, most especially as every Publicity in

London as well as in the Country had been given of it.

I then wrote a Letter to Mr Wright at the Place of Sale acquainting him with the Substance of your Letter to me in your own Language, and requiring him to consider such Communication as a further Notice from you to prevent and Stop the Sale.

The Letter was conveyed to him by Messenger. Beyond this and the Steps you had previously taken I am not aware that more cod not well be done under the Circumstances. Without the slightest Desire to move out of my Province I wod just take the Liberty of observing that if I am taking a correct View of the Matter it stands thus—

Mr Butt at this Moment is wholly incapacitated to manage his Affairs and is under necessary personal Retirement and Confinement. Mrs Butt, his Wife certainly it shod seem without an Legal Power or Authority, but it may be not with any improper Motives, has proceeded to the sale of his Property. You as the natural and lawful Uncle of his first family feel deeply interested in their Well-being, and consider the present Proceedings not only illegal and Unconselary, but of an injurient Tendency. It strikes me to be exceedingly desireable, that you shod without Delay take a Journey hither and make yourself thoroughly acquainted with the Transaction, unless indeed you receive a Satisfactory Explanation of it from Mrs Butt, herself.

You may rely on my seeing Mr Wright immediately on his Return from East Garston and acquainting you with the Result of my Interview with him.

Without a Application to the Court I do not see how you can clothe yourself with any efficient Authority. I need only add that any further Communications which you may think proper to make to me, shall receive my best Attention.

I am Sir Your Faithful & Obedient Servt
Hen: Woodham

Two days later Woodham writes to Congreve informing him that the sale will be closed on the November 15. Mr Wright thinks that it will realise about £300.[290] Marten had a valuable library much of which he had inherited from his father. Furthermore, Mrs Butt has assured the auctioneer that 'she has not the slightest Wish to receive the Money.' Woodham will send Congreve the sale catalogue with the prices and because of his nephew's concern all the most valuable of the books from Marten's library have been withdrawn 'but to the great Discomfiture and Dissatisfaction of several Book-buyers from a Distance, who immediately indicated their Determination to bring Actions against the Auctioneer.' Jemima went to see Mr Wright on November 17. She had reiterated that she had no wish to profit from the sale. Woodham continues by suggesting that as a first step the proceeds from the sale should be deposited either in a bank or with someone of known Character and Responsibility.

This would give a pause during which there is:

> … perhaps, the reasonable Hope that Mr Butt may become sufficiently convalescent to receive guarded Communication of what has been done, and to signify his wishes upon the subsequent Arrangements, and if that shod not be the Case, Time will be afforded to yourself and Mrs Butt, and any others of the Family who might think it proper to consult on such an Occasion to exercise a deliberate Judgement.
>
> Mr Wright, I should hope, will be ready to pay the Money to Mrs Butt and yourself upon having your joint receipt for it.

In a letter dated November 26, 1833, Jemima writes to J. F. Congreve to justify her actions. She goes into some detail about the auction and the outstanding debts:

> Dear Sir
> As I was not able to perform my journey at the time I mentioned I think it right to inform you of this delay lest any letter which you may have addressed to me elsewhere may not seem to meet with the attention it ought—I likewise thought it right you should know the particulars of the sale as you have thought it your duty to demand the produce. The money is in the hands of the Auctioneer & though I do not mean to distract from his character as a respectable man I suppose it will be necessary to add that a more safe custody than his wd be advisable—Had I been allowed to make the use of the money I had thought right—I shd have used it to pay those debts which encumber & disturb my mind & prevent our income from being free to finish George's education, an object which I have much at heart to accomplish but wh will be entirely impossible to me whilst impediments are raised to our income being cleared of debts—You must be aware that with our expences & numerous family much economy is requisite to make our income answer the necessary demands & little can be left to pay debts—since dear Mr Butt's affliction upwards of 3 years I have continued to live £50 under our income & have within £43 paid all of the small debts but there still remain £80 at Bunby & Slocock's Bank £50 Mr Harbent these borrowed to finish poor Marten's last yr at college—likewise £100 borrowed of Mr A Cameron when Congreve's stipulated apprenticeship was put an end to & he became pupil at the infirmary—now that the furniture is sold the salary of the Curate is increased now to £100 per anm—My dear husbands [?] him at least another £100—& for three years to come £50 per anm for Henry besides £20 each of them for clothes namely Eliza George & Henry [children of Anne, Marten's first wife] heavy expences of repairs in the Vicarage which have been [?] of late &c these leave little or no surplus with the most self denying economy wherewith to disemburden the family with debts—I should not have thought of disposing of either furniture or books if the destruction of both had not been threatened by delaying the trying duty—Now that they are sold I had hoped to have benefited & not imposed our circumstances which by yr requirements will be

the case as I understand that no individual of the family has any claim by law to make any use of the sum arising from the sale witht the consent of all the family—I have no idea that all will consent to appropriate it to pay those debts which none feel the presence of but myself—I therefore submit to yr judgment as Executor to yr poor Sister's children if the interest of this sum may be appropriated towards the completing the education of George? There are some items in the catalogue witht price annexed & these Mr Cornwall the present curate has taken in the light of fixtures valued at £33—the books bought in or not sold are locked in a dry place with a promise of care from the curate & two inventories one in my possession & one in his With kind regards I am Dr.

    Sir Yrs sincerely

    J Butt

On April 4 the following year Congreve wrote from London to his uncle, J. F. Congreve. In the letter he explains that he has not been able to visit him at Stoney Stratford as he has been waiting to hear whether he was successful in obtaining a post as an assistant to a surgeon in Worcester. He has visited his step-mother, Jemima Butt, to discuss the financial situation of the family.

Mrs Butt told me that she had been informed the money from the sale had been paid into the Newbury Bank in her name jointly with mine. She was so positive of this that we drew out some cheques for myself for £78 to defray some debts including Mr Woodham's & to enable me to finish in London, a second to Mr A Cameron for £50, a third to Mr Sherwood for £12 with an arrangement for the remainder to be paid into the Newbury Bank to defray a debt to the bankers there.

They had drawn cheques for £140 anticipating receiving £300 from the sale. In fact the sale only realised £130–13/3. The discrepancy may have been caused by the withdrawal from the sale of Marten's books. The letter continues on the subject of various debts called in by the Newbury Bank which will not accept an offer of £40 against a previous debt of £80. Clearly the financial situation is muddied and complicated. Congreve did little to help and applied for a 'Commission in Lunacy'. This would have enabled him to have the right to his future inheritance at the expense of his stepmother. He was thwarted as his action was opposed by the rest of the family. In debt, he had no alternative but to convey his expectations on Marten's death to one of his creditors. Congreve would die in 1844. His father, Marten, died two years later but he had been lost to their world for so many years as husband, father and brother. In his will, made in 1824, he left books, furniture and effects to Jemima – with interest during her life on his investments – which were to be shared between the surviving children on her death.

After her husband's death in 1846 Jemima moved to live in Pimlico, London and the following year sent this letter to the Bishop of Salisbury.

> 1 Trelleck Terrace, Pimlico, London.
>
> My Lord,
>
> Having understood from the Bishop of Oxford that you would be so kind as to endeavour to procure admission for me into the Widows' College in case my testimonials should be satisfactory, I beg leave to submit the accompanying for your approbation. The copy of the baptismal register I have not been able to obtain from the circumstances of being separated very young from my parents and I cannot learn at which church my name was entered. I therefore hope that your Lordship will feel satisfied as to my age from the testimony of a relative with whom I resided in my youth. The two daughters upon whom I have settled £12 per annum named in Mr Devey's certificate are entirely dependent upon me for their maintenance, and in addition I have to support my son while he is qualifying for the medical profession from which he can obtain no emolument for three years. Your Lordship from these circumstances how very grateful I should be if you can favour my reception.
>
> I am My Lord, your obedient servant,
>
> Jemima Butt.
>
> October 25th, 1847.

The next letter reveals that Jemima had been adopted.

> My Lord,
>
> I beg to certify that I have known Mrs Jemima Butt since the year 1796 at which time she was four years old, and being a relative of my father's was then adopted into our family, in consequence of her parents going to America where they both died. If the exercise of every Christian duty and trials borne with exemplary patience can entitle the widow of a truly pious and learned clergyman to the benefit of your excellent charity I know no one more deserving of it.
>
> I am, My Lord, your obedient servant,
>
> Eleanor Devey. October 23rd, 1847.
>
> St. Paul's Terrace, Wolverhampton.

This then makes Jemima fifty-five years of age. Jemima also submits a letter, dated October 19, signed by G. B. C. Cave, Incumbent of St. George's, Wolverhampton and W.A. Newman, MA, Curate of St. George's certifying that Jemima's conduct has been exemplary in her attendance at

St. George's church, Hanover Square.

Also included in the above letter is a letter dated October 25, 1847 from James Kelly [?], Minister of Charlotte Chapel, Pimlico in the Parish of St. George's.

> Mrs Butt, widow of the Revd. John Martin Butt, has attended this Chapel for the last twelvemonth and it has given me sincere pleasure to learn that she has now met with an opening into the Widows' college, New Sarum. I am quite satisfied from my knowledge of her religious habits and character and the testimony I am familiar with from all quarters of her uniform respectability, that all the requirements on this head for admission to the benefits of the institution will be fully answered by her.

J. Kidd, a friend of Marten's from Westminster school, writing from Oxford also on October 25, offers his support and sends a letter extolling Jemima's virtues as wife and mother:

> … Having been well acquainted with Mrs Butt during the last thirty years, I can with truth say, that in all those relations of life which she has been called to fulfill, her conduct has been most exemplary, more particularly during the period of her husband's derangement, throughout which period, at the same time as she fulfilled all the duties of a mother in attending to the religious education of her children, one son and three daughters, [William Boyne, Jemima, Emily and Matilda, Marten's children by Jemima] she curtailed the expenses of herself and family to the utmost, in order to afford her husband all the comforts in her power, which his unhappy situation required.

Frederick Nicholls Devey, writes from Ely Place, London also on October 25:

> I hereby certify that the income of Mrs Jemima Butt, widow of the Reverend John Marten Butt, lately amounted to the sum of £51–11/6 a year: but that she has now agreed out of the same to give up absolutely, the sum of £12 a year to two of her daughters: Emily Martha Whittingham Butt and Matilda Butt. And I further certify that I have acted as solicitor for Mrs Butt, and consider myself to be acquainted with the nature and extent of her income; and that I verily believe she has no other income, except from the Widows' Relief Charity, than the income above mentioned, which does not amount to £40 a year.[291]

Jemima confirmed her daughters' allowances the same day:

> In consideration of natural love and affection and for facilitating the obtaining the Benefits of Bishop Ward's Charity, I hereby agree out of my income under the Deed of Settlement executed by my late husband, the Rev'd John Marten

Butt, to give up absolutely the sum of twelve pounds a year during my live [sic]
to my daughters Emily Martha Willingham Butt and Matilda Butt equally to
be divided between them and to execute every deed and instrument that may
be reasonably required for effecting the above maintained agreed and if
requisite to appoint my son William Boyne Butt and my son-in-law, John
Edwards Trustees of the fund so agree to be given up. Dated this 25th day of
October 1847
        Signed Jemima Butt.[292]

Jemima was elected a Matron of Seth Ward's College on Monday,
November 22, 1847 at a meeting of the Dean and Chapter of Salisbury
Cathedral. The College of Matrons[293] in Salisbury was an alms-house for
ten widows of clergy of the Salisbury diocese funded by the Bishop
Ward's Charity. It is heartening that Jemima, who acted in the best
interests of her mentally ill husband and all their children, should, after
financial hardship and seemingly having been somewhat cold-shoul-
dered by Marten's family, find security within the family and love of her
church to which she and Marten had devoted their lives.

Britannia Square

Happily the Sherwoods' understandable anxiety about Sophia's delicate health was proved wrong. Sophia married Dr. Streeten, the widower of Emily. After a short period the newly married couple came to live with the Sherwoods in Britannia Square, Worcester, much to the delight of Mary, 'for it was the warmest wish of my heart to have them always to myself.'[294] Dr. Streeten's widowed mother and his unmarried sister 'with the youthful members of their family, took the house next door to us; so that when we met, which was very often – two or three times a week – we made a large and cheerful party.'[295] The Sherwoods were also fortunate that their son, Henry, was now curate at White Ladies Aston, a village lying some six miles east of Worcester, so they were able to visit him and his wife regularly at the beautiful vicarage. Henrietta, the Sherwoods' eldest daughter, to whom Mary was less close, probably because of the early separation from her parents she had suffered when they left for India, still lived at Eccleshall near Stafford. Henrietta produced nine children whom the Sherwoods saw and entertained regularly.

One day Mary was surprised when a large parcel arrived from America. When the parcel was opened many beautifully bound volumes of her works were revealed. They had been sent from America by a group calling themselves 'Universalists' who claimed in their journals that Mary and Sophia adhered to their beliefs. Mary was outraged and promptly instructed Dr. Streeten to repack the books and dispatch them immediately back to where they had come from. Mary sent a letter disclaiming any such connection with the group: 'I believe their doctrines, as far as I know them, are a denial of the Holy Scriptures, as they say that the mercy of God is bestowed upon man without the ransom being obtained by Christ.'[296] Mary's beliefs were very different.

There was some opposition locally in Worcester to her views on religion. Mary believed in universal salvation which brought her into disfavour with the Evangelicals, and this was the cause of much opposition and discussion among them. Mary defended her views robustly when confronted. In August, 1835 she had received a letter requesting her to cease her visits to the workhouse as:

> One of the reformed penitents who had been set to watch me had brought a charge against me of having asserted that our Lord would in due time save all mankind. I had certainly not done this directly, but probably had done so by inference. This charge was only the first drop of the hailstorm which was speedily to be discharged against me. I was vexed at being disappointed of my quiet Sunday walks, but other wise not much troubled with the matter.[297]

Mary's literary output continued unabated. In 1835 *The Garland*, a collection of seventeen moral tales, based on woodcuts, had appeared. Mary would employ the same method of writing a story to represent the image of a given woodcut in *The Juvenile Forget-me-not* which was published as an annual in 1841. She was also still writing for *The Youth's Magazine or Evangelical Miscellany*. She continued to contribute to the periodical until 1848, having begun writing articles and tales as well as tracts since 1822. James Harper, of the House of Harper Brothers, New York, wrote to Mary from London on July 2, 1836, heaping praise and informing her that they had by then published 13 volumes of her collected works[298] which he was sending to her:

> for such has been the very great popularity of your books in our country that thousands, tens of thousands, and I may safely say hundreds of thousands copies of some of them have been sold, for I may add that in every hamlet and in every mother's boudoir they may be found, and I think I may safely say that almost every Sabbath-school scholar in America has beguiled many, very many an hour with poring over them, whose head and heart, I trust, has been greatly improved. You not only receive praise from the white man and his child, but the red man of the forest has learnt to lisp your name, and the black man in the South—his heart has been made to dance for joy that his Heavenly Father ever put it into your heart to plead his cause.[299]

Mary, in spite of opposition and hostility towards her strongly expounded beliefs which she maintained had led her to see the truth, was not about to relinquish them. She now felt that 'the veil of goats-hair has been removed from the face of the Sun of Righteousness.'[300] For some, her views were regarded as heresy and she began to quarrel with certain friends. She was visited at home by an American who 'made himself very disagreeable' and also by the incumbent of a certain chapel, who regarded Mrs Sherwood as a heretic and 'poured forth such vehement threatenings whenever he saw me, that I thought it best to withdraw my attendance there.'[301] Having been asked to no longer visit the workhouse because an inmate had reported her heretical teaching, Mary was now forced to spend the Sabbath indoors because of the local hostility her views engendered. In spite of censure of her religious views from some quarters, her books continued to be best sellers. In 1837 she was criticised, on the publication of the fourth part of *Henry Milner* in which the doctrine of regeneration is strongly emphasised. Mary took the criticism in her stride and continued to write.

Lucy Cameron's Deep Waters

I have passed through deep waters this year, such as I had wellnigh sunk in...[302]

The year 1836 brought a great change to Lucy Cameron's life. In 1831, her husband had become rector of the newly built St. Nicholas' church at Swaby, in Lincolnshire. Although he had resigned Donnington Wood he continued to serve as curate there and they had remained living at Snedshill. Their eldest son, Charles, had been ordained to the curacy of St. George's church, Donnington Wood in 1832. The Camerons finally left Snedshill for Louth, set in the Lincolnshire Wolds near Swaby, in 1836. They lived in lodgings for three years while a new parsonage was being built. This was to be their home for the foreseeable future. The following year their second daughter, Mary Anne, aged twenty-seven, was married in St. James' church, Louth to the Reverend J.C. Moor, who was vicar of Clifton near Rugby. Lucy continued with her Sunday school work and her writing.

Both Lucy and Mary record the coronation, on June 28, 1838, of the young Victoria, just nineteen, the niece of William IV who had died on June 20 the previous year. He left no surviving legitimate children. Mary and Henry celebrated the great day at White Ladies Aston with their son, Henry, and daughter-in-law. It was a happy occasion in spite of showers forcing the celebrations to take place indoors. Cake had been laid out in huge baskets:

> ... piled up like the bricks of the Tower of Babel in a child's story book. Round this room, on chairs placed against the wall, was a goodly assemblage of the dames of every dairy in the parish, with one or two smarter females from Droitwich; and there we sat and took tea and discussed the circumstances of the day, and spread our pocket-handkerchiefs over our knees to save our best

gowns ... Our repast being concluded, and the company being reported to be assembled in the barn, thither we repaired, and found that long boards and forms were set out, and all the appliances for wholesale tea-drinking. This was provided with no sparing hand.

Henry showed me the first child he had ever christened, with much delight, and a sweet baby she was. I must not forget to say that dear Henry read a chapter and prayer before we sat down to tea. After tea the musicians, of whom two had been secured at very great trouble, struck up a lively tune, and all the company set to and capered and jigged in the most surprising style ... The treat was finished by draughts of cider, and still more plum cake.[303]

With eleven surviving children much of Lucy Cameron's time and interest centred on her large family. She visited her old home at Snedshill, Shropshire, in September to celebrate the wedding of her eldest daughter, also called Lucy, who was married on September, 1838 in the church where not so many years previously her father had preached and all her siblings had been baptised. Like her sister, Mary Anne, Lucy had married a clergyman, the Reverend S.R. Waller. They were to live at Ettingshall in Staffordshire. After the ceremony the parishioners came together and drank tea. Two days later Lucy Cameron set off for Rugby by train to visit her other married daughter, Mary Anne. There still remained five unmarried daughters and four unmarried sons. In the spring of 1839 the Camerons finally moved into the new rectory in Swaby. It had been three years since they had lived in a home of their own. She was delighted when in July 1841 her son-in-law, the Reverend Waller became one of the curates in Dr. Butt's old parish of Kidderminster.

Both Lucy and Mary were saddened by the death of their much-loved cousin Thomas Butt who lived at Trentham and who had been so kind to the family. It may well have been Thomas's position at Trentham that had influenced Marten Butt's being placed for treatment at Spring Vale, close to Trentham.

The Camerons were beset by ill health in the family. Lucy's happiness in her daughter, Lucy, living at Kidderminster was short-lived. She died three hours after giving birth to her second child, a daughter, on May 15 1842: 'I put away my coloured clothes, never to wear them more.' Lucy was buried beneath the shade of trees which had been planted by her grandfather. The baby was taken to Swaby ten days later and christened in the presence of her grieving father, the Reverend Waller, and eight of the Cameron's children. In the Spring of 1843 their third daughter, Eliza, went to look after the Reverend Waller and the two older children of his marriage to Lucy, Stephen and Lucy, who both fell seriously ill. Mrs Cameron went to Kidderminster and nursed Eliza, who had also fallen ill, and her three grandchildren for almost two years.

> I am living for a time in this place again, amidst all its lovely scenery. In the pulpit, which my father occupied, I see my son-in-law; and in the same town, where my grandfather visited us, I see my grandchildren.[304]

That summer her husband and their daughter Amelia joined her. Death came again. This time in the form of scarlet fever scything down two of her grandchildren. Lucy writes a moving letter to her eldest son Charles on November 2, 1843:

> … Many, indeed, and very trying have been our warnings lately, more especially the loss of that lovely baby, who had entwined herself around our hearts as if she had been our own. Nor can it be wondered at that she should, when we consider the circumstances under which she was laid in our arms; and we had anxiously watched her through what we considered as the most trying period of her life, and were rejoicing in the blooming health with which she returned to her father's home,–and the mower's scythe, at one stroke, has cut down this fair flower.[305]

Lucy admits that the death of the baby following the death of Stephen, the baby's elder brother, almost overwhelmed her and her husband. Her religion saved her. She believed in a heaven where one day she would be reunited with all those dear to her who had died.

For Lucy the year 1844 started on a more optimistic note. Her family's health seemed to be improving. Eliza had grown strong enough to be taken to London to seek medical advice. Ewen, the Cameron's second son was in practice at the Chancery Bar in London and George, their youngest son, was ordained by the Bishop of London in St. Paul's Cathedral in May. While in London Lucy met Malan who had influenced much of Mary's religious belief. Lucy also met with Jemima Butt who she refers to as 'dear Mrs Butt.' The two women enjoyed a drive in one of the London parks together and no doubt discussed Marten and his state of mind.

In July 1844 Lucy and Mary learnt of the death of George, Lord Mountnorris, the loving companion of their youth at Stanford, who had remained their friend. That autumn the Camerons returned to

Worcester where they stayed for six months. Lucy's husband, Charles, had taken temporary charge of St. Clement's parish in Worcester.

On May 6, 1845 Mary Sherwood celebrated her seventieth birthday. She invited Lucy and her unmarried daughter, Amelia, to join her on a visit to Stanford which brought back idyllic memories of their childhood together:

> ... my sister and myself, separating ourselves from the rest of the party, visited together the haunts of our early days,—the bee meadow full of cowslips, the coppice above the parsonage, which is now greatly altered with walls and coach- houses, that it does not look like the place we were born. We sat down together on a block of wood, reviewing days whose joys no more return, and looking forward to those days whose joys shall pass away no more, and agreeing after all our recollections, that though many be our trials since our early days, greater had been our blessings, and that old as we were, we were far happier than we had been in the days of our childhood.[306]

While on a visit to London, Charles Cameron had been approached to find a suitable lady to take on the management and teaching of young women at an East Indian institution in Madras. The Camerons agreed that Eliza, now recovered from her illness, should go but that she should be accompanied by Emma, daughter number four. The two young women sailed on August 4, 1845. It was a hard parting from her two daughters for Lucy who would have been fully aware of the hazards the two women would face. On a happier note her son, Ewen, married the daughter of the late Consul General of Venice at Cheltenham.

The following year brought more sadness: early in January Ewen died in Brighton and was buried in Hove. Lucy grieved once more. Her son so recently married: 'so wise, so good; prosperity opening up before him; rising in his profession' had been suddenly taken from her. His death was, according to Lucy, caused by overwork. But Lucy's woes were not at an end. She had been nursing Charlotte, a younger daughter, at Brompton for the past six months. There is a growing acceptance on her part that her lovely young daughter is dying. When Charlotte dies on June 10, 1846, Lucy once again finds comfort in her strong religious faith and conviction that she will be reunited with Charlotte in the world which awaits the true believer. She had needed this strong faith for 1846 delivered cruel blows to her. Not only had she lost a son and daughter but her brother, Marten, had died that January at Spring Vale.

Lucy needed all her religious and physical strength once more in 1847 when two more of her children died: Mary Anne on May 14 followed four months later by Eliza who had returned from India in a delicate state of health. Lucy had now lost four daughters and one son. In her journal she does not reveal what caused their deaths but tuberculosis would seem to be a likely cause. Her daughter, Emma, remained in India, having married the Reverend Frederic G. Lugard, a chaplain in the East India Company and a clergyman at a church in Vepery, Madras, that year. Lucy now had five surviving children in England: Amelia and Sophia and three sons. Both Charles and George were clergymen. George was curate of St. Ebbes, in Oxford. In September Lucy witnessed her youngest son, Frank, being ordained at Lincoln cathedral.

A Hive of Writing

In 1842 Hatchard had published the second part of *The History of the Fairchild Family*. Part I, published in 1818, had brought universal approval with its narrative of the Fairchild family in which moral lessons were taught and naughty children strictly disciplined for misdemeanours. Mary's publisher and readers had keenly awaited the appearance of a second volume but Mary had made them wait. Instead she had offered *The History of Henry Milner* – published in four parts between 1822 and 1837. When the second volume of *The History of the Fairchild Family* recounting the further religious and moral education of the Fairchild children appeared in 1842 it was markedly less Evangelical in tone than the first part. The children now have 'a new and divine nature, which works against your evil natures, causing you to know when you have done wrong, and making you truly and deeply sorrowful when you have committed a sin.'[307] Gone are the terrifying scenes, like the gibbet scene in Part I, and also the children's moral depravity; furthermore the parental role has changed to a much softer one. Like Part I each chapter ends with a prayer and hymn but unlike Part I when 'she was convinced of the deadly and almost ineradicable nature of Original Sin ... a belief in Saving Grace has softened her outlook.'[308] Mary writes:

> It was for the purpose of declaring that my whole trust and confidence are on the righteousness of my Divine Saviour that I then set out to work to write a statement of my belief, which I did in the story of Evelyn, in the third volume of "The Fairchild Family."[309]

In 1847 Mary would complete Part III with her daughter, Sophia Streeten, as joint author. In the preface Mary acknowledges Sophia's input as being 'of especial service to me.' The story of the Fairchild family continued to be popular although by the turn of the century the more

Part of a Letter from Mrs Sherwood to Mr Darton, March 24, 1847

gruesome aspects of the stories were revised in Part I. Part II remained largely intact apart from prayers and hymns being deleted, and the death scene and funeral appearing as *The Story of Evelyn* in a much shortened version. The parents became the arbiters of correct behaviour and 'the Victorian cult of the family was reinforced in a way that Mrs Sherwood had never intended.'[310]

Mary continued producing chapbooks in penny and twopenny series and tracts, commissioned by Darton, illustrated with woodcuts. She could write a tract in a few hours and would often create the tract to fit the wood engraving. Many were less than fifty pages in length

MY DEAR MRS DARTON,—I cannot begin on the work Mr Darton has kindly sent to us til you answer the following questions. Must there be one distinct story to each design, or may the four be worked into [one] story, which would be the easiest to perform? Is there to be no more letterpress than in the little pattern volumes sent? For what age should the story be suited? I write in haste but with every feeling of kindness to you, your husband, and the dear little ones.—Yours ever, most sincerely M. M. Sherwood.[311]

Sophia became more closely involved, assisting her mother during the 1840s and 50s. Together they produced such titles as *The De Cliffords* (1847), *Brotherly Love* (1851), *Boys Will be Boys, or The Difficulties of a Schoolboy's Life* (1854). Mary acknowledges the joint authorship in a preface dated 1846 to the first title: 'It has been further arranged by Providence, that this daughter, Mrs Streeten, has inherited from me, a turn for composition.' Sophia claimed the work as her own after Mary died, writing she had been 'assisted by Mrs Sherwood.'

~

Both Dr. Streeten and Henry were keen members of the Worcestershire Natural History Society whose meetings were held in Worcester. The Society published *The Magazine of Natural History and Journal of Zoology, Mineralogy, Geology and Meteorology*. In 1849 a book by Mary, *The Story Book of Wonders*, published by Nelson, appeared. The book had a serious purpose which is explained in the preface: 'the design of the authoress … is to furnish a series of interesting and instructive readings for the young on the Wonders of Nature. Her aim has been, while conveying useful information in as pleasing and attractive form as possible, to lead the youthful mind to the great Creator of all.' This suggests that Mary took an interest in the proceedings of the Society and would certainly have had access to their magazine. Included in the book are poems and music, perhaps to lighten the tone of the book for the young reader.

During this happy period of Mary's life at Britannia Square, Robert Streeten helped Mary check proofs of her works and joined his wife and father-in-law in the great work of creating the *Type Dictionary*, something which was still dear to Mary's heart:

> My son-in-law, Dr. Streeten, and his wife, and my beloved husband, all studied together with me the original languages of the Scriptures, and sweet, most sweet, were the beautiful promises that were daily unfolded to one or other of us, from the exquisite metaphors or types, of which the Eastern Languages are such rich wells of holiness and love—living waters which never fail.[312]

The house was a hive of writing and research: so much so that at times Robert forbade Mary to work, insisting that she must rest. On one occasion he instructed Sophia to remove the pen and ink and forbade Mary to read. Mary, as is so easily imagined, was extremely frustrated. She always had some form of written work in process. In order to placate her Sophia found an old bag which her husband's sister, Ellen Streeten, had filled with pieces of material intended for patchwork. Much to Mary's delight among them were pieces she had sewn for the children of Mary and Sally, her two adopted daughters, and the children of servants who had worked for the family and with whom she remained close. Once, or sometimes more often, each year Mary would visit Mary and Sally, whose lives would have been so different if she had not rescued them. Together they would reminisce happily about those far off days in India which held such rich memories for them all and which Mary had drawn on so profitably in her writing.

'I am dark and sad, and confused'

Both Mary and Henry appeared to be in good health and enjoying their life together with Sophia and her husband. Financial worries were a thing of the past thanks to Mary's prolific output and popularity as an author. Family ties remained strong: their other two children, Henry and Henrietta were established with families of their own and were living relatively close to them which meant visits could be made to see the grandchildren or they came to visit their grandparents in Worcester. In the summer of 1846 the first intimation of what would occur the following year made its sudden appearance.

One hot day Mary and Henry set out by carriage from their home in Britannia Square. Henry was dropped off en route to discuss some business with a tenant while the carriage went on to Abberley where Mary was paying a social visit to a friend. When Henry found that the tenant was out he decided to walk back to Worcester, a distance of about ten miles. He expected that Mary would overtake him in the carriage on his way home. It was one of those very hot summer days with no wind and as Henry walked he became over-heated and tired. He finally arrived home feeling faint and looked very flushed. This was unusual as Henry habitually took regular exercise in the form of long walks. After lying down for a couple of hours he joined the family for dinner as usual, showing no ill effects from the walk. However, the following night, about midnight he had his 'first attack of illness.' What the illness was Sophia does not say but she does report extreme breathlessness. Dr. Streeten, concerned about Henry's symptoms, had called in a colleague of his, Sir Charles Hastings.[313] Clearly Henry was in expert hands. Mary appeared calm as her husband lay gasping for breath. The prognosis looked serious but Sophia writes: 'The next day all bad symptoms had passed away.'

Two years later, on April 28, 1848, Henry had another attack. The previous year Mary and Henry had stopped dining in the evening with company, preferring to eat in the room upstairs before retiring to bed early. Mary, who was then almost seventy-three, remained calm as if she was resigned to his death. Her attitude caused Sophia to write: 'I have myself no doubt now that she felt too deeply for utterance, and that those two nights of suffering were too much for her.'[314] Mary was exhausted with helping nurse 'my beloved' as she now referred to her husband. Once again Henry recovered and resumed his daily life: going to the reading rooms and Worcester Cathedral. Calm descended on the household once more. Mary and Sophia embarked on writing *The Mirror of Maidens in the Days of Queen Bess* which would be published in 1851 by Hatchard. However, Sophia records how their relationship had changed:

> At first all the principal ideas were all her own, and the most important composition, also the revising and correcting. Little by little this had become reversed, as age came on with her, and maturity of mind with me; in this our last great work together our relative positions were altogether changed.[315]

Sophia later claimed that she was the main author of the work.

Robert Streeten was only forty-eight when in November 1848 he became ill with influenza. He failed to fully recover during the rest of the winter so it was decided that he and Sophia should go to Torquay in April in the hope that the sea air would improve his health. They stayed with his brother, Edmund, a clergyman. However, rather than improving, his health further deteriorated and the couple returned to Worcester after two weeks. His doctors were of the opinion that he was getting stronger when they attended him on May 10 but that evening, after eating a light supper in his room, he was standing in front of the fire to warm himself when he remarked to Sophia that he felt better and would now recover his health. The next moment he exclaimed: "Oh, hold me," before collapsing dead on the floor. Mary came rushing in to the room having heard him fall and Henry, who was in bed in the next room, struggled into some clothes to get medical help. A doctor, who lived opposite in Britannia Square, arrived but by then Robert had no need of him. It was Henry who now needed medical help. He was having another of his attacks in which he could not get his breath. In one room lay Sophia's dead husband; in another, Sophia, her mother and the doctor tended to Henry for the remainder of the night.

It was decided that the Sherwoods and Sophia needed to move to a smaller house which would be more suited to Henry, now an invalid. Mary was no longer the robust figure she had once been. Robert Streeten's financial support had gone and the life style they had enjoyed with servants in a large house had to be changed for something more economically viable. Mary and the newly-widowed Sophia, aged thirty-four, tried to find a house in Worcester which would meet their new situation. However, on a business visit to London in 1849, Sophia was advised by Robert's two brothers, who lived there, to move to Twickenham, near Richmond. Sophia was concerned as to how the move would affect Henry's health but in fact he bore no ill effects for the first two months. They settled, with Ellen, Robert's sister, at Isleworth in the house of friends, the Misses Coxon, who were travelling abroad. It was a comfortable house and the Sherwoods liked the area. Henry had one or two episodes of varying intensity of his chronic breathlessness but was able to enjoy life in a restricted manner. Then the Sherwoods and Sophia moved into a house in Twickenham. On October 20, Henry 'took to his bed.'

> From that time to his death, December the 6th, all was suffering, intense suffering. Occasionally he had spasmodic attacks, and his effort to breathe could be heard all over the house. He could no more lie down, and he hardly ever slept; for one of the most distressing symptoms of his complaint was a constant wakefulness. He required to be perpetually moved from his bed to an easy chair and back again, for in no position could he find ease.[316]

Henry was constantly demanding that they read to him, pray with him or to be comforted. He also talked incessantly in a changed voice to the one they were familiar with and failed to end his words. Mary had grown slightly deaf and, as she could not hear what his demands were, Sophia decided it would be better that she did not spend too much time with him. Henry was now becoming incoherent in his ramblings and at times failed to recognise Mary. Sophia persuaded Mary to go and stay with their friends at Isleworth from time to time, for, although she seemed composed outwardly, she was beset by inner demons. She commented to Sophia:

> Your dear father has no fear of death, but rather hopes and prays for it; but I am dark and sad, and confused, and stupid, groaning within the prison of the flesh.[317]

It was at dusk that Mary found her situation most difficult to bear: she had been so confident about meeting death with equanimity but now admitted fear. Henry died on December 6, 1849. He was seventy-two. Mary's husband of forty-six years and her companion through so many life-changing events had gone.

Henry was buried at Oak Lane Cemetery, Twickenham where the inscription on his grave read:

> Sacred to Henry Sherwood of Lower Wick formerly Captain of His Majesty's 53rd Regiment of Foot and late Captain in the Brunswick Hussars who died in this parish on the 6th of December 1849 in the 73rd year of his age.
> Blest are the dead which die in the Lord, ever so safe the spirit for they rest from their labours. Rev. 14. v.13.[318]

Mary was persuaded by Sophia to go and stay at Isleworth for a time, with the Misses Coxon who loved her dearly. Lucy, her sister, came down to London to provide further consolation and support and the two sisters found comfort in each other's company. Mary now lived a retired and ordered life at Twickenham: breakfasting at an early hour before going to her study and working on her Scripture Types till after midday. She would then select a hymn, which she sang in her still sweet voice, and read a passage from the Bible before having lunch at two o'clock. After lunch she would rest and read an amusing book for three hours. Then, in the summer, she would go out in her Bath-chair, whilst in the winter she would read aloud to Sophia and Ellen Streeten. She would conduct family prayers, to which the servants came, just before going to bed at nine o'clock. Mary kept to this division of her day somewhat rigidly although she did receive her friends who called on her regularly.

'Sickness of Heart'

Mary was still able to visit friends, many of whom had shared references from their time in India. One of these friends was Lady McCaskell whose husband Sir John had been in the 53rd with Henry and to whom Henry had been close. Living nearby was Mrs Mawby, the wife of General Mawby, Henry's commanding officer in India. Visits to Lady McCaskell at her home at Westbourne Terrace in Paddington meant taking a fly – drawn by a single horse with the driver above and with two or three passengers behind – to Richmond station and then by train to Paddington. Mary and Sophia had arranged to stay with Lady McCaskell for a few nights in April 1850. Mary was looking forward to seeing her friends but the day before they were due to set off they received news that there had been a fire at Lady McCaskell's home. She had fallen down some stairs whilst going to help one of her grandchildren who was calling for help. Both had fallen. The child was uninjured but Lady McCaskell was now confined to bed.

Mary had been looking forward to the trip and so it was decided that she and Sophia would travel up for the day, visit Lady McCaskell and then call on Mrs Mawby. Sophia had been worried for some time about how tired Mary seemed and, with this in mind, the Misses Coxon travelled with them in the train up to London. The party settled into their carriage but soon after the train left the station Mary fainted, causing great alarm. When she recovered she was still very weak but was given some water by a young man who leapt out at the next station to get it. It was clear that Mary was very ill so Sophia and the Coxons decided that they should continue to Paddington where she could be removed from the train and where help would be more readily at hand. There she was given a glass of hot wine and water before she was placed in a carriage which took her to Hatton Garden where Mrs Darton, the wife of the publisher of so many of her books, lived. Mary was placed on a couch and ministered to by Mrs Darton and Sophia. They were now faced with a predicament as to what was best for the patient. It was decided that Mary, in the care of Sophia and the Coxons, should return home where she could be nursed and would be in surroundings familiar to her. Mary remained confused and unaware of the drama. She remained very weak and confused for the next two months expressing great anxiety as to Sophia's welfare. Sophia, who was still mourning the loss of her husband, was now fully aware that her mother might soon die.

Gradually Mary regained some strength. Her diary which once was so fully written with descriptions, comments and hopes was largely neglected but on the first anniversary of Henry's death she confides:

> I hoped no one remembered this day, and that no one would speak of it; neither did they, though they most kindly managed not to leave me all day, and to amuse me and divert me to the last. But, oh, my beloved one! Not lost, but gone before, I have been parted from you one year, one whole year, and I even miss you more than I ever did. Alas! alas! My heart sinks within me thinking of the days which are gone. With how much pain do I begin another year, the revolving season reminding me so forcibly of that which has been, and that which was only this time two years, that I have attempted to go on with my diary, more than once, and have left it off from very sickness of heart.[319]

A moving reminder of her loss.

Now, largely confined to her home, Mary once again began working on the dearest project to her heart: the *Type Dictionary*. It was an escape from the depressing world which was beginning to envelop her in spite of Sophia's and friends' attempts to cheer her. In a letter to her friend, Lady John Somerset, she reveals the importance of this faith confirming work in which she had been engaged for many years and in which Henry had been so involved:

> I thank God that I am able once again to return to my old and favourite 'TYPICAL DICTIONARY'. When I am sad, I find such lovely things concealed under the figures of natural things, that I am ready to weep for very joy; they are like violets hidden under dark leaves, or precious stones buried in the rock.... Very sweet thoughts are sometimes vouchsafed to me, when I take a pen in hand, perhaps I sometimes become tedious in recording them.[320]

Finally on March 27, 1851 Mary announced to Sophia that she had finished the first draft of the work which had occupied her for thirty years. Now Mary, with Sophia's help, began checking the manuscript and making any necessary revisions. One of Mary's eyes was growing dim so the revision was slow and Mary tired more easily. Sophia had an announcement of her own: in July she became engaged to Dr. Hubert Kelly. They were to be married from Hubert's brother's house near Hampstead Heath. The news cheered Mary: one of her great anxieties since Henry's death had been the uncertain future for her widowed daughter. Now all she wished for was to see Sophia married and to be able to move into the couple's home at Pinner with them. This would seem to open a promising and happy new chapter for Mary and she began to plan for the removal. She would have her own sitting room to which she could retire; the arrangement of furniture in her rooms occupied her thoughts; where all her books and manuscripts would go needed careful thought too. To her delight she would have the luxury of her own pony carriage to take her out – she no longer liked expeditions in the Bath-chair.

Henrietta's daughter, Sarah, who was delicate, had been staying at Twickenham with her grandmother. Unfortunately Sarah became ill. This distressed Mary so Sophia wrote to Henrietta asking her to come down to Twickenham in order to take Sarah home. As Henrietta was herself unwell, Sarah set off by herself only to find that her mother had by then set off for Twickenham. When Henrietta arrived it was the first time that Mary and her eldest daughter had spent time alone together for many years. Both Mary and Henrietta treasured this reunion. Henrietta's presence was also a practical comfort to Sophia who needed to be resident in the parish of Hampstead where she would be married. On September 3 Sophia left Twickenham for Hampstead.

Mary was in good spirits. She had decided to delay further correction of the first draft on the *Type Dictionary* and instead was working from woodcut prints sent by Mr Darton. The twelve prints were of animals and Mary was writing penny books on each one which she then gave to Sophia to correct before publication. A morning's work would produce a book which she would then read aloud to Henrietta. Mary was impatient for her move to Pinner and often spoke of it with Sophia. With this in mind she decided to visit Henry's grave at Twickenham cemetery before she moved. As she stood by his grave her thoughts turned to her own death and how she would join her beloved husband.

On September 14 Sophia saw her mother who appeared to be in good health. Mary entreated Sophia to marry that same week:

> "My dear Sophia," she said, "you know not, you cannot comprehend the strange feelings I have about it. What matter the arrangements respecting this or that? Do let the ceremony be performed this week."[321]

However, Sophia wanted her brother, Henry, to be present on this important day. Henry was still at White Ladies Aston and it would be impossible for him to leave at such short notice. Sophia left Mary in a state of anxiety about the wedding arrangements and caught the train back to Hampstead.

> I was called away; the train would be starting shortly to town. I left her, soothing her as well as I could. I thought her anxiety on this affair attributable to the timidity of age. I anticipated nothing. I feared nothing, and I went. To say I was thoughtless would not be true; for I never parted from my mother, even for a few hours, in later years, without a feeling of uneasiness that the occasion often did not warrant…
>
> But I was to return to her in four days more. Alas! What a return was that! I cannot enter into it. I cannot enlarge long upon it; for it would be but sorrow upon sorrow I should have to recite.[322]

Sophia and Ellen Streeten returned from Hampstead to their home in Twickenham, arriving at about four o'clock.

Henrietta met her with the distressing news that Mary was not well and furthermore that her doctor, Dr. Barry, was then in Ireland. Henrietta turned to Sophia for advice as to what should be done. Sophia went immediately to Mary's study. Her mother was lying on a couch and was pleased to see her daughter. Sophia and Ellen had tea with her and told her excitedly about the plans for the wedding. Later, with the benefit of hindsight, Sophia realised that Mary had heard nothing, but unaware of this, and, as their mother did not appear to be in pain, they continued to describe what had been happening since they last saw her. It was only when they decided that Mary should be prepared for bed that they realised how ill she was. They undressed her on the couch on which she lay but when they attempted to stand her up she fainted. On regaining her senses she pointed to the spot at the end of the room where Henry had died and said: "Is it there you want to lay me?" Between them the three women managed to take Mary to the nearest bedroom which was Henrietta's. Mary slept deeply and the next day was sufficiently alert to discuss Sophia's plans for the wedding the following week. During the day as she lay in bed she several times expressed a wish to see Hubert, Sophia's future husband. Sophia explained that although it was Saturday he had a patient whom he had promised to visit twice that day so would be unable to drive across to Twickenham. However, he would be with them all after the morning service on Sunday. On the Saturday night a local nurse looked after Mary. In the morning Mary asked the nurse if she would visit Henry's grave after she died.

When Hubert Kelly arrived on the Sunday afternoon Mary asked to see him immediately. He confirmed that Mary was now dying but it was decided not to telegraph Henry, her son, as he would be busy with his Sunday service which they felt should not be interrupted by such tragic news. That night, before Hubert sent Henrietta and Sophia to bed to get some rest while he and a nurse cared for Mary, he gave Mary some port wine to sip. After drinking it she kissed his hand and asked his Christian name. Then turning to him she took both Sophia's and his hands in hers and said:

> Hubert, you will be my son, my dear son; you will be very kind to my dear child; you will be her protector, and you will be very tender to her, for she has been used to tenderness. You will love me, too, and I shall be very happy with you at Pinner. God is very good.

Then bending her face over their joined hands she uttered these words:

> Remember this, my children, that God is love. He that dwelleth in love dwelleth in God, and God in him.[323]

Henrietta and Sophia then went to bed. They were called at four o'clock on the Monday morning, September 22, 1851. Mary still was able to know Sophia and called out her name before she died. She was seventy-six. Henry, her beloved son, arrived too late to say his final farewell to his mother.

All three of her surviving children were left with many treasured memories of a remarkable woman who had happened to be their mother.

Mary also left behind a huge canon of literary and religious work which continued in its popularity into the next century.

As late as 1912 *The Fairchild Family* and the lessons it held for children was a classic:

> Almost every English child brought up during the period between 1820 and 1870 began his or her literary education with it. From its perusal our fathers and grandfathers derived untold mental and moral stimulus and it is in demand to this day.

Plaque to the Memory of Mrs Sherwood in Worcester
Cathedral

Epilogue

Lucy Cameron

Lucy received the news of her sister's death by letter, dated Thursday, September 25, 1851. She had shared the same upbringing as Mary, the elder sister she adored and who had told her entrancing magical stories on their walks in the woods of Stanford when they were children:

> Oh day of sorrow! A letter brought me the news of my loveliest, my beloved sister's death. The blow, being so sudden, quite overpowered my bodily frame. Oh, my sister, my sister! Were we not nursed upon the self-same hill, fed the same flock by mountain, wood, and rill? ... Oh sweet sister and brother! but we shall soon meet again; and circling our happy parents stand, our husbands and children with us ...[325]

Encouraged by her father, Lucy had started to write at an early age like Mary. When only seventeen she had written *Margaret Whyte* which enjoyed success, and both she and her sister, inspired by Hannah More, produced many tracts and chapbooks during their time in Bridgnorth. In 1803 Lucy wrote *The Two Lambs* a simple allegorical narrative. This was not in print until 1816. Mary commented that it was 'a beautiful little work of my sister's, but, like many of my own early works, defective in doctrine.' Mary sent the tract to be translated into Hindustani the following year. It became highly popular in Sunday schools even though the lamb, named Inexperience, is represented as innocent rather than being portrayed with the Evangelical doctrine of original sin. Lucy continued to find the time to write throughout her life.[326] Like Mary she could write a small book rapidly in a morning and, like her sister, incorporated events and scenes around her. *The Raven and the Dove* (1817) took her just four hours to complete and was sold for sixpence. After a visit to an old house belonging to the Earls of Powis her attention was caught as she went up a staircase. This had given her the idea for Lady Harewood in a story called *Emma and her Nurse* (1821). Lucy had dedicated much of her time to Sunday school and visiting the poor in her husband's parishes. Like Mary she had a strong work ethic whether it be writing improving stories for young people, managing her large family or doing good works in the church. It was perhaps because of Mary's over-shadowing literary success that she was not so widely known as her sister.

Lucy, the youngest of George and Martha Butt's children, was herself growing old. Grief enveloped her in February 1852 when she learnt that Emma, her daughter, who had said farewell to her in 1845 when she set out to Madras, had died there from cholera. She had now lost five daughters. Lucy's widowed son-in-law, Frederic Lugard, did not return to England until 1855.

However, the next few years brought great happiness. In July 1853 there was the joyous reunion with Sophia, her youngest daughter. Sophia had gone out to Adelaide in South Australia and married the Reverend T. P. Wilson who was the Principal of St. Peter's Collegiate School. The couple stayed with the Camerons at Swaby before moving in 1854 to Bardsley in Lancashire where the Reverend Wilson had been appointed to a living by the Hulmean Trustees. Lucy also had the pleasure of seeing her three surviving sons together.

The summer of 1854 saw the Camerons paying a visit to Scotland. A nephew of theirs was living in Glen Urquhart in Inverness-shire. The journey up there had taken a week and they stayed in both Edinburgh and Glasgow. The Scottish scenery, with its mountains and lochs, appealed to Lucy who particularly enjoyed a steamship trip on which she looked across to Ardrossan and the mountains. Lucy and her husband celebrated fifty years of a happy marriage in June 1856. Her children and grandchildren joined in the celebrations which also included the chris-tening of her most recent grandson, Theodore. The Camerons had now lived at Swaby for twenty years. Later in the year she attended the wedding of George Butt, her late brother Marten's son, now the vicar of Chesterfield. After the ceremony the Sunday school children held nosegays which they threw down for the bride to walk on as she left the church.

In September the Camerons went to Cumberland for a holiday. One day they went for a sail on Ullswater and were caught in a sudden heavy

Lucy Cameron in old age. Cameron, *frontispiece*

shower. Drenched through, Lucy caught a chill. When they returned home she remained confined to her room until mid-October. She never fully recovered. In May 1858 she went with her husband to Woodhall Spa in Horncastle, twenty-two miles from Lincoln, in order to take the waters and bathe. She was under the care of a Dr. Scott. From there she wrote to her grandson a charming letter on May 29:

My dear Charley,

I am going to write to you to-day to thank you for the nice birthday letter you sent me, and the pretty nosegays you and your dear little sisters sent me; [her birthday was 29 April] and in return I shall send you four lilies, which your aunt gathered with her own hand, yesterday, out of a wild wood, and not a garden.

We came here last Thursday; not by the train, but across the country, quietly, with our own horse, and enjoyed the journey so much, and had several adventures from not knowing the way; and we had some trouble finding the Bath Cottage, but we did find it at last, and looking very much prettier than we expected, with a very pretty garden which opens into the hotel gardens; in which there are the finest lilac trees I ever saw, loaded with blossoms; and there is green grass, and seats, on which your dear mama would like to sit.

There is a field opposite to us, and on one side of the field is a little wood, and a path leading down to another wood, where the lilies grow.

There is a very civil gentleman living here, called Dr. Scott, who is a physician, and he tells us how much water to drink, and when to bathe; and I have a great tumbler brought to me to drink, every morning, about an hour before breakfast, and I think it does me good …

And our house at home is having its face and hands and feet washed quite clean while we are out; and then, I hope, being washed quite clean, as we shall be, in large copper and marble baths here, that our friends and neighbours will not be afraid of visiting us on our return

… Please to give my love to your dear papa and mamma, and thank them for their letters, which were ready to welcome us here. With kisses to your sisters, I am, dear Charley,

Your affectionate grandmother
L.L. Cameron.[327]

Sadly her health did not improve after she returned home but death held no fear for Lucy. She had often written about it in her journal and had faced it many times when called to nurse her sick children. In July she grew worse and she was confined to bed, where, through the open window, she could hear the cooing of a woodpigeon, her favourite sound, and the shouts from a nearby field as corn was being gathered. Lucy expressed her concern for her husband's well-being after her death but was comforted by the fact that: 'We shall meet again.' Lucy Cameron, the last of the Reverend George and Martha Butt's children, died peacefully, surrounded by her loving family on Monday, September 6, 1858. She was seventy-seven.

∽

Sophia Kelly

Sophia and Hubert Kelly continued to live at Pinner where Mary had looked forward so much to living with them and sharing in their life. Mary had clearly liked Hubert during the brief time she knew him. He died in 1867 aged fifty-six. He was described as an 'ebullient doctor' by a patient. After the death of her mother Sophia continued to write books with the same moral message as her mother and aunt. She did claim that she had been responsible for the major part of some of Mary's later books.[328] Sophia saw Mary's great work on scripture types published in 1866 with the title: *Types from the Hebrew and Greek Scriptures as illustrated in the colours of the rainbow.* But *The Spectator*, March 30, 1867, was not complimentary: 'The less said of this strange patchwork the better. Mrs. Kelly does not seem to reflect that the colours of the rainbow are not motley.' Sophia did not achieve the great success through her writing as her mother had: she died in 1899 aged eighty-four.

∾

Henry Martyn Sherwood

The longest living of Mary and Henry's children was their son, Henry: the little boy who had arrived after a long and eventful journey from India, with its jewelled colours, to the strange cold foreign land of England in 1816, speaking fluent Hindustani and only a few words of English. Like Lucy he had been born in Meerut and, like his sister, had survived his early days in India. Henry was married twice: first in 1834 and secondly in 1864.

He served his church, St. John Baptist at White Ladies Aston, well and was much-loved by his parishioners. In 1861 a new North aisle and vestry were built, and new pews installed thus increasing seating from 73 to 155 to accommodate the increase in his congregation. The same year twenty-two yew trees were planted on the path leading to the church: one for each year of Henry's incumbency. He saw the building of a church porch in 1864 dedicated to the memory of his first wife. In 1904 two of his daughters by his second wife, Emily and Mary, funded the building of a Village Hall.

When he had become vicar of White Ladies Aston in 1839 witchcraft was still widely practised in the surrounding countryside. Henry described the area as:

> The place was a nest of poachers and thieves. Morality was hardly existent. The roads were so bad as to be almost impassable in winter. No one dared to go out after dusk. The whole place had been pauperised and degraded by the Poor-law system. Many villagers use openly to keep a special pair of breeches or a petticoat in which to appear for their dole. As for the clergy few of them attended to their duties at all. The vicar of one neighbouring parish of mine lived in Devonshire; that of another in London. One who lived as near his charge as Worcester used to arrange for all marriages and christenings to take place on Sundays so that he need not go near the parish during the week. Even on Sunday there would be no service if it were rainy and cold. The parson contending that the fireside suited both him and his flock better.[329]

When he first arrived at the age of twenty-six Henry's sermons were not popular with his congregation but, through his devotion to them and their welfare, and his broad view of life, they revered him until his retirement at the great age of ninety-seven. During his time at White Ladies Aston he saw parishioners whom he had christened obtain old age pensions for which Henry signed the necessary paperwork. Henry had lived to see the reigns of six monarchs and could recall the unfortunate Queen Caroline being turned away by soldiers and police, weeping, at her husband George IV's coronation on July 19, 1821.[330] However, for Henry it had been a happy day as he was joined by his mother and father to celebrate with his parishioners. Henry had always loved the countryside and enjoyed shooting and fishing till late in his long life. There is an amusing account in 1868 of Henry's adventures on a velocipede:

> Villagers in White Ladies Aston were amazed to see the Reverend Henry Sherwood balancing on a two-wheeled metal framework which he propelled along the muddy village streets by pushing foot-pedals attached to the wooden front wheel. It is understood that the Vicar has acquired this machine, of which there are only two in Worcestershire, for pleasure trips. Popular Village Carrier and butcher Mr Samuel Andrews told our reporter "Unfortunately The Reverend keeps falling off. He frightened my horses on my last Saturday journey into Worcester. He'd do better to stick to a pony. I can't see this is a sport which will ever prosper. I wish he'd keep to his shooting and fishing."[331]

When he retired, after the death of his second wife, Mary, in the autumn of 1910, he moved to live with his married daughter and her husband, the

Rushers, in Pershore, near Worcester. Henry continued to explore the countryside in his Bath chair until he abandoned that mode of transport and took to riding in the side car of motorbikes driven either by his son or his son-in-law.

In January 1911, just over a year before his death, Henry and his mother were reunited in *The Spectator*: 'The Literary productions of Mrs Sherwood have shown a remarkable vitality, she seems to have communicated the same quality to her son.'

Whether Mary would have chosen the quality of vitality to have bequeathed to Henry is doubtful. She would have been far more likely to have chosen her belief in the enveloping power of God's love and righteousness which their shared religion brought: not only for her beloved son, Henry, but her entire family, and their belief that they would once again be reunited after death embraced them.

Born on July 1, 1813, Henry had a long life. He died at Pershore on January 21, 1912 just six months short of his centenary. He had been vicar of White Ladies Aston for seventy-one years.

Bibliography

Primary Sources

Butt, *Correspondence*. (1847). Transcribed in 2013 from: Butt Papers. Berkshire Record Office, Refs.: D/EZ/106/3/6/36 and D/EZ/106/3/7/1/1–10.

Butt, Jemima, re. (1847). *Chapter Act Book*, Monday 22nd November 1847, Meeting of Dean and Chapter, Chapter Records, Acc. 15, bundle 22, Salisbury Cathedral.

Sherwood, Henry. *Diaries of Henry Sherwood*. Transcribed in 2013–14 from originals in Shropshire Archives, Shrewsbury, UK. Ref. 5624/1-2.

Sherwood, Mary Martha. *Letter to Mrs Commins*, Worcestershire Archive & Archaeology Service. Ref. 705:936 BA 8720/1(ii)32.

Sherwood, Mary Martha. (ca. 1811). Fragment of a letter from Mrs Mary Sherwood, India with transcript: Henry Martyn Centre, Westminster College, Cambridge, Ref. MAR 8/3. From their original ref. MA12/1 by permission of the Master and Fellows of St John's College, Cambridge

Sherwood, Mary Martha. (1824). 31 Sunday letters to a pupil, Lydia Commins, Dorset History Centre. Ref. D/PLR/F57 1824.

Secondary Sources

Annesley v Annesley. Greater London Record Office: London Metropolitan Archive. Ref. GLRO DL/185.

Annesley, George Viscount Valentia. (1809). *Voyages and travels to India, Ceylon, the Red Sea, Abyssinia, and Egypt in the years 1802, 1803, 1804, 1805, and 1806*, 3 Vols. London: Miller.

Avery, Gillian. (1975). *Childhood's pattern: a study of the heroes and heroines of children's fiction, 1770–1950*. London: Hodder and Stoughton.

Bowker, John, ed. (1999). *The Oxford Dictionary of World Religions*. Oxford:Oxford University Press.

Breckinridge, R. J. and Cross, A. B., eds. (1837). *The Baltimore Literary and Religious Magazine for 1837*. Vol III. Baltimore, USA. For notes on Swiss Momiers pp. 58–73.

Burney, Frances (Fanny). (1782). *Cecilia. Or, Memoirs of an Heiress*. 5 Vols. London: T Payne.

Burney, Frances (Fanny). (Published anonymously) (1778). *Evelina, or, A Young Lady's Entrance into the World*. 3 Vols. London: T. Lowndes.

Cameron, Lucy Lyttelton. (1873). *The Life of Mrs Cameron: Partly an autobiography, and from her Private Journals*, Revised and edited by George Thomas Cameron. 2nd edition. London: Houlston.

Chaudhuri, Nupur. (1994). *Memsahibs and their servants in nineteenth-century India. Women's History Review*, Vol. 3, Issue 4, pp. 549–562. Routledge.

Corley, T. A. B. (2009). *Mrs Sherwood's Secrets: Jane Austen's Boarding-school at Reading in the 1790s*. Jane Austen Society Report: pp. 136–42.

Corrie, Daniel. (1847). *Memoirs of the Right Rev. Daniel Corrie, LL.D. the First Bishop of Madras*. London: Seeley, Burnside, and Seeley.

Crittall, Elizabeth. (1962). *History of the County of Wiltshire*, Vol. 6: pp. 168–178, in Salisbury Charities. London: University of London & History of Parliament Trust. Online Resource.

Cutt, M. Nancy. (1974). *Mrs. Sherwood and her Books for Children*. London: OUP.

Cutt, Margaret Nancy. (1979). *Ministering angels: a study of nineteenth-century evangelical writing for children*. Wormley: Five Owls Press.

Dangerfield, J. (1826). *A Stenographic Lecture as delivered to the Royal Institution on the 1st of March 1825 and at the Mechanic's Institution on the 22nd of June 1825*. London: Jaques & Wright.

Darton, F. J. Harvey. (1932). *Children's Books in England, Five Centuries of Social Life. 3rd Edition (1982). Cambridge: CUP.*

Darton, F. J. Harvey, ed. (1910). *The Life and Times of Mrs Sherwood*. London: Wells Gardner, Darton & Co.

Dawson, Janis. (1996). *Mary Martha Sherwood* in *Dictionary of Literary Biography*. Detroit: Gale Research. Vol. 163: pp. 267–281.

de Courcy, Anne. (2012). *The Fishing Fleet, Husband-hunting in the Raj*. London: Weidenfeld & Nicholson.

Demers, Patricia. (2004). (online edn. 2011). *Mary Martha Sherwood (1775–1851)* in *Oxford Dictionary of National Biography*. Oxford: OUP.

Dow, Gillian. (2009). *The Imagined Female Academy, Mary Martha Sherwood*. Cambridge: Lucy Cavendish College.

Dow, Gillian. (2010). *Northanger Abbey, French fiction, and the affecting history of the Duchess of C***.* in *Persuasions: The Jane Austen Journal*, Vol. 32, Annual, 2010. Jane Austen Society of North America.

Eaton, Barbara. (2005). *Letters to Lydia: 'beloved Persis'.* Penzance: Hypatia Publications.

Eaton, Barbara. (2012). *Yes Papa! Mrs Chapone and the Bluestocking Circle.* London: Francis Boutle.

Edgeworth, Maria and Edgeworth, Richard Lovell. *Practical Education.* 2 Vols. London: J. Johnson.

Fielding, Sarah. (1749). *The governess; or, little female academy. Being the history of Mrs. Teachum, and her nine girls. With their nine days amusement. Calculated for the entertainment and instruction of young ladies in their education. By the author of David Simple.* Dublin: Bradley and James.

Gawler, John Bellenger, *Valentia, Lady. (1799). Trial for adultery: the whole proceedings on the trial of John Bellenger Gawler, Esquire, for criminal conversation with Lady Valentia, in the Court of King's Bench, before Lord Kenyon … . Journal of The House of Lords*, Vol. 42. London.

Gilchrist, Isabella, ed. (1907). *The Life of Mrs. Sherwood, The Author of "The Fairchild Family, etc."* London: Robert Sutton.

Good, James I. (1913). *History of the Swiss Reformed Church Since Reformation.* Philadelphia: Publication and Sunday School Board of the Reformed Church in the United States.

Hudson, Giles & Jackson, B. D. (2004 rev. 2014: online edn. 2014). *Mary Martha Sherwood (1775 1851)* in *Oxford Dictionary of National Biography.* Oxford: OUP.

Hunt, Peter. (1994). *An Introduction to Children's Literature.* Oxford: OUP.

Ilbert, Sir Courtenay. (1922). *The Government of India: A Brief Historical Survey of Parliamentary Legislation Relating to India.* pp. 76–8. Oxford: Clarendon Press.

Kelly, Sophia, ed. (1854, & 2nd ed. *1857). The Life of Mrs. Sherwood, (chiefly autobiographical) with Extracts from Mr. Sherwood's Journal during his Imprisonment in France & Residence in India Edited by Her Daughter.* 1st & 2nd editions differ. London: Darton & Co.

Kilmer, Paulette D. (1996). *The Fear of Sinking: The American Success Story in the Gilded Age.* Chapter 5, Why Children Read Success Tales. University of Tennessee Press.

Lees, E. (1831). *The Worcestershire Miscellany*, Supplement. pp. 155–7. Worcester: Lees.

Lushington, Charles. (1824). *The History, Design, and Present State of the Religious, Benevolent and Charitable Institutions Founded by the British in Calcutta and its Vicinity.* Calcutta: Hindostanee Press.

Malcolm, John. (1833). *The Government of India.* London: J. Murray.

Moore, Peter. (2013). *Damn His Blood, being a true and detailed history of the most Barbarous and Inhumane Murder at Oddingley and the quick and awful Retribution.* London: Vintage.

Nelson Evening Mail, Anon. (1912). *The Rev H. M. Sherwood.* Article in *Nelson Evening Mail*, Volume XLVII, 5 January 1912, p. 3. National Library of New Zealand: Paperspast website.

Palgrave, Mary E. (1902). ed. Introduction. *The Fairchild Family.* London: Wells Gardner, Darton & Co.

Plymley, Joseph. (1803). *General view of the agriculture of Shropshire, with observations: drawn up for the consideration of the Board of Agriculture and Internal Improvement.* London: G. & W. Nicol.

Raffles. (2000). *Sir Thomas Stamford Raffles 1781–1826.* Raffles Museum of Biodiversity Research, Department of Biological Sciences, The National University of Singapore. Online article.

Rowland, Clarissa M. (1973). *Bungalows and Bazaars: India in Victorian Children's Fiction.* Article in *Children's Literature*, Vol. 2, 1973, pp. 192–6. Baltimore: Johns Hopkins University Press.

Royde-Smith, Naomi. (1946). *The State of Mind of Mrs. Sherwood.* London: Macmillan & Co. Ltd.

Salt, Henry. (1814). *A voyage to Abyssinia, and travels into the interior of that country, executed under the orders of the British government, in the years 1809 and 1810.* London: F. C. & J. Rivington.

Sherwood, Bryan, ed. (2012). *Press Cuttings from The White Ladies Aston Chronicle Incorporating The Churchill Chanticleer.* (1848–1868). *During the incumbency of the Rev. Henry Martin Sherwood.* Printed in *The Sherwood Forest*, Vol 7, No. 3, Spring 2012.

Sherwood, Henry. Bond, Andrew, ed. (1981). *The Value of Bread, a Memoir By Henry Sherwood Who, as a Teenager, Resided in France During the Years of the Revolution.* London: Saint George Orthodox Information Service.

Sherwood, Mary Martha, Mrs. (1834 - 57). *The Works of Mrs. Sherwood in a Uniform Edition*, 16 Volumes: New York: Harper & Brothers.

Sherwood, Mary Martha. (1839). *The Indian Orphans. A narrative of facts: including many notices of the Rev. Henry Martyn, B.D., and the Right Rev. Daniel Corrie, Lord Bishop of Madras.* Berwick: Thomas Melrose.

Skultans, Vieda. (1987). *Asylums: a historical survey*, in *The Oxford Companion to the Mind*. Oxford: Oxford University Press.

Smith, Leonard D. (1993). *To Cure Those Afflicted with the Disease of Insanity: Thomas Bakewell and the Spring Vale Asylum* in *History of Psychiatry*, IV, pp. 107–27.

Spurrier, Lisa. (1997). *East Garston's Mad Vicar* in *The Berkshire Echo – The Newsletter of Berkshire Record Office*, No. 3, Autumn 1997.

Stowe, Harriet Beecher. (1852). *Uncle Tom's Cabin, or Life among the Lowly.* Boston: John P. Jewett & Company.

Trumbach, Randolf. (1998). *Sex and the Gender Revolution*, Volume 1: *Heterosexuality and the Third Gender in Enlightenment London.* Chicago: University of Chicago Press.

Voltaire, F. M. (1759). *Candide or Optimism.*

Walpole, Horace. (1765). *The Castle of Otranto, A Story. Translated by William Marshall, Gent. From the Original Italian of Onuphrio Muralto, Canon of the Church of St. Nicholas at Otranto.* London: Tho. Lowndes.

Yule, Henry and Burnell, Arthur Coke. (1886). *Hobson-Jobson: being a glossary of Anglo-Indian colloquial words and phrases and of kindred terms etymological, historical, geographical and discursive.* London: John Murray. New edition. (1994). Sittingbourne: Linguasia.

Appendix 1

Works of Mrs M. M. Sherwood

Writings of Mrs Mary Martha Sherwood (Mary Martha Butt) 1775–1851.
Including collaborations with her daughter Sophia, later Mrs Streeten then
Mrs Kelly.

The Traditions, a Legendary Tale written by a Young Lady 2 Vols.	1795–6	Book
Margarita 4 Vols.	1799	Book
The Traveller	1800	Book
The History of Susan Gray as Related by a Clergyman: designed for the Benefit of Young Women going into Service	1801–2 1836	Book Works III
The History of Theophilus and Sophia	1811 1836	Book Works III
The History of Lucy Clare as related by a clergyman and intended for the use of young women	1812–4 1836	Book Works III
Stories Explanatory of the Church Catechism 1st in Calcutta	1814	Book
Stories Explanatory of the Church Catechism	1817	
The Ayah and her Lady, an Indian Story in Hindi	1814	Book
The Ayah and her Lady, an Indian Story also as *The Lady and her Ayah*	1816	

The History of Little Henry and his Bearer Firstly anon. then Mrs Sherwood	1814 1836	Book Works III
The Infant's Progress from the Valley of Destruction to Everlasting Glory also as: *The Infant Pilgrim's Progress ...*	1814? 1834 1887	Book Works V
Memoirs of Sergeant Dale, his Daughter, and the Orphan Mary	1815 1836	Book Works III
The Indian Pilgrim or the Progress of the Pilgrim Nazareenee from the City of the Wrath of God to the City of Mount Zion, delivered under the Similitude of a Dream Formerly Goonah Purist or the Slave of Sin, An adaptation of John Bunyan's *Pilgrims Progress*. Known translations: Telugu 1840, Hindustanee 1844, Urdu 1847, Marathi 1848	1815 1834	Book Works IV
The History of Emily and her Brothers	1816 1837	Chap-Penny Works XIII
The History of Little George and his Penny	1816	Chap-Penny
An Introduction to Astronomy	1817	Book
The Infirmary	1817? 1837	Tract Works VIII
A Drive in the Coach through the Streets of London	1818	Chap-Penny
An Introduction to Geography	1818	Book
The Busy Bee	1818	Chap-Penny
The Little Woodman and his Dog Caesar	1818 1834	Book Works IV
The Rose. A Fairy Tale	1818	Chap-Penny
The History of the Fairchild Family, or the Child's manual: being a collection of stories calculated to shew the importance and affects of a religious education	1818 pt I 1818 pt I 1834 pt II 1842 pt II 1847 pt III	Book Gutenberg Works II Book Book
The Friendly Visitor. No author credits given but credited elsewhere. Then: *The Children's Friend, A Monthly Juvenile Magazine Devoted to the Best Interests of the Young.*	1819–24 1824–	Journals Tracts

A General Outline of Profane History from the *beginning of the world unto the present period*	1819	Book
The Errand Boy	1819 1837	Chap-Penny Works VIII
The Hedge of Thorns	1819 1836	Book Works III
The History of Henry Fairchild and Charles *Trueman* extract from *The Fairchild Family*	1819	Book
The Little Sunday School Child's Reward	1819	Chap-Penny
The Orphan Boy	1819 1837	Chap-Penny Works VIII
The Wishing Cap	1819	Chap-Penny
The Two Sisters, or Ellen and Sophia Religious Tract Society Series	1819? 1827 1837	Tract Tract Works VIII
Little Arthur	1820	Chap-Penny
The Golden Clew Nos. 41–2 of William Whittemore's tract series	1820 1834	Tract Works IV
The Governess, or The Little Female Academy by Sarah Fielding, edited and adapted by Sherwood	1820 1834	Book Works VI
The May-Bee	1820	Chap-Penny
Abdallah, the Merchant of Bagdad Religious Tract Society Series	1820–5? 1836	Tract Works III
The Fountain of Living Waters Religious Tract Society Series	1820–5?	Tract
Mary Anne Religious Tract Society Series	1820? 1834	Tract Works IV
The Flowers of the Forest Religious Tract Society Series	1820? 1834	Tract Works V
The History of Little Lucy and her Dhaye	1820? 1836	Book Works III
The Nursery Maid's Diary	1820?	Tract
Procrastination, or The Evil of Putting Off till *tomorrow which ought to be done today* No. 23 of William Whittemore's tract series also as *Procrastination or, The Evil of Delay*	1820? - 1834	Tract Works VII

The Young Mother No. 24 of William Whittemore's tract series	1820?	Tract
The Iron Cage No. 27 of William Whittemore's tract series	1820? 1834	Tract Works IV
The Lambourne Bell No. 28 of William Whittemore's tract series	1820?	Tract
Waste Not Want Not Nos. 35–38 of William Whittemore's tract series	1820?	Tract
The Blessed Family No. 2 of William Whittemore's tract series	1821 1837	Tract Works XIII
Charles Lorraine, or The Young Soldier drawn from scenes of real life Nos. 5–9 of William Whittemore's tract series	1821	Tract
Little Robert and the Owl	1821	Chap-Penny
Mrs. Sherwood's Primer, or First Book for Children includes *Margery*	1821	Book
The History of George Desmond, founded on the facts which occurred in the East Indies and now published as a caution to young men going to that country	1821	Book
The Recaptured Negro, Susannah 2nd edition	1821 1836	Book Works III
The Young Forester Nos. 1–4 of Houlston's New Series of Religious Tracts	1821–2? 1837	Tract Works VIII
The China Manufactory No. 5 of Houlston's New Series of Religious Tracts	1821–2? 1837	Tract Works XIII
Blind Richard	1821?	Book
The Village Schoolmistress	1821?	Book
Easy Questions for a Little Child	1822	Chap-Penny
The History of Henry Milner, a little boy who was not brought up according to the fashions of this world, Part I	1822	Book
Henry Milner, The History of, Part II	1826	Book
Henry Milner, The History of, Part III	1831	Book
Henry Milner, The History of, Parts I, II, III	1834	Works I
Henry Milner, The History of, Part IV	1837	Book
Henry Milner, The History of. Part IV	1837	Book
Henry Milner, The History of Part IV	1856	Works XV

The Orphans of Normandy, or Florentin and Lucie	1822	Book
	1822	Works II
	1828	Book
The Poor Man of Colour, or The Sufferings, privations and death of Thomas Wilson in the suburbs of the British metropolis	1822–3	Tract
The Penny Tract No. 1 of William Whittemore's tract series The Penny Tract	1822–3?	Tract
	1837	Works XIII
The History of Mary Saunders No. 11 of William Whittemore's tract series	1822–3?	Tract
The Blind Man and Little George No. 13 of William Whittemore's tract series	1822–3?	Tract
The Potter's Commons, or The Happy Choice Nos. 15–18 of William Whittemore's tract series	1822–3	Tract
	1837	Works XIII
The Youth's Magazine This periodical brought out tales, tracts, and articles by Mrs. Sherwood for over twenty-five years signed at first M.M., and after 1827, M.M.S. The earlier tales were rapidly reprinted by Houlston, Darton, Melrose, Knight and Lacey and the R.T.S. [Religious Tract Society], as well as by various American publishers	1822–48	Periodicals
The Bitter Sweet Nos. 19–20 of Houlston's New Series of Religious Tracts	1822?	Tract
	1837	Works VIII
Common Errors No. 21 of Houlston's New Series of Religious Tracts	1822–5?	Tract
	1837	Works VIII
Père La Chaise first in *The Select Magazine*	1822	
	1823	Book
	1834	Works VI
The Infant's Grave a story of the Northern part of France first in *The Select Magazine*	1822	
	1823	Book
	1837	Works XIII
The Guinguette and *The Noble Allamont* written but no record found of publication	1822?	
The Child's Magazine	1823–4	Periodicals
Old Times Nos. 23–4 of Houlston's New Series of Religious Tracts	1823–7?	Tract

The Lady of the Manor, being a series of conversations on the subject of confirmation intended for the use of the middle and higher ranks of young females 7 vols 30 chapters	1823–9	Book
The Lady of the Manor (1825–29)	1825–9	Book
5 vols 28 chapters	1836	Works IX
The Lady of the Manor, Volume I: 1836	1837	Works X
The Lady of the Manor, Volume II: 1837	1836	Works XI
The Lady of the Manor, Volume III: 1836	1835	Works XII
Content and Discontent	1824	Tract
The Children's Friend, A Monthly Juvenile Magazine Devoted to the Best Interests of the Young. Successor to:	1824–	Journals
The Friendly Visitor. No author credits given but referred to elsewhere.	1819–24	Tracts
The Bible Teacher's Manual	1824	Book
The History of Mrs. Catharine Crawley	1824	Book
	1837	Works VIII
The Spanish Daughter by Sherwood's father, corrected by her.	1824	Book
The Little Beggars	1824–	Tract
Nos. 29–30 of William Whittemore's tract series also as *The Children of the Hartz Mountains*	1834	Works IV
Bible History, or Scripture its own Interpreter	1825	Book
Clara Stephens, or the White Rose	1825	Book
	1834	Works IV
Emily, a tale for young persons	1825	Book
Juliana Oakley, an autobiography	1825	Book
Part 2 as *Ermina* 1827	1834	Works V
My Father and his Family Religious Tract Society Series	1825	Tract
My Uncle Timothy, an interesting tale for young persons	1825	Book
	1834	Works VI
Poor Burruff	1825	Chap-Penny
Preface to Scripture Exercises	1825	Assorted
Julian Percival	1826	Chap-Penny
	1837	Works VIII
The Captive in Ceylon	1826	Book

The Gipsy Babes, a story of the last century also as *The Two Gypsy Babes*	1826 1829 1834	Book Works VII
The History of Emily and her Mother, an extract from *The Governess*	1826	Book
The Soldier's Orphan, or The History of Maria West	1826	Book
The Two Dolls	1826	Chap-Penny
A Chronology of Ancient History	1826–7	Book
Joan, or Trustworthy Nos. 31–2 of Houlston's New Series of Religious Tracts	1826–8? 1837	Tract Works VIII
The Cottage in the Wood Nos. 41–2 of Houlston's New Series of Religious Tracts	1826–8?	Tract
The Turnpike House Nos. 51–2 of Houlston's New Series of Religious Tracts	1826–8?	Tract
The Hop-Picking Nos. 61–2 of Houlston's New Series of Religious Tracts	1826–30?	Tract
Do Your Own Work No. 67 of Houlston's New Series of Religious Tracts	1826–30?	Tract
Do What You Can No. 71 of Houlston's New Series of Religious Tracts	1826–30?	Tract
False Colours No. 72 of Houlston's New Series of Religious Tracts	1826–30?	Tract
It Is Not My Business No. 81 of Houlston's New Series of Religious Tracts	1826–30?	Tract
A Series of Questions and Answers Illustrative of the Church	1827	Chap-Penny
A Series of Questions and Answers Illustrative of the Church Catechism	1827	Chap-Penny
Edward Mansfield, a narrative of facts	1827 1837	Chap-Penny Works VIII

Ermina, or the second part of Juliana Oakley also as *Ermina in the East Indies*	1827	Book
Le Fevre, a True Narrative	1827 1837	Book Works XIII
Religious Fashion, or the History of Anna	1827	Book
Susannah, or The Three Guardians	1827	Book
The Birthday Present	1827 1837	Book Works VIII
The Dry Ground	1827	Chap-Penny
The Lady in the Arbour	1827	Chap-Penny
The Pulpit and the Desk	1827	Book
Arzoomund	1828 1837	Book Works VIII
Home	1828	Chap-Penny
My Aunt Kate	1828 1834	Book Works VII
Soffrona and her Cat Muff	1828	Chap-Penny
Southstone's Rock	1828	Book
The Broken Hyacinth	1828	Works IV
The Fawns	1828	Chap-Penny
The Hills	1828	Chap-Penny
The Idiot Boy	1828	Chap-Penny
The Rainbow	1828	Chap-Penny
The Rosebuds	1828	Chap-Penny
The Thunder Storm	1828	Chap-Penny
Theophilus	1828	Book
The Crows' Nest Nos. 45–46 of Houlston's New Series of Religious Tracts	1829	Tract
Darkwood Court No. 47 of Houlston's New Series of Religious Tracts	1829	Tract
The Apprentice No. 48 of Houlston's New Series of Religious Tracts	1829	Tract

Emancipation	1829	Book
	1834	Works V
Little Sally	1829	Tract
The Butterfly. A Melrose Tract	1829	Tract
	1834	Works VII
The Golden Chain. A Melrose Tract	1829	Tract
The Little Orphan	1829	Tract
The Millennium, or Twelve Stories	1829	Book
The Mourning Queen	1829	Chap-Penny
	1834	Works VII
The Orange Grove	1829	Chap-Penny
An Illustration of the Prophecy of Hosea Mrs T Best, Preface by Mrs Sherwood	1830	
Dudley Castle, a tale	1830	Book
	1837	Works XIII
Intimate Friends	1830	Chap-Penny
	1834	Works VII
Katherine Seward	1830	Chap-Penny
	1834	Works IV
Lucy's Going to School	1830	Chap-Penny
Obedience. A Melrose tract	1830	Tract
	1834	Works VII
Sequel to the Oddingley Murders	1830	Tract
The Father's Eye. A Melrose tract	1830	Tract
	1837	Works XIII
The Mountain Ash. A Melrose tract	1830	Tract
The Oddingley Murders	1830	Tract
The Red Book Religious Tract Society Series	1830	Tract
	1837	Works XIII
The Two Paths. A Melrose tract or *The Lofty Way and The Lowly Way*	1830	Tract
The Useful Little Girl and The Little Girl Who *was of no Use at all.* A Melrose tract	1830	Tract
	1837	Works XIII
Hard Times	1830–1	Tract
Roxobel, or English Manners and Customs *Seventy Years Ago.* 3 vols.	1830–1	Book

A Mother's Duty	1830?	Chap-Penny
The Babes in the Wood of the New World	1830? 1834	Book Works IV
The Hidden Treasure	1830?	Chap-Penny
The Stolen Fruit	1830?	Chap-Penny
The Stranger at Home	1830? 1834	Book Works VI
Ermina, a tale of Calcutta	1831 1834	Book Works V
Everything Out of its Place	1831	Chap-Penny
Lamentations of Old Hospitality included in Marshall's Christmas Box	1831	
Scripture Prints with Explanations in the form *of familiar dialogues*	1831	Book
Emmeline. A Melrose tract	1832 1834	Tract Works VII
Alune, or Le Bächen Hölzli, A Melrose tract *Alune, or Le Bächen Hölzli* *Aleine, or Le Bächen Hölzli* in *The Garland* Note: published both as Aleine and Alune	1833 1834 1835	Tract Works VI Story
My Godmother. A Melrose tract	1833 1837	Tract Works XIII
The Convent of St. Clair. A Melrose tract	1833 1837	Tract Works XIV
The Latter Days	1833 1833 1834	Book Book Works II
The Little Momiere	1833 1834	Book Works VI
The Nun, a Narrative	1833 1834	Book Works VII
The Rosary or Rosée de Montreux. A Melrose tract	1833 1837	Tract Works XIV
Victoria	1833 1837	Book Works VIII
A Visit to Grandpapa	1833?	Chap-Penny
The Ball and the Funeral	1833?	Tract
English Mary	1834	Works VI

The Basket-Maker. A Melrose tract	1834	Tract
	1834	Works VII
The Monk of Cimiés	1834	Book
	1837	Works XIV
The Works of Mrs. Sherwood 16 Vols.	1834–57	Works I-XVI
Caroline Mordaunt, or The Governess	1835	Book
	1837	Works XIII
Sabbaths on the Continent	1835	Book
	1836	Works XV
Saint Hospice. A Melrose tract	1835	Tract
	1837	Works XIV
Shanty the Blacksmith, a tale of other times	1835	Book
Social Tales for the Young	1835	Book
The Garland, A Collection of Moral Tales Includes: *The Red Morocco Shoes, The Lofty and the Lowly Way, The Father's Eye, The Mountain Ash, My Godmother, Obedience, The Useful Little Girl, The Golden Chain, The Violet Leaf, Emmeline, St. Hospice, The Rosary, The Roman Baths, Aleine, The Convent of St. Claire, The Basket Maker, The Butterfly*	1835	Collection
The Lofty and the Lowly	1835	Tract
The Old Cobler of the Cottage translated from the French of Madame Montolieu	1835	Book
The Red Morocco Shoes. A Melrose tract	1835	Tract
The Roman Baths, or The Two Orphans. A Melrose tract	1835	Tract
	1837	Works XIV
The Violet Leaf. A Melrose tract	1835	Tract
	1837	Works XIV
Biography Illustrated	1836	Book
Contributions for Youth	1836	Book
Cottagers going to church	1836	Rustic Exc. Essay
Frank Beauchamp or the sailor's family	1836	Book
Hay-makers in a Storm	1836	Rustic Exc. Essay
Indian sagacity	1836	Rustic Exc. Essay

Ploughing	1836	Rustic Exc. Essay
Rearing of Ducks	1836	Rustic Exc. Essay
Rustic excursions for tarry-at-home travellers, a series of interesting tales, having a strictly moral tendency, and designed for the instruction of children Includes: *The cottage girl fetching water, The summer storm, The shepherd, The reaper going to labour, The turnpike gate, The gleaners, Ploughing, The cottager's funeral, The fox hunt, Indian sagacity, Cottagers going to church, Haymakers in a storm, Rearing of ducks.*	1836	Book of Essays
The Cottage Girl fetching water	1836	Rustic Exc. Essay
The Cottager's Funeral	1836	Rustic Exc. Essay
The Fox Hunt	1836	Rustic Exc. Essay
The Gleaners	1836	Rustic Exc. Essay
The Last Request of Emily. A Melrose tract	1836	Tract
The Reaper going to labour	1836	Rustic Exc. Essay
The School Girl. A Melrose tract	1836	Tract
The Shepherd	1836	Rustic Exc. Essay
The Summer Storm	1836	Rustic Exc. Essay
The Turnpike Gate	1836	Rustic Exc. Essay
The Well-Directed Sixpence. A Melrose tract	1836	Tract
Uncle Manners, or Self-Will Cured	1836	Book
The Cloak to which is added the Quilting Sherwood wrote only *The Cloak*	1836 -	Book
Economy	1837	Works XIII
Hoc Age	1837	Works XIII

My Three Uncles	1837	Works XIII
Obstinacy Punished	1837	Works XIII
Old Things and New Things	1837	Works XIII
The Happy Grandmother	1837	Works XIII
The Hours of Infancy	1837	Works XIII
The Mailcoach	1837	Works XIII
The Old Lady's Complaint	1837	Works XIII
The Parson's Case of Jewels. A Melrose tract	1837	Tract
The Shepherd's Fountain	1837	Works XIII
The Swiss Cottage	1837	Works XIII
The Lily of the Valley	1837 2Ed	Book
Scenes from Real Life. Includes *The Old Lady's Complaint, The Mail Coach, Economy, The Swiss Cottage*	1838	Book
Sea-Side Stories	1838	Book
The Bible	1838	Chap-Penny
The Happy Family	1838	Chap-Penny
The Little Negroes	1838	Chap-Penny
The Wild-beast Show	1838	Book
Adelaide and Antoinette	1839	Story
False Kindness	1839	Story
The Indian Orphans. A Melrose tract	1839	Tract
The Little Girl's Keepsake Includes *Adelaide* and *Antoinette & False Kindness*	1839	Collection
A Visit to Sherwood forest, Newstead ...	1840	Book
Former and Latter Rain	1840	Book
Master Alfred Seymour	1840–47	Book
Comfort in Death	1840–50	Chap-Penny
Conceit Checked	1840–50	Chap-Penny
Dangerous Sport	1840–50	Chap-Penny
Eyes and Ears	1840–50	Chap-Penny
Going to the Fair	1840–50	Chap-Penny
Horses and Coaches	1840–50	Chap-Penny

How to Please	1840–50	Chap-Penny
Land of Snow 1	840–50	Chap-Penny
Let Me Take Care of Myself	1840–50	Chap-Penny
Susan's First Money	1840–50	Chap-Penny
The Blind Gentleman	1840–50	Chap-Penny
The Child is but a Child	1840–50	Chap-Penny
The Druids of Britain	1840–50	Chap-Penny
The Flood	1840–50	Chap-Penny
The Honey Drop	1840–50	Chap-Penny
The Indian Chief	1840–50	Chap-Penny
The Parting Cup	1840–50	Chap-Penny
The Shawl	1840–50	Chap-Penny
The Useful Dog	1840–50	Chap-Penny
What Could I Do Without Grandmother?	1840–50	Chap-Penny
What's the Use of That?	1840–50	Chap-Penny
Willy Cary	1840–50	Chap-Penny
Yours is the Best	1840–50	Chap-Penny
Martin Crook and the Lost Purse	1840–7	Book
The Fall of Pride	1840–7	Book
The Heron's Plume	1840–7	Book
The Quadrapeds' Pic-nic	1840–7	Book
The White Pigeon	1840–7	Book
Duty is Safety, or, Troublesome Tom	1841	Story
Jack the Sailor Boy	1841	Book
Julietta di Lavenza	1841	Book
Sisterly Love	1841	Book
The Holiday Keepsake Includes *Sisterly Love, The Traveller, Duty is Safety, Jack the SailorBoy*	1841	Collection
The Juvenile Forget-me-Not Includes *Think before you act, Frank Beauchamp, Grandmama Parker, Uncle Manners*	1841	Book
The Joys and Sorrows of Childhood	1841–7	Book
The Loss of the Rhone	1841–7	Book

Robert and Frederick	1842	Book
The Last Days of Boosy, the Bearer of Little Henry. Sequel to *Little Henry and his Bearer*	1842	Book
Wreck of the Walpole	1842	Book
Grandmamma Parker, or The Father's Return	1844	Book
The Good Nurse	1844	Book
The History of John Marten, A Sequel to *The Life of Henry Milner*	1844 1846	Book Works XVI
The Lost Trunk	1844	Book
Sunday Entertainment, a collection of little pieces calculated to teach important truths to the reader	1845	Collection of 9
The Rose and The Nightingale	1845	Book
A Soldier's Life	1847	Story
Old Man's wanderings	1847	Story
The De Cliffords, an historical Tale by Sherwood and her daughter Sophia Streeten	1847	Book
The Keepsake – not all tales are by Sherwood: Contains *A Soldier's Life, Caroline Mordant, Old Man's Wanderings*	1847	Annual Collection
The Fairy Knoll	1848	Book
My Prize Book	1848–62	Chap-Penny
The Golden Garland of Inestimable Delight by Sherwood and her daughter Sophia Kelly	1849	Book
The Story Book of Wonders	1849	Book
The Blessings of Peace is by Sherwood and her daughter in *The Young Lord and Other Tales*	1849–50	
Victorine Durocher is by Sherwood and her daughter in *The Young Lord and Other Tales*	1849–50	Collection
Think Before You Act	1850	Book
Brotherly Love, Shewing that as merely human it may not always be relied upon by Sherwood and her daughter	1851	Book
Home Stories for the Young	1851	Collection
Jamie Gordon or The Orphan	1851	Book
The Harvest Home by Sherwood, in *Green's Nursery Annual*	1851	Collection

The Mirror of Maidens in the Days of Queen Bess by Sherwood and her daughter	1851	Book
The Two Knights, or Delancy Castle	1851	Book
Boys Will Be Boys, or The Difficulties of a Schoolboy's Life, a schoolboy's mission by Sherwood and her daughter	1854	Book
Maria and the Ladies and Other Tales "by Mrs Sherwood, [or rather by her daughter Sophia Kelly*"	1855	Book
Grand-Aunt's Pictures	1854–62?	Book
John and James and other tales by Sherwood and her daughter	1854–62?	Book
Mary and her Grandmama	1854–62?	Book
Must I Learn, and Other Tales	1854–62?	Collection
The Golden City and Other Tales by Sherwood and her daughter	1854–62?	Book
The Greedy Boy, and Grateful Dog, and Other Tales	1854–62?	Collection
William and Henry	1854–62?	Book
The Idler	1856	Works XV
Grand Aunt's Pictures and other tales Mrs Sherwood but all stories signed by-lined Sophia Kelly	1858	Book
Frank and the Christmas gifts	1860	Story
Mrs. Sherwood's Popular Tales	1860	Collection
Shanty also as *The Maid of Judea*	1860	Story
Mrs. Sherwood's Juvenile Tales	1861	Collection
My New Story Book	1861	Collection
The Hog and Other Animals	1862	Book
The Lily Series 6 Vols	1869	Collection
The Juvenile Library by Mrs Sherwood	1880	Collection
What is the world? in fifty-two stories of pluck, peril and romance for girls ed. H A Miles	1896–1905	Collection
Margot and the Golden Fish extract from *The Fairchild Family*	1908	Book
The Rational Exhibition	no date	BooK

Sources of book list

The Works of Mrs. Sherwood in a Uniform Edition, 1834–67. 16 Volumes: New York: Harper & Brothers. Referenced above as Works I-XVI.

Mrs Sherwood and her books for Children. Nancy M Cutt 1974. Lists all editions known to her then.

The Cambridge Bibliography of English Literature. ed. Joanne Shattock, CUP 1999.

Rowland, Clarissa M. *Bungalows and Bazaars: India in Victorian Children's Fiction. Children's Literature*, Vol. 2, 1973.

Worldcat.org a catalogue of library stock.

Books available online by Mary Martha Sherwood:

openlibrary.org has free ebooks.

gutenburg.org Project Gutenburg has free ebooks.

http://onlinebooks.library.upenn.edu/webbin/book/lookupname?key=Sherwo od%2c%20Mary%20Martha%2c%201775%2d1851&c=x Lists Sherwood's texts.

archive.org has several books as scanned text though often poor OCR.

books.google.com has several books in scanned original form including *The Complete Works of Mrs Sherwood* in 16 volumes, I - XVI published 1834–57 – which is not complete but is useful – listed as Works - in table above as Works I, II etc.. 7,305 pp in total.

Appendix 2:

Works of Mrs L. L. Cameron

Writings of Mrs Lucy Lyttelton Cameron (Lucy Lyttelton Butt) sister of Mrs M. M. Sherwood.

Protestant Episcopal Tracts 4: 46 Tracts by various authors including Cameron & Mrs Sherwood	?	Tracts
The Three Books; and other Tales	?	Book 2/6d
The Two Baskets; and other Tales	?	Book 2/6d
The History of Margaret Whyte: or *The Life and Death of a Good Child*	1803	Book
The Lost Child, a Christmas Tale *Founded on a Fact*	1810	Book
Dialogues for the Entertainment and *Instruction of Youth.*	1813	Book
The Two Lambs, an Allegorical History	1817	Tract
The Raven and the Dove *The Raven and the Dove and the Stork*	1817 1825	Chapbook 6d Tract
The History of Fidelity and Profession	1817	Book
The Holiday Queen	1818	Book
The Caskets; or The Place and the Church	1818	Book 1/-
The Lost Child	1818	Chapbook 6d
The Nosegay of Honeysuckle	1818	Book 1d

The Mother's Grave	1820	Book 1/6d
The History of Marten and his Two Little Scholars at a Sunday School	1820	Book 1/-
The Polite Little Children	1820	Chapbook 6d
The Three Flower Pots	1820	Book 2d
The Little Dog Flora and her Silver Bell	1818 2nd Ed	Book 1d
Memoirs of Emma and her Nurse; or The History of Lady Harewood	1821	Book 2/6d
Sophia; or The source and Benefit of Affliction	1822 1829 3rd Ed	Publ. in parts Book 1/6d
The Oaken Gates Wake	1822	Chapbook 6d
The Strawberry Gatherers	1820 2nd Ed	Book 1d
The Warning Clock; or The Voice of the New Year	1820 2nd Ed	Book 1d
Memory	1824	Book
The Pink Tippet Parts I & II and Parts III & IV	1824	Chapbooks 6d
The Willoughby Family	1824	Book 1/6d
The Caution; or Infant Watchfulness	1824	Book 1/-
Memory	1824	Book 1/-
The Mountain of Health; or The Hour Improved	1824	Book 1d
The Two Mothers; or Memoirs of the Last Century	1824	Book 5/-
Forms of Pride; or The Midsummer Visit	1826	Book
The Baby and the Doll; or Religion and its Image	1826	Book 1/-
The Berkshire Shepherd	1826	Book 1/-
The Workhouse; or, A religious life the only happy one: being an interesting history of Susan and Esther Hall	1826	Book
The Fruits of Education	1827	Book
Amelia	1820 7th Ed	Book 3d
The History of Little Frank and his Sister	1827	Book 3d
The Sister's Friend, or Christmas Holidays at Home	1828	Book
Addresses to Children on the Beatitudes	1828	Book 1/-
The Mother's Nosegay	1828	Book 3d
The Bunch of Violets	1828	Book 1d
The Broken Doll; or The Trial with Two Faces	183–?	Book 3d

Title	Year	Format
The Girl's Book. Stories By Cameron & others	1830	
Visit to an Infant School	1831	Book 2d
The Careless Little Boy also as *The Careless Boy*	1835	Book 2d
The Faithful Little Girl	1830 6th Ed	
The Use of Talents; or The Two Guardians	1837	Book
Lectures to Children (Lectures for Little Children)	1836 2nd Ed	Chapbook 6d
Our Neighbourhood	1839	Book 2/6d
Fourteen Chapbooks Contains 18 chapbook parts	1840?	Chapbooks
Englishwomen in Past and Present Times	1841	Book
Worldly Conversation in *Englishwomen*	1841	Book
Ancient and Modern Old Maids in *Englishwomen*	1841	
Georgiana Mansfield in *Englishwomen*	1841	
Sophia Mansfield in *Englishwomen*	1841	
Farewell in *Englishwomen*	1841	
The Farmer's Daughter	1843	Book 2/6d
The History of Fanny and Marten	1847	Book 2/6d
Lucy and her Robin	1848	Book 3d
The Two Virginian Nightingales	1850	Book 3d
The Kind Little Boy	1850 new ed.	Book 1d
A Gift from the Mountains; or The Happy Sabbath Margaret Graves Derenzy & Cameron	1857–69	Book 1/-
The Bright Shilling and other Tales	1873	Book 2/6d

Note: Prices in shillings and pence taken from a contemporary advertisement eg:- 2/6d.
       A shilling is now 5p and was divided into 12 pence. 2/6d would be worth about £8 in
       2014.

Appendix 3:

Works of Mrs S. Kelly

Writings of Mrs Sophia Kelly (formerly as Miss S. Sherwood, Mrs Sophia Streeten) daughter of Mrs M. M. Sherwood.

The History of the Fairchild Family, or the Child's manual: being a collection of stories calculated to shew the importance and affects of a religious education Parts I & II by Mrs Sherwood, Part III jointly with Kelly	1818 pt I 1834 pt II 1847 pt III	Book Book Book
Edwin and Alicia, or The Infant Martyrs by Miss S. Sherwood	1834	Book
The Scarlet Lobelia. Founded on Fact	1836	Book
The Drooping Lily by Miss S. Sherwood	1839	Book
The Fortescue Family: a tale for young persons, in which the principle of Christian charity is familiarly illustrated and explained	1840	Book
The De Cliffords, an historical Tale by Mrs Sherwood jointly with Kelly as Streeten	1847	Book
The Golden Garland of Inestimable Delight by Mrs Sherwood jointly with Kelly	1849	Book
Victorine Durocher by Mrs Sherwood and Mrs Streeten in *The Young Lord and Other Tales*	1849–50	Collection
The Mirror of Maidens in the Days of Queen Bess by Mrs Sherwood jointly with Kelly	1851	Book

Brotherly Love, Shewing that as merely human it may not always be relied by Mrs Sherwood jointly with Kelly	1851	Book
The Life of Mrs. Sherwood, (chiefly autobiographical) with extracts from Mr. Sherwood's journal during his imprisonment in France ed. Kelly in 2 editions	1854 1857	Book Book
Boys Will Be Boys, or The Difficulties of a Schoolboy's Life, a Schoolboy's Mission by Mrs Sherwood jointly with Kelly	1854	Book
John and James and other tales by Mrs Sherwood and her daughter	1854–62?	Book
The Golden City and Other Tales by Mrs Sherwood and her daughter	1854–62?	Book
Maria and the Ladies and Other Tales by Mrs Sherwood, or rather by her daughter Sophia Kelly	1855	Book 6 parts
Mrs Sherwood and Henry Martyn	1855	Book review
Grand-Aunt's Pictures and Other Tales	1858	Book
The Red Hand of the Ford of the Dee. A tale of Old Cambria.	1860	Book
Jessie's Bible, or The Italian Priest	1860?	Book
The Anchoret of Monserrat: a Tale	1861	6d Book
Types from the Hebrew and Greek Scriptures as illustrated in the colours of the rainbow	1866	Book

Appendix 4:

Rules of the Calcutta orphanage for European girls

Extracted from History, Design, and Present State of the Religious, Benevolent and Charitable Institutions founded by The British in Calcutta and its Vicinity. Charles Lushington Esq. of the Bengal Civil Service. Calcutta: Printed at the Hindustanee Press, 1824.

European Female Orphan Asylum.
This most interesting Institution owes its origin to the vigilant benevolence of the Reverend Mr. Thomason. The destitute conditions of the female orphans of European Soldiers belonging to the King's Regiments in this country having attracted his notice and commiseration, Mr. Thomason took an opportunity of calling the attention of the public to their generally distressing case, and pointed out the ignorance, neglect or cruelty of which, at their tenderest age, they were too frequently the victims. That deprived of their natural protectors, and left to the casual mercy of successive individuals, if they happily escaped the dangers of infancy, they were then constantly exposed to the corrupting influence of scenes of profligacy, until arrived at maturity, and familiarised with vice, they irrevocably gave themselves up to dissolute habits. To preserve such friendless Children from contamination, and to afford them the advantage of kind treatment and decent education, Mr. Thomason proposed to the community the establishment of the Female Orphan Asylum.

In the confidence that encouragement would be given to the plan, ten female orphans were taken from the 66th regiment and placed, on the 1st of July, 1815, under the care of a Mistress, in a house on the Circular Road, and the public sympathy aided by allowance of 3 rupees per mensem granted by Government for each orphan* (* footnote: This allowance was afterwards commuted for a consolidated donation of 200 Rupees per mensem.) soon provided the means for a permanent Establishment. Donations and Subscriptions poured in. Within two years from the period above mentioned, nearly 14,000 rupees had been received in Donations, and above 7,000 in monthly Subscriptions. An additional number of children having been admitted, it became necessary to remove them to a new situation, the premises originally occupied being now too small for their accommodation. The Managers of the Institution, therefore, encouraged by the countenance so liberally manifested by the public, ventured to purchase on mortgage, a capacious house and grounds for the sum of 37,000 Rupees. The number of children was at this time augmented to 26; within a year it rose to 34, most of them of a tender age, one having been received at the age of 15 days, and another before she was a week old. The list has continued to increase until it has risen to 76.

With this multiplication of demands on the services of the Institution, the beneficence of the public seems to have kept a more than equal pace. According to the latest accounts of the Institution, the debt increased by the purchase of the premises, even after defraying the expense of some recent extensive additions to them, had been liquidated, and a balance exhibited in it's favour. Still further necessary augmentations of the premises will, however, temporarily turn the scale against the Institution. The Asylum appears, from the commencement, to have become a peculiar favourite with all classes of Europeans, among whose subscriptions, the contributions of the officers and men of His Majesty's Regiments, and the Honorable Company's European Troops, as was natural, have been distinguished for their liberality.

The rules of the Establishment, being in considerable detail, are inserted in the Appendix.

[There follows a list of the military donations, omitted here.]

It was the avowed intention of the Managers, from the commencement, to afford such education and treatment to these children of private soldiers, as was most suitable to them, and which they would have enjoyed in their native country; that they should be brought up as much as possible independent of servants, and that they should learn every detail of the management of a house and the care of younger children, in order to their earning their livelihood in any way the governesses may think proper to dispose of them. These views were sensible and judicious, and it is understood that, as far as the internal practice of the Asylum goes, they have been satisfactorily accomplished. For some time, however, it would appear that a small number of the girls obtained situations out of the Institution than the age of some of them, and their practical education and knowledge of household affairs would have induced the public to hope. The Committee, nevertheless, are far from being inattentive to this essential object, and have latterly been more successful in carrying it into execution. The first class have for some time past, as alluded to in the account of the Ladies Society for female education, been instructed in Bengallee, with the view of their being employed to superintend native Schools, under that Association, and four of the girls have been placed as assistants in those establishments; six have been suitably married, and one respectably apprenticed.

The affairs of the Asylum are excellently administered by the Committee of lady Managers, who have also the aid of Mrs Thomason's more particular and unremitting supervision. The proficiency and good conduct of the girls, bear testimony to the judicious instruction imparted to them by Mr and Mrs Schmidt, Mr Cameron, an able Physician in the Company's Service, affords his gratuitous services to the Asylum.

Appendix No: 16

Rules of the European Orphan Asylum

I. The objects and nature of the Institution:
1. This Asylum is established for the reception and education of Female European Orphans; principally those of the King's regiments in India.
2. Those children only are admissible, whose fathers and mothers are Europeans.

3. The objects of this charity are admissible (if under ten) whenever they become Orphans – at however early an age.

4. The Asylum, though established expressly for orphans strictly so called, that is, those who have lost both parents, may also receive those who have lost one parent only, provided the Committee of Management, on careful examination of the circumstances of the case, shall think proper to admit them.

5. In cases, however, where the surviving parent is a mother, it is to be understood as a general rule that such children are inadmissible; exceptions to this rule may be admitted under peculiar circumstances, of which the Committee of mangers will judge.

6. The orphans, after admission, are placed at the entire disposal of the Managers and trustees; and not removable from the Asylum, without their concurrence.

7. The admission is to be conducted on the principles of the Church of England; and is to be plain and suitable to their prospects in life; such as shall tend to make them good and useful members of society, whether they become housekeepers or servants.

8. For the double purpose of economy, and in bringing up the orphans in habits of useful labour, all the business of the house is to be conducted (as far as may be expedient and practicable) by a number of the senior children, who shall take their various departments of labour in rotation, under the direction of the Head-Mistress.

9. It is an important object that the institution furnish its own teachers; which must be therefore ever kept in view in the training of the orphans; who will, it is hoped, provide a succession of mistresses, well qualified by previous discipline, to carry on the whole business of the institution.

10. It is important also that they should contribute by their manual labour, as far as this may be practicable, (of which the Lady Managers will judge) to the funds of the institution; care however being taken that this object be considered subordinate to that last mentioned.

11. DIVINE SERVICE is to be regularly performed on Sundays, according to the Liturgy of our Established Church.

12. The friends of the children are allowed to visit them once a month, on Saturday, but on no other day, without express leave from one of the Managers, who must supply the person with a ticket to be presented to the Head Mistress.

II General Government

The Government of this institution is vested in a Committee of Gentlemen Trustees, and a Committee of Lady Managers, under a Lady Patroness.

III Committee of Trustees

1. The Committee of Trustees to consist of five Gentlemen.

2. The landed property of the institution to be purchased and held in the names of the Trustees, for the benefit of the Asylum.

3. Every proposition respecting additions or alterations in the buildings of the Asylum, or the purchase of houses and land, is to be submitted to the Trustees for their approbation, after having obtained the concurrence of a majority of the Committee of Managers.

4. In all questions respecting the disposal, or placing out of the orphans, reference is also in like manner to be made to the Trustees, after the measure has passed the Committee of managers.

IV Committee of Managers

1. The Committee of Managers is to consist of ten Ladies.

2. The Ladies forming this Committee will take charge of the superintendence of the institution, comprehending all matters which usually fall under the heads of education, expenditure, and examinations of the children, giving rewards or censures, and whatever else may belong to the general executive management.

3. In the event of any member resigning her situation, the vacancy is to be filled by the remaining Members.

4. The Committee will meet at the Asylum on the first Saturday of every month, in order to examine and pass account, hear the report of the mistress, and adjust the business of the institution.

5. Applications for Admission to be decided at the monthly meetings; but in rare cases of emergency, any two members are competent to make such provisional arrangement as may appear expedient, subject to the decision of the Committee at their next meeting.

6. Three members of the Committee shall constitute a quorum for the transaction of current business.

7. Two members of the Committee are to be considered as visiting members for the month in rotation, not however to the prevention of other members – for the frequent attendance of the members of the Committee as they have opportunity, must materially contribute to the prosperity of the institution, – but to secure some permanent regular inspection of the establishment.

8. Such remarks and observations of the visiting members as may affect the arrangement of the institution, shall be submitted to the monthly meeting through the Committee, by their Secretary to the Mistress.

9. The Secretary is ex officio a member of the Committee.

V Alteration of Rules

None of the above rules shall be altered, and no new rules adopted without the concurrence of a majority in each of the Committees. References, when judged needful by the Committees, is to be made to the Lady Patroness, whose decision shall be final

Notes

1 Sarah Trimmer (1741–1810). High Church Anglican who lived in Brentford, Middlesex. Influenced by Robert Raikes and set up schools for the poor. Wrote The *Oeconomy of Charity* which set out rules for behaviour in church and *The Teacher's Assistant* which was a practical handbook for teachers.

2 Hannah More, (1745–1833). Wrote plays and poetry before starting her philanthropic work. In 1789 founded schools for the poor in Somerset and between 1795–97 produced *Cheap Repository Tracts*. By 1796 two million were sold in England, Scotland and Wales. They were sold cheaply and distributed by chapmen or pedlars.

3 Sir Walter Bagot (1702–1768) of Blithfield Hall, Staffordshire. MP for Newcastle under Lyme, Staffordshire and Oxford University.

4 Sir Edward Winnington (1728?–1791). MP for Bewdley, Worcs. 1761–1774.

5 Kelly. ed. (1854). *The Life of Mrs Sherwood*. p. 32.

6 Anna Seward (1742–1809). Often referred to as the 'Swan of Lichfield'. Lived at the Bishop's Palace-her father was Canon Residentiary at Lichfield Cathedral. She remained there after his death. She surrounded herself with a coterie of writers and thinkers and was a close friend of Erasmus Darwin. She wrote romantic poetry and was an inveterate letter writer. She never married. Her reputation and work divided opinion.

7 Richard Lovell Edgeworth (1744–1817). Had radical ideals and educational theories to promote rationality: *Practical Education* (1798) in which he modified the educational principles of Rousseau and de Genlis. Met Darwin and member of the Lunar Society, so called because it met when full or near full moon. Lived at Stowe House, Lichfield before moving to Ireland where he inherited a family estate. Very interested in Rousseau's theory of education in children. Married four times. On his first wife, Anna's death in 1773, he married Anna Seward's cousin, the very beautiful Honora, the same year. Anna Seward, with whom he had carried on a flirtation, never forgave him. When Honora died in 1780 he married her sister, Elizabeth, who died from consumption in 1797. Maria Edgeworth (1767–1849) was a famous author, daughter by first wife, Anna.

8 Darton, F. J. Harvey, ed. (1910). *The Life and Times of Mrs Sherwood*. p. 15.

9 Arthur Annesley, Viscount Valentia (1744–1816), 1st Earl of Mountnorris (1793). His son, George Annesley, became a pupil of George Butt.

10 Darton, p. 16.

11 Edward Winnington (1749–1805). MP for Droitwich, Worcs.

1801–1805. m. Anne, the daughter of first Lord Foley. 12 children, 5 sons.

12 Darton, p. 18.

13 George Annesley, (1769–1844). Viscount Valentia (1793–1816). 2nd Earl Mountnorris; Son of Arthur Annesley,1st Earl Mountnorris, and the Hon. Lucy, daughter of George Lyttelton. In 1802 travelled to India via the Cape accompanied by Henry Salt, the son of Alice Salt, Mary's aunt. Salt's paintings illustrated Lord Valentia's *Voyages and Travels to India*. 1809.

14 Kelly, (1854) p. 41 & (1857) p. 39.

15 Ibid. p. 18.

16 Darton, p. 8.

17 Ibid. p. 50.

18 Gilchrist, Isabella ed. (1907). *The Life of Mrs Sherwood*. London: Robert Sutton. p. 19.

19 Cameron, George Thomas. ed. *The Life of Mrs Cameron*, 2nd edition (1873), p. 6.

20 Darton, p. 88.

21 Ibid.

22 Ibid. p. 89.

23 Frances (Fanny) Burney (1752–1840).

24 Darton, pp. 81–2.

25 Lady Anne Courtenay, (1774–1835). Daughter of William Courtenay, 2nd Viscount Courtenay.

26 Darton. p. 84.

27 Kelly, (1854) p. 90 & (1857) p. 85.

28 Darton, pp. 123–4.

29 Kelly, (1854) p. 92 & (1857) p. 86.

30 Darton. p. 128.

31 Cameron. p. 17.

32 *Tatler*, founded by Richard Steele in 1709. Steele used Isaac Bickerstaff as nom de plume and invented a half sister, Jenny Distaff. She first appears in No.10 and was the author of several issues in which women's issues were examined. Mary had read *Tatler* from an early age in her father's library.

33 Darton. p. 160.

34 *The Traditions. A legendary tale. Written by a young lady*. London: William Lane, 1795. Her first book was written at the age of eighteen. 'The Critical Review commented on its romantic elements, saying it ought to have been called *The Superstitions*, but it approved the book's moral and its sentiments.' p. 117 in Cutt, Nancy. (1974). *Mrs Sherwood and Her Books for Children*.

35 Kelly. (1854) p. 125. & (1857) p. 119.

36 Darton. p. 165.

37 Ibid. p. 165.

38 Kelly, (1854) p. 126 & (1857) p. 120.

39 Ibid. p. 132 & (1857) p. 126.

40 *Margarita*. Printed at the Minerva Press for William Lane. 4 vols.

41 Kelly, (1854) p. 216 & (1857) p. 204.

42 Darton. p. 169.

43 Kelly, (1854) p. 156 & (1857) p. 146.

44 Darton. pp. 169–70.

45 Kelly. (1854) p. 156 & (1857) p. 146.

46 Ibid. p. 159 & (1857) p. 149.

47 Ibid. p. 159 & (1857) pp. 148–9.

48 John Bellenden Gawler (1764–1842). First called John Gawler: captain in the 2nd Regiment of Life Guards. Had to leave army in 1793 due to his pro French Revolution sympathies. In 1804 George III granted him a licence to take the name of Bellenden Ker. Charming and witty he had several affairs. In 1801 he published a book on botany and contributed to botanical magazines. (DNBO).

49 Trumbach, Randolph. (1998). *Sex and the Gender Revolution*. Vol.1. pp. 420–21. University of Chicago Press, Chicago. 1998.

50 Greater London Record Office: London Metropolitan Archive ref: GLRO: DL/185: Annesley v Annesley. Quoted in *Sex and the Gender Revolution*, Vol.1 p. 420–21.

51 Journal of The House of Lords Vol. 42.

52 This original letter is a much fuller

account of Henry's adventures and the hardship he faced in France than the edited account published in *The Value of Bread*. The editor, Andrew Bond, had produced the text from an edited copy made by Sophia Kelly, Henry Sherwood's youngest daughter, in 1892.

53 *Diaries of Henry Sherwood*. Shropshire Archives, 5624/1, 1790–95. I have kept his syntax, spelling and punctuation throughout.

54 The Sallee Rovers were Berber pirates operating out of Salé on the coast of Morocco opposite Rabat.

55 *Liberté, Liberté, Cherie* is a line from the French National Anthem *La Marseillaise*.

56 The Feast of St. Blaise falls on February 3.

57 *Ça Ira* was an emblematic song of the French Revolution.

58 Jacobin: member of the Jacobin Club, a revolutionary political movement; used more generally for all supporters of the French Revolution.

59 paid per diem or per day.

60 Maximilien Robespierre (1758–1794). Executed July 28,1794. Member of radical political group who sought to change France from a monarchy to a democratic republic, took power in 1793 and began the Reign of Terror in which thousands were sent to the guillotine.

61 *The Value of Bread* has: 'she at once returned to the friendly nuns, one of whom was in St. Vallery, & I saw her no more in France.'

62 Cameron, p. 30.

63 Robert Raikes (1736–1811). Philanthropist. The Sunday School Movement began in 1780.

64 Cameron, p. 78.

65 *Diaries of Henry Sherwood*

66 Mr Lilley Smith of Coventry. Successful grocer. Friend of Henry's grandfather and executor of his

will, trustee of the fund under the will for all of the grandchildren.

67 Mr Reynolds was a partner of Henry's grandfather in the silk trade.

68 Mr William Henry Maskall. Calenderer and packer. Henry's maternal uncle, brother of Henry's mother Margaret. Lived at 3 Mitre Court, Milk Street, Walthamstow, London.

69 Henry's father filed a suit unsuccessfully against Smith and others having been cut out of Henry's grandfather's will. Henry's siblings by his father's second wife, Mercy, successfully sued Lilley Smith, Henry and Margaret, and Mary, Lucy and Marten Butt. Sherwood v Smith 1801 was an important case as maintenance of minors was allowed for time past as well as time to come.

70 *Diaries of Henry Sherwood*.

71 Ibid.

72 Ibid.

73 Ibid.

74 Ibid.

75 The Morf was a hill common 5 miles long and 3 miles wide near Bridgnorth. Joseph Plymley, 1803. *General View of the Agriculture of Shropshire*. Richard Phillips: London.

76 *Diaries of Henry Sherwood*. There is a longer version of this letter also copied in *Diaries of Henry Sherwood*.

77 This is Margaret his father's daughter by his first marriage.

78 Orphris, Orchis & Epidendrum are all Orchids.

79 Seapea: *Lathyrus maritimus*.

80 Manincheel: Poison guava tree.

81 A gecko commonly found in buildings.

82 Castries, the main town on St. Lucia

83 'Yellow fever is a serious viral infection that's usually spread by a type of mosquito known as the Aedes aegypti mosquito. Typical

symptoms of yellow fever include: high temperature (fever), headache, nausea and vomiting, muscle pain, including backache, jaundice – yellowing of the skin and the whites of the eyes caused by liver damage.' www.NHS.uk/conditions/yellow-fever. 2014.

84 The Morne, south of Castries, known as Morne Fortune was one of the principal battle sites between the French and British. Fort Charlotte was captured by the British in 1796 and became the principal base for the British in St. Lucia.

85 West India Regiment (WIR), infantry unit of the British Army recruited from, and normally stationed in the British colonies of the Caribbean between 1795 and 1927. The Carribean soldiers were better able to cope with tropical disease and climate than the British soldiers.

86 Treaty of Amiens, March 27, 1802 between Britain, France, Spain and the Batavian Republic (Netherlands) brought peace in Europe for 14 months during the Napoleonic wars. *Encyclopaedia Britannica.*

87 Antoine Richpanse. (1770–September 1802). French Revolutionary General, died of yellow fever in Guadaloupe.

88 Pigeon Island, St. Lucia, once the base for pirates. In 1778 Admiral George Rodney built a fort there, Fort Rodney.

89 Carenage, a safe anchorage.

90 Squince Bay, near Skibbereen, on the south coast of Ireland, a notoriously difficult bay to navigate.

91 Royal Hospital Haslar at Gosport, opened in 1753 as a naval hospital; closed in 2009.

92 The Light Company of an infantry regiment went in front of the main body to delay the enemy.

93 *Fête champêtre*, a garden party with entertainment.

94 Cameron, p. 67.

95 Kelly, (1854). p. 221.

96 *The Works of Mrs. Sherwood*, Uniform Edition, vol. III. pp. 203–4.

97 Henry Salt, (1780–1827). Born in Lichfield and trained as portrait artist. 1802 became secretary and draughtsman to Lord Valentia. Accompanied Valentia to India in 1803. His paintings illustrated *Voyages and Travels to India* (1809) by Valentia. Salt also explored the Ethiopian Highlands in 1805 and returned there in 1809 on a government trade mission. Published *A Voyage to Abyssinia, and travels into the interior of that country, executed under the orders of the British government in the years 1809 &1810*. Widely travelled: Egypt and Ceylon. 1815 British consul-general in Cairo. Egyptologist: sponsored excavations of Thebes and Abu Simbel. Built up important collection of Egyptian artefacts.

98 As Dudmaston is north of Bridgnorth and Arley is well to the south, it seems that there may be some mistake here.

99 Darton, p. 203–4.

100 *Diaries of Henry Sherwood.*

101 Napoleonic Wars 1803–1815.

102 Kelly, (1854). p. 246.

103 Ibid. pp. 250–51.

104 Elizabeth Carter, (1717–1806). Classicist, writer and respected member of the Bluestocking circle.

105 See Eaton, Barbara: '*Yes Papa!' Mrs Chapone and the Bluestocking Circle.*

106 Cameron, p. 108. In 1845 two of Mrs Cameron's daughters, Emma and Eliza, went out to Madras to manage a missionary institution. Emma died there.

107 *The Government of India: a brief*

historical survey of parliamentary legislation relating to India: pp. 76–78.

108 Darton, pp. 226-7.

109 A ship's carpenter earned £3 to £5 a month so 30 guineas was an enormous bonus.

110 Diaries of Henry Sherwood.

111 Ibid.

112 Darton, p. 243.

113 Ibid. p. 246.

114 Diaries of Henry Sherwood.

115 Ibid.

116 Ibid.

117 Ibid.

118 1 rupee, then worth about 2s/8½ d, equivalent in 2014 to £8.90 by the UK retail price index or £110 UK average earnings. http://www.measuringworth.com

119 Ayah, an Indian nanny.

120 Diaries of Henry Sherwood.

121 Ibid.

122 Darton, p. 271.

123 Diaries of Henry Sherwood.

124 Darton, p. 272.

125 Kelly, (1854). p. 307.

126 Darton, p. 282.

127 Yule, Henry and Burnell, A.C. Hobson-Jobson: A Glossary of Colloquial Anglo-Indian Words and Phrases.

128 Diaries of Henry Sherwood.

129 Darton, p. 276.

130 Margery appeared in Mrs. Sherwood's Primer, or First Book for Children published in 1821.

131 Darton, p. 294.

132 Kelly, (1854). p. 327.

133 Darton, pp. 301-2.

134 Nulla, Nullah, a creek, watercourse or dry river bed.

135 Henry Martyn, (1781-1812). Completed first translations of the New Testament into Urdu, Farsi and Arabic. See Eaton, Barbara, Letters to Lydia: 'beloved Persis'.

136 Diaries of Henry Sherwood.

137 Daniel Corrie (1778-1837). First Bishop of Madras.

138 Darton, p. 323.

139 Diaries of Henry Sherwood.

140 Kelly, (1854) pp. 354-6.

141 Eaton. Letters to Lydia: 'beloved Persis', p. 140.

142 Darton, p. 348.

143 Diaries of Henry Sherwood.

144 Gilchrist, p. 183.

145 Darton, p. 370.

146 A small copper coin, 1/64 rupee.

147 Translations published in India include: Telugu 1840, Hindustanee 1844, Urdu 1847, Marathi 1848.

148 The Indian Pilgrim or, The Progress of the Pilgrim Nazareenee. 1818. Wellington: Houlston & Son.

149 Kelly, (1854). p. 424.

150 Eaton, Barbara. Letters to Lydia: 'beloved Persis'.

151 Martha of Bethany was burdened with worries. Luke 10:38-42.

152 Darton, p. 389.

153 Kelly, (1854). p. 434.

154 'A copy of a letter dated about 1811': Westminster College, Cambridge. MAR 8/3. Original at St John's College Cambridge, ref. MA12/1.

155 Diaries of Henry Sherwood.

156 Darton, extract from a letter; p. 390. This is a paraphrase of Henry's detailed account in his diary.

157 Topy: hat.

158 Gilchrist, pp. 195-6.

159 1 anna was 1/8 of a rupee, or 8 pice.

160 Darton, p. 402.

161 Darton, p. 405-6. In Kelly's 1854 edition, p. 450, she writes: 'the once blooming boys, who were slowly sacrificing themselves to drinking, smoking, want of rest, and the witcheries of the unhappy daughters of heathens and infidels.' She continues by imagining their mothers praying and weeping in England.

162 Diaries of Henry Sherwood. Officers had to make their own living arrangements.

163 Ibid.

164 Ibid.

165 Darton, Appendix B. p. 501.

166 Ibid. p. 502.

167 Ibid. p. 504.
168 Kelly, (1854). pp. 468–70. The letter was not sent till after Henry's return in 1815 as Mary thought it would distress her mother.
169 Ibid. p. 480. A copy of part of a letter he wrote to Mrs Mawby in Meerut.
170 Ibid. p. 480.
171 Darton, p. 409.
172 There is some discrepancy on dates between the 1854 edition and the edition edited by Darton. I have taken the dates from Henry's diary.
173 *Diaries of Henry Sherwood.*
174 Henry had sent it in a letter to Lucy Cameron. She sold the copyright for £5 to Houlston, a bookseller in Wellington, Shropshire. It became a runaway bestseller, establishing Houlston's reputation as well as Sherwood's. By 1840 it had gone through 30 editions. By 1866 it had sold upwards of 250,000 copies and been translated into several languages. Also written during this Evangelical period were: *The Ayah and the Lady* (1816), *The Indian Pilgrim* (1818) and *The Infant's Progress* (1821). In *The Literary World*, 4 December 1852, New York, an unsigned article, *The Uncle Tom Epidemic* examines the use in Uncle Tom's Cabin: (1852) by Mrs Harriet Stowe of several of Sherwood's devices: 'the religious discussions between Boosy, the Indian servant, and Little Henry, the white English child, are mirrored in those of Eva and Uncle Tom; the heartless mother; and the haircutting scene of a dying child.'
175 Darton, p. 414.
176 Lord Moira, 1st Marquess of Hastings, (1754–1826). Governor General and Commander in Chief in India from 1813–22. Then became Governor of Malta until 1826. Fought in the American War of Independence and then in France. Successful campaigns against the Gurkhas, the Gurkha War, 1814–16; ended with the Gurkhas suing for peace and the Sugauli Treaty: and the defeat of the Marathas in 1818. Married in 1804 to Flora Campbell, Lady Loudon, sixth Countess of Loudon.
177 In Henry Sherwood's diary there is a note by his great grandson, also a Henry Sherwood, who served with the IX Battalion, The Middlesex Regiment in India in 1915: 'While I was confined to bed in MARCH 1915 with a badly poisoned thigh (poison from a saddle) I received by mail from my father at home extracts from this diary which I was persuaded to send to the Statesman (cutting above). Resulting from its publication I learnt from the wife of a retired judge from Patna that my great grandmother founded a home in CALCUTTA in 1815—the year the Sherwoods returned to ENGLAND—for the sons and daughters of soldiers with the object of keeping them away from barrack room life! Later I received an invitation to go to CALCUTTA to be shown over this building which was then celebrating its centenary but under existing conditions I did not feel justified in accepting. I also received an invitation to BERHAMPORE where a public memorial to "little Henry" existed.'
178 Kelly, (1854). p. 505–6.
179 *The Indian Orphans. A narrative of facts: including many notices of the Reverend Henry Martyn, B.D. and the Right Reverend Daniel Corrie, Lord Bishop of Madras* (1839). The book is dedicated to Lieut.-Gen. Sebright Mawby: 'This simple narrative of facts, entitled Indian Orphans, is dedicated, as a small token of respect and esteem; and is a humble testimony of remembrance of innumerable acts of kindness and condescension shewn by him to persons whose

lowly condition must ever have precluded any hope of temporal recompense.' In the introduction Mrs Sherwood writes that it 'is taken from memoranda, written from day to day, during a residence of many years in India ... ' The first chapter starts: 'The condition of the children of European parents in India, when deprived of their natural protectors in infancy is, generally speaking peculiarly pitiable; and when the parents were in humble circumstances, there was, even as late as the beginning of this century, hardly a refuge left for these orphan children, either from untimely death, or, in the case of females, from infamy worse than death.'

180 See Appendix for the Rules governing the orphanage.

181 First published in *The Youth's Magazine*, 1822. Dhaye daye, dhye, is variously spelt.

182 *Diaries of Henry Sherwood*.

183 Darton, p. 421. A holystone was a large block of soft brittle sandstone used for scouring and whitening wooden decks of ships.

184 Custom House waiters were the staff who administered the weighing of goods and duties chargeable.

185 The diary ends with: 'so ends for the present the Voyges [sic] & Travels of H.S'. Henry's diary has their arrival at Liverpool on May 31, Mary on June 1. The latter date is given by *Lloyds Register of Shipping* and the *Indian Shipping Intelligence*.

186 Darton, pp. 422–3.

187 Ibid, p. 418.

188 Published in 1814 by Houlston it was sold initially for 2s.6d. *Lucy Clare* (1815) went through twenty-two editions by 1835. It was sold for 1s.6d. *The Memoirs of Sergeant Dale* (1815) sold for 1/- and went through twenty-two editions by 1838. All the books were received

enthusiastically by the critics but all were published anonymously. Each of the books was sold for £5 to Houlston and on the back of their popularity Houlston became a prominent publisher.

189 Cameron, p. 117.

190 Ibid. p. 119.

191 Ibid. p. 120.

192 Ibid. p. 139.

193 Darton, p. 430.

194 *The Oddingley Murders* and *Sequel to the Oddingley Murders*, both tracts,1830 by Mary. Between 1818 and 1830 Mary's tract writing was prolific. She produced almost 100 and they were printed by different firms. Mary varied her style to fit her readership which included servants, children and adults and varied in length from simple chap books to books of almost 100 pages, illustrated with delightful woodcuts.

195 Cameron, p. 148.

196 Ibid. p. 155.

197 Kelly, (1854). pp. 518–9.

198 Sarah Fielding (1710–68). The sister of Henry Fielding. *The Governess or the Little Female Academy*. (1749). Mary's version was published in 1820.

199 She sold it for £25. Published in 1818 and by 1838 had gone through eight editions.

200 Cameron, p. 169.

201 Darton, p. 439.

202 *An Introduction to Geography* (1818). p. 60.

203 Ibid. pp. 19–20.

204 Ibid. p. 63.

205 Ibid. p. 59.

206 William Wilberforce (1759–1833) was a politician, Evangelist—he knew many of the Clapham Sect which encouraged missionaries in India—a social reformer and a leading abolitionist: the Slave Trade Act (1807).

207 *The China Manufactory* was published 1821–2? by Houlston in

the New Series of Religious Tracts which started in 1821.

208 Chapbooks: pocket–sized booklets.

209 Cutt, (1974). pp. 117–120. 1974.OUP.

210 Ibid. p. 27.

211 Houlston promptly paid her £25 for *The Indian Pilgrim*. Houlston's list for 1818 showed fifteen titles by Mary and twelve by her sister Lucy Cameron.

212 *The Fairchild Family*, 20th edition: (1854). pp. 55–7.

213 Ibid p. 146.

214 *The History of Henry Milner, a little boy who was not brought up according to the Fashions of this World*. Part I, 1822. The Millenarians, whose beliefs Mary Sherwood shared, approved of it.

215 *Emile, or On Education*. Published in 1762 when it was banned in Paris and Geneva and publicly burnt. It is a treatise on education and divided into 5 books: 1–3 deal with the young Emile's education; 4 deals with adolescence and moral education; 5 describes the education of Sophie and civic and domestic life.

216 Darton, p. 445.

217 'Papist' 'anti-papist' and 'papacy' were at this time common terms used by Protestants about Roman Catholicism and while derogatory they were not generally seen as offensive as now. As the terms were used by Mary, I use them in her sense.

218 *Père la Chaise and The Infant's Grave* were first published in *The Select Magazine* in 1822 and then published by Houlston in 1823; *The Blessed Family* by William Whitmore in 1821, by Houlston in 1824.

219 Kelly, (1854). pp. 531–2.

220 *The Guinguette* and *The Noble Allamont*. I have found no record of publication of these stories.

221 Penitentiary here is used to describe a workhouse, not a prison.

222 Worcester Record Office has no further information of a penitentiary committee.

223 Elizabeth Fry, (1780–1845). Born in Norwich to a rich Quaker family. Married Joseph Fry, a banker. They had eleven children. Initially focused on convict children before turning her attention to women prisoners. Prison conditions were dire and she describes her impressions after her first visit to Newgate prison in 1813: 'the filth, the closeness of the rooms, the furious expressions of the women towards each other, and the abandoned wickedness, which everything bespoke are really indescribable.'

224 Dorset History Centre: D/PLR/F57 1824.

225 Stream of Time diagrams represented nations and historical events and were popular in the nineteenth century.

226 Carrying palms, olive or willow boughs appears in the Old Testament on the Feast of the Tabernacles: Leviticus 23:40 'And you shall take to you on the first day the fruits of the fairest tree, and the branches of palm trees and boughs of thick trees, and the willows of the brook.'

227 Worcester Record Office. Letter to Mrs Commins, ref. 705:936 BA 8720/1(ii)32.

228 Darton, pp. 454–55. These were the boys she taught in Cawnpore.

229 Romney's *The Gower Family* is at Abbot Hall Art Gallery, Kendal.

230 Darton, footnote, p. 460.

231 Kelly, p. 541. Darton comments that Pownall's marriage to Thomas Bird was not a very satisfactory one for various reasons but does not elaborate.

232 Darton, pp. 460–1.

233 *Emancipation*, 1829. Houlston & Son, Wellington, Salop.

234 *Worcestershire Miscellany*, 1831, pp. 155-7. Quoted in Cutt, (1974) p. 86.

235 *Emancipation* p. 107.

236 Ibid. pp. 116-7.

237 Ibid.pp. 149-50.

238 *Roxobel*, (1831) Houlston. p. vii.

239 Kelly, (1854). p. 543.

240 Cameron, p. 202.

241 Henri Abraham César Malan (1787-1864).

242 John Calvin (1509-64). Broke away from the Catholic church about 1530. After violent attacks on Protestants in France he fled to Switzerland where he was a member of the Reformed church. He taught the centrality of the Bible and salvation was through God not good works on earth.

243 *History of the Swiss Reformed Church Since the Reformation*: p. 374.

244 Ibid. p.387.

245 *The Baltimore Literary and Religious Magazine*, Vol. III.

246 Royde-Smith. *The State of Mind of Mrs Sherwood*: p. 202.

247 Quoted in *Sir Thomas Stamford Raffles 1781–1826* (2000): Raffles Museum of Biodiversity Research, Department of Biological Sciences, The National University of Singapore.

248 Kelly, p. 550. *The Little Momiere* was published by Hatchard in 1833.

249 Darton, p. 468.

250 Ibid.

251 Sir Walter Scott (1771-1832). Scottish historical novelist and poet. Wrote: Waverley (1814) which was published anonymously. Scott's Waverley novels and subsequent novels enjoyed huge success. He entered the legal profession and became Clerk of Session and Sheriff-Depute of Selkirkshire. Scott was financially ruined by the banking crash of 1825-6. He had invested in the Ballantyne printing press which failed. He refused financial help, placed his home, Abbotsford, and income in trust to his creditors, determined to settle his debts through his writing.

252 *Victoria*, (1833). pp. 63-6.

253 *The Little Momiere*, (1833). p. 20.

254 *The Nun, A Narrative*, (1833). R.B. Seeley and W. Burnside, London.

255 *The Monk of Cimiés*, (1834). William Darton and Son, London.

256 *The Nun*: p. 71.

257 *The Monk of Cimiés*: p. 129. Mary includes a footnote: 'Jesuits' Catechism.'

258 Ibid. p. 169.

259 Cutt, (1974). p. 73.

260 *Sabbaths on the Continent*, T. Ward & Co. London (1835). I have used *Sabbaths on the Continent* in *The Works of Mrs Sherwood*, Vol XV, pp. 331–403 on Google Books.

261 Ibid. p. 332.

262 Ibid. p. 353.

263 Ibid. p. 358.

264 Theodore Beza (1519-1605). A French Protestant theologian and a disciple of Calvin. Settled in Geneva circa 1558.

265 *Sabbaths on the Continent: Works* XV, p. 359.

266 Jean-Jacques Rousseau (1712-78). Philosopher and writer on education and religion. Author of *Emile, or On Education*. His books were banned in Geneva in 1765.

267 François-Marie Voltaire (1694-1778). French writer of polemics, plays, poems and stories. Satirist: *Candide or Optimism* (1758). Moved to Ferney. Deist and attacked Catholic religion as 'the most ridiculous, the most absurd and the most blood-thirsty ever to infect the world.'

268 *Sabbaths on the Continent*: Works XV, p. 397.

269 *Shanty the Blacksmith*, (1835). Darton, London.

270 *Caroline Mordaunt or the Governess*, (1835). Darton, London.

271 Kelly. (1854). p. 545.

272 'Some have supposed that Moses formed the Hebrew letters from Egyptian writings, and it must be admitted that Egyptian emblems, Hebrew emblems, and Hebrew letters, have a very remarkable similarity in their form, and it has been, I believe, proved satisfactorily, that all or nearly all the old Hebrew letters have some natural meaning, and some resemblance to well-known objects. Many of the Jews believe that the Hebrew letters, and even the vowel points, were revealed to Moses by the Almighty on Mount Sinai, when he delivered to him the two tablets of the law. Others think that Ezra invented the vowel points after the Babylonish captivity: probably he did invent some of them, and some seem to have been in use before his time. Among Christians, many Hebrew scholars imagine that the vowel points were invented more than a thousand years after the Hebrew language ceased to be a living one.' Dangerfield: *A Stenographic Lecture as delivered to the Royal Institution on the 1st of March 1825 and at the Mechanics' Institution on the 22nd of June 1825.* p. 5.

273 'Millennialism or Millenarianism in the narrowest sense, the belief in a future millennium, or thousand-year reign of Christ. The main source of the belief is Revelation 20. Its adherents are pre- or post-millennialists, according to whether they conceive Christ's second coming (parousia) as coming before or after the millennium. Post-millennialists are accordingly the more optimistic about the progress of history toward the millennium.' *The Oxford Dictionary of World Religions*: (1999). ed. John Bowker. OUP.

274 *Henry Milner*, Part III (1837). pp. 152-3.

275 Ibid. p. 139.

276 Ibid. pp. 249-50.

277 Kelly, pp. 569-70.

278 Ibid pp. 570-71.

279 Ibid. p. 542.

280 Ibid. p. 564.

281 *Henry Milner, Part I* was published in 1822; Part II, 1826; Part III, 1831 and Part IV, 1837. '*The History of Henry Milner* was well received in America. The Universalists found in it confirmation of their belief that Mrs Sherwood and Mrs Streeten had joined their ranks; and sent a gift of tastefully-bound books (her own) which they had reprinted. They did not make her denials public. *Henry Milner* was also appreciated by the Millenarians, among whom Mrs Sherwood could certainly be counted.' Cutt, Nancy. (1974), p. 137.

282 Kelly, p. 565.

283 Ibid. p. 566.

284 Lisa Spurrier: *East Garston's Mad Vicar*. The Berkshire Echo—The Newsletter of Berkshire Record Office: No. 3 (Autumn 1997).

285 Vieda Skultans: *Oxford Companion to the Mind*. (1987).

286 Smith, L.D: *To Cure those afflicted with the disease of Insanity: Thomas Bakewell and the Spring Vale Asylum. History of Psychiatry*, iv pp. 107-127. (1993), p. 109.

287 Ibid. p. 110.

288 Ibid. p. 111.

289 All the letters are held at Berkshire Record Office: D/EZ 106/3/7/1 -10.

290 £300 in 1833 = £25,000 in 2013 by RPI. Measuringworth.com

291 *Chapter Act Book*, Monday 22nd November 1847, Meeting of Dean and Chapter. Chapter records. acc.15, bundle 22. Salisbury Cathedral.

292 Berkshire Record Office, Butt Papers, D/EZ 106/3/6/36.

293 Founded by Seth Ward, (1617-1689). Bishop of Salisbury

1667–89. Built at his own cost in 1683 it provided an almshouse for ten widows of priests in the diocese of Salisbury. 'Matrons were to receive a weekly pension of 6s each. Candidates for admission were to be at least 50 years old, and to possess an income of less than £10 a year.' *A History of the County of Wiltshire*: ed. Elizabeth Crittal. (1962). Vol. 6. pp. 168–78. *Salisbury Charities*. The charity now offers 14 flats and cottages and caters for 'single ladies resident in the area, able to live independently. Preference is given to widows and unmarried daughters of ministers of the church of England.' The age for new residents is now 55 and it is heartening that 'both cats and dogs are generally accepted, but not to be replaced (dogs by prior agreement).'

294 Kelly, p. 572.

295 Ibid. p. 574.

296 Ibid. p. 575.

297 Darton, p. 479.

298 *The Works of Mrs Sherwood*, 16 vols. Published 1834–57. Three volumes were published after this letter.

299 Darton, p. 480.

300 Royde-Smith, p. 186.

301 Ibid. p. 187.

302 Cameron, p. 263.

303 Darton, p. 481.

304 Cameron, pp. 238–9.

305 Ibid. pp. 241–2.

306 Ibid. p. 251.

307 *The History of the Fairchild Family, Part II*: pp. 9–10.

308 Royde-Smith, p. 64.

309 Kelly, p. 575. In fact Evelyn and her story appears in two parts in Part II of the book.

310 Cutt, (1974). p. 80.

311 Darton, p. 462. Darton includes: 'The stories thus written to order were remarkably original and fresh—a rare feature produced under such arbitrary limitations. Mrs Cameron took a large share in these labours.'

312 Kelly, p. 575.

313 Hastings was a doctor at Worcester Infirmary and had founded the Provincial Medical and Surgical Association (PMSA) in 1832 at a meeting in the board room of the Infirmary. The PMSA would later become the British Medical Association. The purpose of the PMSA was to share information between doctors. Robert Streeten was the Dispenser at the Infirmary and also the secretary of the Association as well as editor of the PMSA weekly Journal which would later become the British Medical Journal (BMJ).

314 Kelly, p. 582.

315 Ibid.

316 Ibid. p. 585.

317 Ibid. p. 586.

318 'The cemetery is now closed, and many of the monuments have been so damaged by time and weather erosion that they are illegible (including this one). 1930.' 8th Hussars Regimental Museum, New Brunswick.

319 Darton, p. 484.

320 Ibid. pp. 484–5.

321 Ibid. p. 488.

322 Ibid.

323 Ibid. p. 491.

324 National Library New Zealand: Paperspast. Nelson Evening Mail, Vol. XLVII, 5 January 1912. p. 3.

325 Cameron, p. 283.

326 See list of Lucy Cameron's works in Appendix 2.

327 Cameron, pp. 311–2.

328 See list of Sophia Kelly's books in Appendix 3.

329 National Library New Zealand: Paperspast. Nelson Evening Mail 5 January 1912, p. 3.

330 George IV and Queen Caroline had lived separately for many years, their marriage having been a disastrous union of two people unsuited to each other. George

forbade Caroline to attend the
coronation so when she did appear
to claim her right as consort she was
publicly humiliated when turned
away.

331 *The White Ladies Aston Chronicle*:
summer 1868

Index

Barbara Eaton lives on The Lizard in south-west Cornwall. She is a graduate of Manchester University in English and Philosophy, Edinburgh University in Education and MSc of Aston University in Applied Linguistics. Married, with two grown up children, she lists her interests as writing, theatre, gardening, cooking and walking her two boxer dogs. She has travelled widely throughout Asia and the Middle East. Her first book, a historical biography of Henry Martyn, *Letters to Lydia: 'beloved Persis'* was published in 2005 and was the non-fiction runner-up in the 2006 Holyer an Gof Awards for Literature of the Cornish Gorseth.